PRETTY CAN BE UGLY

AUTOBIOGRAPHY OF KIMIKO LEWIS

"Always remember your current situation is not your final destination"
-Miko

real, inspiring, raw... COMING OF AGE LIFE STORY

Pretty Can Be Ugly
All Rights Reserved.
Copyright © 2021 Kimiko Lewis
v4.0

The opinions expressed in this manuscript are solely the opinions of the author and do not represent the opinions or thoughts of the publisher. The author has represented and warranted full ownership and/or legal right to publish all the materials in this book.

This book may not be reproduced, transmitted, or stored in whole or in part by any means, including graphic, electronic, or mechanical without the express written consent of the publisher except in the case of brief quotations embodied in critical articles and reviews.

Paperback ISBN: 978-0-578-24663-5

Cover Photo © 2021 www.gettyimages.com. All rights reserved - used with permission.

PCBU Reads

PRINTED IN THE UNITED STATES OF AMERICA

Table of Contents

Acknowledgments I
CHAPTER ONE 1
CHAPTER TWO 11
CHAPTER THREE 21
CHAPTER FOUR 31
CHAPTER FIVE 38
CHAPTER SIX 45
CHAPTER SEVEN 55
CHAPTER EIGHT 62
CHAPTER NINE 69
CHAPTER TEN 77
CHAPTER ELEVEN 84
CHAPTER TWELVE 91
CHAPTER THIRTEEN 97
CHAPTER FOURTEEN 109
CHAPTER FIFTEEN 115
CHAPTER SIXTEEN 123
CHAPTER SEVENTEEN 128
CHAPTER EIGHTEEN 136
CHAPTER NINETEEN 143
CHAPTER TWENTY 149
CHAPTER TWENTY-ONE 156
CHAPTER TWENTY-TWO 163
CHAPTER TWENTY-THREE 173
CHAPTER TWENTY-FOUR 184
CHAPTER TWENTY-FIVE 193
CHAPTER TWENTY-SIX 203
CHAPTER TWENTY-SEVEN 210
CHAPTER TWENTY-EIGHT 220

CHAPTER TWENTY-NINE	230
CHAPTER THIRTY	239
CHAPTER THIRTY-ONE	247
CHAPTER THIRTY-TWO	254
CHAPTER THIRTY-THREE	263
CHAPTER THIRTY-FOUR	270
CHAPTER THIRTY-FIVE	276
CHAPTER THIRTY-SIX	283
CHAPTER THIRTY-SEVEN	291
CHAPTER THIRTY- EIGHT	299
CHAPTER THIRTY-NINE	309
CHAPTER FORTY	319
CHAPTER FORTY-ONE	328
CHAPTER FORTY-TWO	337
CHAPTER FORTY-THREE	346
CHAPTER FORTY-FOUR	354
CHAPTER FORTY-FIVE	363
CHAPTER FORTY-SIX	374
CHAPTER FORTY-SEVEN	381
CHAPTER FORTY-EIGHT	389
CHAPTER FORTY-NINE	400
CHAPTER FIFTY	409
CHAPTER FIFTY-ONE	419
CHAPTER FIFTY-TWO	430
CHAPTER FIFTY-THREE	439
CHAPTER FIFTY-FOUR	448
CHAPTER FIFTY-FIVE	456
CHAPTER FIFTY-SIX	465
CHAPTER FIFTY-SEVEN	473
CHAPTER FIFTY-EIGHT	483
CHAPTER FIFTY-NINE	494
CHAPTER SIXTY	502
CHAPTER SIXTY-ONE	511
CHAPTER SIXTY-TWO	520

CHAPTER SIXTY-THREE 528
CHAPTER SIXTY-FOUR 536
CHAPTER SIXTY-FIVE 544
CHAPTER SIXTY-SIX 553
CHAPTER SIXTY-SEVEN 561
CHAPTER SIXTY-EIGHT...570
CHAPTER SIXTY-NINE...579
The Beginning 587

Acknowledgments

I want to give thanks and glory to the almighty Jesus Christ himself. Through Jesus Christ every mission will be complete. Every question will be answered and every curse will be broken. I'm not a saint but I carry an abundance of faith in my pockets. In life you need something to believe in, to motivate you to carry on. When afflictions are blowing through the wind. You'll need faith and internal strength to get through the turbulence. Pretty can be Ugly is a publication that goes into details and events that occurred during my adolescent years. I'm thankful for the adversities and distress that consumed my childhood because it blossomed me into the woman I am today. It presented an opportunity for me to tell my story through this autobiography.

I'm grateful for family and friends who are there when most needed. Support is so valuable and vital to each of our lives in every aspect you can think of. It breaks my heart to know that some people feel and believe they walk this earth alone. In some cases, to numb the agony inside people use drugs, sex, and sometimes bullets for closure. Depression is real and if you're feeling victim to any of this kind of pain. I want you to know, you're not alone. God is with you and he will protect you if you let him.

I want to give a special thanks to one of my good friends Tink, for being one of my first proof- readers. You don't know how much it means to me that you took the time out to assist me, free of charge, with such a big project. Shout out to a couple of my besties, Daquann and Nadiya for expressing how much they hated my book cover. I deeply appreciate the honesty and tough love from the bottom of my heart. Also, I want to give a huge thanks to my work family at Channel 3 News for the premature preparation, guidance and all around love and support.

I pray you as the reader can find inspiration, motivation, and *appreciation through my story. Whatever you're going through, just keep in mind you're not at your final destination. The bumps on the road are only preparing you for the smooth ride. Love yourself, encourage yourself, and support one another.*

CHAPTER **ONE**

MY LIFESTYLE IN the city of Detroit as a kid is not your typical "ring around the rosy" childlike game. Gaining strength, courage, and especially maturity faster than the typical kid puts me outside of the box in a lot of categories. The reason I say strength is because attending Detroit public schools or not, you have to be tough in this neck of the woods. If people sense an inch of weakness, humiliation is going to be waiting for you at the door. Having a sister that's five years older than me introduced me to maturity quicker than the blink of an eye. I haven't had to face much humiliation in the neighborhood or in school, but I definitely have witnessed it at a young age. I witness hardcore fistfights and bullying almost daily in elementary school. Luckily, I never had to face any of that, which is surprising to me, being that I'm the "pretty girl" the boys like in elementary school. Usually, the "pretty girl" is the girl the boys love, and the girls hate, but it isn't like that in my case. I make friends easily, and nobody picks on me; girls and boys are friendly towards me, and I'm friendly in return.

Academy of Southfield Lathrup Village is a school I enjoy going to. It's not in Detroit, so my mom thinks it's a better choice for us. I'm in the second grade, and my older sister is in the seventh grade. Going to school with my older sister Karin — a.k.a Key — is a blast.

PRETTY CAN BE UGLY

All of the middle school kids know me because I'm Key's little sister. Some people don't believe that we are related because of our dissimilar features. Key is brown-skinned, tall for a girl her age, with nice long legs, short hair, and a pretty face. I, on the other hand, am a lot shorter, of course, because of my age, light-tinted skin, and skinny with naturally long hair. People always ask if we have the same parents, and we always respond, yes. My father raised Key and accepted my mother and her first child long before I was born. So, my father is the only father my sister knows, and she is his oldest daughter.

I'm Mrs. Johnson's teacher's pet; she is in her early to mid-fifties with a short natural haircut. She wears really thick square glasses and chooses red as her everyday lip color. She reminds me of my Granny in a lot of ways, being that she is so nice to me and always wears red lipstick. My two best friends are Samantha and Trisha. Samantha is the outgoing one, with lots of friends and always keeps a boyfriend. Trisha is more on the shy side and very specific about picking her friends. I fit right in the middle of their extreme personalities. I'm not super outgoing or shy in school. I'm cool with you if you're cool with me.

Recess approaches right after lunch, as the second and third graders play outside. The girls play hand games and make up secret girl stuff to seem like they have so much business while the boys run around playing racing games.
  "Kimiko, come play "Slide" with me, Alex, and Brittany so it can be four of us!" Samantha calls from a distance.
  "Me and Trisha about to go play on the monkey bars!" I yell back.

She rolls her eyes at me with an attitude, and I proceed. She always wants me to follow after her, but I always do what I want to do, which causes us to feud a lot of the time and forces Trisha and I to grow closer. Samantha and Trisha are both my best friends, but they aren't best friends towards one another. They just deal with each other because of me.

"She always want you to listen to her." Trisha mutters under her breath.
I shrug my shoulders, "I know, and she just mad because I don't want to play with them."

We continue to play on the monkey bars, and as soon as the fun starts, it was time to go back into our portables for class. As everyone settles in, I glance at Brandon, who is being bad and talking back to the teacher. He is dark-skinned with a nice round head with straight white teeth. He is so cute to me, and I have a secret crush on him, but I've never confessed it to anyone.

"Since you want to continue to talk back and keep disturbing the class, go stand in the corner!" Mrs. Johnson shouts.
Brandon blustered back, "I'm not standing in the corner again; I'm tired of standing in the corner, you not my mama!"
Mrs. Johnson jumps out of her seat as quickly as possible and confronts Brandon, grabs his collar, and pulls him out of his seat, then snatches him to the corner of the classroom. As the class is laughing, I think to myself, *why is he so bad? Do his parents not care if he gets in trouble? If I got in trouble in school, I would get a beating as soon as I turned the knob of the screen door to my house.* My parents, especially my mother, don't allow bad behavior or bad report cards. After the rift raft in class, three o'clock arrived sooner than expected, which is good news. *I have to use the bathroom*, I think to myself as my stomach begins to growl. I never do the number two at school. I will hold it until I feel like I have to throw up, which isn't smart, but I let the embarrassment get the best of me.

"Kimiko, what's your number so I can call you later?" Trisha ask as she pulls out a piece of paper.

"It's 313-543-**** call me around five o'clock," I stammer.

"Ok, see you on Monday!" Trisha excitedly yells while leaving the portable.

Trisha's older sister is about the same age as Key. She comes to pick Trisha up from the classroom at the end of every day. As I'm walking out of the portable to go find Key, I notice Samantha behind me.

"Hey, Samantha, where you about to go?" I ask curiously.

She walks past me hastily, ignoring my question to meet with Kayla, whose class had already been let out. Kayla is Samantha's other best friend that she grew up with, and she listens to whatever Samantha says. If Samantha say jump, Kayla would say from where? She even cries if Samantha is mad at her or if she acts mean towards her. It is kind of ridiculous to me and sort of funny. I continue to go about my merry way after feeling the cold shoulder from Samantha. Refusing to suck up or kiss anybody's ass, I find Key and her ugly boyfriend. His name is Joseph, and he is about the same height as Key, brown-skinned with a haircut, really big lips, and a huge gap in the middle of his top teeth. I don't understand what she sees in him.

"Kimiko!" I hear a scream calling from a distance.

I turn around, trying to follow which direction the voice is coming from, and I find my friend Mya standing behind me.

"What's up," I say with a smile.

"Do you have latchkey?" Mya ask as she plays with her gum.

I shake my head, "Nope, I don't."

"Oh, how did your hair get so long?" she asks, gazing at my long ponytails.

"I don't know," I answer quickly, knowing Mya is shocked at my hair length because it is not the most common trait for young black girls like ourselves.

"Are you mixed?" she asks seriously, not letting the topic go.

"No," I answer confidently.

"You gotta' be mixed with something. Are those real gold rings?" Mya continues with the nosy questions, admiring my hands.

I touch the perfectly fitted shiny gold bands around my fingers. "Yeah, they real." I'm relieved when my mom pulls up in our dark green minivan, and it's time for me and Key to leave.

"See you later!" I wave heading for the car.

When Key and I get in the car, I have a strong feeling our mom is going to be talking our eardrums deaf about her marriage problems. My mom's name is Joyce, and she is a hell of a character. As soon as we enter the car, my mom checks Key.

"Who is that boy you were talking to?" Mom looks at Key with an uneasy facial expression.

"He's just my classmate," Key responds quickly, lying because my mom doesn't allow us to have boyfriends.

"Yeah, well, don't get your little ass beat," mom scolds Key.

Damn she can't even have a conversation with a boy. I roll my eyes in the back seat where no one can see.

Then comes the awkward silence that's making everything that much weirder. I know that is Key's boyfriend, but I would never tell my mom. I know a lot of things about Key that I don't tell my mom. Key and I's relationship is so legitimate and tight; nobody can come in between us. We have each other's back and would never stab each other in it. Our relationship with our mom is sort of different. From my point of view, Key is kind of a "mama's girl" and believes almost everything Mom says. Even if Key knows my mom is making something up, she will still find some type of truth out of her lies. Me, on the contrary, is more of a "daddy's girl." I love being around my dad. The more my mother tries to force it in my head to hate my father. It only strengthens my bond with him.

Key paused, sensing an argument, or something worse if she attempts to question my mom, so she continues with another topic.

"Today, Kim got caught making out with her boyfriend in the boys' bathroom," Key snickers.

It is always easier for my mom to talk about other people's children and their problems, but when it comes to her own children, no boys are allowed. Key can't even tell her she has a little crush.

"Oh my god!" mom burst out laughing.

"Did they get suspended?" mom asks curiously while turning down the radio.

"I think so; she was crying when I saw her at her locker," Key responds, less excited by the lack of not being able to express her own puppy love to her mother.

"That is so crazy! I remember being that young, kids are so bad!" mom giggles at her puberty sprouting daughter's school gossip. Surprisingly, she turns the radio up and proceeds to the route.

"Where we about to go?" I ask tiredly from school, hoping she says home or somewhere where I don't have to get out of the car.

"To the grocery store," she quickly responds.

Fuck! I hate going to the cold ass grocery store! I pout.

"I need to grab a few things for dinner tonight; hopefully, Jihod joins us," she sarcastically hisses as she continues to drive.

Jihod is my father, though she talks about him, specifically to us, like he's our brother. I hate it when she talks bad about him. It makes me feel sad and out of place. I love my dad so much. When he comes home, everything is so fun, and I can tell it makes my mom happy sometimes. I say sometimes because half the time she's happy when he's home. Other times she wants to start arguments and drag Key and me into it. If she didn't drag us into the argument as it was happening, she would find a way to speak through us at random times to get her point across to him. This is stupid to me because whatever she needs to talk about to her husband should be said out of her own mouth.

Pulling up to our home is relieving until I'm reminded that I have to bring all of the groceries in, and to put the icing on the cake, it's raining outside. Mom never helps us with the groceries, which is so aggravating. She always makes excuses about her back hurting. She does have a bad hip and scoliosis, but I have scoliosis, too. My back never hurt, and I'm never in pain. She lies so much that I don't know what to believe sometimes.

"Y'all hurry up with these groceries so I can close the door; its cold out here," she adds, cutting off the car and running to the door.

"She never help us with the groceries. It wouldn't take so long if she helped sometimes!" I exclaim with my six-year-old attitude.

"I know, with her lazy ass! She gets on my fucking nerves." Key hops out the car, slamming the door.

After getting all of the groceries out of the car and into the house, I make it my business to run upstairs to the bathroom. The bathroom is always my escape, for not helping with putting the groceries away. I stay there for about twenty minutes, then go to my room and start my homework. When it comes to homework, I don't like asking anybody for help. Both of my parents are too tempered for me to feel comfortable asking for help with homework. So, what I do is pay close attention in class and write down notes so I can avoid asking my parents for help.

After finishing up my Social Studies homework, I go downstairs for a change of scenery. Feeling like Sonic with my math homework in my hand, I zoom downstairs as fast as I can almost falling, jumping from the third or fourth step towards the end of the staircase, and mom yells from the kitchen.

"Stop running down those motherfucking steps like that!" Turning the corner, I see her eyes bucked and eyebrows frowned like I just committed a crime.

My mom is very mean looking to me; she has very big eyes, high yellow skin tone, and tall with long hair. She always wears swoops with every hairstyle to cover up her big forehead. She also has a lot of piercings in her ears from the start of her earlobe to the top of her helix and a nose piercing. When she's in her nice moods, she tells us stories about the old days when she used to wear an earring in every earhole. People are always saying how pretty she is, but she looks mean to me. Maybe she looks mean to me because she is a mean person in my eyes. She may be a pretty person on the outside, but she's a dark person on the inside. People don't know her like I do.

My math homework is a piece of cake because math is my favorite subject. While doing math homework in the dining room, I tuned into the conversation mom and Key are having in the kitchen.

"And he is never fucking here! I told him to go over Rock's house with that shit." she sternly explains to her twelve-year-old daughter.

"You right, he not ever here then he want us to come with him when he get here, over to Big Mama's house or something. It's boring over there," Key responds while stirring the mash potatoes.

That's all they do, sit around and gossip about my dad. All of the negative bullshit drives my mood to the ground. I wish I could live in a regular household where the parents let the kids be kids, and the parents love and help the children. I wish I enjoyed being here in the place I call home. I hate it here. Most of the time, I just want to leave, but where would I go? I can't control the parents God blessed me with, and I especially can't control the way the adults in my family act. That's exactly why I can't wait until I get older. Nobody is going to be able to control me. I'll be in charge of my own life.

The reason Key doesn't like going over Big Mama's house is because my mom is always forcing her to say something to somebody or the total opposite. Mom will literally threaten us not to speak to anybody over my Big Mama's house until somebody speaks to us first when we walk through the door. If we don't do exactly what she says, we will get a whooping when my dad leaves the house.

Another reason Key doesn't like going over there is that her "real" boyfriend Cory lives across the street from our house, and she hates to leave him. She loves being around him and his family, plus she's best-friends with his sisters, Patricia and Porsha.

"Miko, do you like going with him?" my mom asks sternly, wanting me to say no, but I did the total opposite.

"Yeah," I respond nervously, hoping not to get in trouble.

"Well, that's too damn bad, and when he get here and ask you if you want to go with him, you better say no, or when you get back, you are going to get fucked up," mom rapaciously responds, serious as a heart attack.

That's the way my mom controls us, by whooping us with belts all the time, over the smallest things. Instilling fear in us, so we have no other choice but to do what she says while keeping the abuse and the mind control a secret.

With her being our mom, that mental control is hard to fight, especially as a child. I'm still in my training years, and Key is already well trained. I'm a harder shell to crack, but she doesn't know it yet. In my opinion, I have more mind control over her. As I finish my homework, the phone rings.

"Hello," my mom answers. "Hey, Ma."

It's my granny, calling from North Carolina. They just moved a few years ago in this nice ranch house. I love going down south to visit them! We always have some type of activities planned, and the neighborhood is so pretty. Granny is a very nice lady, sweeter than sweet tea, I'd say. She is very soft-spoken and polite. She stands about 5'6 tall brown-skinned with a body out of this world. She's shaped so curvily, despite her old age. I could only imagine how she looked when she was younger. My mom hands Key the phone.

"Yeah, I'm doing good," Key responds gently.

"Tell her our furnace is broken," mom whispers spitefully.

Mom knows my dad didn't want anybody telling my grandparents about the furnace being broken and that he would fix it soon. Both of my parents know that if Key told my grandparents about anything needing to be fixed that they would have it fixed in no time. Or if we need anything, we know our grandparents could get it, and my mom knows her parents have it. Dad specifically didn't want my granddaddy knowing because I guess he wants him to know he can take care of his own family. Dad didn't want their support this time. Mom knew it would cause drama between Key and my dad when he comes home, and the furnace is fixed. It is always some type of drama within my household; that's probably why my dad stays away for days at a time.

CHAPTER **TWO**

SATURDAY MORNING GREETS us with shiny skies and nice September weather. It is still warm enough to go outside, but a jacket is needed. The sun always makes the day better, and Key and I are excited to be able to go outside. We love going outside and hanging with our friends on the block. Going outside is like our therapy. It leaves all of our worries, guilt, stress, and depression inside the house. Outside waiting for us is Ron from next door, Patricia, Porsha, and Cory from across the street, Jena and Joe from down the street, and others that I don't recognize.

Ron lives right next door to us with his grandparents. He seems like the only child most of the time, but he claims to have siblings we never met before. Patricia, Porsha, and Cory are siblings; they're kind of close in age, and they are Key's favorite. Patricia and Porsha are Key's best friends, and Cory is her boyfriend—her *real* boyfriend. Maybe even her first love. Jena and Joe are siblings and they are always butting heads and getting into arguments, which is entertaining most of the time. These are the main people we associate with on the block, being that we're not allowed to go far.

Patricia and Porsha approaches us first as we walk toward the crowd.

"Where y'all been?" Porsha bluntly asks.
"Over our Big Mama house and stuff," Key responds cool and calmly.

My mom doesn't let us go outside on the weekdays, so we are stuck in the house with her and her pity party. So instead of us explaining and complaining about our dysfunctional family, we just play it off sometimes.
"We about to walk to the store, are y'all coming?" Patricia asks.
"Miko, go ask mama if we can walk to the store," Key rushes me.

I run in the house trying to hurry up because I want to go too. Mom is watching her soap operas she recorded earlier in the week.
"Ma, can we walk to the store with Patricia, Porsha, and them?" I ask nicely.
"Yeah, but don't go anywhere else. Come right back," my mom answers sternly.

We are the only kids on the block that have to ask to go to the corner store, which is kind of embarrassing and played out. Running back outside, we head to the corner store right off of 7 Mile and Meyers. Every time we go to the store, everybody always buys Hot Cheetos. Everybody buys at least four bags because each bag only costs twenty-five cents.

"I bet you won't steal these Twizzlers," Joe whispers to Jena humorously.
"How much you want to bet?" Jena challenges him.
"A dollar," Joe responds quickly.

On the way back to the block, everybody is talking and having separate conversations. Porsha and I are talking about something funny. She keeps me laughing all the time. She is one of the funniest people I know. She is a couple of years older than me and she's the closest to my age out of the group. Key and Cory are sharing snacks. Ron and Patricia are having a crazy conversation about a mutual friend. While crossing the street, Inez calls Patricia's name and tells all of us to come here. Inez is a girl that lives at the corner, and she is kind of fast in the pants. She is a pretty brown-skinned girl with slanted eyes, long hair, and a shapely body for one so young.

"Where y'all coming from?" Inez asks Patricia, overly interested.

"From the store," Patricia quickly responds.

"Have you heard from that Jamal guy from around the corner?" Inez asks with a mysterious smile.

"Nope, I heard he got into a fight the other day, though." Patricia goes along with her conversation, trying to find out more information.

"Yeah, I heard about that, too. My brother's friends don't like him, but he is fine as hell to me," Inez grins slightly as she licks her lips.

"Key and Cory always together, they gon' get married," Inez switch the topic, then walks over to the rest of the crowd.

"Cory, you and Key gon' get married when y'all get older?" Inez giggles putting Cory and Key in the spotlight.

Cory responds quickly and confidently in a charming tone, "Hell yeah me and 'Key Wee' getting married, what kind of question is that?"

Cory can be a schmoozer at times. He is about the same height as Key, more so on the light-skinned side of the scale, nice waves in his hair, and very cute. Everybody knows Key and Cory are boyfriend and girlfriend because they don't keep it a secret. His parents know as well, the only people who don't have a clue are my parents. Key loves how affectionate Cory is toward her and how he shows no shame to their puppy love no matter who is around. Key is just watching Inez and Cory have their conversation, soaking up every little thing Cory said as he brags about her. She is watching Inez's every move and body language because everybody knows how Inez gets down and how fast she is. Not intimidated at all, Key stands next to her boyfriend knowing Inez didn't have anything on her and that she wouldn't dare step to her but still keeps her eye on her.

"Y'all so cute!" Inez expresses insincerely.
"We know! We know!" Key rubs Inez's fake compliments in her face.
"Dang, yo, sideburns thick as hell!" Jena changes the subject out of nowhere.

Everybody is laughing unbearably at Jena's random comment.

"Her sideburns thicker than Joe's pubic hair!" Jena continues to clown Inez's sideburns while she sits there looking embarrassed.

Inez's reaction to the comment is what's making everything funnier. It's odd that Inez doesn't have anything to say about Jena, being that Jena's looks are far from perfect. Jena is sort of tall for her age, dark-skinned, and fat with short hair. Inez could have said anything about her. There are a lot of funny things to tease Jena about. Instead, she is just standing still looking stupid as all of the attention is on her extremely thick sideburns.

Jena could be sort of a bully sometimes, but she knows who to pick on and who not to pick on. She has no other choice but to be tough because she fights with her brother Joe all the time. Inez has an older brother, too, but she doesn't have any real fight in her, which is obvious.

The evening is coming to an end, and Key and I are still outside, which is surprising. My mom usually would have called us in by now. Five minutes later, I hear my dad coming down the street in his black Cadillac. He always blasts the music loud enough so he and the people outside of the car could hear it. It is always a bittersweet feeling when my dad comes home. I like it when he's home because I love his company and spending time with him. He is so funny and such an easy person to talk to. At the same time, I don't like it when he's home because there is a huge chance that he and my mom will get into a big argument, and the tension in the house will be extremely high. What makes it even worse is when they do get into an argument, my mom always acts like she needs a teammate. That's when she drags Key or me into the argument, and that becomes a scary situation. Most of the time, she calls Key in the room to defend her because she is the oldest. If she calls us into the room while they're arguing and ask a simple question, Key and I know if we didn't take her side, when he leaves, we would get a beating.

"Hey, Uncle Jihod!" Patricia and Porsha coincidently wave at the same time in their Ice Cube and Smoky voices, reminding me of the movie *Friday*.
"What's up, y'all! Dad smiles as he walks confidently in the house.

All the kids on the block and in our family love my mom and dad. He's the uncle that every kid wants to leave with after every gathering. He can be stern at the same time, so kids and adults know their limits. He stands six feet tall, caramel-skinned complexion with individual braids that hang a little past the nape of his neck, soft textured hair, and toned up with a muscular body. People say he favors the rapper Ludacris, but I don't see it. Watching him walk inside our three-bedroom house, my little petite body shivers inside wondering *what is it going to be today?*
About fifteen minutes went by, and my mom comes to poke her head out the front door and screamed for us to come in. Dreading to go into my own home, I wave goodbye to everyone.
"You should ask if y'all can spend the night," Porsha suggests
"Ok, I will," Key responds quickly, loving the idea but knowing my mom wouldn't let us.

Key kisses Cory goodbye and follows me to the house. As soon as I enter the house, I could taste the tension. I head straight to my room and close the door behind me. I'm forced to hear the hysterical argument that is happening in the room diagonal from mine. They are arguing about the furnace being fixed, which I should have expected. When Key talked to my grandparents about our broken furnace, they immediately got it fixed. As soon as we enter the house, my mom calls Key inside the room.

"So why did you tell your grandparents that the furnace was broken when I specifically asked you not to?" dad angrily confronts Key.
"Because we were cold in here for too long," Key response well prepared as good as she practiced with mom.
"But I told you not to fucking say nothing about it to them, I don't need them for shit!" Dad barks back.

He can get very hostile quickly if you take him to that point. It's weird because he doesn't know that my mom controls us and is behind a lot of things that we say to him. Key lied and said it was her idea to tell my grandparents that the furnace was broken when really my mom told her to tell my grandparents.

My mom is sitting back, watching my dad and my sister argue like they're a married couple. I don't understand why she forces Key to argue with my dad, but one thing I do know is that it is affecting their relationship in a negative way slowly but surely. I know for sure my mom wants us to hate our dad, and if that isn't true, then she makes it hard to think otherwise. She tries to brainwash us into believing all sorts of things. Since she is my mother, I have to listen to her, but I never believe her and I don't let her get in my head. I have my own mind and I know even at age six, that being here deep inside doesn't make me happy. How can I be, with the way my mom treats us?

After the ranting and raving and everybody calmed down, my dad comes and knocks on my bedroom door.

"Mik, you want to come ride with me?" he asks friendly and welcoming.

"No, I'm tired," I respond, restraining the truth.

"Come on, Mik, you can roll, we will be right back," Dad grins, with hope in his eyes that I will change my mind.

"I'll come next time. I'm about to go to sleep," I lie regretfully.

"Alright, Mik Mik, good night boop. See you later."

He closes my bedroom door and the dam breaks. Tears flood my cheeks. Lord knows I want to go with him every chance I get, but the Lord also knows I will suffer the consequences when I come back home. Out of fear, I just obey my mom's hateful ways and decline my dad's request, which tares me apart inside. Most of the time, when he leaves, he doesn't come back for a few days. I miss him so much, and when nights like this occur, I don't get to spend much time with him because they spent all night arguing. Times like these made me want to write something mean in my diary, but I cry myself to sleep instead.

Sunday went by kind of drowsy, and things around the house are back to quiet. Playing in my room most of the day, in my world of dolls and imagination made the day fly. That is my way of coping with my unhappy home. I have dollhouses, Barbie cars, adult Barbie dolls, and Barbie kids, too. I love playing with dolls so much because I enjoy the feeling of controlling my own world. Being able to pick the wife and her husband and the kids that they share excites me. No one telling me what to do, what to say, and how to feel; it is my world, and I'm in control.

Key is across the street over at Patricia and Porsha's house as usual. If my mom knew what I know about Key, she wouldn't even be allowed to be friends with them. It's funny because everything our parents don't know about Key and Cory's secret romance, his parents are fully aware of. Their parents are much more lenient than ours; they are able to express themselves to their parents and have more than just a child-parent relationship with them. I like going over there, it is fun and free, but I don't like how junky they keep the house. My mom has her ways, but one thing she does right is clean. Our house is always squeaky clean, not a crumb on the floor.

Most of the time, we do the cleaning, of course. Key does the regular chores like washing dishes and vacuuming. I clean my crowded room weekly. My room is pretty small, and I have a myriad of toys that clutters my room quickly, so I have to keep it organized. Both of us wash the walls, scrub the windows, clean all of the glass tables and coffee tables, and any other glass surfaces. We wipe down the furniture and water the plants on a weekly basis. On our cleaning days, Mom just watches us clean to make sure we are cleaning everything efficiently. She sits around and orders us like a slave master or something.

One thing I do regret about choosing to stay in the house today is that my mom consistently calls my name to do things for her.

"Miko!"
"Huh?" I run to her room.
"Go get me a glass of ice water," she demands.
"Ok."

Putting my play world on hold, with an attitude, I whisper to myself when I get downstairs. *She is so irritating! I can't even complete a thought before she calls my name again.*

Catching the ice from our refrigerator door, I think about dropping one piece of ice on the floor and putting it in her glass, but the good side of my conscience got the best of me. The idea is inspired by the movie *Friday* when Craig's father kept calling him to do stuff because he was too busy watching TV. Craig mistakenly dropped an ice cube on the floor. Instead of throwing it out, he put it in the glass of water he was making for his father. I giggle at the thought of the comedy as I walk upstairs quickly.

Mom grabs the glass, but before taking a gulp of water she asks "Why you didn't go outside today?"

"I didn't feel like it," I shrug my shoulders.

"Key loves going outside over to Patricia and Porsha's house, don't she?" she asks with a slight attitude.

"Yeah," I respond, unable to deny the facts.

"I'm about to tell her to come inside in a minute. It's almost dark out there."

Not giving my mom any information about Key's puppy love, I exit her room and resume living in my pretend world of happiness. The night finally arrives, and I'm still locked in my room. Key is home in her room, playing music with her door closed. Mom doesn't like us to stay outside on the porch or across the street for too long, but when we come in the house, we stay up all night, weekdays and weekends. Sometimes we'll be up talking to my mom or watching movies, or sometimes in our rooms doing our own thing.

Pushing Key's door open, I hear the lovely sound of Aaliyah's voice seeping through the speakers. We are huge Aaliyah fans, especially Key; she has posters of her on her walls and tries to mimic her style sometimes. Her room is much bigger than mine, and she has a full body mirror on the back of her door, which I adore. I notice her in the mirror, messing with her teeth.

"What you doing with those rubber bands? Eating them!" I sarcastically answer my own question.

"Putting them in my teeth like braces so I can close my gap."

"That's not gonna work," I'm unconvinced.

"We will see." She wraps another around her two front teeth.

"How many do you have in there?" I try to look in her mouth like a dentist.

"Like four," she responds in a funny way.

We look at each other with a straight face then burst out in laughter at her weird creativity.

"Mama kept calling my name earlier," I roll my eyes.

Key burst out in laughter.

"See, that's why you should of came with me," Key sounds sure.

"Right, she is so irritating, and then she was talking about 'Key love going across the street,'" I gossip, knowing Key would have a mouthful to say.

Key cops a quick attitude, "I sure do, they family is so different from ours. Cory can talk to his parents about anything. Everything is out in the open. I feel comfortable over there, sometimes more comfortable over there than over here. I do love being around their family, and they are very open to me and treat me like family."

I respond jealously, "Right…"

Sometimes I feel like Key likes Patricia and Porsha's parents better than ours. She is so close to them, and they seem to like her and Cory being together. Key glorifies the relationship Cory, Patricia, and Porsha have with their parents and how they don't get in trouble about every little thing, like we do. Sometimes I feel like Key likes Patricia and Porsha better than me too.

CHAPTER **THREE**

MONDAY MORNING COMES too soon, and it is time to wake up at six-thirty in the morning. I like going to school, mostly to get away from home, but the process of waking up is brutal. When my mom taps me, I wake up easily. I can be a light sleeper at times. The fear of my dolls makes it harder for me to sleep in my room at night after seeing the movie *Dolly Dearest*. I usually sleep in my mom's or Key's room.

My dad is home this morning, lying on the couch. *I wonder why he's lying on the couch. I hope him and mom not beefing like usual.* I'm so happy he's home, and I can't wait to wake him up. He drops us off at school in the morning when he's home. To wake him, I turn on my "Wake-Up Song." The Wake-Up song consist of me yelling extremely loud, saying, "WAKE UP...COME ON, COME ON...WAKE UPPP!!?" for about a minute straight. I turn my Barbie recorder volume to the maximum and place it on the arm of the couch right next to his ear. When the loud screaming comes on, he pops up quickly in defense mode like he's ready to fight.

"Turn that shit off!" dad yells with a frown on his face.

I almost fall trying to restrain my laughter. I quickly press the stop button, and the music shuts off abruptly.

"That shit not funny," he looks mad, then he smirks, finding some kind of humor out of it, too.

I love it when he drops us off at school because he listens to the sweetest music. On the ride there, "Soon You'll Understand" by Jay Z is playing through the speakers pretty loudly. Sitting in the back seat and looking out the window, it looks like the winter is coming sooner than expected. All of the trees stand naked, not a leaf in sight, with a light brush layer of white snow hardly sticking to the trees and ground. Bobbing my head to the good music, I ask dad from the backseat.

"What's the name of this album?"
"This Jay Z new album, The Dynasty: Roc La Familia."
"I like this song," I bob my head happily in a good mood.

We arrive at school too quickly, and my dad drops us off at the front door. Entering my classroom, I see Mrs. Johnson shuffling around her desk, looking busy. Will is right behind me, walking quickly as if he's running from the cold weather. Will is like my boy best friend. He's high yellow, chubby with big ears and wears glasses. He is very smart, too. Sometimes we help each other with classwork, and we always talk and share laughs. I'm almost sure that he secretly has a crush on me, but he's too shy to say anything to me about it. I never asked him because I don't look at him in that way, so I don't feel like it's something to talk about. Even if I did feel that way about him, I still wouldn't say anything to him about it because I'm sort of shy myself when it comes to these things.

"It's cold as fuck out there, ain't it?" I ask Will, giggling.
"Hell yeah... I almost started running as fast as I can," he begins laughing.
Class is going by smoothly and everybody is going easy on Mrs. Johnson, she seems like she's not having the best day. She keeps coughing and her eyes keep watering. I'm happy everybody is on

their best behavior and not giving Mrs. Johnson a hard time, she is such a nice lady. Before recess is over, I make sure I tell Samantha and Trisha about my birthday party that is coming up.

"When is your birthday again?" Samantha asks.

"In a few weeks, November thirteenth, and I'm having a basement party," I explain to Samantha and Trisha.

"I'm going to ask my mom if I can come," Trisha smiles.

"Me, too," Samantha quickly adds playing in her hair.

The end of the day is approaching, and everybody is complaining about how they can't wait to go home. I'm ready for school to be over, but I'm not necessarily ready to go home. I miss my grandparents with all my heart. Since they moved to North Carolina, we don't get to see them as much as we're used to. It also causes us to be at home way more, which really sucks ass. We used to go over to their house almost every other weekend when they lived here in Detroit. My grandparents have no idea how my mother treats us, either. I wonder what they would say if they knew. Snapping back from daydreaming, while waiting on my mom to pick us up, one of Key's friends named Jarvis greets me.

"Little Key Key, what you over here doing?" Jarvis smiles.

"Nothing, waiting on my mama." I put my hands in my coat pocket.

"Why you look so much better than Key?" he asks in an amusing way.

I giggle at his flattering question—I know it isn't supposed to be taken seriously. He is so cute though, and he is short for a boy his age, which makes him closer to my second-grade height. He is light-skinned with nice teeth, full lips, and he has a short afro cut. I know in my mind that he is too old for me. I'm not sure if he is in Key's grade or a year older or younger, but I know for sure that he is way older than me. Key walks up out of nowhere.

"What is you over here talking to my little sister about?" Key jokingly checks Jarvis.

"I was just asking her why she looks so much better than you," Jarvis gives her a goofy look.

"Boy, shut up! You irritating!" She hits him as both of them share laughs.

People say those kinds of jokes to us a lot, but Key never shows any type of offense or jealousy, which makes me feel comfortable. After joking with Jarvis, my mom pulls up, banging some old school music. When getting in the car, I immediately recognize the song that was just a cloud of bass outside of the car. She is playing one of her favorite old school songs called, Take Your Time by The SOS Band. Mom always finds time to play her old school music. Sometimes she hogs the radio and listens to her old school music the entire time we're in the car. It doesn't bother me much because I like most of her old school songs. Both of my parents are music lovers like me and have really good taste when it comes to music.

On the way home, my mom seem to be in a good mood, so that made me happy. She is singing and dancing in the driver's seat, making Key and me laugh. When we have birthday parties and sleepovers, music always features the events, and we always end up singing, dancing, or mimicking some type of song or movie that have singing in it.

"Y'all don't know nothing about this!" Mom is dancing in her driver seat, doing some kind of ticking moves with her shoulders and arms.

Key and I are dying laughing because she gets so serious when she dances. Her eyes buck, but not in a mean creepy way, like when she gets mad, but in a playful, funny way. We enjoy watching her dance on the low because she can really dance. It's just that the dances she does are old school dances, which makes her look old and silly because those dances aren't popular anymore. It's a little embarrassing when she dances in front of our friends, but they think it's funny, too. I try to smother myself in these times because they don't last long. Most of the time, she seems so mad and unhappy. It makes me feel like I have to be on guard all the time.

Running to my place of peace, I close my bedroom door in a good mood.

"Stop running around this goddamn house! If I have to tell you again, you're going to get your little ass whooped!" mom yells from downstairs.

I immediately give her the two middle fingers, rock star style as if she's standing in front of me. "Yeah… yeah… suck on these!" I flop on my bed.

My birthday is coming soon and I still haven't told anybody what I want. Rushing to my backpack ripping a piece of paper to write down my birthday wish list, it includes:

<u>Birthday Wish List</u>
American Girl Doll
Clothes
Shoes
Games
Baby alive
Barbie dolls

My list isn't long, but it is sort of expensive. Out of everything that is on my birthday wish list, what I want the most is an American Girl doll, which I do not own one yet.

My granny created a monster when she introduced me to the American Girl Dolls catalogue. The American Girl Dolls are dolls that are supposed to symbolize younger girls from as far back as the 1700s and maybe even further back into time that witnessed historic events. They aren't little girls who lived in real life, but the concept of the meaning of each doll would make one think they were real little girls who lived once before. That's what's so sweet about them.

These dolls are more like collectible dolls, as opposed to playing dolls. They range from one hundred to two hundred dollars, not including accessories. Each doll comes with a book that explains the type of historical event that happened around the time the fictional character was a kid. Another thing that's intriguing about the books and the dolls is that the little girls are the same age as me. That's what immediately sparked my interest and connection with American Girl Dolls.

Sometimes I hate my birthday because it's so close to the first report card marking. Even though bad grades are never allowed in my household, it's pressuring because if I receive a bad report card, I might not get what I want for my birthday.

The phone begins ringing at a distance, so I run to answer it.

"Hello?"

"Hey, Mickey," I catch granddaddy's stern, deep voice.

"Hey, granddaddy," I respond with a slight giggle.

"How are you doing?"

"I'm doing good! You know my birthday is coming up!" I politely remind him, hoping they didn't forget.

"Yeah, I know, what do you want for your birthday?"

"I want an American Girl Doll and other kinds of Barbie dolls, too," I answer excitedly.

"American Girl Doll?" He sounds confused at what I'm talking about.

"Yeah, Granny gets the magazines for the dolls," I explain.

"Oh, okay, I have to tell her about that, then. Is it one doll or a bunch of them?"

"It's a bunch of dolls, and all of them are from different places and were born in different periods of time. But the first one I want is Josefina; she's the prettiest one."

"Okay, well, I'll tell your granny. When do you get your report card?"

"In a couple of weeks," I dryly respond dreading the turn this conversation just made.

"Well, you know you have to get a good report card if you want that doll," he adds with a little more bass in his voice so I know he's serious.

"I know, I will," I add less excited.

"Okay, well, let me talk to your mom."

November thirteenth came faster than expected. I'm turning seven-years old today in the year 2000. I'm super excited about my party we're throwing today and I'm hoping everybody will be able to show up. We always throw basement parties for my birthday. All of the family and friends gather downstairs in the basement and share laughs, memories, and food. My favorite part is the good music that's going to be played. There are things I hate about my parents, but their taste in music is the bomb, plus they know how to throw a party.

My dad picked us up from school today, and that alone brightened up my day. He brought me home to a bunch of gifts, but there is this one box that is sticking out the most. It is the biggest and the tallest; it's almost as tall as me. While opening up gifts, trying my new clothes and shoes on that my parents bought for me, everyone seemed to be in a good mood. My mom is cooking and dancing, getting everything prepared for tonight while the music through the speakers plays loud and clear. I waited to open up the biggest gift for last. I grab a sharp knife to open my last gift. As soon as dad notices the knife in my hand, he grabs the knife from me before I could even think about what to do with it.

"Let me see," he adds giggling at me.

I laugh because of how fast he grabbed the knife out of my hand. I closely watch as my dad cut the clear tape that's keeping the tall brown box sealed.

My dad pulls out a rectangular box displaying a light tinted Mexican looking doll by the name of Josefina. She is prettier in person, and her book is lying right beside her. The box also includes some of Josefina's accessories. She has two other outfits with jewelry to match and an extra book to go with one of the outfits.

I'm so excited to read these books! I'm currently at the end of one of my Mary-Kate and Ashley books. It's a mystery/drama kind of story. I love the Olsen twins, too. I have so many of their movies when they were all kinds of ages. Most of the movies I own are the ones when they were between the ages of seven and ten years old, which makes me feel like we're around the same age, but in reality, they're closer to Key's age.

Everybody is slowly but surely arriving for my basement party. My mom cooked mostly hand foods for our guests like hot dogs, hamburgers, and tacos. Mom left it up to the rest of the aunties and uncles to bring side dishes. Family and friends are showing up with gifts and food, my best friend Samantha is here too, which is surprising because we're only in the second grade. Most parents are overprotective of their little ones, but her mom seemed to like my mom a lot. Samantha's mom dropped her off and is coming back to pick her up later. Of course, Patricia and Porsha are over, considering they live right across the street. By the time everyone had settled in, after playing games, my mom starts a dance contest with the kids.

"Come on, y'all! Get in a soul train line," mom yells overenthusiastically.

Everybody gathers around and forms a two-sided line with a space in the middle, and one person from each side goes down the center. While my mom is hyping all the kids up to dance, my friend Samantha is kind of confused about what is going on, which is so hilarious. My cousins and friends from the neighborhood know how my mom is so everybody is prepared and geeked up. We dance all the time, so it isn't anything new to us. To get the party started, mom plays one of the popular mixed CDs. Mix songs are popular in the neighborhood. Anytime the mix songs come on, everybody knows entertainment was about to hit the fan. The first song that comes on is "Bounce That." I don't know who's rapping on this song or the DJ, but I do know it's good dancing music with exclusive beats. After everyone got all riled up, my mom's favorite mix song comes on, "Let me bang," and then she begins to get extra excited.

She have to stop herself from getting up and out-dancing all the kids. My boy cousins are here, too, but they aren't having as much fun as the girls because they don't find it fun to dance as much. My mom made up this dance where you pat your body up and down like you are about to battle somebody in a dance competition and had all of the kids doing it to each other down the soul train line. She made my cousin Raven and I go against each other in a dance battle. Raven is a couple of years older than me, and she has a younger sister named Micha that is my age. I'm guessing she had us go against each other because we both are skinny and can dance really well. Her sister isn't much of a dancer. She is more on the tomboy side of the fence. Raven and Micha aren't our blood cousins. Their mom, Tina and my mom, are best friends and claim each other as sisters. What makes it even more convincing is that we all favor each other. We are all on the light-skinned side, tall, skinny with nice textured long hair, so people assume we're blood related anyways.

After I won the dance battle, the mix song "Push it" comes on, which is one of our favorites. As the song slowly begins, Key and Patricia pulls their shirts up, revealing only their stomachs and start to Hip-roll. Hip rolling is a popular dance that everybody in the neighborhood have mastered, even the boys hip roll. Typically, when the girls Hip-roll it is cute, but when a boy starts to "roll" as we call it for short, it is sort of sexy. After my mom geeked Key and Patricia up, everybody starts hyping me up to Hip-roll. At first, I'm sort of shy being that all of my friends and family are here. Everybody is surrounding me, as I get more nervous, my dad gets out of his seat to record me on the video camera.

"Come on, Miko, stop acting shy!" mom yells and I can tell she's getting a little annoyed.

Swallowing all of my bashful feelings, pulling my shirt up only to expose my stomach. I take a quick glance at my best friend Samantha from school, and she looks so surprised. Like she can't believe I'm about to start hip-rolling. When I start rolling my small hips to the rhythm of the beat, the basement full of friends and family begin to roar out of excitement, which boost my confidence. As the night proceeds, I open gifts, we sing happy birthday, and have cake and ice cream.

The night went on and eventually comes to an end. I'm so happy I got a grade point average of 3.8 on my report card. My parents probably would have cancelled the party if I had gotten a low average. As my parents cleans up after our guests departure. Key and I are upstairs, minding our own business in our own rooms. Josefina made my entire birthday. I love the way she looks in real life and her accessories that my grandparents paid extra for. I'm so happy my grandparents came through. The peace and quietness that's surprisingly consuming the house is delightful as well. I'm sure the peace won't last for long. Surely as it stands, I fall asleep in my room, reading the book that Josefina came with.

CHAPTER **FOUR**

CLASS IS BORING on this Wednesday morning. We have interesting bell-work; we have to write a paragraph about if we believe in Santa Clause and why. Then after writing our beliefs, we have to present it in front of the class. I'm usually nervous to talk in front of the class, but this is a good topic, and I'm anxious to get up and give my opinion. My teacher gave us about fifteen to twenty minutes to write and prepare for presentation. When the time is up, we start on the left side of the room and end on the right side. Luckily, I'm sitting on the left side of the classroom, so it will be my turn sooner than later. I'm the third person to present; walking up to the front of the classroom is nerve-wracking, but when I start to talk, the nervous feeling in my stomach disappears.

"Well, I don't believe in Santa Clause because of two reasons," I speak confidently.
"And why is this, Ms. Lewis?" Mrs. Johnson eagerly asks, waiting on my response.
"Because when I go to different malls. At some of the malls Santa is black and at others he's white. Everybody knows that you can't be black and white at the same time or on different days.
Trying to hold her laugh in, Mrs. Johnson utters, "And what's your second reason?"

"I noticed that when I'm opening up gifts on Christmas, on the to and from sticker, it usually says it's from one of my family members and not from Santa Clause."

Walking back to my seat, I just know in my own head that I'm right, and I have good enough reason to believe Santa isn't real. As Mrs. Johnson proceeds to the next student. I begin daydreaming about seeing my grandparents on Christmas day. Christmas is in just a couple of weeks, and I'm so happy my Grandparents are coming to town. I miss them so much, and I know when they visit, they are going to stay with us. That means if they stay with us, my parents will put on their fake happy faces and act nice to each other.

On top of that, I miss my granny's cooking, and I know she will cook every day that she is here. She is always trying new recipes and doing new things with different kinds of food and desserts. I'm also looking forward to my grandparents coming to town because I know they will take us shopping. I'm a November baby, so I've been building my Christmas list since my birthday passed.

The end of the day comes soon enough, and my dad is outside early. It feels good not to have to wait in this cold weather today. It's only fun to wait on a ride during the summertime. It always makes me happy when my dad picks us up from school because most of the time, my mom picks us up. When Key and I get in the car, we immediately speak to my dad, and his response is so energetic.

"What up, doe!" he yells in a joyful manner.

His sense of humor is so embarrassing at times that you can't help but to laugh.

"What's so funny, Busta?" he asks me in a less serious tone.
"Nothing," I add while getting comfortable in the back seat.
"Y'all want to play basketball, test y'all abilities?" he asks, looking

at Key as she sits in the passenger seat, looking as if she's having unsure feelings.

Interested and anxious, I speak up. "I want to play basketball, that would be fun!"

"My girl, Mik Mik, I knew you would want to play!" he adds with his hands out, initiating a high five.

Key never answered his question, so he probably is assuming that she's not interested in playing, but I know different. Basketball probably wouldn't have been her first choice of all sports to play, but I know she has to check in with my mom first. Since I'm younger, my mom goes a little lighter on me, but Key knows better. On the rest of the ride home, we listen to music by the Fugees. I love the sound of this band. The few songs I'm familiar with are very soothing to my seven-year-old ears. Watching my dad bob his head while rapping the lyrics to the song "Ready or Not" made me enjoy the song even more. Seeing his strong emotions to specific songs help me understand music and words better. Having two parents that love music gives me no choice but to love and appreciate the world of music.

Pulling up to our house, I notice a dark blue truck sitting directly in front of the house. Thinking nothing of it, I grab my backpack and follow my dad and Key into the house. Walking inside the door and being greeted by my granny is one of the best feelings in the world. My grandparents are in town early, and that's a joyous feeling.

"Hey, Mickey, you're getting so big." granny smiles from ear to ear hugging me tightly.

"Hey, Granny, I thought y'all wasn't coming until next week."

"We wanted to surprise you," she speaks softly with her ruby red lipstick painted on perfectly.

"I miss you, boo," granny adds smiling from ear to ear.

" I miss you, too! I wish we could just come over y'all house," I admit less excited by the inconvenience of them living out of town.

PRETTY CAN BE UGLY

Granny bends down on one knee to be closer to my height. "You can... just come over, we're just a flight away."

Key rolls her eyes, adding under her breath, "They always use that line." Key continues with a little more sarcasm than me, "It's not as easy as just driving over your house."

"Well, we will pay for you guys to come down during the summer, and whenever other time y'all want to come down," Granddaddy jumps in the conversation with his casual frown on his face.

Key avoids an argument and continues to go upstairs to her room. My granddaddy is a very tall, long-legged, dark-skinned macho man. Tall like a basketball player and weight like a football player, they call him Big Jim or Pudding. When it comes to my granddad, it is his way or the highway, similar to my mom. Granny is the opposite, nice, soft backbone sort of personality. People always say opposites attract, and they are definitely opposites.

As the day goes on with love and laughter in the air, I'm not locked in my room because of the company of my grandparents. My dad is present and chilling around the house with the family. I noticed my granddaddy didn't have much to say to my dad, but that didn't seem to intimidate my dad at all. Even though there is a permanent tension between my dad and granddad, they still show respect towards one another, which keeps the peace and unity within the immediate family. Granddaddy never liked the choice of men and people my mom involved herself with. I know because I've overheard conversations my grandparents had about her. He hates the fact that she's married to a drug dealer but respects the fact that he can financially take care of his responsibilities and protect his family. Mom was adopted when she was a newborn. My grandparents are the only parents she knows. Being raised by two hard-working parents, I'm sure they wonder where her wild/lazy side comes from, or maybe they don't. We know mom is adopted because she told us. Far as features, Granny and Granddaddy don't look like they would create my mom anyway. To be honest, Mom sort of favors my granddaddy in a hard to explain kind of way, and their mean ways mimic each other to the tee. By the love and support they show her and us, I don't think blood would make us any closer.

As the day goes on with no drama throughout the house, Granny decides to bake some peanut butter cookies and a red velvet cake. I assist her in the kitchen while my mom is hanging by the bar area, which separates the kitchen and the dining room. Granddaddy and Dad are in the living room watching sports and Key is coming down the stairs.

"Can I go outside?" Key pops her head in the dining room where we are.

Mom looks at her like she's agitated, "Where do you want to go outside?"

"Across the street," Key answers dryly because she knows mom knows where she wants to go.

"No," my mom cuts the conversation short.

Key quietly goes back upstairs to her room. I know she's mad that my mom said she couldn't go outside. She's probably cursing my mom out in her head. Even though Key is a mama's girl, she still gets as annoyed with my mom as much, if not more, than I do. Sometimes I wish Key would just stand up to my mom. But the fear that's been embedded in us takes over.

"She always want to go across the street. She probably be over there with that little boy," Mom looks at me while I try my hardest not to lock eyes with her.

Granny responds off guard, "What boy?"

"You know, Porsha and Patricia's brother Cory. The kids from across the street," mom explains.

Remembering the names, Granny answers, "Oh, okay, they're her friends, right?"

Mom snaps, "She only like going over there because they can do whatever they want over there. Their parents let them run wild like little hoodlums."

Granny giggles at my mom, "Hoodlums?" as she sips on something that looks like cold clear water.

Granny acts so late and kind of clueless about slang words at times. It's so funny because she's so nice, so when she gets serious, it's hard to take her seriously.

"Can I have some of your water?" I ask as the mist from the cold temperature fogs the outside of the glass.

"This isn't water, boo," she moves the glass away from me.

"What is it?" I ask knowing the answer.

"It's a drink for grown-ups?" she responds quickly with a straight face.

"Can I see what the drinks for grownups taste like?" I smile.

"No," she says firmly.

Mom and I are giggling.

"Ma, let her taste a little bit of it," mom suggests in a humorous way.

"No, I'm not," Granny stands by what she said.

I don't think my grandparents know that sometimes my mom lets us taste her drinks. Little does she know, I know what she's drinking is nasty as fuck because it's alcohol. As the day goes by, the family is just chilling and catching up.

"Where did Key go?" Granddaddy asks curiously, since she hasn't been in sight within the last few hours.

"Locked in that room. She act like since she can't go outside, she has to bury herself in her room." Mom frowns.

I understand why Key wants to bury herself in her room. The difference between her and me is when family is around or visiting, I enjoy being around my family. As far as for Key, she desires to be with her boyfriend and his family no matter the occasion.

My mom goes on about Key getting on her nerves as she pours herself another glass of wine for company, while Granny and I listen and continue to bake. I get nervous when my mom starts drinking because she becomes so aggressive, and you just never know what she's going to do or say. What makes it so astonishing is that she doesn't have to drink too much to reach her maximum level. One glass of anything that is stronger than pop is enough for her—even I can see that, so I know she must be aware of her own tolerance.

Then again, nobody else says anything about her low tolerance for drinking either. So, that's probably why she thinks it's fine. She doesn't drink all the time, but when she does, you never know what's going to happen next.

"Jim, you want to try some of this cake?" Granny politely asks.

"What do you think, Mary?" Granddaddy sounds fed up over nothing.

"Well, I just asked." Granny huffs.

"You heard what I said, Mary." Granddaddy shoos her off.

Most of the time, Granny ignores his mean attitude but listens to what he says. When Granddaddy starts to drink, he becomes really mean, especially to Granny. When he is sober, he's still mean to her, but it's worse when alcohol enters the picture. Granny's attitude is a bit more feisty than normal when she starts to drink, but only for good reasoning. I think the alcohol gives her more confidence to stand up to Granddaddy and everybody else. She never get's too carried away with it, her or my dad. They can handle their tolerance for smoking and drinking pretty well from what my seven-year old eyes have seen.

CHAPTER **FIVE**

THE MORNING SEEPS through with the delicious smell of breakfast. Instantly, I know it's my Granny's cooking. Filled with excitement, I rush downstairs to hear The Spinners playing through our speakers singing "The Rubberband Man." Skipping to the dining room, I see everybody's up before me. I'm usually the first person to wake up so this is kind of weird.

"Morning, Mickey," granddaddy speaks in his baritone voice.
"Good morning," I smile as big as Mickey Mouse.
"Mickey you want some breakfast?" Granny asks nicely.
"Yeah, y'all eating without me?" I frown feeling a little left out.
"No, nobody has eaten yet, the food just got finished," Granddaddy corrects me.
"Go and brush your teeth first, Mik Mik, before you eat." Dad looks like he's in a good mood.
"Ok." I rush to the bathroom.
"Make sure you brush your tongue, too," mom yells as I leave the room.

After eating breakfast, everybody parts ways. Dad left to handle some business as always. Key is going to stay with mom. I'm guessing she's staying home so she can go outside. My grandparents are going to visit some family members. I'm hoping my mom lets me go with my grandparents, since she never lets me go with my dad.

"Ma, can I go with granny and granddaddy?" I cross my fingers behind my back.
"Yeah, I don't care," she answers quickly like she's annoyed with me wanting to go with them.

That is music to my ears! I hurry to get in the shower so nobody would have to wait for me. When I'm finished showering, my mom had my clothes laid out on my bed. After putting on my clothes, I had to let mom do my hair. I hate it when she does my hair for two reasons. For one, she never lets me choose my hairstyle. For two, she parts my scalp so hard, as if she's intentionally trying to hurt me. It doesn't make it any better that I'm tender headed. Mom never shows any compassion for how heavy handed she is. She always styles my hair in ponytails; the fewer the ponytails means the faster she can get out of my head. Today, I guess she is feeling lazy and only gives me two ponytails, which is more than enough for me. As she finishes, she puts four to five rings on my small hands. I wish these rings could magically stick to my fingers. Sometimes I get nervous wearing all of this jewelry. The memory of getting a beating for letting my friend at school wear one sticks like glue. Before letting me leave her room, she subtly adds:

"Don't be telling your grandparents our business either," mom squints her eyes, looking deep in my soul.
"Ok," I nod my head, knowing if I were to say anything about how she treats us to anybody she would give me the punishment of a lifetime.

Out of fear, I never speak a word to my dad, grandparents, or to anybody. The same thing goes for Key. We don't tell anybody our family business. What is mind-boggling to me is that everybody, including family and friends, are judgmental towards us. They assume that we live this perfect life. I guess they judge us by the way we carry ourselves and how well-dressed we're kept. But it is way deeper than that. Life is not always about how you look. It's about how you feel, and I realize this early without an advisor or a counselor. But the way family, friends, and strangers show their fascinating *ouuss* and *ahhs* help me understand that a lot of people don't look at life like that.

After visiting one of my granny's brothers, we had everybody meet us at George's, which is a Coney Island restaurant my granddaddy loves going to. If you don't know anything about Detroit, please note that the best Coney Island's and Corned beef spots are here. When they come to town, they make sure they make a trip to Coney Island and White Castle, which I think is funny because they aren't fancy restaurants. Waiting on Key and my mom, I break the silence.

"Why do y'all like Coney Island so much?"

Granny giggles, and granddaddy answers, "Because we don't have Coney Islands down south."

Bursting out in laughter, I say "What do you mean?"

"Just what I said." Granddaddy giggles at my question.

"So, there are no Coney Islands down south at all?" I confirm.

"Not where we live," granny looks sure.

"So, Mickey, what do you want for Christmas?" granny switches the gear to the conversation.

"An American Girl Doll," I smile in fascination.

"American Girl Doll?" Granddaddy asks in an irritated tone of voice.

"Yeah," I laugh because I know he knows what I'm talking about this time.

"Which one?" Granny ignores his obvious little attitude.

"Addy, the black girl," I explain, as my granny is taking note to every little word I speak.

"Oh, you want the black girl this time, huh?" Granddaddy adds sarcastically.

"Yeah," I nod my head.

"Why didn't you want the black girl at first?" he inquires in a less serious way.

"I don't know. I guess I wanted the one that favored me the most the first time."

Granddaddy laughs. "That Mexican doll does look like you."

Walking through the door is my mom and sister. The waiter directs them towards our table. When they're seated, we order our food, share a couple of laughs, and gossip about each other's day. Granddaddy took the tab when everybody was done eating, and we head home. As the night goes on, everybody talks about exchanging gifts and what they want for Christmas. Key sticks around for the family time, which is relaxing and cool. Granny isn't in the kitchen, which is irregular, so I take advantage of every time she isn't busy to find my way to snuggle her arm fat. I'm infatuated with her fat on her upper arm. Most of the time, she lets me squeeze and rub her arm fat, but sometimes she acts appalled. So, when she acts funny style, I navigate to my granddaddy's earlobes. Sometimes I play with my granny's earlobes too, but she gets irritated a little faster with me playing with her ears as opposed to her arm.

While rubbing on granddaddy's earlobe, he asks quickly "What's up with you and people's ears?"

"I don't know. I just notice everybody has fat earlobes except for me. Mama don't really have fat earlobes either," I shrug my shoulders.

Granny giggles taking a sip from her straw, "Fat earlobes? Oh is that why you like playing with my arms? Because you think they're fat?"

"She is always playing with somebody's ears and fat, that's so annoying," Key blurts out.

"Why don't you just play with your own?" Granddaddy continues while letting me play with his ears.

"Because mine are too small. I don't even have fat on mine." I showcase my small earlobes for the room full of people to see.

"Wake up, Mickey, it's Christmas Eve!" Granny exclaims.

Waking up slowly but surely, I hear music coming from downstairs, which gives me a mixed feeling of comfort and excitement. Looking out the window, I see snow coming down very slow and daintily.

"Mickey, are you going to bake some cookies for Santa?" Granny smiles.
"For Santa, granny?" I ask with a straight face.
"Yeah," Granny doesn't crack her smile.
We can make some cookies for me. I don't know about Santa, crazy lady! I think quickly to myself.
"Ok, we can make some." I go along with it, not wanting to be a "Debbie Downer."
"We'll make some tonight before everybody goes to sleep." It's obvious granny is way more excited than I am about leaving "Santa Clause" some cookies, but I enjoy her holiday spirit.

As the day goes on, I'm enjoying Christmas Eve in the house, embracing everybody's company, while my granny and granddaddy make little smart remarks towards each other per usual. My parents aren't really speaking to each other at all. I notice small things like that between them two but didn't let it bother me. I would rather they not speak to each other than to be yelling in each other's faces. Key and I are spending a lot of time with each other playing hand games and Mancala. When ten o'clock hit, all of the adults heads downstairs to the basement. I stay upstairs to watch the last batch of cookies that we were making for "Santa". Curious to see what everyone is doing downstairs, I creep down to the basement and see they are wrapping gifts. I approach my dad while coming down the stairs, since he's the first person who locked eyes with me. A tall brown box that looks similar to the box Josefina came in grabs my attention.

With a smile slipping through the corner of my mouth, I ask "Who's the tall brown box for?"
"Go back upstairs, sneak-Ko!" my dad jokes.

Running back upstairs, I gossip to Key about them wrapping gifts and that I might be getting my second American Girl Doll.

"Was it a lot of gifts down there?" Key asks intrusively.
"Yeah, it was a whole bunch of stuff, but daddy told me to come back upstairs."

We share some giggles amongst each other and continue to play games. Soon after, Key and I went to sleep earlier than usual, growing too excited for Christmas. I had a plan to wake everyone up as early as possible to open presents. Before going to sleep, I do Josefina's hair and sit her on top of my dresser gently.

"Wake up. It's Christmas!" I sing waking my grandparents up first.

Next, I walk to my parent's room, to wake them up as well. After waking the household up, everybody head downstairs to open gifts. I was trying my hardest to find a tall, sort of narrow box. Giving up, I quickly reach for the gift that's closest to me. The first gift I open have two perfectly folded Guess outfit sets inside. The second gift I open is the Xbox and a Star Wars game that came with it, which is surprising because I didn't have this on my list. The Xbox had just come out, and even though I wasn't crazy about it, I'm still happy to have it.

While everyone is opening gifts, the bottom of the Christmas tree is getting empty. I'm finally able to see the box I was looking for. Seeing the tall box creates a bubbly feeling in my gut. Before opening the gift that has my name on it, I secretly pray to myself that it is Addy, the second American Girl Doll I'd been dreaming about. I swiftly begin ripping the wrapping paper off of the box like I was being timed in a race. Once the wrapping paper is clean off, I still need to get past this tape that sealed the familiar box. After having a hard time with opening the big box, it's finally open, revealing my American Girl Doll, Addy.

Addy is an African American who lived in the 1850s as a slave. She despises the fact that blacks worked for whites and were considered to be beneath whites. She came with a book as well, and the clothes that she is wearing are very identical to the clothes I have seen slaves wear in movies. Her hair is on the coarser side like African Americans. She is so much different from Josefina, and I love both of them. Josefina is closer to my skin complexion, and Addy have a dark skin complexion. Both of them are my favorite compared to the other American Girl Dolls. That's why I made sure I asked for these two first.

Being that I woke everybody up so early, I thought everyone would go back to sleep and wake back up. I was wrong. Everyone stayed awake trying on clothes and trying out their new gadgets. I'm so hype to play with my new Xbox.

However, I'm less excited that my grandparents will be leaving in a couple of days. With them being at the house, I was able to escape from my mom. On top of that, it is so peaceful in the house with them being here, but I know when they leave, it will go back to the crazy normal.

CHAPTER **SIX**

THE LAST DAY of class is bittersweet. I'm going to miss my close friends and especially Mrs. Johnson. I am excited for summertime and starting dance school though. Speaking of *friends*, my best friend Samantha is mad at me because I didn't want to let her see my favorite pencil. The last time I let her borrow my cute Mickey Mouse notepad, I never got it back, so she's making it her business to try to avoid me.

"Bye, Mrs. Johnson, I'll make sure I come to visit you next semester," I wave.
"Okay, Sweetie, you make sure of that! Are you coming back to this school for third grade?"
"Yeah, I think so,"
"Well, I will see you in September, pretty girl," she gently touches one of my ponytails.

After I said my goodbyes to Mrs. Johnson, I proceed with my goodbyes to my friends and classmates. As all of us walk out of the classroom, I notice Samantha is still being petty and ignoring me. When I find Key and her friends, I tag along with her until one of our parents show up. While waiting, I see Samantha standing by herself, so I decide to go and talk to her before one of us leave for the summer.

"Hey, Samantha, where you about to go?" I ask, trying to lighten up the tension, but Samantha didn't even look at me twice, which made me say fuck it. If it takes the smallest things for her to get mad and act like she doesn't want to talk to me or be friends anymore, maybe it's just not meant for us to be friends. I'm not about to keep kissing her ass. Right before walking away from Samantha's mad ass. My mom shows up out of nowhere with a camera.

"Hey, my two favorite Power Puff Girls! Y'all say *cheese* for the camera!" Mom snaps a quick picture on the disposable camera. *"fuck this bitch"* I think to myself as Samantha and I stand next to each other awkwardly.

After taking pictures with friends, Mom, Key, and I head to the car. Mom seems to be in a good mood, which made me happy inside. I try to soak up her good mood days.

"Ma, can we go to McDonald's, I'm hungry?"

"Yeah, we can go there." Mom nods her head as she turns on the radio.

I'm looking forward to McDonald's. I'm so happy she said we can go to McDonald's, because we never eat a lot of fast food. When we pull up to the drive-thru, my mom orders.

"Yes, can I have two number ones, Key what you want?" Mom giggles.

"I want a number one and one extra Big Mac."

"And another number one meal with an extra Big Mac on the side," my mom yells.

"Extra cheese and extra mac sauce," Key twiddles with her fingers.

"Put extra cheese and extra mac sauce on all of the Big Macs," mom speaks clearly to the microphone.

"Miko, what you want?" Mom looks back at me from the front seat.

"A chicken nugget meal with sweet and sour sauce."

"And can I have a chicken nugget meal with sweet and sour

sauce, please, and a strawberry milkshake, and that will be all." Mom drives to the next window.

After we pay for our food, mom immediately pulls around to park so we can eat in the car.
"Can I try some of that milkshake?" I flop to the center of the backseat.
"Yeah."
Mom hands me the milkshake. Before taking a sip, I flip the straw around so I wouldn't drink off the same side my mom is drinking off of. When she heard the sound of the straw coming out of the cup. She turns around quickly from the front seat with a major attitude.

"I'm your motherfucking MOTHER! You came out of my PUSSY!" She expresses with rage.
"Must you remind me?" I think in my head, unbothered.
"I don't know why she act like that!" she finally turns around to finish her meal, talking to Key like I'm not in the car.

I know where I came from, so I don't really get why she made that comment. What I don't know is what she does with her mouth or what any of my other relatives do with their mouths. My household family looks down on me because I don't like eating after them. I feel like they judge me because of it. They try to make me feel bad about it, all of the time. They often try to make it seem like I think I'm better than them because I don't eat after them. Even though I'm the youngest, I don't let their antagonizing, strong opinions change my mind. I continue not to eat or drink off of them or anyone else. I personally think it's nasty, and it's one of the most disgusting things people casually do.

"Whatever, they'll get over it," I shrug my shoulders and continue eating my nuggets.
"She think we have rabies or something." Key giggles instigating

the topic.

"Exactly, I don't know who the fuck she think she is." Mom frowns as if she's fed up.

"And I don't give a fuck!" I respond in my head.

She's really mad about me flipping the straw around. Like, girl, when are you going to get over it? I can't wait until I get older so I can say how I really feel and not be in fear of getting in trouble. *"When I get older, I'm not lying on the bed to wait on her to whoop my ass. Watch!"* I think sternly in my head as I continue to eat my food.

"Next week dance school start and we have to see what classes y'all want to take." Mom finally changes the topic.

"At what dance school?" Key asks.

"Wendy School of Dance. You know the first dance school we went to go visit sometime last week."

"Oh, okay, well I know for sure I want to take hip hop and jazz class." Key does a silly dance.

"Miko, what you want to take?"

"I don't know," I make sure I'm short with my response since I'm still annoyed.

Key and mom continue to talk while we all finish eating. Mom is going on about a cousin that we don't remember who she recently ran into. She's explaining how he did something so small to her when they were kids, and how she's still mad to this day.

"He tried to speak to me, and I walked right past his ass. The nigga' must of thought I forgot," mom adds with confidence.

"When did this happen?" Key asks, sounding lost.

"When we were in, like, high school," Mom answers confidently.

And you're still holding anger in your heart against this man? I roll my eyes in the backseat, continuing to make comments in my head. *Again! Get the fuck over it!!*

Mom is explaining an incident that happened over twenty years ago as if it happened last week. She's a good grudge holder, and it's really sad. After her hate story, we proceed on our trip home while the newest music plays on the radio. We arrive home pretty quickly, and surprisingly none of our friends are outside. It's probably too hot for everybody, or maybe everybody is over someone's house. As soon as we park the car, Key asks if she could go outside. I started to follow, but I want to play on my Xbox for a little bit. I will find out where she is later and go with her.

"Yeah, you can go, but come back around eight o'clock because I'm going out tonight."

"Alright," Key smiles.

"Jihod is coming to pick y'all up tonight to drop y'all off over Big Mama house," Mom speaks loudly so Key can hear as she walks away.

"I don't want to go over there this weekend." Key sighs, walking back toward the car.

"You just want to stay over here to go over Patricia and Porsha's house! Get out of my face," mom frowns.

Key didn't respond, knowing that it would start up an argument that could last all week. I overheard their short conversation, and I'm excited to go over Big Mama's house. We hadn't been over there in a long time, which is odd because we used to go over there every weekend. I guess ever since my mom and my Aunt Lora got into it last month sometime, my mom didn't want us going over there.

Aunt Lora lives with Big Mama with her two twin sons and one daughter. Her and my mom doesn't have the best relationship, but they deal with each other due to the circumstances. Their relationship with each other doesn't affect the way Big Mama or Aunt Lora treats us. Even though they don't have the best relationship with my mother, they still treat Key and me with love and affection. Another reason I like going over to Big Mama's house is that all of my cousins are always over there. All of my Big Mama's children drop their children off at her house every weekend, and that's how we all see each other so often. I love being around my cousins. They are all different ages, but everybody has someone to play with that are in the same age group. The cousins I hang around are April and Bryon. Bryon's older brother Evin is Key's age, so they hang out. The twins are like four to five years older than Key and Evin, so they have their own friends and most of the time they do their own thing. After accomplishing a mission on Grand Theft Auto, I see Key outside with the crew, so I go outside to see what they are doing.

As soon as I walk outside, Porsha approaches me. "Where you been?"

"I was playing on my Xbox."

"Oh, what game you was playing?"

"Grand Theft Auto."

"I heard that game is fun, we gotta' play one day," Porsha adds.

"Yeah, but it's not a two-player game, we would have to take turns," I respond, unable to hide my stinginess.

"That's cool,"

"Key said Auntie Joyce going out tonight." Porsha switches the topic.

"Yeah, she is." I smile at the thought.

"Y'all should see if we can spend the night."

"Yeah! That would be fun! Is Key going to ask?" I ask

"She said she would. But y'all mama probably gone say no, though." Porsha is starting to catch on to my mom's strict ways.

"Right, she probably is," I agree, less excited.

As the night comes, everybody is outside chilling, telling stories, and gossiping. Key finally built up the guts to ask my mom if Patricia and Porsha can spend the night before my dad comes home because it was past eight o'clock. While we wait for the news, my dad pulls up.

"Aw. It's too late now." I shake my head.

Patricia responds, "Right. That little boy was looking for you earlier, too, Miko."

"Who?" I'm curious as George.

"The little boy from around the corner, I think his name Deonte."

"Oh, eww! What did he want?" I frown with disgust written on my face.

"I don't know. He just asked where you were. I think he like you," Porsha giggles.

"I don't like him; he is not cute!" I laugh

Porsha laughs, "Right, that nigga' look like a little possum."

I burst out with laughter, as Key approaches us.

"What she say?" I speak first.

"She said no," Key looks irritated.

"What took you so long to come back out?" Porsha asks.

"I had to pack my bag. We about to go over my Big Mama house."

"Oh, y'all daddy about to drop y'all off?" Patricia asks.

"Yeah, I don't want to go over there, though." Key folds her arms.

"Why she making you go, then?" Patricia continues.

"Because she's a fucking bitch," Key rolls her eyes.

"You want to go over there?" Porsha asks, looking at me.

"It doesn't matter to me; it's fun over there too." I shrug my shoulders.

We chill with everybody for about ten more minutes, and then my dad calls us to leave. I run to the car as Key gives Cory a quick hug and a kiss before leaving. As soon as we get into the car, my dad ask,

"Y'all wanted Patricia and Porsha to spend the night?"

Key quickly responds, "Yeah."

"Y'all could of stayed here. They could of spent the night," dad adds in a calm way.

"I just asked my mom, and she said no." Key looks annoyed.

"I know, I don't know why she be acting funny sometimes," Dad sound confused.

She act funny all the time!

I know Key is thinking the same thing. The ride to Big Mama's house isn't that long; it's a straight shot up 7 Mile. When we arrive, I see Bryon and the twins outside, and Big Mama is sitting on the porch. It's weird seeing Big Mama sitting outside because she usually stays in her room. She lives in a very small house that stays full of company. Most of the time, she stays in her room and watches TV, so when people come to visit, they go to the back to speak to her. Big Mama's house is fun too because she knows how to cook and she has one of my favorite movies, The Little Rascals. It seems like every time I ask to watch the Little Rascals either her or Aunt Lora have to look for it, which is annoying because they know how much I love that movie, so I don't know why they can't keep it in a safe place. Big Mama is a short, caramel-skinned Indian looking lady. She always dyes her hair blond, which throws the Indian look off. The couple of times I did see her natural color jet black hair, it looks good. Big Mama is completely different from my Granny. She is nice but more so on the feisty side. Big Mama will cuss anybody out in a second if need be. She also isn't as hard as she comes off, but she gets her point across easily.

As the night goes on, Aunt Deanna arrive with Evin and April, whom I was excited to see because we always play together. Aunt Deanna isn't Big Mama's biological daughter, but blood wouldn't make them any closer. Big Mama took Aunt Deanna in as her daughter when she was a teenager. Being that she is my Uncle Nutty's childhood girlfriend and first baby mama made it more intuitive. Uncle Nutty is my dad's older brother and the complete opposite of my dad. Not only are their looks different, but their ways and the way they carry themselves are also distinct too. Uncle Nutty is more so on the conservative side, tall, and dark-skinned. He has a flirty feel to his persona mixed with firmness.

After staying up all night watching TV and eating Oreo cookies and milk. Everybody had fallen asleep before me, so I went to go sleep with Big Mama, and fell asleep by playing with her earlobes. That's another thing I like about Big Mama; she lets me play with her earlobes with no problem. Most people get irritated with it quickly, and others don't even let me touch their ears. One similarity about both of my grandmothers are, both can cook really good, and both of them let me play with their fat for as long as I want.

The morning is here, and the smell of Big Mama's coffee is delightful. She makes the best coffee. It didn't taste too sweet or too bitter, but perfect. She makes her coffee before she makes breakfast, and everybody is up to get a sip.

"Dang, sleepy head, you finally up?" Evin teases as soon as I walk in the living room.

I giggle. "Whatever, because all of y'all went to sleep before me."

"No we didn't, I was the last one up," Bryon adds his two cents.

April burst out in laughter. "Nah, you was more like the first person down!" Everybody laughs at April's joke.

"Make a circle, y'all. Big Mama about to come in with her coffee." Key walks swiftly in the living room from the kitchen like a spy.

Everybody shuffles around forming a circle around Big Mama's seat.

"What are y'all doing?" Big Mama stops in the walkway before sitting down.

"Nothing, we getting your seat ready." I smile, unable to hide my excitement.

Big Mama gives me a side-eye, "Getting my seat ready, huh? Since when do y'all kids care about my seat?"

"Since you started brewing some of that famous, delicious coffee you make." Evin smiles super big.

"Right, that coffee be so good. Can I have some?" I piggyback off of Evin's comment so I can get the first sip.

"Yes, y'all can have SOME. That means to take small sips." Big Mama looks at our circle like a referee.

After I take a couple of sips, I pass the hot coffee mug to April, April passes it to Bryon, Bryon passes it to Key, Key passes it to Evin. After Evin took a gulp, he passes it back to Big Mama.

Big Mama looks into the coffee mug. "Y'all took too many sips!" everybody burst out in laughter. She fusses and yells a lot but never actually punishes anybody. The rest of the weekend over Big Mama's house is fun, and I don't want to go back home. Even though I'm excited about dance school, I don't want to go home with *"Mommy Dearest"*.

CHAPTER **SEVEN**

THE FIRST DAY of dance school at Wendy School of Dance is very interesting. There is a nice crowd of people that attends the school, even though it's such a small building. The dance teachers seem to be nice, and the actual owner Wendy does as well. Wendy has a young daughter, and by her attitude and demeanor, she looks like she is going to be lots of trouble. There are kids of all ages here, which is pretty cool to me. Today everybody is getting all of their classes together and meeting their teachers.

I decided that I'm going to take Little Jazz, Hip Hop, Ballet, Baton, and Tap class. Key and I are only taking two of the same classes: Hip Hop and Tap class. Key decided that she wanted to take Tap, Hip Hop, African, and Modern class. Our teachers begin handing out uniforms and a roster of things we will need for the classes. After our last meeting for Hip Hop class was over, I notice a light-skinned, brown-haired girl who looks around the same age as me coming towards me.

"Is that your real hair?" Her eyes open widely.

"Yeah," I giggle at her facial expression.

"Can I touch it?" she asks in amazement.

"I don't like people touching my hair," I respond as nicely as possible.

"Oh, why not?"

"It's irritating," I shrug my shoulders.

She brushes my comment off and introduces herself. "I'm Shalissa. What's your name?"

"I'm Kee-Mee-KO," I say slowly because it's not the easiest name to pronounce.

Shalissa looks confused, "Kah-Mee-KO?"

At this point, I don't care that she pronounced it wrong because people do it often, "Yeah."

"That's different."

"Are you new here?" I ask.

"Nope, we have been going here for about a year or two now."

"You and who?"

"My older sister Diamond and my cousin Tasha," she points in the direction of a girl who looks about the same age as Key.

"I think Tasha is in class," Shalissa adds.

"Oh, ok, I have an older sister too, her name is Karin, but we call her Key."

"Does she go here?"

"Yeah, she's over there standing next to my mom." I point towards their direction.

"It looks like everybody is taking this class."

Shalissa agrees, "Right, it is a lot of people in here. I think you're taking Tap with me too."

"Yeah, I'm taking Tap class too." I confirm

Before Shalissa could respond, this pretty brown-skinned girl with crooked teeth started to call her name. Instead of coming over to join in the conversation, she is calling Shalissa to her. We are getting ready to leave, so I say bye to Shalissa and follow Key out of the door.

"So, y'all think y'all are going to like dance school?" Mom straps her seatbelt on in the driver seat.

"Yeah, I met a few people today," I answer before Key.

"I did too, our Hip Hop teacher is so cute," Key adds with a smile.

"Yeah, he is," Mom giggles.

"The teachers seem to be nice as well. I was talking to Wendy and she said something about planning on changing the location soon," Mom explains.

"To somewhere further out?" Key asks.

"She said maybe a little further, but not too far. She has a lot of members that have been with her for years, so she's not going to go anywhere too far," Mom continues.

"Hopefully she's looking to expand because the building is very tight," Key giggles.

"Right, that's the same thing I was thinking," I add from the backseat.

"Yeah, that and for a better location," Mom turns the volume up on the radio.

In no time, we are pulling up to Farmer Jacks, and my mood goes from ten to negative ten.

"When we get in here, don't ask for shit and don't touch shit." Mom looks both of us dead in our eyes.

"Can I stay in the car?" I ask quickly.

"No, come on," she opens the door for me to get out.

"Well, if we can't ask for shit, can't touch shit, why do we even have to go in?" I cut my eyes at her behind her back.

Every time we come to the grocery store, it feels like we're in here for literally twenty-four hours. She doesn't want us to ask for anything, and she wants to be in here all day. I wish she had told me we were coming to the grocery store because I would have made sure I brought a big coat to wear. *It's colder than a bitch in here!*

When we get home, Rap City is on BET, so I have to give it my undivided attention. Today, Lil Wayne is in the basement with the host Big Tigger. The best part about this show is the freestyle rapping. The DJ plays a hot beat in a studio looking room and Big Tigger and the day's guest will do a couple of rounds of some freestyle wordplay.

They also show the most popular/hottest music videos. I already know Lil Wayne is about to spit some bars. He's one of the hottest rappers out now. Becoming excited as Big Tigger does his freestyle, I call for Key to come see.

"Key!"

"Huh?" Key yells from upstairs.

"Come here! Lil Wayne on Rap City!"

Key rushes down the stairs as if he was here sitting on our living room couch.

"They started yet?" Key is trying to catch her breath.

"Look, here his part come," I add excitedly at what he's about to say over this sweet Lil Flip instrumental.

It's the year 2001 and Key is turning thirteen today. My grandparents are back in town for the celebration, which is always joyous. It feels like they have been gone forever since the last time we saw them for Christmas. But technically it's only been a few months. They're regretting the fact that they're here in April for the late snow.

"Damn, this is ridiculous. See, it's seventy degrees back in North Carolina," Granddaddy brags about living in the south.

He always makes sure he tells us the temperature, whether we ask or not. I'm guessing that's one of the reasons why they moved from Detroit because of the cold weather.

"Yeah, it's warm back at home," he continues while driving through the snow.

"Man, the snow is really coming down," Granny adds in a soft, delicate voice.

"This shit is crazy," Grandddaddy sounds disappointed.

Him being bothered by the weather is so funny to me. I'm sure to keep my laughs to myself because I know he's annoyed. I don't feel like getting snapped on for nothing. We're on our way to the hall, where the party will be starting. I left to go with my grandparents to pick up extra decorations and a catering order.

When we arrive to the hall, the DJ is here playing music and setting up. Mom, Dad, Key, Patricia, Porsha, Cory, Jena, and Joe are running around trying to get everything ready for the party. Our closest friends from the neighborhood drove here with us to help set up. The only person that is missing is Ron.

Key looks so pretty, with crimps in her hair and her matching Guess outfit. She has all of her gold jewelry on today—mom made sure of that.

"I hate that it's snowing." Key looks nervous.
"I know, it just started snowing out of nowhere," Jena adds.
"Hopefully people still come." Key checks her jewelry.
"They should, but it is snowing bad out there," Patricia shakes her head.
"Don't worry, baby," Cory adds very slickly, looking around and making sure the coast is clear.

Six o'clock comes before our eyes and people slowly but surely are coming in. My dad's siblings and their children are here. Granddaddy's brother and his family are walking in, approaching Key.

"What's up, Mik," Aunt Lora hugs me then kisses my cheek.
"Hey Auntie," I smile.
"Where ya' daddy at?"
"I don't know. He was over there by the DJ a few minutes ago," I point in the direction of the DJ booth.
"Did Big Mama come?" I ask looking around for her.
"Yeah, silly, why wouldn't she come?" she giggles. "I know she

made dessert too. She probably went out to grab it from the car."

Even though the weather is bad, the DJ is good! He's playing all of the new music and he's taking request. More people are walking in now. It looks like some of my mom's friends and their kids are here. Tina brought her three daughters, Breana, Raven, and Micha. Irene brought her daughter Amanda and her niece and nephew. Even Ms. Belk, Diamond, and Shalissa came out from dance school. Some of Key's friends are here from school so I know she's happy. I'm surprised my mom let her invite boys. I think my dad had to talk my mom into being calm about the boys being there. Cory and Joe are boys, but they live on the block and we see them all the time. So, in other words, they don't count, at least not in my mom's eyes.

Everybody is eating, talking, and having a good time, when the DJ switches to the Cha Cha Slide Hustle, everybody and their mama jumps up to do the hustle. This is one of those hustles everybody knows. If you don't know the song, it is really easy to catch on to. After a while, he repeats himself and the moves become repetitive.
"To the left. Take it back now, y'all. Two hops this time, two hops this time, hand on your knees, hands on your knees."
The song goes on, and everybody gets hype on the hands on your knees part because that's where the beat drops. I'm doing the hustle next to Tae, Bryon, April, and Porsha.
"Tae little butt is getting it, on the hands on your knees part! Look!" I laugh to Bryon while trying to get April's attention to look at Tae. I'm having a good time with my family and friends. I hope the party never ends.

"OKAY! I WON'T DO IT AGAIN! I'M SORRY! PLEASE!" Key's screams for mercy cut my skin like a knife.
"Sit still! What did I say? What did I SAY!" mom continues to slash

Key with a belt. Every thrash sounds harder and faster.

I hate when Key gets whippings. I wish I could storm in Key's room and save her. I wish we could just jump that mean ass bitch. Out of nowhere, the slashes of whipping finally come to an end and my door opens quickly.

"And you watch what the fuck you doing around here too! I'm tired of warning your little ass!" Mom looks at me with plain evil in her eyes.

My heart drops and my mouth instantly is dry. "Okay," I nod my head.

Mom walks out of my room with her belt in her hand. I don't understand why she likes whipping on us so much because from what I hear my grandparents barely punished her as a kid. Key just got a whipping for mistakenly knocking over one of her plants. *What kind of bullshit is that?* She uses any excuse to put her hands on us. She makes me sick to my stomach!

CHAPTER **EIGHT**

THE SUMMER IS finally in attendance. The sun is bright; there is no school tomorrow, so that means I can sleep in and stay up all night. Mom and Key are downstairs cooking and gossiping, I assume, not eager to join them till I finish reading my Pokemon book. I always keep my Pokemon book inside of my Pokemon card-holder booklet. I have a huge collection full of cards and golden cards. I'm going to miss trading cards with the boys in my class, especially with Will. Thoughts about school fade as I finish reading.

"Miko!"

"Huh?"

"Don't say huh to me, bring your ass here!" my mom snaps from downstairs.

Noticing her attitude from her tone of voice, I rush downstairs to see what she wants.

"What are you doing?" Mom asks in a nosy way.

"Playing in my room."

"Did you brush your teeth?"

"No."

"Well go brush your teeth, breakfast is ready. Key made Omelets," mom orders.

Mom must have made Key stay in and cook because she would have been ready to go outside as soon as she woke up.

As I am eating and talking to mom and Key, mom is in a throwback mood. She's sharing a story about when she was younger. I pretend to be listening so I wouldn't seem rude or get slapped, but I'm not. Usually, her childhood stories are fun to listen to but this one isn't catching my attention. Most of the things my mom says about herself and others, I never take heed in, anyway. The reason for that is, I don't believe half of the things that come out of her mouth. She is always lying and making us lie to people, so it's hard to judge between the lies and the truth. After she's done babbling along, Key finally ask the drum rolling question.

"Can we go outside?"

I giggle to myself, *"My dog! She was waiting on her as to shut up."*

"Yeah. After y'all clean up," Mom responds quickly.

Key and I already know the drill for a clean-up day. It's at least going to take us about two hours to clean up, so we get dressed first, so when we are finished cleaning, we can go directly outside.

"She doesn't ever help us clean up with her lazy ass," I complain to Key.

"Right, she always standing over somebody like she gone help though. She need some business," Key rolls her eyes.

"I hate washing each window on the front room door! Man, I can't wait until I grow up!" Passion speaks through my words.

"I can't wait until I grow up either. I'll beat her ass," Key exclaims with a giggle.

I burst out with laughter. "It just seem like it's taking me so long to grow up like I've been a kid for so long."

"You are young though," Key looks down at me like I have no hope.

"I know! I'm younger than everybody! Damn!" I smack my lips.

As we are talking, Ron comes outside and walks over to talk to us. Ron has this signature clean scent to himself that I don't think he is aware of.

"What's up, y'all?" Ron greets us in a jokey way.
"You smell good," I compliment him.
"I do?" he sniffs his shirt trying to smell what I smell.
"Yeah, you always smell like that."
"It's probably because I been in the house for too long. My motherfucking granddad getting on my god damn nerves. I had to get the fuck out of there," he expresses, making Key and I laugh.
"We know the feeling, nigga', we know," Key confirms in a joking but serious way.
"You talk to yo girl?" I ask.
"Who?" he looks confused.
"Jena." I smile, unable to keep a straight face.
"I don't like her fat ass! Her Big Worm looking ass!" he replies quickly defending himself.
Laughing uncontrollably, I add, "Well, she like you!"
"I'm sure she want to have me for dinner too! I'm straight!" he continues to crack us up.

What's making his jokes even funnier is that Key and I both know he wouldn't say any of that to her face. She is so much bigger than him, and she is wild. She probably could manhandle him. When he's around her, he doesn't act like he like her, but he doesn't act mean to her either. When she comes around, he sort of just plays it cool and ignores her flirty comments.

Speaking of the devil, as we are talking about Jena, here she comes walking down the street with this other short, fat light-skinned girl she hangs around. The other girl's name is Courtney, and she lives a couple of blocks over. Courtney is Jena's shadow, and she follows everything Jena says and does. Jena bullies her to the point that it is obvious Courtney is scared of her.

"Hey... Ron!" Jena greets Ron with a forceful hug.

"What's up?" Ron replies quickly, not hugging her back but snatching away.

They remind me of "The Parkers." Jena is Nikki and Ron is Mr. Oglevee but less intense. Giggling at my own joke in my head, I ask "Where y'all coming from, Jena?"

"From Courtney house," she answers quickly.

"Y'all seen Patricia and Porsha?" Jena asks.

"Nope," Key answers quickly, mimicking how she just answered my question.

"We just got out here," I add noticing the weird tension they have without Patricia and Porsha around.

When things start to get more awkward than what it already is, everybody heads across the street to see if Patricia and Porsha are home.

Key and Jena have an on and off relationship. Sometimes they are friends and sometimes they aren't. When it comes to Patricia and Porsha, Jena loves them just as much as Key does. Jena acts like she doesn't want to hang out with us unless we are with them sometimes. Key notices how Jena acts funny, so that makes her more distant towards Jena.

"Is Cory in the house?" Key asks.

"Nope, he went with my cousin somewhere," Patricia fixes her curly ponytail.

"Oh, you know if they left the neighborhood?" Key continues.

"No, I don't think so."

"We should go to the park," Porsha suggest out of nowhere.

"Right, we should!" Jena agrees before Porsha could even finish her sentence.

"Why you standing like that?" Jena teases Courtney.

"Jena... Why?" Courtney replies with an attitude.

Jena raises her voice as if she's talking to a little kid. "You the one looking fucking stupid, I'm trying to help you out!"

Everybody burst out laughing, while Porsha is instigating it, which is making it even funnier. I want to go to the park too. I just don't know if my mom will let us.

"Go ask Mama if we can go to the park," Key demands.
"You go ask," I defend myself because I always go and ask.

The park is literally a few blocks over, but my mom still might not allow that. Key goes to ask, and while she is in the house, Patricia asks me "Why y'all always have to ask to do little stuff?"
"I don't know, that's why I be wanting to go with my dad." I turn a long story into a short story.
"Right, yo daddy seem fun," Patricia giggles.
"I be wanting to go with your daddy too," Porsha agrees with Patricia.

Everybody laughs as Key walks back to the group.

"What she say?" Patricia asks.
"She said no," Key looks agitated.
"Y'all still want to go?" Jena intrudes.

Instead of leaving us like Jena obviously prefers to do. Everybody just ignores her question and continues with the gossip for the day. Jena loves having Patricia and Porsha all to herself as if it is a competition.
As the day goes on and the night appears, Cory and his friend arrives from wherever they were earlier. Key and Cory are happy to see each other as if they had been away from each other for a year. Their chemistry is so magical at such a young age. Patricia, Porsha, and I are happy that our older siblings go together. It makes us feel closer like a little family. It is getting boring outside, so everybody heads across the street over Cory, Patricia, and Porsha's house. Of course,

we had to see if we could go inside their house, so this time I went to go ask, and my mom said we could go in.

Patricia and Porsha's house is sort of built like ours inside, but it seems a lot smaller. I think that have a lot to do with how cluttered and junky the house is. They have a lot of people who live there so that's probably why it's so junky. I'm really weird about junky houses and dirty cars. Anytime I get inside of a car with a lot of stains on the seat, it makes me feel itchy. Maybe it's a mind thing, but I know dirty atmospheres make me feel uncomfortable. Our house is squeaky clean at all times, so I'm not used to messy houses or cars. It doesn't seem to bother Key at all. She seems to love being over here, and I can tell she is happy here.

Cory, Patricia, and Porsha live with their grandma Betty. Their parents live here too, so it's like a seven-family household. There is always a full house, and they keep company most of the time. Cory's parents' names are Dona and Tez. They are very cool laid-back type of parents in my eyes. Tez is a very nice looking, dark-skinned man. He always has something funny to say, which makes it obvious where Porsha gets her sense of humor from. Dona is light-skinned with naturally curly hair. She isn't that talkative towards me. Key knows her way better than I do, but she's cool as well. They have a son that is about five years younger than me. His name is Roger; he is practically Porsha's twin. They are a nice-looking family, and what's cute to me is how they all look alike.

"Take off your shoes," Porsha orders in a friendly way.

Not wanting to make anything awkward, I take my shoes off knowing my socks would get dirty. I hate when my socks get too dirty at the bottom, and I really hate when I step in something wet. I have a strong feeling both of those two things are about to happen in no time.

A couple of hours goes by, as the darkness sneaks through. When we get home, mom is putting on the movie Grease. This has been one of her favorite movies since she was a kid. She knows all of the words to each song and almost every word in the script. We like the movie too, so we join her for dancing and singing. After the movie goes off, I fall asleep in my mom's bed while my mom and Key stay up for a "Hate your Dad" lecture.

CHAPTER **NINE**

"SPIN, SPIN, SPIN and flesh," Ms. Wendy directs us in the dance room.

    Little Jazz is not one of my favorite classes because I'm the oldest student in the class. That means I have to babysit the rest of the class. Of course, I catch on to all of the routines faster than the rest of the smaller kids, so I help and guide the class with routines when needed. I'm not big enough in size to be in regular Jazz class, which is sort of annoying. All of my friends that are only a year or two older than me are in Jazz class with all ages. It makes me feel like I'm a baby and too young for Jazz class. For now, I have to tutor these little girls and make the best out of it.
    After Little Jazz, I have Hip Hop class, which I'm excited about because all of my friends are in that class. Key is in that class as well.
    When Little Jazz is finally over, I rush out of class. Wendy's daughter, Francesca, beats me to the door.

    "Francesca! Come here! Stop running from me!" Wendy is struggling to catch her.

    Francesca doesn't budge and keeps running as fast as her little feet can go. As I watch Wendy chase after her daughter, I imagine

PRETTY CAN BE UGLY

myself doing that to my mom. Then that thought immediately expires because I wouldn't be able to run from my mom. Even though she is younger than me, she knows better than that. She's a five-year-old and very disobedient. If I were to ever *think* about running from my mom, I would get the worst beating from hell. As I continue to watch Francesca damn near fight her mother, Shalissa and the same brown-skinned girl I usually see her playing with walks up to me.

"Hey, y'all," I wave.
"Hey, Kimiko," Shalissa responds.
"Francesca bad, look at her," I giggle, pointing in her direction.
Shalissa laughs, "She always acting up like that. My mama wouldn't let me fight her like that."
I laugh. "I was just thinking the same thing."

As Shalissa and I continue to talk, Shalissa notices how quiet her friend is the whole time.
"Oh yeah, Kimiko, this is my best friend Kyra. Kyra this is Kimiko."
"Hi," I speak first.
Kyra responds dryly, "Hi."

I ignore Kyra's unfriendly demeanor, as Shalissa and I continue to talk and get to know each other. When we get to Hip Hop class, I see Key mingling with some girls who looks her age. Our Hip Hop teacher is so cute. He is tall, light-skinned, and muscular with a nice smile. His name is Mr. Jessie, and what's even better is he is really nice. There is only one boy in our class, and he looks like he is my age.

"Do you know that boy over there?" I asks Shalissa.
"Yeah, that's Jaylen, he's Kyra's boyfriend." Shalissa smiles, waiting on Kyra's reaction, but Kyra doesn't respond.
"Oh, ok," I giggle, brushing off their moment.

Jaylen is about a little taller than me, brown-skinned, with curly hair. He is cute to me, but I don't know him, so I don't feel any type of way about him.

We change into more relaxed clothing for Hip Hop class and stretch before we start our new routine. We practice on a dance we will be performing at an activity center. After class, when everybody's parents begin to show up, Mr. Jessie explains what kind of uniforms will be needed for the performance.

Time in class went by so fast because it is lots of fun. While everybody is leaving, Key calls me.

"Miko."

"Huh?"

"Oh! That's your sister! She is so pretty!" A very pretty tall, high yellow, curly-haired girl who looks around the same age as Key compliments me.

"Hi," she waves.

"I'm Jasmine. What's your name?"

"Miko."

She smiles, "Aw, can you be my fake daughter?" Jasmine smiles.

"Yeah," I return the smile.

I didn't find it odd that she asked to be my fake mom because she's not the first teenager to ask me that. Jasmine is so pretty, and after speaking to her, I got a feeling that she is a little bit older than Key.

Jasmine introduces me to her grandmother shortly after we met. It's funny because her grandmother favors my Big Mama. She is brown skinned with short blonde naturally curly hair.

"Grandma, she is so pretty, right?" Jasmine shows me off like a gold metal.

"Yes, she is a doll. Who is she?"

"My play daughter, Miko," she spins me around.

"Hi, sweetie." Jasmine's grandma reaches out to shake my hand.

"Hi." I return the nice smile.

After I met Jasmine's grandmother, I found Key and Mom talking to Shalissa's and Diamond's mom. When I notice my mom isn't ready to leave just yet, I begin looking for Shalissa. I find her playing with Kyra and Jaylen in the tap-dancing classroom. After joining them, I notice that Kyra is still acting very distant towards me, but I didn't let it bother me. Ten minutes went by, and it was time to go, everybody said bye to each other and head home.

We made it home around nine o'clock and the block is hot on 7 Mile. Everybody is outside and, to top it off, it is a nice summer night. Before we park the car, I'm praying that my mom will let us stay outside.

"Can we stay outside?" Key pops the question.
"Yeah, but stay in front of the house." Mom grabs her purse before getting out.
"Okay," Key looks happy.

When we approach the crowd that is standing in the middle of the street. It is the same crew that we always hang around. There are a few extra faces that I'm not familiar with. Joe and Jena's cousin Dave is present. Dave is tall and caramel-skinned with a preppy personality. He's not a new face, he just doesn't live in the neighborhood. When he comes to visit Joe and Jena, he's fun company. Cory's cousins are here too, one looks familiar, and the other one doesn't.

"Where y'all been?" Patricia meets us in the street.
"Dance school." Key plays with her hair.
"Oh yeah, I forgot y'all go to dance school." Porsha smiles.

Later in the night, Cory and his cousins put on a mix CD in the car and turns up the volume to the maximum. They put some fast mix songs on so they could "Jit." Jitting is another dance that is very popular in the city of Detroit. It's more popular for guys to "Jit," but some girls are good at it as well. The dance is a fast-paced dance that includes a lot of movement within the feet. It's sort of a hard dance, but Cory and his cousins are good at it. They got everybody hyped up as they start to dance. Everybody crowds around them like there is about to be a fight as they dance to the beat.

Most of the time people Jit to mix songs because most mix songs are fast instrumentals. There are mix song with lyrics, but the lyrics are repetitious. Mix songs are dancing songs, so nobody really cares about the lyrics. One of my favorite mix songs is the one that says:

"Bounce that, roll that, freak that, shake that, pop that, roll that, now stop that, hold that."

It keeps repeating those exact words over an exclusive beat, and it makes all the kids and people who love to dance go crazy in a good way. I'm surprised mom doesn't hear the music. She probably would come outside to bust a move or two. It's getting really late outside, so everybody heads in the direction their houses are in until we meet tomorrow.

The morning comes, and Key, Mom, and I are getting ready to watch the soap operas. My mom's favorite channel is sixty-two. Young and the Restless, Bold and the Beautiful, and As the World Turns, all air on that channel, in that order. One day, mom wouldn't let us go outside, so we watched the soaps with her out of boredom. We've been hooked ever since. After I brush my teeth, I flop on my mom's bed, getting ready to watch Young and the Restless. As soon as I get comfortable, the door from downstairs opens.

"If he asks y'all to go anywhere, say no," my mom whispers sternly with her eyes poked out of her face to let us know she's not playing.

See, this type of shit is what make me hate her ass! She so fucking mean and controlling. I put my attitude in my pocket.

I want to run downstairs and give him the biggest hug a young girl can offer, but I know I would probably get a ten-hour lecture about it when he leaves with a side of *ass whopping*. Not wanting to go through one of my mom's dreadful "talks" about my dad and what she's mad about, I continue to watch TV. My dad comes upstairs to say hi, and my mom is the only person that didn't speak to him. Once I finish watching TV, I go to the basement to see what my dad is doing, and he is nowhere to be found. Seconds later, I hear my dad and someone else coming through the side door to come downstairs to the basement. I hide in the pantry to be sneaky and listen to what they are talking about.

"Man, what do you want now?" dad asks, sounding fed up.

I didn't recognize the guy's voice, and I couldn't really hear him clearly. They didn't have a long conversation.

"Oh yeah, let me get some socks," the guy adds.

After exchanging some things, the guy leaves and I come out of the pantry, to the other side of the basement to meet dad.

As soon as he sees me he can't hold his laugh, "Sneak-ko, what are you doing?"

"Let me get some socks," I mimick the man who was just in our basement.

Dad cracks up, "You heard him say that?"

"Yeah."

"What else did you hear?" he smiles.

I just stood there with a guilty grin as if I heard everything, but I really didn't.

"Where were you hiding?" he asks smiling, but curious.
"In the pantry," giggling as if it was cool to eavesdrop on him.
"Don't do that no more, Sneak-ko," he grabs my nose. "What do you want to do today?"
I want to do anything that consists of leaving this mother fucking house, but I lie instead, fearing the consequences. "Nothing."
"Why y'all don't ever want to do nothing, especially Key," he shakes his head.

I sort of ignore his comment out of fear of telling him that my mom told us not to go with him.

"I'm going to visit Big Mama later on. You want to come?" Dad tries again.
"Nah, can you stay here and watch that Mary-Kate and Ashley movie with me?" I ask, praying he says yes.
"I already watched that movie with you," he takes a deep breath while giggling.
"No you didn't, you fell asleep," I quickly remind him.

We both share giggles because we both know that he always falls asleep on my Mary-Kate and Ashley movies.

"Ok, what's the name of the movie again?"
"Holiday in the Sun," I jump for joy.
"That's the same movie we watched last time!" he laughs, trying to get out of watching the movie.
"No, it's not, we watched "Billboard Dad" last time. I mean I... watched it last time," scolding him.

Dad ends up staying home and watching half of the movie with me. It doesn't make me mad that he falls asleep on the Mary-Kate and Ashley movies. I enjoy watching them with or without company. I can watch the same Mary-Kate and Ashley movies repeatedly and still get a kick out of it. So, when my dad goes to sleep, it just gives me an excuse to drag him through the next movie again.

CHAPTER **TEN**

AS MY JOSEFINA book gets good, I can smell the food Key is cooking downstairs. After a couple of chapters in, I hear my mom and dad yelling extremely loudly at each other.

"Well, where the fuck did it go?" my dad screams.
"I don't know!! I don't smoke weed!!" Mom snaps back.
"Somebody in this motherfucka' smoke weed, because nothing would be missing!" dad yells.

They continue to yell, and I decide to stay in my room away from the drama. It scares me so much when they argue. That's probably one of the reasons why he stays gone for days at a time because when he comes home, they fight like cats and dogs. When they argue, it's never a small disagreement. It's always an extreme argument.

Surprisingly, this argument didn't last all night, and when dinner is ready, my mom calls.

"Miko, come and eat!"

Key fixed baked chicken, mac and cheese, and broccoli. When it is time to eat, dad didn't join us. He left. That was the cause of the quiet noise that lingers throughout the house. I hate when he leaves but it's relieving when he's gone. I know the longer he stays, the longer the drama would continue.

My mom always fixes our plates with so much food on it. What's even more irritating is she makes us eat every bite of food on the plate. It doesn't matter if we sit at the table all night, she doesn't let us get up if we aren't finished with our food.

"I'm full," I express.

"You better eat the rest of that fucking broccoli," mom looks serious.

Key is done with her food and is upstairs in her room. Mom is cleaning up in the kitchen and supervising me. I hate eating vegetables, especially broccoli. That is the only thing left on my plate. I'm waiting on my mom to go upstairs so I can put the broccoli in the garbage can. I sit in my seat at the dining room table for at least an hour. Mom is finally finished with whatever she is doing and makes her way upstairs. I wait for ten minutes or so, making sure that she is upstairs for good, then I hurry to put my broccoli in a plastic grocery store bag before throwing it away to hide it in the trash. Then I put my dishes in the sink and head to Key's room. Key have her music playing as usual, this time she's listening to TLC.

"You finally finished your food?" Key jokes.

"Ya' think?" I respond shortly with a slight attitude.

Key burst out with laughter.

"I hate broccoli!" I flop on her bed.

She giggles, "Why? It doesn't even taste like nothing."

"It's nasty," I add with a frown on my face.

"I can't believe she made you sit down there for so long." Key shakes her head.

"I was happy when she came up here because I threw the rest of that shit away," I whisper.

"Hopefully she doesn't look through the trash," Key overthinks.

For the rest of the night, Key and I gossip and share secrets until we fall asleep. I always feel comfortable telling her secrets because I know she wouldn't tell anybody. We always share our opinions with each other. Good or bad, we voice our opinions, but never to our parents. Our parents aren't accepting of our opinions and how we feel, especially my mom. If we were to ever disagree with her, she would be rebellious and lash out. She never lets us express ourselves, and that is one of the reasons why I secretly don't like her. My dad is the opposite; he isn't as mean as she is. However, he doesn't let us get away with saying too much or get too carried away.

The morning arrives and the sun is shining. I'm surprised Key let me sleep with her because sometimes she doesn't like when I get sleepy and rub my eyes. The moisture in my eyes make sounds when I rub them, and it irritates the fuck out of her. Rolling out of bed, I look out the window to see the crew. Wondering why Key isn't out there, I skip downstairs to see where she is. When I get downstairs, I find her in the kitchen with a long face.

"What's wrong?" I sit down in the chair.

"Mama getting on my nerves, she won't let me go outside." Key rolls her eyes.

"Everybody is out there, too!" I rub it in her face on the low.

"She said we about to go over Renee's house."

"I don't know why she won't let you go outside until it's time for us to go," I frown.

"I know, stupid bitch," Key whisper.

Letting the information marinate, I leave the kitchen and Key's pity party because I really don't care about going outside. I like going outside, but I don't mind when we leave to go other places. Key just doesn't want to leave Patricia, Porsha, and Cory. She never wants to go anywhere else. If it were up to her, she would stay on

Manor and 7 Mile every day, all day.

After I brush my teeth and take a shower, mom is waiting to do my hair.

"Can you do it in two ponytails? One at the top and one at the bottom?" I ask.

"No, I'm giving you six ponytails," she answers without hesitation.

Uggghhh, I hate this bitch! I think to myself, getting ready for the pain.

While combing my hair, I get more and more annoyed.

Is she doing this on purpose? Jealous hearted hoe!

She is so heavy-handed. When she parts my hair, it's as if she's carving my scalp hard and slowly. When she grabs my sectioned hair to put the ponytail in, she grabs my ponytail super tight for no reason. After making the small ponytail, she yanks my hair downward to twist my long ponytail as if she's trying to pull my ponytail out, then closes it with barrettes at the end.

"Joyce! Your daughters are so pretty! I remember seeing Key, but I forgot about Miko. She looks just like Jihod, girl!" Renee smiles.

"Let me introduce y'all to my daughters."

We follow Renee into a very small house. The neighborhood is a rough-looking area, but Renee seems to be a nice lady.

"This is Shay, and Raquel," Renee nicely introduces us.

There is no one here my age, which is less exciting. Renee's daughters are older. One is Key's age and the other one is older than Key, with a child. There are other people here as well, but nobody brought their kids, so I immediately feel the urge to want to go home, which is unusual. After everybody makes their plates, Key, Renee, Shay, my mom, and I sit down at the kitchen table. They're having girl talk, reminiscing, and eating.

"When I was your age, I used to be so fast," Shay confesses while giggling with Key.
Renee adds quickly, "Yes, she was; I had to stay on her ass!"
"I used to be sneaking guys into the house and sneaking out all the time," Shay laughs.
"I'm glad Key not like that! She would be getting her ass beat from here to next week!" my mom intrudes as if she's so confident in Key's behavior.
"Key don't have a boyfriend or nothing," mom continues to brag.
"Well, that is so good. It's good not to be all boy crazy," Shay continues while passing the blunt to her mom.
I pray my mom don't hit the blunt with her low tolerance having ass.
Renee intrudes, "Joyce, you think I wasn't getting on her ass? This one had a very hard head," Renee hits the blunt of weed.

They continue to talk and I'm almost sure of what Key is thinking about my mom right now. Little does my mom know, Key is doing the same exact things Shay is saying she used to do.
The day goes on and on, and eventually, it seems like it's never going to end. I figured when twelve o'clock came, we would be close to leaving. My mom is nowhere to be found. Key is somewhere talking to Renee's daughters, and I'm stuck on the couch looking dumb. Out of nowhere, my Uncle German shows up coming from the back with Renee.

"Hey, Guh!" Uncle German speaks in his country accent as Renee leans on him as if she can't keep her balance.
He is so country, I think to myself before speaking. "Hey."
"Where ya' mama at?"

"I don't know," I shrug my shoulders.
"You ready to go home, little mama, ain't you?" Renee ask nicely.
"Yes," I respond shyly.
"She is so gorgeous," Renee expresses to Uncle German as if he can't see. "Look at all this jewelry she has on. Joyce keeps her kids dripping in gold," Renee giggles.
"That's Joyce's daughter," Uncle German adds, sounding drunk.
Renee giggles, "I know who she is, silly. That's what I just said"
"Do all the kids try to play in this pretty long hair of yours at school?" Renee continues to converse with me.
"Yeah," I answer quickly not interested in talking to her.

I know in my head that they are drunk and that my mom probably is too, which makes me nervous. Mom gets so aggressive and mean when she is drunk. About ten minutes goes by, and my mom shows up chewing as if she never ate anything in her entire life. She approaches my Uncle German and Renee, stumbling, and discombobulated.

"Joyce, where you been?" Renee asks.
"I went to go get something to eat," mom slurs her words.
"Joyce, the kids are ready to go home." Renee sounds like she's concerned.
"She can't drive home," Uncle German adds.
"I can drive home, I sobered up," mom tries to defend herself.
"Are you sure, Joyce?" Uncle German second-guesses her decision.
"Yes, we don't live that far anyways," she continues to slur her words as her eyes blink slowly.

It is obvious that she shouldn't get behind anybody's wheel, but no one steps up to her, so she calls Key to the front to get ready to leave. Anyone with two eyes can see that she shouldn't be driving, especially with us in the car.

"Come on, I'm ready!" she yells at me like I'm getting on her nerves.

"And what the fuck were you doing?" she confronts Key face to face as Key walks from the back of the house.

"I was sleep," Key defends herself.

"Well take your ass to the car," Mom demands.

"Joyce, the girls were waiting on you," Renee takes our defense.

Walking to the car, I'm so scared for her to drive.

What if we get into a really bad car accident and die?" My mind is racing.

"She is drunk," I whisper to Key.

"I know," Key replies sounding disappointed.

I'm praying we get home safely as Uncle German and Renee walk us to the car.

"Call me when you get home, Joyce," Uncle German demands.

Uncle German is my granny's youngest brother. Granny has four brothers, and Uncle German is the one we see the most because mom hangs with him the most. Every time we see Uncle German, he is drinking or already drunk.

The drive home is the scariest drive ever. It feels like a maze from the Scooby-Doo cartoon, never-ending. Mom is swerving from lane to lane. I wish the police would come out of nowhere and pull us over and drive us home.

CHAPTER **ELEVEN**

I'M SO HAPPY Key let me sleep with her last night, being that my mom was sloppy drunk. She fell asleep in the car in the driveway of our house and got mad every time Key tried to wake her up. She wouldn't give us the keys to go into the house, so we sat there waiting on her to wake up in the car. I'm so thankful that something bad didn't happen to us in the car last night. I mean, it's not like we live in the suburbs. We live in the city of Detroit, and anybody could have tried to take advantage of a drunk woman and her two young daughters in the car.

Instead of reading this morning, I'm writing in my diary. My diary is pink and white with a lock on it, and I'm the only person who has a key to it. When I write in my diary, I usually write about how I'm feeling or what I want to feel. Most of the time, it's about bad things and about happy feelings I wish I could feel. Writing helps me relieve stress, and it also keeps me in my right mind. Being in my room alone and writing brings me peace. I don't have many pages left in my diary, since I try to write in it every day. No one knows that I write in my diary on a regular basis. It's not a secret. I just don't talk about it.

When everybody wakes up, my mom didn't even mention last night. She didn't apologize for it or for anything. Sometimes she put us in the worst scenarios and never speaks about it after as if it never happened. Even if it's not an apology, she never shows any signs of remorse when it comes to us.

My dad is gone again, and I miss him so much. I want to tell him what goes on around here so bad, but I hate seeing them argue. I don't want to be in the middle of anything, and I don't want to get in trouble either. Once he leaves, I'll just end up with mommy fucking dearest.

After I finish taking my emotions out on the pad and pencil, I go see what my mom and Key are up to. They are in my parents' room, talking about my dad again, which isn't surprising. Key is fully dressed as if she is ready to go outside after the "Dad Hating" coaching.

Once I notice how intense the conversation is, instead of entering the room, I walk past it to the bathroom. Avoiding the hate session, I just brush my teeth and begin to get dressed so I can go outside with Key. Finishing just in time, I catch Key in her room doing her hair, watching music videos.

"You getting ready to go?" I ask, flopping on her bed.
"Yeah, she irritating as fuck," Key adds with an attitude.
"Where you about to go?"
"Across the street," Key answers quickly.

As she finishes up with her hair, I notice the way Jennifer Lopez has her bun in the "I'm Real" video.

"Can you do me a bun like that?" I ask, pointing at the TV screen.
"Yeah, it's just a simple bun with some swoops in the front. You have to see if mama will let me do it."
"She probably gone say no," I roll my eyes.
"Right." Key shakes her head.
"With her hating ass," I add before going to ask her.

Once I get downstairs I see mom sitting on the couch watching TV.

"Ma, can Key do my hair in a bun?"
"What kind of bun?" mom frowns.
"A bun on the top of my head?"
"Yeah, whatever," she brushes me off.

Surprised that she said yes, I fly back upstairs to Key's room out of excitement.
"What she say?" Key looks curious.
"She said yeah!" I express happily.

Mom is very strict about us asking for things. We have to ask for every little thing. If we want to eat something out of our own refrigerator, we have to ask. If we want any kind of snack, we have to ask. If Key would have done my hair without her permission, both of us probably would have gotten in trouble.

When Key is done with my hair, it turns out really cute! She slicked all of my hair up to the top of my head and made a nice sized bun. To top it off, she brushed my baby hair down very smoothly, just like Jennifer Lopez's. I like it when she does my hair because it doesn't feel like she is trying to pull my hair out of my scalp. When my mom does my hair, it feels like she is trying to hurt me intentionally. Even when I say "ouch" or make obvious hurting sounds, my mom doesn't ask if I'm okay or say sorry.

I was happy to go outside with my hair done differently. I never wear my hair in simple styles like this, so I feel confident and pretty.

Gazing at Porsha's naturally slick, wavy hair, I ask, "What do y'all put on y'all hair to lay it down?"

"Just gel, your hair would look like this if you used it too," Porsha answers.

"Her hair probably can't go in an afro because it's too long, though," Patricia adds.

"Oh yes it can," I correct her quickly.

People assume that my hair texture is soft and fine because it's long. Nobody ever sees my natural hair wet because my mom makes sure we go to the salon and get our hair straightened every two weeks. When water hits my hair, it instantly changes texture. It goes from straight strands to big kinks because it's so long. People think my hair is wavy and doesn't form into an afro because of how straight it gets without a perm, but that's not the case at all.

It is getting dark out, and it is time for Key and me to be in front of the house. It is so embarrassing that we are the only kids on the block that have to be in front of the house when the streetlights come on. We don't get teased about it, which makes it better. All of our friends just come down to our house, and while everybody is chilling on our porch, my mom comes to the door. I immediately thought that she was going to tell us to come in.

"What y'all out here doing?" mom ask in a friendly way.
"Nothing, Auntie Joyce," Porsha responds.
"Y'all want to play "Questions?" she asks excitedly.
"Questions?" Jena asks, as she eats her chips.
"Oh yeah, that one game we played when we spent the night," Patricia giggles.
"Is that the same game y'all was telling me about the other night?" Cory asks, scratching his head.
"Yeah!" Porsha gets excited.
"How you play it?" Ron jumps up from the porch stairs like he's ready.
"Okay, so it's just how it sounds. The game is called Questions, and you have to ask whoever's sitting next to you a question, without answering it," Mom explains.
"Make sure it's the person to the right of you," Key adds.
"So, you can't answer the question?" Joe asks in a confusing way.
"Nope. If you answer the question you have to take a sip of my special drink," Mom looks sneaky.
"Alright, let's play!" Jena claps as if she's going to win.
"There's one more rule. You can't stutter, pause, or laugh. If you

do, you have to take a sip of my special drink," Mom looks at everyone slowly.

"What? So, we can't think about what we want to ask?" Ron looks surprised.

"Nope, you have to know what you're going to say before it's your turn," Key giggles.

"And you said we can ask anything, right, Auntie?" Cory confirms.

"Yeah, y'all can ask anything y'all want. For example, Are you black? Are you gay? Do you lick toes?" Mom goes on, while everyone burst out in laughter.

"Y'all want to play?" Mom asks for the last time, and everybody is down to play.

"Alright, I'll be right back with my special drink." Mom goes back into the house.

"This game about to be so easy," Ron brags.

"What is the special drink?" Daniel looks nervous. "It's whatever she make it out of," Porsha answers Daniel's question quickly, making a nasty facial expression.

"Last time she made it out of a whole bunch of nasty stuff," Patricia laughs.

"She be putting worms and ants in the drink too?" Ron asks in a humorous but serious way.

"Nah, fool!" I answer while laughing.

"Oh, cause I was about to say, 'What kind of Fear Factor shit is this?'" Ron continues, joking.

Two minutes later, mom comes outside with this dark raspberry red type of drink. Every time she makes the drink, she makes it in a clear glass for us to see the nasty looking color and texture.

"Alright y'all ready?" mom has a mysterious smile on her face.

"Man, what's in that drink?" Cory ask, letting Ron's curiosity get to him.

Before she answers, she put the glass drink in the center of the porch. "Water, Apple Juice, red Kool-Aid, ketchup, mustard, hot sauce, and a little bit of pepper."

The crowd moans out of disgust.

"Remember, no pausing, thinking, or stuttering. You can ask any kind of question, but don't answer it. Questions do consist of who, what, when, where, and how," Mom explains quickly.

"Oh, so we can ask who, what, when, where, or how alone?" Jena asks.

"Yeah, but if that's the only thing you keep asking in every round, you gotta' drink," mom confirms.

"Alright, y'all, let's go! Make sure the person next to you is sitting right beside you so nobody won't get skipped." Mom have everybody shuffle and shift around our porch.

Since I'm the youngest one, I go first, then Ron, who is on my right. To his right is Jena. Sitting on Jena's right side is Patricia. Key is on Patricia's right side. My mom is on Key's right side. On the right of my mom is Daniel. On Daniel's right sits Joe, on his right sits Cory. Porsha is sitting to Cory's right, and I'm on Porsha's right side.

"Do you stink?" I ask Ron confidently.

"Why are you so big?" Ron giggles while asking Jena his question.

Jena didn't ask Patricia anything because she was too busy trying to fight Ron, as everybody is laughing at his question.

"Alright, Jena, you gotta' take a sip," my mom reminds her in a silly way.

"Dang!" Jena expresses while picking the glass up slowly as if something is living inside of it.

"He got you, Jena!" Mom laughs as she takes a sip from the glass while holding her nose.

"Dang, it's hot!" Jena sticks her tongue out, making everybody laugh. Jena starts the game, since she messed up.

"Are you a gay bob?" Jena asks Patricia.

"What?" Patricia asks Key.

"Why you look like that?" Key asks my mom.

"Are you an African booty scratcher?" Mom asks Daniel.

"Who?" Daniel asks Joe.

"Huh?" Joe stutters.

"You gotta' drink. 'Huh' is not a question!" Mom picks up the special drink and hands it to Joe. Joe takes his sip like a "G", and we proceed with the game.

"Are you an African booty scratcher?" Joe asks Cory.

"Is yo' mama an African booty scratcher?" Cory asks Porsha.

Porsha burst out laughing and ends up having to take a sip.

"Dog, don't come on my mama like that," Porsha playfully checks Cory about their mom.

The night goes on, and we play questions all night until the mosquitos are tired of us.

Nights like these never get old for any of us. Our neighborhood friends love my mom and think she is so much fun. She is fun twenty percent of the time, especially when we are around company. She knows how to be nice when she wants to. She makes all the kids call her "Auntie Joyce" and she's so nice towards them. But when it comes to Key and me, it's a different story.

CHAPTER **TWELVE**

IT'S THE END of the day for dance school, and everybody is getting ready to leave. We have a performance coming soon in Downtown Detroit that everybody is excited about. My mom and Shalissa's mom are chatting as usual. Once I started to get bored I begin looking for Shalissa and find her in one of the dance rooms practicing for a routine. Kyra and two other girls are practicing with her. They are way better dancers than me. They've been in dance school since they were very young, so they are very flexible and extremely athletic. They have older sisters that are extremely experienced too. Dance school is something new for Key and me. We aren't the weakest links, but we aren't stomping with the big dogs either. I sit and watch for about five minutes, then I feel a tap on my shoulder.

"Hey," Jaylen speaks confidently.
Responding shyly, "Hey."
"Are you new here?" he asks curiously.
"Yeah."
"Oh, my name is Jaylen," he smiles.
"I'm Kimiko," I go along with the conversation as if I don't know who he is already.
"Are you finished with yo' classes?" Jaylen ask.
"Yeah, I'm just waiting on my sister."

"Oh, well, I will see you later. I'm about to go. Bye." Jaylen runs off waving.

"Bye!" I wave back.

Trying not to smile or blush, I noticed Kyra taking a quick glance at me from a distance. *She's going to think I like him*, I think to myself. A few minutes fly by, and I hear Key's class let out. Going to meet them, Jasmine, my play mom, runs to scoop me off of my feet.

"Hey, boo!" she gives me a huge hug and swings me around.

"Hey, what you happy about?" I giggle at her excitement.

"I miss you, daughter, did you have class today?" she asks politely.

"Yeah, I'm finished for the night."

"Aww... I love you!" she shares a quick peck on my cheek and put me down.

She never told me why she likes me so much more than the rest of the kids that are my age, but I like the attention she gives me. Running to Key and Diamond as they pack up, I listen in to what they are talking about.

"I don't really care for the routine," Key expresses.

"Key, your little sister is so pretty!" Diamond adds, changing the topic as soon as she notices me walking up.

Key and I look at each other and giggle as if we have a top secret because we hear this all of the time.

"Look at all of this hair," Diamond goes on.

"Miko!"

Turning around to see who is calling me, I see it's Shalissa.

I run to go talk to her. "I like y'all routine!" I add as soon as I'm close enough.

"Ms. Phee is still trying to come up with the ending, everybody catching on so fast," she brags.

"That's good, and it look like y'all have it down pat," I continue.

"Y'all should see if y'all can spend the night," Shalissa changes the topic.

"My mom is probably going to say no," I hint in a sad tone of voice.

"She don't let y'all stay over at people house?"

"Sometimes," I respond in a less persuasive way, knowing she doesn't even let us spend the night across the street half the time.

"You think she would say yes if I ask?" Shalissa tries to plot.

"I don't know," I shrug my shoulders.

Before I could say anything next, I watch Shalissa prance to my mom, asking if we could spend the night.

Smiling and grinning pretending to be nice, I overhear my mom reply, "Well, they need clothes and stuff. Maybe next time they can come over."

"And you didn't even ask if they could come over, Lissa," Ms. Belk giggles while checking Shalissa.

Ms. Belk looks and seems genuinely nice. After Key finishes getting dressed, we leave and say bye to everybody. Driving in the car on the way home, Mom turns the radio down.

"Don't EVER have anybody ask me can YOU do something! You come and ask YOUR DAMN SELF!" she announced strongly and sternly as if I disrespected her or did something bad.

"I didn't tell her to ask. She asked on her own," I defend myself.

"I DON'T GIVE A FUCK! Don't let it happen again!" her eyes get bigger and bolder as she gives me a serious stare through the rearview mirror.

I can't stand that bitch! I yell in my own head.

The ride home didn't last long. We don't live far from the dance school, and I can't wait to get to my room.

As soon as we arrive home, I run up to my place of peace, then mom calls.

"Miko!"

"Fuck," I mouth with my lips but silently to myself. I go downstairs to see what she wants.

"Grab my shoes and bring them upstairs." Doing as told I grab her shoes, wondering why she can't pick them up herself. I didn't attempt to question her though. I know she has a bad hip, but it can't be that bad. When I get to my room, I just feel like being alone. Ironically, I feel like sleeping in my own room. I usually sleep with Key or my mom, but instead, I want to sleep in my own bed. Tears slowly strolling down my cheeks as I get in the bed. I begin to think about my dad and how much I miss him. He leaves for days at a time, and we don't hear from him or see him. I wish I could just leave for days - away from this place I hate calling *home*.

"I want to go home!" cries my little cousin Malik.

"Okay, well, your mom will be here in a minute!" I catch a quick attitude.

"Why do we have to stop playing?" Malik pouts.

"Because it's late and we have to clean up before your mom get back." I pick the toys up from my bedroom floor.

I can't wait until I hear the alarm system beeping for the front door because I'm ready for my three little cousins to leave. Malik is the bad one and the first to cry about something. Mario is the oldest; he's a pretty chill type of kid, and Heavenly is the baby girl. Key is "babysitting" because my Mom and their mom, Shalonda went out. It feels like I'm doing the babysitting. Since they are younger, they want to hang out with me, so I'm doing all of the work. I'm occupying and entertaining these kids, making sure that they are having fun while Key is in her room, talking on the phone, and looking in the mirror. When the money comes in, it goes to Key's hand. I deserve most of that cut. I'm going to bring it up to my mom one of these days. I'll press the issue if they start to come over too often.

The sound of the alarm sounds like Heaven right now. After cleaning up the last area of my room, I gladly bring the kids downstairs to their mom and their shoes.

"Hey, guys! Were they good, Miko?" Shalonda asks with a clear, soft speech.

"Yeah, they were," I drag.

"Where is Key, she's probably tired?" Shalonda ask, as my mom vulgarly adds:

"She's never fucking tired of going outside!" I watch her as she is hardly able to keep her balance to stand. "Key, bring yo' ass down here!" Mom yells and frowns as if she's mad at Key for no reason. Key runs downstairs, as Shalonda approaches Key.

"Thank you for watching the kids, Key. I really appreciate it. Did they treat you nicely?" Shalonda smiles.

Key giggles. "Yeah."

"Well good, here's fifteen for you." Shalonda hands Key the money, and then she digs in her other pocket and leans over to me. "And here is five for you."

"Thank you." I grab the money with a huge smile painted on my face.

"Well, let me get these kids in the bed, Joyce I'll call you tomorrow," Shalonda picks Heavenly up and makes sure the boys are all set, then leaves for the door.

I wake up the next morning earlier than everybody, so I decide to write in my diary and play with my American Girl Dolls. Soon after, it sounds like Key is waking up from the tossing and turning. When I enter her room, she is still lying down.

"I was so happy when it was time for them to go home last night," I confess.

Key giggles. "Why?"

"Because Heavenly kept trying to play with my American Girl dolls and Malik kept whining about everything."

"Did you let her play with them?" Key asks, knowing the answer.

I look at Key like she's stupid "No, those dolls cost too much money for me to let people play with them."

"You so stingy," Key shakes her head.

I respond quickly out of defense, "Well, she is too young to play with my American Girl Dolls."

"You don't let Patricia and Porsha play with them when they come over either," Key proves her point.

"Like I said, those dolls are too expensive," I mutter, shrugging my shoulders.

"Like I said… S.T.I.N.G.Y. I wish they could've came over last night," Key continues.

"Mama was so drunk," I change the subject.

"Yes, she was." Key rolls her eyes. "It was obvious she was way drunker than Shalonda."

"I wonder why she let herself get like that. She must think it's cute," I egg the conversation on.

"She's a fucking fool if she think that!" Key adds with disgust in her tone of voice.

I burst out in laughter at Key's joke.

CHAPTER **THIRTEEN**

"DANG, WHAT TOOK y'all so long to come outside?" Porsha asks impatiently.

I'm surprised she doesn't know the answer to that by now.

The whole day damn near went by and my mom wouldn't let us come outside for no apparent reason. It's not like when we come outside she doesn't know where we are.

"We came out for a quick minute but, we didn't know where y'all were," I lie.

"We walked up to Boubien Park then met up with Jackie from around the corner." Patricia fixes her hair.

"Is Auntie Joyce going out tonight, again?" Porsha asks with excitement.

"Probably, I should ask if y'all can spend the night," Key adds like she's in deep thought. Then she continues, "Miko, go and see if she is getting dressed or if she have clothes out."

I do as told and proceed toward the house. I know that both of my parents are much harder on Key, so most of the time I don't mind going to ask for stuff. When I walk through the door, I can tell from the darkness that she hadn't been downstairs. I can see the luminous sunset beaming through the living room window and the shadows of the blinds placed in between. I run upstairs out of fear of being in the dark. I find mom laying across the bed, watching something I'm not familiar with. She doesn't have any clothes out. From the looks of it, she's not going anywhere anytime soon.

"Ma."

"What?"

"Patricia and Porsha wanted to know if they can spend the night, can they?" I ask, expecting her to say *no*.

"Yeah, they can, but make sure y'all clean up y'all rooms," she yells as if I'm far away.

"Ok," I rush back outside to share the good news.

Everybody is standing near Patricia and Porsha's house by the streetlight, waiting on me.

"What she say?" Key asks with a stiff look on her face.

"She said no," I fold my arms, shaking my head with a serious facial expression.

"Dang, that's bold!" Porsha sighs. She always shows more emotion than Patricia.

"Sikkke…" I yell, dancing around in circles.

Key cracks a huge goofy smile on her face. "She said yes?"

"Yeah," I giggle as everybody laughs.

After about thirty minutes, Key, Patricia, Porsha, and I go to pack Patricia's and Porsha's overnight bag. Everybody is so excited that we're having a sleepover. One would think that we are long-lost sisters who hadn't seen each other in years. As Porsha grabs her last few items, Patricia goes downstairs, and Key goes into Cory's room.

"Is Auntie Joyce going out tonight?" Porsha asks.

"Nope, I don't think so, she didn't have any clothes out," I add.

"Last time she went out, it was fun being home alone!" Porsha grin.

"Yeah… it was fun! She might go out, but I don't know," I shrug my shoulders.

As Porsha and I head for the stairs, we hear Tez talking about something, cracking jokes. Patricia and Dona are laughing at him while Betty is in the kitchen, smoking on a cigarette. It seems like that's the only time she comes out of her room.

"And look at Porsha's goofy looking self," Tez adds with a cute smile on his face.

"Look at you," Porsha jokes back.

"Where is Key?" Patricia asks.

"She's upstairs with Cory," Porsha answers quickly, smiling.

"She love her some C, huh?" Tez asks like he's sure.

Dona giggles, instigating while bragging, "Right, she love my oldest son!"

They continue to make jokes as Key and Cory come downstairs.

"What's up, Holiday Hearts!" Tez jokes.

Key and Cory are coming down the stairs slowly, blushing and looking embarrassed. We sit and chill with Patricia and Porsha's family for a while, and then we head to my house before it gets too late.

When we get to the house, my mom seems to be in a good mood. She has the house lit, with all the lights on and her stereo playing.

"Hey, daughters!" Mom seems like she's happy to see all of us.

Everybody kind of speaks at the same time, but the only person's voice who stands out is Porsha's voice, "Hey, Auntie Joyce."

As everybody settles in, my mom is still in her friendly talkative mood "Y'all want some wine?" Mom offers in a sneaky but goofy way.

"Yeah!" Porsha blurts out with no hesitation.

Everybody burst out in laughter at her hasty response.

"That's my baby!" Mom adds while cracking up.

We follow her into the dining room, and we all sit around the circular dining table. Waiting on my mom to pour us some glasses of wine. Everyone is so happy, and our bubbly facial expressions are exposing all of our feelings. Mom uses miniature wine glasses for us as she pours a little bit of wine in each of our glasses.

"Now, y'all, don't tell y'all parents I let y'all have a little bit of drinky drink," Mom adds for assurance.

"We won't," Patricia confirms.

"We can keep it on the down low," Porsha winks one of her eyes.

"On the DL," I add giggling.

After chatting it up with my mom, we go upstairs to play school. After that got boring, we play with our hair styling mannequins all night while listening to the CDs.

"Make sure y'all clean up the rooms after y'all finish," mom orders, unable to hide her clean-freakish ways.

"Ok, Auntie Joyce," Porsha blurts out. "Dang, Miko, why you don't ever let me play with your American Girl Dolls?" Porsha asks with a slight attitude.

Key answers before I can utter anything. "Because she stingy."

I ignore Porsha's question and Key's remark. "How did you braid it so neat like that?" I ask Patricia, since she's the only one not irritating me right now.

"You take three pieces, then every time you go under with each piece, you grab extra hair," she explains while demonstrating a perfect French braid on the mannequin.

Key and Patricia can braid very well. When they are finished with each braid, it comes out super neat and pretty. Porsha can braid, too, but her braids don't come out as neat as theirs. I'm learning pretty quickly, but my braids are too loose. As the night goes on, we continue to do hair and have girl talk until everybody falls asleep.

The next morning when I wake up, everybody is out of the bed. I can smell a mouthwatering aroma throughout the house coming from downstairs. Surprisingly, mom don't have her old school music on. Listening hard, I don't recognize the music, so I decide to go downstairs.

"Dang, sleepy head, we were just about to come and wake you up," Patricia adds enthusiastically as I walk down the stairs slowly.

"Y'all the sleepy heads, all of y'all fell asleep before me last night," I smirk, defending myself.

Mom screams from the kitchen, "Y'all go wake Miko up!"

"She already up!" Key answers from the living room.

"Auntie Joyce cooking breakfast! I can't wait!" Porsha smiles, rubbing her hands together like lotion is on them.

I went to go brush my teeth before my mom told me to. By the time I finish, the food is well prepared and it is time to eat. While we are eating, my mom questioned everybody about what is going on "the gossip," and everybody spilled the beans. She always wants to know what is going on with everybody else's kids, but there is so much she doesn't know about her own kids.

After everybody finishes eating, my mom goes upstairs and Key washes the dishes before my mom told her to. For most of the afternoon, we all chill in the living room playing the PlayStation while listening to R. Kelly 12 Play album. Everybody knows all the words to every song on this album. I know the words because it is Key's CD, and she always listens to it. I think Patricia owns her own copy as well. I nod my head rhythmically to the beat of the music, as Key sings, "See I'm wise enough to know…" Patricia and Porsha sing the ad-libs, "My body's calling for you."

We play all kinds of games, from fighting games to driving games. I love playing the driving games because we have a separate wheel and pedal that you can plug into the PlayStation console, which emulates a real car. After playing video games, we play on the Pinball machine in the basement for a few. Then we all decide to get dressed and go outside after being in the house got boring.

For the rest of the day, everybody chilled in front of my house, joking and gossiping. Not too long into the conversation, we see a car pull up to Patricia and Porsha's house. It's their Auntie Toot and her sons. As they get out of the car, I immediately feel the urge to want to go in the house. Her oldest son, Ira, is my age, and he has a crush on me. He comes over often because Betty is his Grandma, too. Most of the time, he acts so weird it makes the vibe between us awkward, so I try to avoid him as much as possible. Patricia and Porsha goes over to speak to Toot, and as soon as I notice Ira walking across the street to come over to speak to Cory, I walk straight inside the house. I'm not good at letting people down when the feeling is not mutual.

You could easily just say I don't like you like that. Like most little girls, I think to myself, but I would feel bad. I'm not like most little girls anyway. I figure he would get the point sooner or later and begin to act normal towards me. Walking upstairs, hoping when I walk past my mom's room, she wouldn't say anything to me.

"Miko," mom calls.

"Huh?" I peek my head through her bedroom doorway.

"Tell Key to come in the house."

"Ok." I go downstairs to tell Key the news knowing she would have an attitude about it.

My mom has my dance bag packed and loaded for tomorrow. I forgot we have a performance in downtown Detroit at the Hart Plaza. Standing in the center of my bedroom, I replay every dance routine in my head. The Hip Hop routine is my favorite routine. The song we're doing the routine to is an electronic dance song called Trommeltanz (Din Daa Daa). The routine isn't complicated. My favorite part is at the end of the routine when we snatch our polyester jogging pants off. Our uniforms include leotards, colored stockings, jogging pants, and flat black shoes. During the entire routine, we keep our jogging pants on. Then, at the end, we snatch them off on a specific part. Last time we practiced the routine, I had a problem with snatching my jogging pants off at the right time. The jogging pants are very lightweight with buttons along the side. The buttons on the side of the pants made it easy to pull off. For some odd reason, there were times when I could pull them off at the right time, and other times, I couldn't. I continue to practice snatching my pants off, and tonight I'm doing well at it; hopefully I can perform well tomorrow.

The nice sunny afternoon, is complimenting the energy around the house. My dad came home last night, which made me feel good and even more excited about the performance. I'm super excited my dad is joining us, and that the energy is positive throughout the house. No one is fighting or arguing, which made the day go by much smoother.

When we met up with the rest of the members, everybody is anxious and getting ready for the first show. Ms. Wendy is in charge of the performance schedule, so she's prepping the next acts.

"Okay, the Little Jazz is going to be the first show from the Wendy School of Dance."

"That's your routine, Miko!" Key taps me with excitement.

"How do you want me to do Miko's hair?" Mom asks Ms. Wendy.

"Let's do the girls' hair in a ponytail at the top and the rest of the hair hanging down in the back. I have some white flower hair accessories for the girls when you guys are done," Ms. Wendy shuffles around.

My mom made sure she asked about the hairstyle to insinuate that no one was putting their hands in my hair. She hates for other people to touch or play in my hair. She always tells me, *"Don't let people touch your hair or it will fall out."*

The music coming from outside is very loud, and the sound coming from the crowd is full and in effect. Looking at my costume for the Little Jazz performance gives me butterflies in my lower stomach. My spotless white leotard compliments my sparkly white tutu. The sparkly tutu has silver sequins all over it. After I get dressed and my mom finished doing my hair, I go to look for my friends. Shalissa and Kyra are getting their makeup done for their next routine. Their performance is after the Little Jazz performance.

"Hey Kimiko, it looks like y'all going first," Shalissa smiles.

"Are you nervous?" Kyra asks as if she's scared for me.

"Yeah, a little bit. I hope the little girls don't make me mess up."

"Right," Shalissa agrees with a giggle.

I guess Kyra is starting to get used to me. She's not being as distant and she's starting to speak to me more.

"Daughter!" I see Jasmine from a distance walking towards me.

"Hey!" I wave, standing still expecting for her to pick me up.

When Jasmine approaches me, she picks me up quickly and swings me around a couple of times. I think Jasmine shows me more love and affection than my actual mom. I low key wish she was my real mom. It's so funny because she looks like a younger, prettier version of my mom.

"The Little Dance is getting ready to perform, and they're waiting on you, boo!"

Jasmine carries me to the front of the line where Little Jazz members are gathering.

"Good luck! You got this!" She gives me a friendly smile and kisses my cheek before I go on stage.

As I lead the six girls to the stage, the massive amount of people in the audience catches me by surprise. I try to find my dad in the crowd, I know he has a video camera and is going to be recording the show. The girls seem to find their places on the stage quickly. I center myself before the younger girls, and begin the routine. Walking out is very nerve wrecking, but I'm more comfortable after the first few minutes passes. The little girls are following my lead graciously as we perform on the huge stage.

Before I know it, the routine is over and we are walking off stage with the audience roaring with lots of excitement and energy. The reaction from the audience gets me anxious and confident for my next performance. As we walk towards the back, everyone is applauding our performance. Shalissa runs to me right before I could look in her direction and lands a huge hug on me.

"Y'all did really good!"

"Thank you, and I didn't mess up either!" I smile proudly.

"Is it a lot of people out there?" Shalissa's tone of voice drops as if she's scared.

"Yeah, more people showed up from earlier. It's more people than what I was expecting," I warn her.

"Did you see anybody you know out in the audience?" Shalissa continues.

"No, I was looking for my dad because he's recording the show, but there are so many people in the audience I couldn't find him," I explain.

"Jazz is up next, everybody line up!" Ms. Wendy calls.

"Gotta' go, wish me good luck!" Shalissa jogs away.

"Good luck! Good luck!" I yell, crossing my fingers.

Key jogs from behind me, "Good job, Miko!" Key passes me quickly to line up for her performance.

"Thank you Key Money!" I smile.

After walking around for a couple of minutes looking for my mom, I wasn't successful, so I go to watch the performance from backstage. I ended up running into my mother standing by Ms. Belk watching the performance. When my mom notices me coming, she gave me this serious face as if she wants to smack the shit out of me.

"Where were you?" she asks discreetly but seriously. Then when Ms. Belk turns around mom lightens up.

"I was looking for you," I'm sure to answer mom's question.

"Wendy said Baton is next up, so we have to get you dressed," Mom walks towards where we have our things, and I follow. Last time we had dance practice, I didn't have Baton class, so hopefully I can remember the steps and tricks.

When Key's performance is over, everybody in Jazz had to hurry and get dressed for Baton. The baton costume includes skin-toned shiny stockings, a one-piece bathing suit, and white gym shoes. The extra accessories include the baton and a circular floaty that we have to wear throughout the whole routine. The floaty is cute, but it doesn't fit my small body correctly. It falls off my waist when I stand, so I know once I start dancing, it's going to give me a hard time. After I finish putting my costume on, I grab my baton and practice the dance.

Jaylen walks up to me out of nowhere. "You're supposed to bring it up and throw it. See, like- is this your baton?"

I correct him, "No, that's Key's baton."

"Can I show you how it's supposed to be done?" he asks nicely while bragging with his chest out like he's the man.

"I know how the dance go, we have different parts. When you're doing something, I might be doing something completely different, but go ahead," I giggle, letting him show off.

He's spinning the baton extremely fast and crisp. He's catching it just in the right time frame for his speed while turning in circles. He's doing all kinds of tricks that are not apart of the routine. He is pretty good with the baton, and he's doing a good job showing off.

"This baton feels different!" he proclaims.

"That's because it's for bigger people like your older sister," I explain while smiling.

We continue with the small talk and he shows me more cool tricks, then his mom calls him, so he had to leave.

"Baton line up!" Ms. Wendy announces.

Everybody gathers to the front of the backstage to prepare to run out on stage.

Shalissa runs behind me. "Do you remember this dance?"

"I remember some parts. Do you?" I nervously admit.

"A little bit, there are a lot of parts I don't remember. I'm just going to follow what Kyra do," Shalissa shares an embarrassing laugh.

The song we are dancing to sounds like a fun car washing song. When we run out, I'm not too confident because I forgot how the beginning of the dance starts, so I follow Shalissa. It seems like everybody is everywhere and nobody is really sure of anything. I'm happy this dance is more of a fun dance because it helps the mistakes look less obvious.

The boys coming out, is the hint that the middle of the routine is approaching. Then when the older people come out for a short period of time, I know we are at the end of the routine, and it is going to be over soon. Soon enough, the routine is over, and we strike our pose to initiate just that. Once everybody got backstage, the jokes and bombs dropped, and my stomach start to hurt from laughing so hard.

"I was looking at you, and you was looking at me!" Kyra expresses, laughing uncontrollably.

"Man, I told Kimiko I didn't remember the dance and that I was just going to follow you," Shalissa laughs.

"I locked Emily out of the track line we made," I add, laughing embarrassingly. "I saw that!" Kyra adds, laughing.

"And that other little girl! They both were just looking like... what to do?," Shalissa laughs.

"They took too long to get in!" I admit while laughing uncontrollably.

"They didn't even know when to come in!" Jasmine adds with her outgoing personality.

"Right, I'm like I think this is the part where we come in," Key agrees with a laugh.

"Hip Hop is up next in a few minutes! Everybody hurry and change! " Ms. Wendy announces.

The Hip Hop routine is the last routine we are performing for the afternoon, and it is my favorite dance. Everybody loves this dance and is super excited to perform.

"Din Daa Daa Din Doh Doh," I sing, doing a robot type of movement with my arms.

Key giggles while watching me then sings "Da- Da- Da- Da- Da," then she begin making this sound while rolling her tongue mimicking the song to a tee.

"Da!" We both blurt out at the same exact time, and I unsuccessfully pull my pants off.

"Dang!" I pout.

"You have to grip them tight and pull out instead of pulling forward," Key tries to help me.

"Man, I'm going to stand somewhere in the back just in case I don't pull them all the way off," I give in.

In this routine, we didn't have a specific placement. Mr. Jessie just encouraged shorter people in the front and taller people in the back. It's time to perform. I'm excited but a little discouraged.

"Kimiko, you ready?" Shalissa asks with so much excitement. I didn't need to exchange the question.

"Yeah," I nod my head less excited.

"We're going to go to the front of the stage," Kyra adds with big happy eyes.

"Are you coming, too?" Shalissa askes.

"Yeah, I might," I lie, not wanting them to know about my issue with pulling off my pants.

We all gather to our places on stage before the music comes on. I place myself towards the back-left side of the stage. A lot of people are in front of me, so I feel more comfortable if I mess up. When the music comes on, the crowd begins to roar at the song by George Kranz called Din Daa Daa.

So far, I'm doing well with no mistakes yet. As we proceed, the part I'm most intimidated by is coming up.

"Da!" I rip my pants smooth off.

Damn it! I should of stopped being scared and went up to the front, I think to myself as we walk off the stage. Everybody is so happy and cheerful like we won a Grammy. After everyone got dressed, Ms. Wendy passes out small trophies while making her announcement.

"Today was our first time performing as Wendy School of Dance for the season. I must say, you guys wore it on your shirts well! Everyone performed at their very best today! I want to say great job and keep up the great work!"

After the show, everybody met up at Pizza Hut to celebrate. Shalissa and Kyra wanted me to ride with them to the restaurant, but of course Mom didn't let me go, so I just waited to see everybody when we got there. Everybody enjoyed each other's company over pizza and punch.

CHAPTER **FOURTEEN**

ON THE WAY to Big Mama's house, the radio is slapping. All of the mix songs that we dance to are coming on back to back. My mom loves this kind of music, so when they play it on the radio, she always turns up the volume.

"Let me bang" comes on loud and clear through the speakers.

My mom is dancing in the driver seat, and Key and I are waiting for the first verse to start.

"This track is for the playa haters lying on they d***. Cock-blocking punks. Front for a b****" me and Key sing the radio version as they bleep out the curse words.

"Big booty b***** that talk a lot of smack. Bend yo' a** over let me hit it from the back. Hit it from the back -Hit it from the back -Hit it from the back- Hit it from the back- Let me bang."

A few more mix songs comes on before we get to Big Mama's house. Now my mom is geeked up.

"Y'all want to go to the Kiddy Disco tonight?" Mom looks excited.

Key smiles shyly, "I don't care."

"Alright, I'm going to see who else is over Big Mama's house. I might call Tina and see if Raven and Micha want to go too," mom adds.

"Patricia and Porsha might want to come, too," Key suggests.

"Right, my girls might want to," Mom smiles at Key's input.

Big Mama's side door is always open. No one ever has to knock to get in; if you aren't a stranger you know to walk right in. As we enter the house, Aunt Lora is sitting in the living room smoking a cigarette, watching Tae and Kyler. Tae is Aunt Lora's only daughter. She's a pretty baby and looks nothing like Aunt Lora. She's the spitting image of her dad. I don't think Aunt Lora and Tae's dad are together because I only saw him around a couple of times. Kyler is around the same age as Tae, so they play together. Kyler is Uncle Nutty's youngest son, and he's a pretty chill baby. I'm shocked Adrian isn't over here playing with Tae and Kyler. Adrian is Evin and April's younger brother. He's the same age as Tae and Kyler. Usually, Adrian wants to go home with his mom, and tonight is probably one of those nights.

"Hey Aunt Lora," I wave.
"What's up, Mik?" she smiles with her arms out gesturing for a hug.
"Hey, Auntie," Key speaks after me.
"Hey, Key," she smiles and gives her a kiss on the cheek.

After speaking to Aunt Lora, I go to see who's in the back. In the hallway, I see April and Bryon.
"How long y'all been over here?" I ask.
"We just got over here not too long ago," April responds while playing with her beads in her hair.
"We been over here all day. I think we spending the night," Bryon answers.
"I think we spending the night, too," April adds.
"Who? You, Evin, and Adrian?" I ask.
"Nope, just me and Evin. Adrian staying with my mom," April continues.
"You spending the night?" April asks.
"I don't think so. Let me go speak to Big Mama," I cut our

conversation short.

"Hey, Big Mama," I sit on her bed.

"Hey, Miko," she smiles. "When did you get here?" she asks in her raspy voice.

"We just got here."

"Who?" Big Mama asks.

"My mom and Key."

"Oh, okay, your daddy was here earlier. I don't know if he's still here, though," she takes a puff of her cigarette.

That's the only thing I don't like about coming over here, the smell of cigarette smoke. Big Mama and Aunt Lora smoke a lot. The smell is just something I'm not used to.

"Hey, Big Mama," mom speaks, from the doorway, while Key is in front of her walking to give Big Mama a hug.

"Is Jihod still here?" Big Mama asks.

"Yeah, he's downstairs with the Twins," Mom replies.

The Twins are Aunt Lora's oldest sons. Their names are Damon and James. They don't favor Aunt Lora much either; they're extremely tall, brown-skinned complexion with braids. They favor Aunt Lora more than Tae does. I've never seen their dad before, but I'm sure they look more like him, too.

"Y'all want to go to the Kiddy Disco?" Mom asks excitedly.

"Yeah!" April stands up as if she's been before.

"Bryon, you coming too?" Mom asks, not wanting to leave him out, even though he's a boy.

"Yeah, I guess," Bryon responds in an, *I don't care* type of way.

"Is your brother here?" Mom asks April.

"Yeah, he's in Aunt Lora's room. I'll go get him," April runs off.

So, it's me, Key, Evin, April, and Bryon in our green Mercury Montego SUV. Of course, my mom and dad are the chaperons. My parents are the parents that don't mind taking all of the kids to go have fun. That's probably why all of the kids in my family love my parents. When we get in the car, the radio is still bumping with all of the hype mix songs.

"In the club and on the streets, we keep banging; we keep banging the beat. Banging, banging, banging, banging, banging the beat" is playing loud through the speakers. The mix songs always bring a happy mood to the weekend. My dad is doing some dance with his arms in the passenger seat, thinking he's cool.

"We on our way to the Kiddy Disco?" I ask, excited to be with everybody.

"We about to go pick up Patricia, Porsha, and Cory first," Mom replies.

Key's face glows up when she hear those words. My mom included Cory's name, which is kind of surprising, being that my parents try to act like they don't approve of the fact that Key and Cory may have a crush on each other.

When we pull up on the block, we see the regulars and extra people in the middle of the street.

"Hey, Auntie Joyce!" Porsha walks up to my mom's window before Patricia.

"Hey, boo, y'all want to come to the Kiddy Disco with us?" Mom asks immediately.

"Yeah, y'all rolling or y'all strolling?" dad throws a curve joke.

Patricia giggles, "I'm about to go ask real quick!"

"I hope y'all can come," Key adds from the backseat window.

"I know, right?" Porsha agrees while looking in the truck to see who's inside.

"Where Miko at?" Porsha asks.

"She back here," Key gestures towards the trunk of the car.

Patricia runs back outside. "They said we can go!"

Patricia and Porsha hop in the trunk with April and me.

"Come on, Cory!" Key waves him towards the car.

Standing still unsure of if he's invited, mom speaks up "Get in, Cory," Mom confirms, and he doesn't think twice to jump in.

"Auntie Joyce, can we come, too?" Jena asks with a long face.

"Y'all can come next time when it's not so many people in the car. We got a full car, my nieces and nephews, in here too, boo," Mom explains, feeling bad we only came to pick up Patricia and Porsha.

The Kiddy Disco is on the East side of Detroit and we live on the Westside, so the drive there is a nice ride. The radio is still playing all of the popular mix songs and it's getting everybody excited to dance.

"If you bald-headed and you proud of it, just get on the dance floor," is coming through the speakers while everyone is talking and cracking jokes. We didn't have to introduce anybody because everybody already knows each other through us by coming to our parties. When we arrive at the Kiddy Disco, there are a lot of people inside, and the dance competitions are getting started. In no time, my mom registered all of the girls in the dance competition to win a prize.

"I'm nervous. I didn't know we were going to be in a dance competition," Porsha confesses with a smile.

"I'm not that nervous. It's not that many people here. April, you nervous?" I ask quickly.

"A little bit," she giggles, looking around.

"I think we all going up there at the same time," I add trying to make everybody feel comfortable. .

"I hope they play a song we all know when we go up there," Patricia adds while smiling at Evin.

Key agrees, looking overjoyed, "I know, right?"

As we continue to walk into the disco, they call out specific age groups to the stage. After all of us went on the stage, my mom was right in the front crowd rooting for everyone who rode with us. Once the night got older, my parents takes everyone home, and then we proceed home.

PRETTY CAN BE UGLY

There are a lot of things we don't like about our parents, but all of our friends and cousins our age love our parents. Out of all of the adults, my parents are the ones who don't mind watching the kids or doing kid friendly things. What our friends and family don't know is what goes on daily. Thankfully, when we get home, everyone is on a good frequency. After I put on my pajamas, I walk into my parents' doorway.

"Can I sleep in here with y'all?" my hopeful tone of voice exposes my scaredy-cat ways.
"Yeah," dad answers first.

I hop in the bed in between both of my parents. I'm secretly happy that my mom didn't say no because my dad is home. Any other time when he's not here, she doesn't mind me sleeping with her.

CHAPTER **FIFTEEN**

EVERY TIME WE have a hair appointment, we go super early in the morning. Since I slept in my parents' room, my mom wakes me up first to get ready to go. When I get finish getting dressed, my stomach is craving some cereal. That's one of my favorite breakfast meals. We have Honeycombs and Frosted Flakes, and I'm guessing Key opened the Honeycombs already, but I want some Frosted Flakes, so I open the Frosted Flakes to eat before we leave for the salon.

"Your hair is so thick and long," the lady that's blow-drying my hair complains.

Everyone in this room that's getting their hair washed or blow-dried has a perm. If you have thick and kinky hair, a perm will make your hair straight and manageable. Mr. John's is a family-owned hair salon. We're here every two weeks faithfully. Mr. John is the owner, and he's an extremely handsome old man. He's tall, brown-skinned, with a long, silky, grey slicked-back ponytail. His oldest daughter, Marcia, works at the front desk. She makes appointments and sells their company products. Mr. John's hair products are supposed to be miracle-working for people who have damaged hair.

Tony is his other daughter, and she's a stylist at the salon. Tony is a short woman with a short burgundy haircut. Marcia and Tony don't resemble each other much to be sisters. Key and I look more alike than they do. Tony does my hair when John Jr. is too busy to take me. Most of the time, John Jr. styles my hair. I usually get a press and curl for a style. I've noticed most of the clients that come to this salon mainly get press and curl. It's probably because this salon is strictly for hair care. The lady that's blow-drying hair today doesn't know what she's doing. She's being so rough and pointing the blow drier directly in my face, causing me to have shortness of breath.

"That hurt," I complain with an attitude.
"Oh, I'm sorry, your hair is dry. But your scalp is still a bit wet, I'll just let you sit under the drier".
"Thank you Jesus!" I almost scream aloud.

Key is getting her hair pressed in another room right now. I'm just ready to get this over with. I love the results of getting my hair done, but I hate the process of getting it done.

"That baby hair is so pretty and long," I overhear an older woman express to a lady that washes hair.
"Yes, it is, and she's even prettier," the lady that washes hair giggles to the older woman.

Waiting for about another fifteen to twenty minutes under the drier, John Jr. finally comes to rescue me from the washing room. John Jr. is Mr. John's son and one of his only sons who work in the salon. John Jr. is a handsome man, too. He's tall, brown skin, and he wears his hair just like his dad, in a slicked-back ponytail.

"You ready, Kimiko?" John Jr. approaches me, pronouncing my name slightly wrong.
"Yeah, and you can just call me, Miko," I correct him as he lead the way to his suite.
"Okay, that's a little easier," he giggles.

"Yeah, everybody call me Miko anyway," I admit.

"Oh really?"

"Yeah, the only people that call me by my full name are the people I go to school with," I explain. "And they don't pronounce it right either," I add before letting him respond.

He giggles while placing a fresh hair cape over me. "Well, how is it properly pronounced?"

"It's (Kee-Mee-Ko)" I say slowly so that he can hear every syllable.

"Oh, okay that's different. Miko is much more simple. I'll call you Miko as suggested," he continues to giggle.

Before putting my head down so John Jr. could start on the back of my head, I see Mr. John walking into the room.

"You ready to go back to school yet?" Mr. John asks in a smooth voice.

"No, it seems like we just got out," I reply.

"The summer will be over sooner than you know it," Mr. John continues while touching the ends of my hair.

"She's going to need a clip," Mr. John sounds sure.

"Understood," John Jr. nods his head.

"How is her dandruff looking?" Mr. John rubs my scalp softly.

"I just checked on it" John Jr. replies. "It's looking better than her last appointment."

"The change in shampoos must have made a difference," Mr. John adds.

"Yeah, but you know her mom and her sister have really dry scalps as well; it may be genetics," John. Jr. adds.

"Right, okay, well I'll see you before you guys leave," Mr. John walks out of the room.

Applying the same technique over and over again, adding oils and grease, then pressing with a hot pressing comb, John Jr. is finally fucking finished. My hair is as straight and shiny as it's going to get. I walk to the waiting area where Key and my mom are sitting.

"Your hair look pretty, Mik!" Mom compliments as she gets up to go pay for the services.

"Thank you, when did you guys want to schedule for your next appointment?" Marcia seems happier than usual.

"In two more weeks on Thursday," Mom replies.

"Okay, I have you guys down for the Thursday after next. What time?" Marcia smiles.

"Eight-thirty" Mom answers quickly.

"Alright, y'all are all set! See you in two weeks!"

"Alrighty!" Mom adds, walking out the door as we follow.

"What was she so happy for?" Key puts on her seat belt.

"Her daddy probably gave her a raise," Mom mimics Marcia's voice.

We all laugh getting ready to pull off.

"And what don't your daddy do for you?" I take up for Marcia in my head.

The only reason we're able to afford getting our hair done every two weeks is because my grandparents pay for it. She don't even have a job. Her little disability checks are nothing. I'm ready to get back to playing with my Barbie dolls. Right now, in the Barbie world of mine, Barbie and Ken have their dream house, and now they have their dream family. I got the kid baby dolls for Christmas, so Barbie and Ken have a baby now.

By the time we get home, I can tell it's still early because no one is outside yet, not even the sun. As soon as we get inside the house, I keep straight ahead for the stairs. Not too long after, I get all of my dolls out.

"Miko!" Mom screams from downstairs.

I hurry down the stairs to see what she wants. When I walk into the dining room looking at my mom through the kitchen, she looks angry, and buck eyed evil.

Mom walks up to me quickly "Did you open the Frosted Flakes?" she yanks my collar.

Scared to admit but petrified to lie over something so small, I utter, "Yes."

"I should whoop your little ass! Don't open one cereal box until the first one is finished!" she orders sternly damn near throwing me across the kitchen.

"Ok," I respond quickly so I won't get in more trouble.

After pushing me away to put the cereal back in the cabinet, I figure it's safe to go back to my room. *What is the big fucking deal?* Closing my door, I add loud enough for only me to hear, "That's why I don't like her ass now. Mean as bitch." Flopping on the floor with my toys, "I can't wait until my daddy get here," a couple of tears roll down my cheeks slowly.

"We always getting yelled at or whooped for nothing." I wipe my tears, take a deep breath, and continue to play.

After I got bored with playing with my dolls, I switch to play my Star Wars game that came with my Xbox. It's one of those games where you have to complete missions while working with your teammates. It's a pretty cool game, but I don't like it better than the driving and fighting games we have on PlayStation.

"Miko..." mom calls.

"What the fuck do this bitch want?" I throw my controller on the bed.

"Huh?"

"Pick that black thing up from off the floor for me," she points in the direction less than five inches away from her feet. She literally can bend over and reach it herself.

I pick this hard piece of black plastic up. Rolling my eyes because

PRETTY CAN BE UGLY

my back is facing her.

"Where did Key go?" I ask quickly.

"She went outside," she said with a slight attitude. "She's lucky I let her ass go out today," Mom speaks aloud but not directly to me as I walk back upstairs.

I continue to play my Star Wars game that is getting better as I learn different tricks and shortcuts. After playing for about thirty minutes, surprisingly, I pass the first mission. Before I begin the second mission, I put in my Lil' Romeo CD that I got for Christmas in my stereo.

I love Lil' Romeo, but it seems like Lil' Bow Wow is a bit more popular than he is. Or if not more popular than maybe more liked by people I know personally.

As the song "Little Star" plays, I continue to play my Star Wars game and pretend Lil' Romeo is talking to me through the speakers.

When I hear the door close, and I immediately pop up, hoping it's my daddy. I run to the stair railing to listen to who came through the door, and it's just Key coming up the stairs.

"Where you about to go?" I ask Key quickly.

"Back outside," she answers, quickly walking past me to her room.

"It look like it's about to rain," I follow her to her room.

"Yeah, that's why I'm changing my shoes," Key flops her shoes off.

I laugh, "Y'all fooling! Who else out there?" I can't believe y'all about to stand outside in the cold rain."

"Everybody," she answers walking past me, heading out the door.

Attempting to follow but not really feeling up to it, I go back into my room of comfort.

"Plus, we just got our hair done. I'm surprised mama letting her do that," I say to myself as I enter into my room.

Becoming bored with the game, I turn it off along with my stereo. Next up is my American Doll Addy book. Her story is very interesting because the time framing is in slavery days. Addy and her family are slaves. The book is based on her life as a slave and trying to survive the trauma and hardships.

One thing I love about the American Girl books is the family tree. The American girls are usually in the middle, and above them are photos of their parents. On the side of them are their siblings, if they have any. Below are other family members that play a part in the book, like a grandparent or an aunt or uncle. What is super cool is, sometimes they will include a best friend or a neighbor in the family tree as well. It reminds me of my neighbors and the people we see every day. We're almost like a small family; we're together all the time, and everybody knows everybody's parents.

As I read about her everyday life, and how she has to take orders from white people, gives me a mixture feeling of sorrow and anger. Addy is being described as a brave, loving, and kind child. She was separated from her family at a young age due to slavery. Thankfully, they were able to reunite, and she remained tied closely to them. Addy does not like slavery or the hard work she is enduring. Addy doesn't think it is fair or right that white people own and abuse black people. Her Papa describes her as being of the age where a child learns they are a slave. The hope that she had as a child is being broken by the daily burdens of being a slave.

This is so hurtful to read. Addy is my age, and she has to take orders and watch people suffer just because of her skin color. If I were in her position, I wouldn't know how to handle being a slave. I mean, I have my issues with my family, but if I was ever taken away from them, I'd die. I would miss my family knowing that they were out in the world, and I couldn't see them. I couldn't imagine doing someone else's daily yard work or housework. I can hardly take my mom calling me from upstairs to pick something up that's sitting right in front of her fucking face. I can only imagine the pain and suffering she has to go through every day, physically, mentally, and emotionally.

I feel connected to Addy's personal life story because I'm African American. I know black people used to be enslaved, tortured, and held back from resources and still are to this day. But today's slavery is communicated much differently. This is why my dad personally doesn't like white people and we have small talks about how the white man have been stealing and taking advantage of black America for centuries. Dad gets so serious talking about this sensitive topic, but that lets me know its truth behind his words. I also learn about our black history in school, too. After reading a couple of chapters, I put my Addy book and my American Girl dolls away. I noticed that Key is back in her room earlier than expected.

    Walking into Key's room without knocking, I see her in the mirror.
"Mama made you come in huh?"
"Yeah," she answers quickly and somewhat sad.
"Y'all were in front of the house, right?" I sit down on her bed.
"Yeah, we were right on the sidewalk. She just wants somebody to sit in here and be miserable with her ass," Key cuts her eyes.
    "Key, come here!" Mom yells from downstairs.
    "Then she can't stop calling my fucking name…" Key gets up and storms out the room.

    I wait for a few minutes for Key to come back upstairs, but it took her longer than expected, so I go downstairs. My mom is having Key prepare a meal for us, so I just sit at the bar and chime in to what mom have to say. At first, Key had a dry face like she wasn't in the mood to cook, but then she lightens up. Key is such a mama's girl; she gets mad at my mom but never for too long. On the other hand mom doesn't allow us to have attitudes with her. She will punish us even harder if she senses a problem. Sometimes I think Key believes most things my mom says about my dad and about other people. She's more easily manipulated by my mom than I am. When my mom is talking to me about my dad, I listen with my ears, but I don't let it get to my head. I act as if I agree with her, but deep inside, I don't. At the end of the story, once she lets me leave the conversation, I throw everything she said in the garbage.

CHAPTER **SIXTEEN**

"SO, WHAT WERE they talking about outside?" Mom smiles because she knows she's being nosy.

"Nothing, really. Joe and Jena got into it, as usual," Key laughs.

"What happened?" I ask giggling, feeling kind of mad I missed it.

"I don't even know. I was coming from down the street with Sherri, then I saw them tussling like they were about to start fighting," Key explains.

"Who is Sherri?" I've never heard this unfamiliar name.

"That's the same girl I told you I just met a couple of days ago. She lives down the street." Key adds some water in a bowl.

"Oh, yeah, the girl that's your age?" I ask, making sure I was talking about the same person.

"Yeah, and Patricia and Porsha was acting so nonchalant like something was wrong with them." Key stirs around something in another deep bowl.

"What were they doing? Make sure you mix it good." Mom guides Key.

"They just wasn't talking to me much. I introduced them to Sherri, so I don't know what was wrong," Key explains with confusion on her face and in her voice.

"It sounds like they were jealous of the fact that you found a new friend," Mom adds as if she's positive that's the case.

"Sherri was even trying to start a conversation with them, and they were acting so standoffish." Key still looks confused.

"They wasn't acting like their usual friendly selves," I add finishing off Key's explanation.

"Right," Key replies.

"It's because they were jealous that you brought someone new to the crew," Mom adds, chewing on some food. Looking around to see what's cooking in the kitchen, I smell chocolate. Key is mixing a chocolate cake or brownie mix. I'm in a good mood because chocolate is my favorite flavor.

"Are you putting chocolate icing on the cake, too?" I'm praying Mom say yes.

"Yup!" Mom answers just as excited as I am.

"Chocolate cake and chocolate icing?" Key asks still confused.

"Yeah!" Mom and I respond at the same time, as everyone laughs.

"Don't this Sherri girl have a little brother?" I continue with the conversation.

"Yeah, his name is Dominic," Key responds.

"And what do you want with the little brother?" Mom turns the conversation upside down.

"Nothing. I was just asking," I frown.

Key giggles, trying to even out the awkward tension, "Her brother is not cute at all. He's like a dark-skinned boy with two buckteeth. He got the thickest pair of glasses I've ever seen a little boy wear."

Mom laughs, "Is he half blind?"

"I don't know, but I know when you look at him through his glasses, his eyes look two times smaller than their natural size," Key laughs at Mom's laughter.

"Damn!" Mom blurts out while laughing uncontrollably.

Sometimes, Mom can be funny with the way she expresses herself or her reactions to things. I just don't understand why she has to be so mean all the time. She's always making us lie to people. It's not only to our dad, but it's to her parents and her friends for no apparent reason. I wonder what's her reason for lying so much. Sometimes the lies are small, and sometimes they're big lies. I wonder, did my Granny use to make her lie a lot when she was a kid.

As my mind wonders, I tune back into the conversation

"That's why she doesn't have a man now." Mom teases.

"Who?" Key ask quickly. I'm guessing she zoned out with me too, once my mom started rambling.

"Lora," Mom responds with a pause and an aren't-you-listening expression on her face.

"As long as I been around, I've never seen her with a man," Mom goes on.

"Well, what about Tae daddy?" Key asks while waiting on the food.

"I hardly see him, with his Humpty dumpty fell off the wall looking ass," Mom adds while laughing at her own joke, making us laugh.

"If he was to ever fall, that would be a long fall," I add to the joke.

That comment, coming out of my eight-year-old mouth, has Key and mom crying laughing. My mom's pale face is red, and Key is looking like she's about to pee on herself. As everybody catch their breaths mom finally pours the chocolate mix into a pan. That's the part I've been waiting on.

"It seems like ever since Tae was born, I've seen him less and less. I heard he's a married man," Mom continues to gossip.

"Can I have the bowl when you finish emptying the mix?" I try to squeeze my question in the conversation.

"For what?" Mom looks me dead in my face.

"To clean it, you know, like eat the leftover chocolate mix in the bowl," I explain, hoping she let me do it because Granny always does.

"Here you go," she hands it to me.

I grab the big bowl as quickly as I can say bowl.

"Here's a spoon," Mom hands it to me over the bar from the kitchen.

"Then if he's not over to Big Mama's house, he's with Rock and them," she continues to go on and on. "So, when he decides to come home, he expect for everything to go so nice and smooth."

"Right, like he hasn't been gone for days," Key agrees.

"And I'm sitting in here with y'all every day all day. He's not here with me. He wants to be out in the streets," her mood seems to shift in a bad direction.

"Then he doesn't even call most of the time," Mom begins shaking her head.

Five seconds after she made her last comment, I hear somebody walking through the door.

Their conversation ends immediately. It's my dad, and I'm so happy to see him, but I'm afraid to show my feelings. Being that they were just gossiping about him, he's on the shit list.

"What's up, y'all!" Dad walks through the door with a huge garbage bag full of something.

The vibes are kind of awkward, but I speak first. "Hey, Da!" I wave, giving a small smile.

"What are you eating?" he giggles, putting his bag down.

"Chocolate cake mix," I answer while licking the bowl.

"Look at Key! In the kitchen! Cooking up something that's smelling good!" He sings in a happy mood.

Key giggles, unable to resist his sense of humor.

"Joyce in the Rose Royce…" he sings to Mom, wheeling in to give her a quick kiss on the lips.

"I talked to Gee earlier," my mom says in a less agitated tone of voice.

"Oh, okay, everything went alright?" Dad responds walking to the table and pulls this scale out that's usually in the basement.

"Yeah," he said that y'all were supposed to link up sometime today," Mom continues.

"Yup, I seen him already. He was drunk as hell! He almost made me get into it with a nigga'!" he adds with a serious face but a funny tone of voice.

"Really, what he do?" Mom giggles.

"Being sloppy drunk! This guy thought he was about to dog him," he explains while pulling out a hand full of weed and putting it on the table.

"Oh, the guy was trying to fight Gee?" Mom asks, sitting down.

"Yeah, trying to bulldog him, knowing he was drunk. I had to step in and tell dude he better bag the fuck back!" He stops what he is doing to show us he wasn't playing.

Key giggles at his natural animation.

"What you say to the guy?" Mom laughs, anticipating what happened next.

"I told him, 'dog, you see he drunk don't push him like that.' Then the guy said, 'Well, you better get his drunk ass.' I said, "Or what? YOU NOT GONE BEAT MY ASS!" Then he started walking away mumbling, talking about 'You heard what I said.' And I said 'MUTHAFUCHA, AND YOU HEARD WHAT I SAID!'" dad acts the scene out to the tee.

Everybody started laughing because we know he's serious.

When I'm with my dad, I feel so safe and secure. He's like my King Kong. If anyone thinks they're going to hurt me, Jihod's daughter Kimiko Lewis, they thought wrong.

CHAPTER **SEVENTEEN**

IN THE CITY of Detroit, you have to have tough skin. If you don't have tough skin, you at least have to know someone that has tough skin that can have your back. My dad is so tough because he was forced to be. He tells us plenty of stories about how he was the smallest out of everybody growing up. How he always got picked on and had to fight to defend himself, so anytime someone thinks that they're about to get over on him or any of his loved ones, he's always ready for war.

"So, the guy ended up leaving?" Mom asks to confirm that was the end of the story.

"Yeah, his hoe ass left," he continues to put the weed on the scale.

"Where were y'all at when this happened?" Mom continues to question him.

"We were at the store," he replies. "Then it just started raining out of nowhere," dad adds.

"Right," Key adds a little annoyed.

"I had to tell Key ass to come in the house." Mom looks at Key like she's crazy.

"You had to tell her to come in from the rain?" he asks, giggling in disbelief.

"Yeah, she came in changing her shoes and grabbed an umbrella," Mom giggles while talking about Key in front of her face.

Dad bursts out with a loud laugh, "She did?"

"Everybody was out there, though," Key defends herself.

Dad just shakes his head while he continues weighing the weed. I'm surprised that he's weighing his weed on the dining room table; he usually goes downstairs. After dad's ghetto storytelling, Mom starts going on about some story I'm not interested in.

After ten minutes pass, we hear a knock on the door. We have long shaped, cream rectangular blinds covering our dining room window, so as soon as my mom hears the knock, she goes to the far side of the window to peek through.

"Who is it?" Dad asks quickly.

"It's Mars," Mom silently giggles.

"Who?" Dad looks confused.

"Cousin Mars," she repeats herself as if he knows him.

"Oh, y'all invited him over?" He sounds more relaxed.

Key and Mom laugh and whisper like he can hear us from inside the house. "No."

"He just pops up randomly sometimes," Mom explains in a silly way.

"Last time he came over, we didn't answer the door," Key whispers.

"Does he have a car?" Dad asks, seeming curious.

"No, but he can tell you about any car of any brand of any year at the drop of a dime," Mom continues in a low toned voice.

Mars continues to knock on the door after minutes goes by.

"Last time he stood out there for about an hour before he left," Mom giggles, still speaking in a low tone voice.

"Well damn, it is raining out there. Let him in," Dad suggests.

"You think I should?" Mom asks in an unsure way.

"Yeah," Dad sounds sure.

Mars is our cousin on my mom's side of the family. He's my

Granny's nephew from her youngest brother German. I don't know exactly what's wrong with him, but I know he has some type of mental illness. He also has a really bad stuttering problem, and for some reason, he likes my mom. He doesn't have a car, but he makes his way over here just fine and often. He has slowed down from coming over here because Mom doesn't answer the door most of the time. She doesn't like it when company just pops up unannounced. But Mars shouldn't be included since he doesn't have all of his "marbles."

Mars continue to knock in the same rhythm while my mom walks to open the door. Once he comes in, he is standing in the living room by the front door with wet clothes on. He's tall, dark-skinned with a little bit of stubble facial hair within his mustache. He looks uncertain if he wants to come to the dining room where my dad and I are sitting. I guess he's waiting to see where my mom is going to sit. Mom cuts on the living room light so he can sit in the living room where the TV is.

"Mars, where you coming from?" my mom asks in a friendly way.
"I-I came f-from h-h-home."
"How did you get here?" Mom continues.
"I w-w-w-w-walked."
"All the way from Joy Road?" she asks. "Why didn't you ask Uncle German to drop you off?"
"H-he w-w-wasn't at home," he responds emotionless.
"You should've called him so he could have dropped you off because it's raining," my mom suggest. "Did you eat?" she continues to question him.
"No," Mars answers without a stutter.
"Well, Key is cooking Chicken, Rice, and Broccoli. We'll make you a plate, too," Mom confirms.
"K-k-k-key c-c-cooking?" he asks as if he can't believe it.
"Yeah, I'm teaching Key how to cook. Key, come speak to Mars," Mom calls.

Key walks through the dining room from the kitchen to the living room.

"Hey," Key waves politely.

"H-hey, Key!" he looks happy to see Key.

He doesn't show me much attention. Not that I'm upset about it, it's just something I notice. Key is older than I am, and he has known her longer. I'm standing in the walkway between the living and dining room, looking and listening to my mom and Mars conversation. Out of nowhere, I hear a sound coming from behind me.

"ppesss...ppesss," I turn around to see dad bursting out in laughter at me.

"What?" I look dad in the face, with a smirk.

"What are you staring at?"

"Nothing," I respond as Key is laughing at me as well.

"You're just standing there, looking clueless. Are you going to come in here to sit down or are you going into the living room with them?" dad continues to laugh.

"You're just standing right in the middle of the walkway like you're invisible or something," he continues to tease.

"I'm not in the middle. I'm by the wall," I defend myself.

"You're still in the way," he continues as I move to the dining room back to the bar area.

"In who way? It's not like it's a bunch of people here," I catch a small attitude from him putting me on blast.

"Goofball!" he smirks and giggles as he cleans up and goes downstairs into the basement.

My mom walks back into the kitchen to help Key.

"Alright, so that's almost done boiling, you can cut the stove down a little bit. The chicken is almost done, too. It should be enough for Mars," she adds.

"How did he get here?" Key whispers.

"He said he walked all the way from Joy Rd.," Mom giggles, but manages to keep her voice down.

PRETTY CAN BE UGLY

I'm waiting for dinner to be finished so I can get to dessert. The cake took no time to cook. I'm anticipating on eating at least two slices. Mars joins us for dinner and eventually goes back home. My dad offered to take him home, but he insisted that he take the bus back. I don't know how old he is, but he looks like a grown man. I guess he's not afraid to take the bus by himself.

"Let's watch a movie!" I request, hoping everybody would want to join.
"What movie you want to watch?" Mom seems to be a bit interested.
"Mary-Kate and Ashley Mall Party!" I smile from ear to ear.
Before I could even finish, dad interrupts, "Hell Naw!" in a funny tone of voice.
Key is laughing, and mom comments, "Mik, pick something else out, we always watch Mary-Kate and Ashley movies with you."
"But y'all never watch them," what she means to say is that I always want them to watch Mary-Kate and Ashley movies.
"We do!" Dad sounds fed up.
"I know you not talking. You are the first one to go to sleep every time!" I laugh at his audacity. As requested, I go to look for something that all of us are interested in watching. We have so many movies to choose from, the collection is huge.
"I'm in the mood for something funny," I say to myself while skimming through the DVDs.

"Let's watch *Rush Hour*!" I yell while everybody is coming from the kitchen into the living room.
"Okay, pop it in!" Mom seems to like that choice, and my dad didn't rudely interrupt me this time around, so I'm assuming he's cool with it, too. I pop the movie in as everybody gets comfortable. I'm very surprised, but happy that Key stayed downstairs to watch the movie with us. It makes me feel good inside when my family is in the same room without any tension in the air, or without my mom

instigating a fight between Key and dad, or my parents going at it like lions in the jungle. There is no drama, and good vibes are filling the air.

"Do you understand the words that are coming out of my mouth?" Chris Tucker yells at his new Chinese partner, Jackie Chan, who's letting him believe that he doesn't speak English. Everybody laughs at Chris Tucker's dramatic performance because he's all in Jackie's face.

"He is so stupid!" Mom laughs.

"I'm mad he's not in *Next Friday* as Smokey," Key fake pouts.

"Mike Epps as Dae Dae did a good job, though," Dad adds.

"Yeah, he did, but Smokey was super funny! He had a good character," Key continues.

"I think they said something about him not wanting to play those kind of roles anymore," Mom continues.

"What kind of roles?" Dad asks.

"I'm guessing the kind of roles that make him look like he's no good or has no purpose," Mom explains.

"I mean, that movie didn't have a very purposeful meaning," Dad giggles.

Key butts in, agreeing with dad. "Right."

"I mean, *Friday* is a good movie and it is funny, don't get me wrong, but I don't think that out of all the characters in the movie, Smokey looked like the "Ain't shit" person," Dad and Key giggles.

"Maybe they meant like those types of movies then," Mom corrects herself.

"Those "type of movies" are like comedy movies," he challenges her again.

"Black comedy movies," she cuts him off as we all laugh.

"But he brought comedy to *Rush Hour*," Key adds.

"Right, which is good. I hear they are supposed to be coming out with a sequel," Mom adds as if she's telling us the 411 on everything today.

All of us are looking at mom like she's crazy, but my dad manages to speak first. "They did already!" he can barely get his sentence out because he's drowning in laughter.

"The second one is already out! You haven't seen it?" Key asks, as if my mom is joking.

"No, I haven't," she smiles in an embarrassing way.

"We have it down there!" I point towards our movie collection.

"Do we?" she asks as if we're confused.

"Yeah… I bought that movie last year sometime." Dad is trying to catch his breath.

"We should watch *Rush Hour 2* after this goes off," I request.

"I really never noticed that it was down there!" Mom giggles at herself.

The night went on with rain on the outside and laughter and love in the inside. I genuinely cherish these kinds of nights where everybody is on good terms and seems happy. My happiness feeds off of them, and I don't think that they know it. No one surely ever asks, so I don't know how they would ever know how I feel.

After Rush Hour goes off, surprisingly, everybody agrees to watch Rush Hour 2. Key went upstairs eventually, which I'm surprised about. I personally like Rush Hour better than Rush Hour 2, but they're both good movies. After we're done with movie night we head to bed.

"Which one do you like better, Ma?" I ask, walking up the stairs.

"Between Rush Hour and Rush Hour 2?" she asks, making sure we are talking about the same thing.

"Yeah."

"Both of them are good, but I think I like Rush Hour better," she turns on the TV in the bedroom.

"You were falling asleep," she adds.

"And she's always talking about somebody else falling asleep," Dad adds while putting on his pajamas.

"You probably didn't even see me sleep because you were

sleeping," I snap.

"I wasn't sleeping," he claps back.

"You was, I saw you yawning before the movie even started," I tease.

"Why don't you sleep in your own room? How about that!"

"Huh?" Dad continues to tease, as I ignore him.

"Leave my baby alone," Mom joins in defending me, as we get ready for bed.

CHAPTER **EIGHTEEN**

"HERE, TAKE THIS vitamin," Mom places a big vitamin in my hand.
"Key, come take this vitamin," Mom yells.

I don't know how to swallow this big pill at once, so I have to actually bite into mine and taste everything. When I bit into the vitamin, the taste is extremely sour, which makes the sides of my jaws tingle. I hate taking these nasty ass vitamins. Mom doesn't even take them. After Mom got finished *"pulling my hair out of my scalp,"* we get ready to head to dance school. It's still wet and nasty outside from raining last night. This type of muggy, humid weather makes my hair look poofy. As we walk to the car, we see our next-door neighbor, Mr. Taylor, walking out of the house as well.

"Hey, Mr. Taylor," Mom waves as we get into the car.
"Hey," he nods his head.

Mr. Taylor is our friend Ron's granddad. I think Ron's grandparents are stricter than my mom. I hardly ever see his grandmother leave or enter the house. When Ron chooses to speak about his family, I always hear him talk about his granddad or his siblings that I never see. On the way to dance school, the radio is playing old-school music. The song that's playing sounds very familiar. This nice instrumental solo sounds like a saxophone. Following the saxophone is a woman's voice. Then Key and Mom begin singing like they wrote the lyrics..

"Ma, is this Tina Marie?" I ask from the back seat.
"Nah, this is Michel'le" Mom answers in between the song lyrics.

I only have two classes today at dance school, Tap and Hip Hop. I'm the second person to get to class. My mom is always on time for things, so we are always one of the first people to make it anywhere for the most part. As soon as I walk into Tap class, Diamond approaches me.

"Hey, Kimiko," she smiles, going for my hair.
"Hey," I move my head gently, dodging her hand.
"Your hair is so pretty!" she adds, noticing my gesture.
"Thank you. I just don't like people playing in my hair," I explain so she wouldn't think I'm being mean.
"Yeah, no touching on the hair." Shalissa comes out of nowhere with, of course, her sidekick, Kyra.
"Maybe y'all should stop letting people touch in y'all head, so y'all won't be bald-headed," Jaylen tease, hitting Shalissa and Kyra on the head and running.
Shalissa jumps at him as if she's about to hit him but doesn't, and Kyra chases after him to get her lick back.
"Where were y'all at?" I ask, happy to see them.
"We were talking to Ms. Vikki about our routine," Shalissa explains.
"Oh, okay," I add, trying not to show my jealous side.

I'm not jealous of Shalissa and Kyra's friendship because I know they've been friends for longer than they've known me. I'm jealous of the fact that they been dancing for longer than me. They are better dancers than I am, and they take classes that I know I can't take because of my skill level. Sometimes I feel left out, but I try my hardest not to show that I feel that way.

After Tap class is over, I notice everybody is crowed up in the back, so I go to check it out. Squirming by people, trying to get my little body through the crowd, when I finally get to the middle of the circle, I see Key on top of this girl that I see around all the time. Key is repeatedly punching her in her face. It is a one-on-one fight, and Key has full advantage. Just when everything is getting started, Mr. Jessie and somebody's dad broke the fight up. Mr. Jessie grabs Key and takes her to the back where his class is, and the other man grabs the other girl. I follow Key and Mr. Jessie to the back where Mr. Jessie is trying to calm Key down.

"Karin, what happened?" he talks calmly, but seriously.

"She basically kept saying things about me!" Key is trying to catch her breath.

"So, you beat her up, that's it?" Mr. Jessie frowns.

"No, she bumped me on purpose and almost made me fall to the floor just a few minutes ago," Key explains, looking a bit nervous.

"Well, y'all are not going to be able to attend this dance school if y'all can't stand each other and can't control y'all temper. I know y'all don't want to get kicked out and waste your parents' money." Mr. Jessie has a serious look on his face.

Key looks like she just jumped out of a bad dream out of nowhere. "Is my mama here?" She looks at me with a pale face.

"I don't think so. I didn't see her out there," I'm nervous because I know my mom loves to punish us.

"You think I'm going to get in trouble?" Key looks like a tear is going to fall.

"Probably, you know how she is" I respond with a straight face.

"Can you go and make sure she's not here for me?" she stands up to pace back and forth.

As I walk away, I overhear her whisper to Mr. Jessie.

"Look, it won't happen again, and I'll apologize to her if you make sure my mom don't find out about the fight."

Whenever my mom gets the chance, she takes advantage of whopping and punishing us. She was damn near ready to whoop me for opening another box of cereal without finishing the one that was open. I don't know what she will do if she finds out Key got into a fight. What I know she will do is pretend she's not mad in front of everybody, but when we all get alone, she'll show her true colors. Then she'll scare us into not telling anyone what really happened. I'm looking in every dance room class as everybody stares at me like I'm the one who got into a fight. I check in the hallway and in the back where the dressing rooms are. I also check to see if her car is out there, and it isn't.

"Phew!" I feel a little relief for Key. I hate when she get in trouble.

I don't see the girl that Key got into a fight with or the older guy that grabbed the girl. Hopefully they left for the day and doesn't plan on coming back. Hopefully, Key convinced Mr. Jessie to keep his mouth shut so that she won't get in trouble. Walking back to Mr. Jessie's class, my fake mom Jasmine stops me.

"Hey, daughter, are you okay?" she hugs me.
"Yeah, I'm fine."
"Where Key at?" Jasmine looks around.
"She's in the back talking to Mr. Jessie, I'll be right back," I continue to walk back to the dance room.

When I get into the room, I see they let people come into the class.
Key approaches me, "Was she out there?"
"Nope," I smile.
"Where did she go?" Key asks.

"I don't know. I went to go see if her car was outside and it's not," I explain.

"Good! I talked to Mr. Jessie and he's not going to tell her what happened," she looks like a thousand pounds has been lifted off of her shoulders.

"What if somebody else tell her though," I remind her.

"Like who? She doesn't talk to anybody but Ms. Belk and I don't think she's here either," Key sounds convinced.

"Right, I'll tell Shalissa not to tell her mom," I confirm.

"Yeah, and I'll tell Diamond the same thing," she agrees.

Luckily for Key, most of the adults are gone. That's probably the reason my mom left, which is still surprising because she doesn't like leaving us anywhere. The only place she acts like she's fine with us going is over Big Mama's house, and sometimes she acts funny about that.

"Is Key alright?" Shalissa asks.

"Yeah, she's cool."

"She should be because she was beating Monica up!" Shalissa laughs at her own joke.

"I know, right, is your mom here?" I share giggles but change the topic quickly to get to the point.

"Nope, it seem like everybody's parents are gone. You should see if you can come over today," Shalissa suggests,

"Yeah, I'll see, but don't tell your mom Key got into a fight today."

"Oh, okay, but why though?" she asks curiously.

"So she won't get in trouble," I share, embarrassed to admit.

"Oh, okay, I won't, but if I tell my mom not to tell your mom she won't," Shalissa looks sure.

"Okay, that's good and thanks! I think Key is going to tell Diamond as well."

The tension finally went away after the first thirty minutes of class.

The girl that Key fought isn't anywhere in sight. I don't think she's coming back for the day, which makes everything that much better.

"*Mr. Jessie looks so cute doing that move,*" I think to myself, looking at him in front of the classroom.

"So, do we put our arm to the side first?" Amber asks me as she is doing the dance move wrong.

"Nah, you step, one two first, then put your arm out to the side out in front of you," I guide her, demonstrating the movement.

Right after I get finished showing Amber the dance steps, we did one more run-through of the full routine.

"Very good job with the corrections! Y'all are starting to look like one, keep up the good work!" Mr. Jessie announces before class ends.

"Kimiko, you should ask if you can come over," Shalissa suggests for the tenth time, but it doesn't annoy me because I do want to go over her house.

"Ok, I'll see." I try to walk away from her, but she's following me as if she wants to come with me to ask.

"You should stay here while I go ask my mom since you came last time and she said no," I suggest, knowing my mom wouldn't like it if she came with me.

"Right, I was there last time. Okay, I'll stay here," Shalissa changes her mind instantly and walks in the opposite direction.

Once I find my mom talking to Ms. Belk, I figure this would be a good time to ask.

"Hey, pretty girl," Ms. Belk speaks to me nicely.

"Hey," I wait until they are done talking before I go in for the kill.

"Ma, can we go over Shalissa's house for a few hours?" I hope deep down inside that she says yes, but I have a strong feeling she's going to say no.

"Did you or Shalissa ask Ms. Belk if it was okay?" she asks with a smile as if she might be fine with it.

"It's fine. They can come over for a while or spend the night. Shalissa has been asking for her to come over since they first met," Ms. Belk explains as if she's had enough with Shalissa asking the same question.

"Aww, really? I'll let them come over for a few hours, then. I'll come pick them up around nine or ten," Mom finally agrees to let us go for a few hours.

As soon as she said yes, I run to find Shalissa to tell her the good news.

"What did she say?" Shalissa looks nervous as if she doesn't know what to expect because my mom always says no.

"She said next time," I try my hardest not to smile.

"Man, she said that last time," Shalissa smacks her lips in disappointment.

"Sike! She said we can come!" I burst out laughing.

"You play too much!" she looks embarrassed that she got aggravated for no reason.

I continue to giggle, as Key approaches me.

"You seen my mama?" Key walks up to me suspiciously.

"Yeah, she's talking to Ms. Belk. She said that we can go over Shalissa and them house today, too," I jump up and down out of joy.

"For real?" Key asks looking surprised.

"Yeah," I did a little dance to express my happiness some more.

CHAPTER **NINETEEN**

THE NEIGHBORHOOD SHALISSA lives in looks kind of like my neighborhood. The houses are around the same size, and the upkeep is very similar.

"Key, I still can't believe you hit Monica!" Tasha cracks up, not knowing that it wasn't supposed to be brought up in front of Ms. Belk. Tasha is Diamond and Shalissa's cousin, who practically lives with them like a sister.

Shalissa, Key, and I have the "oh shit face", waiting if Ms. Belk is going to catch on or not.

"Key, who did you hit?" Ms. Belk turns around confused.

Key looks nervous to talk so Diamond covers for her. "Umm, okay, ma. Sorry, Key. Key got into a fight today, and she's afraid to tell her mom because she doesn't want to get in trouble," Diamond explains, unable to recover from Tasha's outburst.

"Why would she get in trouble over a fight?" Ms. Belk asks Diamond as if Key isn't sitting right there.

"I don't know, all I know is I wasn't supposed to say nothing about it. Now you have to promise not to say anything to Auntie Joyce," Diamond adds with a serious face.

I roll my eyes at the fact that my mom has all the kids calling her

"Auntie Joyce."

"Okay, I won't say anything if you're going to get in trouble about it," Ms. Belk confirms nice and calmly.

Shalissa looks at me with an I-told-you-so smile. That is so nice of Ms. Belk to be able to keep a secret. It is obvious that Ms. Belk didn't get the point of Key getting in trouble or being punished. I don't either, but any little chance my mom has of disciplining us, whether it's cursing us out or beating us, she takes it. I'll never forget the time I got a beating in first grade for letting my friend wear one of my real gold rings.

"Kimiko!" Shalissa snaps her fingers.
"Huh?" I giggle at how she's looking at me.
"Did you hear me?"
"No, what did you say?"
"Do you want to play Uno?" she asks slowly like I have a hearing problem.
"Yeah," I laugh recovering from my daydream.
"You know how to play, right?" she confirms.
"Yeah, I know how to play Uno, girl" I look at her like she's dumb.

Shalissa, Tasha, and I go into their room to play Uno. Key and Diamond are upstairs probably gossiping and talking about boys. As soon as we start playing, Tasha breaks the silence.

"Kimiko, do you like Jaylen?"
"No, why you ask that?" Tasha catches me off guard.
"I was just wondering, y'all make a cute couple," Tasha adds.
"He goes with Kyra, right?" I continue playing the game.
"No, I don't think so. I think Kyra just has a crush on him," Tasha looks at Shalissa for validation.
"Yeah, I think so, too," Shalissa puts a card down.

"Kyra probably think I like him. That's probably why she be acting weird towards me," I pull a card from the deck.
"I think he likes you," Tasha puts down a card.
"She always act like that when I find new friends," Shalissa pulls from the card deck.

After the small talk about Jaylen, we continue with other juicy conversations about other people from the dance school. Not too long after winning the first game, I hear the doorbell ring.
"It's probably my mom," I take a less excited guess,
"Dang, she came so soon," Shalissa adds as if she didn't want me to leave.

We listen to hear if it was my mom, and sure enough, it is. She's dressed in her jogging suit with a high-end name brand bag to match. Tasha goes out to talk to her while Shalissa and I stay in the room.

"You should ask if y'all can spend the night," Shalissa suggests.
Only if she knew how my mom really is. "She's not going to let us," I respond with certainty. "She might let us next time, though," I try to pick Shalissa's hopes up.

Surprisingly, my mom isn't ready to leave as soon as she walked through the door, so that gave Shalissa, Tasha, and me time to finish our game.

"I'm surprised she's chilling," I admit shockingly, but happy about it.
"Who?" Tasha asks.
"My mom, I thought she was going to be ready to leave as soon as she walked in," I explain.
"Right, me too," Shalissa agrees. "I thought y'all were going to leave as soon as she got here."

"I just hope no one talks about the fight," I give Shalissa a serious look.

"My mom won't say anything about it," she reassures.

"Okay, I guess Tasha is the only one we have to worry about," I joke in a serious way like Tasha isn't sitting there.

"My bad, nobody told me it was on the down-low," Tasha defends herself giggling.

"Yeah, because you were nowhere to be found, in the bathroom taking a shit," Shalissa adds, making all of us laugh.

Tasha laughs then stops abruptly. "I wasn't taking a shit, for your information."

I hold my hand near her face, "Tell it to the hand because the face don't want to hear it," I continue to make fun.

I really didn't want Key to get in trouble over something so stupid. I honestly think I prefer both of us to get a whooping together or at the same time instead of me having to listen to her from the next room getting a whooping, crying and screaming for dear life. Sometimes I think my mom gets a kick out of whooping us. I don't know anyone that gets whoopings as much as we do, especially over the smallest things.

Shalissa and I got to play for a little while longer, and then it was time to go. As we leave, Tasha blurts out.

"Next time y'all have to bring clothes," she smiles.

"Right," Key seconds her comment.

My mom just smiles as she walks out the door, probably thinking *"They will never spend the night."* I hope we're going home and not somewhere where she might want to drink and have fun because those nights are the worst.

"Did y'all have fun over there?" Mom asks while turning the steering wheel.

"Yeah, it was so fun!" I answer before Key answers.

"Do Tasha live with them?" Mom continues.

"Yeah, she shares a room with Shalissa," I add.

"That's so nice that she takes responsibilities of Tasha since that's not her biological child," mom smiles.

"She treats Tasha like her daughter," Key finally adds to the conversation.

On the way to the destination, Mom wants to listen to her old school music. She turns through several songs and stops at a song called "Sara Smile". These people on this song sort of sound like white people. Whatever race they are, I like the sound of the song. It's kind of a sad sounding song, flowing through the speakers.

I'm so happy that we're pulling up in our neighborhood to go home. She asked Key if she felt like going over Uncle German's house. I'm so happy Key said no, and I'm even happier she listened to Key. I'm guessing she asked Key because her and Uncle German's oldest daughter, Cher, are the same age. His younger daughter Aston is about three years older than me. Even though she's a little bit older, when we go over there, I play with her. Uncle German and Mom love partying and drinking together, so we know she's always down to go over there. It's odd that I never see my mom and Aunt Peggy, Uncle German's wife, talking or interacting being that Uncle German and Mom are so cool. I'm not sure, but I don't think Aunt Peggy is a big drinker. If I'm right, that's probably the reason why I don't see them talking as much.

"Man, I'm so happy that mama didn't find out about the fight," Key exclaims.

"I know, that was nice that Ms. Belk didn't say anything," I add with a smile of relief.

"She seem so nice," Key looks down at her fingers.

"Yeah, she does, but they probably think the same thing about our mom," I speculate.

"Right, they be calling her Auntie Joyce," Key giggles.

"Right, Mama love that," I shake my head.

"She always make everybody call her Auntie Joyce," Key adds rolling her eyes.

"Right! That's so irritating to me."

Key giggles. "Nobody else's mom or parents are like that."

"Exactly."

After our 411-discussion, Mom calls us down for dinner. She made chicken, cheese potatoes, and string beans. She always loads so much food on our plates.

I'm not going to be able to finish my food. This time I'm not going to express it to her because I think she's getting tired of me not finishing my food. Last time I got a beating for not finishing my plate. Key just finished her food. As she leaves the table, she gives me this I-feel-bad-for-you look. It's so funny to me because if my dad were here, she wouldn't be so mean to us. I've never gotten a whooping by her while he was here. He doesn't have a clue how mean she is to us. If we were to tell him how she treats us, she would fuck us up when he left. Sometimes I think maybe if he was here more, she would be a nicer person overall. I don't know why she feels like she has to take her anger or frustration out on us.

CHAPTER **TWENTY**

OF COURSE, MOM wakes up extremely early to go uniform shopping. It's 7 o'clock in the morning. I feel like we're on the way to actually go to school. I don't understand why she needs to do everything so early in the morning. If we were to leave around ten or eleven o'clock, that would be an early start as well.

"*Shit pisses me off!*" I cut my eyes as I go to the bathroom to get ready.

When I finish getting dressed, I pop into my mom's room.

"Can Key do my hair in a bun again?" I cross my fingers.

"No. Go and get your comb, brush, and hair bag," Mom doesn't think twice.

"*Bitch*!" I scream in my head.

What's the problem with Key doing my hair in a bun? Mom hurts my head every time she does my hair. Grabbing my barrette case with an attitude from off my dresser made me think about how much I really don't like her.

"That hurts," I mutter, hoping she'd be a bit easier on my hair.

"Shut up," she responds as if I'm annoying her.

I don't know why she is so heavy-handed with my hair. It's not like it's in its natural form. My hair is pressed bone straight, and she's handling it like it's the nappies hair in the world. Almost feeling a tear about to form in my eyeballs, I squint my eyes really hard and quickly to prevent myself from crying. Every ponytail is tight as fuck for no reason. She makes seven ponytails in my head and twists the remaining of my long ponytails.

"What's wrong?" Key asks while making her famous swoops in her hair.
"These ponytails are so tight I can't even think," I give her a blank look.
She burst out in laughter before she could speak. "Why didn't you ask her if I could do it?"
"I did, and she said no." I try to frown, but my ponytail won't let me.
"Why not?"
I stare at Key as she does her own hair, fantasizing about when I'll be able to do my own hair. "Because she's a mean ass bitch."
On the way to go get uniforms in the early morning, my mom seems to be in sort of a bad mood. Usually, when she gets like this, it means she's in her I-hate-someone state of mind. Most likely, it's my dad she hates right now. I could be wrong, though, because there's are a lot of people she has hate for. She's still mad at people from her childhood. I can tell today she's going to be sharing another one of her dreadful stories. Before she begin to talk, she turns on the radio and flicks through the channels. There is an old school song playing.

Bobbing my head to the rocking melody, I ask mom, "Who sing this?"
"This is Maze and Frankie Beverly," Mom smiles and turns the radio up slightly. The smooth ride to the clothing went by pretty quickly. When we arrive to the store, we try on tops and bottoms.

"Mik, look at these?" Mom has a pair of brown and yellow plaid pants in her hand.

"Ugh, I don't like them!" I shut her down immediately.

"Do you see other kids wearing the pants?" Mom giggles.

"Yeah, but not many. Most girls wear the skirts. Some people wear the dresses. I don't like the dresses, either," I explain.

"So, what do you like?"

"I like the skirts and the skorts. Can we try to find some skorts because I don't have any," I ask politely.

"I never seen the skorts, but we can see if they have them here," Mom continues to look through the clothing rack.

Key is trying on some uniforms because her uniforms are getting too small. While we wait to see how the new size fit Key, Mom stops a lady that works in the store.

"Excuse me, do you have the skorts in the brown and yellow plaid?" Mom shows her the skirt with the pattern we're looking for.

"If we do, it will be over here in this area," she guides us to the section she's talking about. "If we don't have it over here, then we're all out," the lady explains.

"Yeah, we checked over here, I didn't see any," Mom expresses.

"Is she your daughter?" the lady's tone of voice changed to a higher pitch as she's looking at me.

"Yes," mom smiles.

"She is gorgeous!" the lady smiles.

"What's your name?" she kneels down.

"Miko," I respond shyly.

"That's pretty, just like you," she adds.

"Thank you," I respond sort of dryly becoming used to these kinds of compliments.

"Her real name is Kee-mee-ko," Mom corrects me.

"Really, that is so different!" the lady looks surprised.

"Thank you. It's Japanese," Mom smiles.

"Is your name Japanese, too?" the lady continues.

"Nope, just my daughters, I have two. The other one is in the fitting room, and I believe she's ready, come on, Miko. Thanks for your help!" We walk towards the fitting room to meet Key.

Key models the new sizes for us and it doesn't look like she's feeling it.

"I think it's too big," Key moves her skirt around trying to find a way to make it fit to her liking.

"No, it's not, turn around," Mom disagrees. "I like that size; I'm going to grab some more shirts and skirts in that size. Hurry up and change so we can go." Mom has her mind made up.

Key did as she was told and put her clothes on in no time. I could tell she didn't want to wear that size from her dry energy. Mom takes the uniforms and hands them to the cashier, the same lady from earlier.

"So, is this your other daughter?" the lady sparks up the conversation.

"Yeah, her name is Ka-ree-ne," my mom speaks slowly, like she always does when she's telling people our names.

"That's pretty, too! She's beautiful as well! I see you spread them apart. How many years?" the lady seems intrigued.

"Five years and I don't regret it," Mom says proudly.

"I only have one; he's two. Everybody keep telling my husband and I that we need to hurry up and have another one, so he can have a playmate," she put the clothes in the bag.

"They play together just fine," Mom giggles, looking at Key and me. "I like their age difference because when I was pregnant with the second baby, the oldest one was able to help and fend for herself. It's hard having two babies," Mom voices her opinion..

"Yeah, that's what I was thinking. I think I might be pregnant as we speak," the lady looks at us with excitement.

"Well if you are, congratulations!" Mom smiles and grabs the bags.

"Thank you, have a good one! Bye, pretty girls," the cashier lady waves goodbye.

"That is so ridiculous that Jihod haven't been home in three days!" she starts the car, and we pull off.

Key is trying to avoid the conversation, so she stays silent.

"You know?" Mom is making Key indulge in the conversation.
"Yeah, that's a long time," Key adds dryly, it's clear she doesn't give a fuck.

Last time my mom wanted to use Key as a marriage counselor, Key answered very short and vague, and Mom hit her in her face. Mom said her reason for slapping Key was because Key was acting like she didn't care about the situation, which she doesn't. Key is only thirteen years old. What thirteen-year old cares about their parents' marriage problems? I don't understand why she chooses to vent to her about their marriage anyway.

"And then he expects for shit to be fine and dandy when he gets home. Like the mothafucka' haven't done anything wrong! Like that's cool or something!" Mom frowns while confiding in Key like she has the answers.
"Right, that's why he doesn't know where anything is when he gets home," Key giggles, trying to find some humor out of the conversation.
"I mean he hasn't even called! He's ALWAYS around Wice and them! If he wants to fuck Wice and Rock and have a family with them then that's what he need to do!" her voice gets deeper.

I can't wait until this conversation is over! No one gives a mother fuck! I complain in my head.
Rolling my eyes in the backseat, watching the traffic through the

window, I wonder why she acts like she can't tell him how she feels herself. She always tries to make Key start the conversation like Key has a problem with him being gone, then feeds off what Key says. She coaches Key before everything happens like this is a sport. They continue to talk about my dad through the entire car ride. This is so annoying, but then again, I must say, I'm happy I'm the one in the backseat who doesn't have to talk about it. I don't have to listen either, but it's kind of hard when the music is silent. They're the only two voices filling the car, so I can't help but listen to the bullshit. I feel so bad for Key. I know she hates being in the middle of my parents' drama.

"When he gets home, just ask him," Mom demands.
"Ask him what?" Key sounds thrown off guard.
"Why he's never home!" Mom yells as if Key should know the answer.
"Then if he says he's out working, say something like 'Betty works every day but she comes home more than you do,'" Mom continues.
"Right, because a lot of people's parents work, and after work they come home," Key tries to make sense out of her future argument.
"Yeah, I wish I could work, but I'm disabled. If I could work, y'all wouldn't see me as often, but y'all would still see me every day," Mom explains.
I wish I didn't see you that often! I comment in my head.

I know deep inside Key doesn't like getting in the middle of their arguments, but it seems like she agrees with my mom a lot. Like now, she's siding with her and making her feel like she's right. But then again, I guess Key has no choice. Look at them, just sitting up there with their matching swoop hairstyles like they dressed each other. When we finally get home, everybody is outside.

"Ma, can we stay outside?" Key asks before we get out the car.
"Yeah, but if your dad comes home, come in so we can talk about

what we discussed," Mom looks serious.

"Okay," Key gets out of the car and I follow.

"I hope my dad doesn't come home today", I speak silently to myself.

CHAPTER **TWENTY-ONE**

"HEY, AUNTIE JOYCE!" Porsha blurts out, and waves as everybody else waves.

"Hey, y'all!" she waves back as she walks in the house.

"Where y'all coming from? The shop?" Patricia answers her own question like she knows our schedule.

"No, look at my hair, I did this. We just came from uniform shopping," Key stands posted.

"Oh, yeah, y'all do go to that far school," Porsha adds.

"We wear the brown and yellow plaid skirts," I add.

"The boo boo and pee pee colors," Ron teases.

"Shut up! It is one of the ugliest plaid colors, though," I admit.

"This summer went by too fast! School starts next week!" Joe complains.

"Damn, school start back next week?" Ron blurts out like he didn't know, making me laugh.

"Yeah, fool," Porsha responds out of nowhere, making me laugh harder.

"That shit did go by fast!" Cory seconds Joe's comment.

"Y'all going back to MacDowell this year?" Key asks Patricia.

"Yeah, this will be my last year there. Then Beaubien, here I come!" Patricia does some kind of silly dance.

"I wish I could go to Beaubien," Key expresses sadly.

"Right! Did you ask your mom if you can?" Cory asks.

"Yeah, but you know what she said," Key gives us the straight face.

"She's always saying no about something. If she let you go there, then you can walk to school with us and she can save some gas," Patricia tries to justify the case.

"I know, it's crazy because my dad said he doesn't care," Key adds.

"Maybe he can talk her into saying yes, then," Porsha adds trying to find some hope in the situation.

Speaking of the devil, right after talking about my dad. Less than fifteen minutes later, he pulls up in the driveway. My heart begins to pound because we're going to have to go inside in a minute for the confrontation.

"You should go and talk to your dad about seeing if you can go to Beaubien," Patricia suggests.

"Yeah," Porsha agrees.

"Alright, we'll be right back," Key takes that advantage to go in as ordered from my mom earlier.

When we get into the house, my mom is sitting in the living room, watching TV.

"This bitch" I look her dead in her face.

Dad is in the basement. Key is sitting in the chair across from my mom, waiting for my dad to come back upstairs. Knowing what was about to happen, I run upstairs, where I'm most comfortable. I decide to play with my Bratz dolls today. I like these dolls, too. I want to start collecting these dolls along with my American Girl Dolls. The Bratz Dolls aren't nearly as expensive as the American Girl dolls, so I'll probably stack up on the Bratz faster than the American Girl Dolls.

In no time, I hear the music coming from downstairs like fireworks. My dad is screaming at the top of his lungs, and Key is challenging him right back. What's so annoyingly funny is that I don't hear my mom's voice at all. She's the reason why they're arguing in the first place. She's just sitting back, enjoying her fire she sparked. I go out to listen to the altercation at the stair railing.

"I DON'T WANT TO HEAR THAT BULLSHIT! DON'T TELL ME WHAT I DO, AND DON'T DO," dad screams at Key, shutting her down.

"But you're never here, even the kids notice!" Mom finally intrudes in the argument.

"Miko!" Mom calls for me.

My heart skips five beats.

"Huh?" I wait, knowing she wants me to come here.

"Come here!" she yells with fury in her voice.

I force my fear into a full bottle of water and walk downstairs a bit slower than usual. When I get downstairs, Key is sitting in the same chair she was sitting in before I went upstairs. My dad is sitting next to my mom on the couch. It looks like a child lashing out on her parents, but the true scenario is never what it looks like, at least in my reality/household.

"Is your dad always gone?" Mom looks me dead in my eyes with a straight face, but I know behind those buck brown eyes of hers that she is expecting me to respond in a certain way.

"Yeah," I say nervously.

"See, so what Key is saying is true," Mom looks at my dad.

"I AM HERE!" Dad is on fire. "SHE NEEDS TO LEARN HOW TO SHUT THE FUCK UP AND STAY IN A CHILD'S PLACE!" he points at Key in her chair

I'm guessing they're done with me, so I take this time to leave the scene and go back upstairs. I don't want to be asked any more questions. I don't want my dad to be mad at me, and I don't want to get in trouble with my mom when he leaves again. My dad is gone a lot, but I wouldn't say that he's absent in our lives. I mean, I know people who don't even know their fathers. I do wish my dad was here more often. Then we wouldn't get in trouble as much, and maybe that would make my mom a happier person. If I were him, I wouldn't want to be around her either or in this house. All she ever wants to do is complain when he's gone and complain when he's here. Nobody wants to hear that all day; he doesn't want to hear it, Key doesn't want to hear it, and I most definitely don't want to hear a peep of it.

The argument didn't last as long as I was expecting. Usually, when Key and dad get into an argument, they argue all night long while my mom sits there and referees it. When the silence goes on for too long, I decide to go see what is going on.

My mom is sitting on the couch watching TV, dad and Key aren't anywhere to be found.

"Did Key go outside?" I ask Mom in a somewhat innocent voice.
"Yeah," she gives me an evil look, squinting her eyes.
"Can I go outside?"
"Go ahead, Miko," she shoos me in the direction of the door

Ignoring her attitude, I run to the entrance of the door where my shoes are and put them on and head out. When I get outside, I didn't see anybody across the street, next door, or down the street. I didn't want to go into the house to ask my mom where she went because she's not in a good mood. Dad's car is still in the driveway, so that means he's not that far. I want to go find my dad, but he's probably not in a good mood either. Plus, I'm sort of nervous to show him any kind of affection right now, being that my mom is mad at him. I don't want her getting jealous or mad that I'm being nice to him because she's mad at him. If she's mad at him, then we are mad at him, and there's no way around it. That's how it has to be, and it really makes me sick.

Key can't be that far, so I walk across the street to see if she's at Patricia and Porsha's house. When I walk in their backyard, I see Key, Cory, Patricia, and Porsha sitting on the back porch.

"I hate fucking living over there!" Key frowns.

"So, you and yo' daddy was arguing over how much he's gone?" Cory looks a bit confused.

"Yeah, but I personally don't give two fucks about how much he's gone," Key does a gesture with her hand.

"So, why we're y'all arguing then?" Porsha sits down.

"Right, you must of said something to him for y'all to be arguing about that," Patricia puts two and two together.

"I had to go in the house when my dad came home and ask him about it," Key explains

"Why?" Cory asks in a pitch higher than his regular voice out of confusion.

"Because my mom told me to. She always makes us say stuff to him or to people," Key looks at me as I open the screen door.

"So…" Patricia tries to get an understanding, but Key cuts her off.

"But I'm the one who always has to argue with my dad," Key continues.

"That's so stupid, why won't y'all mama say anything?" Patricia frowns.

"I don't know. I know I don't like neither one of their asses, though!" Key rolls her eyes.

"She make you say stuff to yo' dad, too?" Porsha asks me in disbelief.

"Yeah," I nod my head.

"That's crazy as hell!" Porsha adds in awe.

"What do she be doing when y'all arguing?" Cory asks with all eyes on Key.

"Nothing most of the time. She'll add her two cents in, and take my side," Key looks at her nails.

"So, you only argue with him because she told you to?" Patricia folds her arms.

"Right, she tells me what to say and how to say it. She lectures me all night sometimes. It's so fucking annoying," Key continues.

"So, what will happen if you tell her you don't want to say it or you don't want to argue with him?" Patricia gets down to the bottom line.

"I'm getting my ass whooped. Point blank period." Key looks at her in her face with buck eyes, imitating my mom.

"That's how she says it?" Porsha lets a small giggle out,

"That's how she be looking?" Cory asks, not letting Key answer Porsha's question.

"Y'all know Auntie Joyce have big eyes," Patricia giggles.

"It's scary, right?" I add to Cory's question.

"Yes, she be so serious, too," Key giggles a little bit.

"Wow! So, if you don't argue with your dad, you're getting in trouble?" Patricia confirms.

"Yup, pretty much," Key looks embarrassed to admit.

"That is so bold," Porsha shakes her head.

"It seems like y'all get in trouble for every little thing," Patricia adds as if this is not the first family story Key has shared.

"Right, then she doesn't like letting us do anything either," Key shakes her head.

"I can't wait until I get older. I'm so tired of them! They better not call me when they get old. I'll end up putting both of them in a home," Key giggles, but she's serious.

"You think she makes you argue with him because that's not your real daddy?" Patricia asks genuinely.

Patricia, Porsha, and Cory are the only people in the neighborhood who know Key and I have different dads. We barely even know if it's true or not because my mom never really discusses it with us, as if it is a private, unspoken secret, except it is dead smack obvious. People always say that Key and Mom look alike, but they don't look that much alike at all, in my opinion. The only feature I can see that both of them share is their big heads. Their skin complexion is different, their eyebrows, eyes, nose, and lips are completely different as well. Key even says it herself that she favors Mom a little bit, but she doesn't favor her enough for my dad to pass as her biological father. Key would have to be identical to my mom for it to look possible.

"Maybe, I'm not sure. Or it could be because I'm the oldest," Key shrugs her shoulders.

"Have you ever asked her who your real dad is?" Porsha asks.

"Yeah, she said my dad is my dad, Jihod," Key makes a "yeah right," expression.

"I wonder why she won't tell you the truth. You don't look anything like him. You don't even favor him a little bit. I don't look like my dad, either, but," Patricia explains.

"But Tez is your dad, though you don't look like him, or you don't look exactly like your mom, but you look like your siblings," Key assures.

"Cory doesn't have the same dad as we do, but it's not a huge secret," Porsha confess.

"Right, and it's obvious that Cory is not Tez's biological son, too," Key agrees.

"I mean, you can look at Miko and tell that he's not your real dad. You and Miko don't favor each other at all, either," Patricia continues.

"I know, people always ask us if we have the same daddy," Key confesses.

"Do you remember meeting him?" Patricia asks.

"Who?" Key looks confused.

"Uncle Jihod," Patricia responds.

"Yeah, I do! That's another reason why I don't understand why she won't just tell me the truth. I met him when I was like five or six." Key rests her head in her hands like she's tired

CHAPTER **TWENTY-TWO**

"I FEEL LIKE smoking. I'll be right back," Cory walks off.
"We should smoke something, too," Porsha jokes.
"Like what, though?" Key seems intrigued.
"Maybe we can make a fake cigarette," Patricia suggests.
"Out of grass and paper or something?" Key adds.
"Yeah," Patricia and Porsha agree at the same time.
"Or we can get some real weed like last time," I give them a daring look.
"I don't think my daddy left any in the basement," Key confirms.

Porsha went inside her house to get some paper while Key, Patricia, and I gather up grass to put inside of the paper. Porsha got back pretty quick with the lining paper.

"Here you go," Porsha hands the paper to Key.
"Okay, cool." Key grabs the paper and puts the grass inside the paper and rolls it up.

"Light di blunt, then smoke di blunt," Patricia adds in a Jamaican accent.
"Then pass di blunt," Porsha finishes her sentence, making Key and I laugh.

When Patricia passes the blunt to Porsha, Porsha seems so excited to get the fake blunt.. Porsha holds the smoke in her mouth, then begin to scoop her head to the left then to the right in a specific rhythm, imitating Smokey off of *Friday*. Surprisingly, lighting the grass inside of the paper made smoke. After Porsha is done playing, she passes it to me. I act as if I'm a pro to the smoking game. Blowing out the smoke made me feel so entitled to what I'm not sure of, but it just made me feel as if I was the man; like I'm the boss dog and nobody can take control of what I'm doing. Since it's not real weed, I'm not inhaling it. I just make sure I let the smoke enter my mouth and come right back out.

"She think she sweet!" Key teases me.

"Right," Patricia agrees with a laugh.

"Bitch, I'm the man," I speak to the fake blunt like we're having a conversation.

"Yoo!" Porsha burst out with laughter. "This my motherfuckin' dog!" she expresses while putting her arm around my neck.

Even though everybody is older than me, they still make me feel like an equal for the most part, which is the prime reason I love being around older people. It makes me feel so mature and cool.

"Where did Cory go?" Porsha looks around.

"Probably to smoke some real weed," Patricia giggles.

"Right," Key agrees laughing.

After we are done fake smoking, we go back to the front so my mom won't notice we're not in sight. As the night goes on, we gossip, chill, and play hand games. I'm going to miss summer nights like these. I'm almost sure when school starts back, my mom isn't going to let us come outside often.

"Let's play 'I like coffee. I like tea,'" I tap Porsha's hand.

"Okay," Porsha stands in front of me with her hands out. Then we both sing while hitting each other's hands in a repeated motion.

"I like coffee. I like tea. I like the colored boy, and he likes me."

"So step back, white boy, you don't shine. I'll get the color boy to beat ya' behind."

"Last night, the night before. I met my boyfriend at the candy store."

"He brought me ice cream he brought me cake. He brought me home with a stomachache.

"I said, Mama Mama, I feel sick. Call the doctor quick, quick, quick."

"Doctor, doctor, should I die. Close your eyes and count to five."

"1-2-3-4-5 I'm alive. You see that house on top of that hill."

"That's where me and my baby gone live."

"Cut the ice cream, cut the cake."

"Come on, baby, let's celebrate!"

Porsha and I finish our hand game, filled with lots of laughs and joy. After we finish, Key and Patricia play Slide. That's another hand game. It's sort of a fast-pace game, and if you mess up, you lose. Eventually, the night gets older, and my mom calls us into the house. We say our goodbyes like we are never going to see each other again. Surprisingly, when I get into the house, I notice my dad knocked out on the couch. Seeing him makes me happy, and I hope I can see him when I wake up tomorrow. Tonight, I'm sleeping with Key so we can gossip.

I close Key's door, so Mom can't hear us. "I'm surprised Daddy didn't leave."

"Right, I hope he stays so she can stay out of my fucking face," Key frowns.

She continues before I can speak. "He's the reason why she's always making me say stuff to him now."

"I know, but she still shouldn't put you in the middle of it," I try to defend Dad.

"Yeah, but she does. So, if he stay his ass home I wouldn't be in the middle of shit," she rolls her eyes.

"It seems like she doesn't say the things that she says to you to him," I continue.

"She don't. With her dumb ass." Key frowns, already annoyed with being in this house.

"I wonder what she would've did if I had said 'Yeah, Daddy is here sometimes,'" I smile viciously.

"You know what she would've did. She would've acted like everything was cool until he left, then it would have been your ass. She wouldn't care if it was five days later. She would've remembered to give you a beating," Key explained confidently.

"Right, she would've held that grudge." What Key is saying sounds about right.

As we lay down in the bed, I try to lighten up the conversation. "That green was good today."

"That green was bomb…" she hypes up my joke.

We share giggles at the fact that we really didn't get high.

As I go next door to my room, I look across the hallway to see my mom and dad watching TV.

I guess that's the reason why she hasn't called our names yet, I think to myself as I walk into my room. Just as I was getting back to my Barbie dolls and Bratz dolls, I hear the phone ring.

"Miko!"

"Huh?" I answer standing in my parents' doorway.

"Granny wants to speak to you," she hands me the phone.

"Hey, Granny!"

"Hey, boo, how you doing?" Granny asks in her usual soft tone voice.

"Good, what you doing," I ask, happy to talk to her.

"Just got finished making lunch."

"Dang, I wish I could have some," I reminisce about her cooking.

"Y'all should have come down this summer," she adds.

"Yeah, I know."

"Do you want to come down next year for the summer?"

"Yeah," I smile unsurely not knowing if my mom would approve or not.

"Okay, we'll make sure we fly you guys down next year," she assures.

"Okay."

"Where is Key?"

"She in her room."

"Let me speak to her."

"Okay, where is Granddaddy?" I ask as I walk to Key's room.

"He's gone Golfing."

"Oh, okay, here is Key," I say quickly.

"Love you," she adds.

"Love you, too!" I speak a little louder as I hand over the phone.

I didn't stick around for Granny and Key's conversation. I wonder why we didn't visit them this year. Ever since they moved, we've been going to visit them every summer. Mom probably lied and made up an excuse for us not to go, or it may be because we started dance school this summer. Anything to keep us trapped around her. I must say, dance school was fun this summer. I met some good friends, and I hope to keep in touch with them. Hopefully, my mom lets us hang out with Diamond and Shalissa before school starts back. Lord knows she's not going to let us do anything while we're in school, as if that's the only thing we need to focus on. Kids play sports and do extracurricular activities during the school year all the time. I guess she prefers us to stay cooped up in the house with her.

As I sit down on the floor to continue with my dolls, thoughts of my grandparents come to mind.

I miss them so much. Then dad's voice interrupt my thoughts.

"Mik Mik!"

I hurry to see what he wants, running to their doorway.

"You want to play basketball this school year?" he asks nicely.

It's like he just read my mind. I hesitate to answer, nervous about what I'm supposed to say and the consequences I might have to face. "Umm, I don't care."

"Come on, you can be sweet like me! I can help you tighten up on your J!" he adds energetically, acting as if he just shot a 3 pointer.

"During the school year or the summer?" Mom questions.

"During the school year," he answers sarcastically.

"Oh, okay, yeah, Miko, learn how to shoot some baskets," Mom smiles in an encouraging way.

I'm guessing that means she's cool with me saying I want to play, so I add "Okay, yeah, I'll do it!" I'm more enthused.

"Oh, so it took for her to say it for you to want to do it," Dad catches a quick attitude and flicks his hand at me as if he's done talking to me.

"She probably just needed somebody to hype her up," Mom sits back smiling, soaking up how jealous he just got.

Feeling a little bad, I head back to my room.

"I can't stand her!" I whisper silently to myself. That's another reason why he stays gone. He probably feels like it's all of us girls against him. Little do he know, I'm on his side all of the time. She might have mind control over Key, but she'll never have mind control over me. I think the way I want to think about people. I don't care what anyone has to say. I have my own mind. But I must admit he's right. It did take for my mom to confirm she was okay with it before I got excited, only if he knew the real reason behind my actions.

I continue to play with my toys. After a couple of hours pass by, I hear Key trying to leave without me, and Joyce is not having that.

"Ma, can I go outside?" Key asks quickly.
"Yeah, and don't leave Miko, either!" she adds semi-sternly.

Key walks quickly across the hallway to come to my room.

"You coming outside?" she asks at the doorway.
"Naw," I answer quickly.

Key goes back to tell my mom that I don't want to go outside, then runs for the door. I don't think Key minds that Mom makes her watch me most of the time because I'm not a snitch and I'm overall a cool little sister. But I'm sure she gets tired of me being in her shadow. Sometimes she shows that she's annoyed by my consistent presence, so I try to give her space. Plus, I'm in my Barbie World, which sometimes can be more fun than going outside with the same people. A few more hours later, I hear Mom from downstairs calling Key in early.
"Miko, come here," Dad calls.
"Huh?".
"You still in your pajamas, Busta?" Dad sees the answer directly in front of him.
"Yup," I smile, assuming he's not mad at me anymore.
"Look, watch this!" he points to the TV.

There's an old school Kung Fu movie on.

"Those Asian mothafuckas don't play no games!" he roars at the fight on the movie.
"That stuff looks hard," I giggle.
"It's all in the mind and body. You have to believe you can do it. Then you have to eat right so you can physically do it and workout to build and gain muscles," he explains so seriously.
"See, it's all a routine." He gets up to show me some moves.
"Damn!" he blurts out, and I burst out laughing.

"Did you see what he just did?" he asks as if I'm not watching it right beside him.

"Yeah, I saw it, that is sweet!" I admit, catching my breath from laughing hard.

"See, that's why I like Asian people and their culture," Dad confirms.

"Why, because they can fight?" I'm confused.

"Yup, they some bad mothafuckas! First and foremost, they stick together as a people; you don't see too many overweight Asian people, meaning that they eat right and take care of their bodies. Always remember your body is like a temple. They're smart as hell; they make way to come over here and make a killing. They just some out-cold mothafuckas, man!" Dad continues.

"So, if you could choose to be another race, it would be Asian?" I pick his brain.

"Hell yeah!" Dad doesn't think twice.

"I'm surprised you wouldn't pick White," I add.

"Fuck them White hillbilly mothafuckas! All they do is lie, steal, and sabotage people and try to take credit for everything," Dad frowns.

"People be asking me, am I mixed with White and Japanese" I giggle, waiting on his response.

"Hell nah, you not mixed with White. You don't want to be mixed with White either. When people ask you what you mixed with, say Indian. You know Big Mama is half Indian," Dad explains.

"Really?" my face lights up.

"Yup, my grandma is a full-blooded Indian woman and Grandddad is Black. Why you think you look the way you look Busta?" Dad giggles.

"Mama be telling us she has white on her biological side of the family," I sit back down on the bed.

"She don't even know her biological people," Dad laughs, calling it a bluff.

"So, you not falling asleep on this, huh?" I catch him off guard.

He giggles before he reply "I don't fall asleep on movies."

"Yeah, right! So, you don't be falling asleep on my Mary-Kate and Ashley movies?" I call his bluff.

"No, all they do is sing and dance!" he does this funny movement with his hands and shoulders trying to be sarcastic.

We share laughs and continue to watch the movie. Not too long after the movie, Mom and Key calls us down for dinner. Key made salmon croquettes, potatoes, and green beans. I can tell by her countenance and her energy that she's not happy. I'm sure it's obvious to my parents too, but they're ignoring it.

We all sit at the table and dad sparks some conversation.

"Me and Miko were watching that Kung Fu movie I just bought," he adds, putting food in his mouth.

"What is it called again?" Mom asks, taking a sip of her water.

"It's called Crouching Tiger," he replies like he's starring in it.

"Was it good, Miko?" Mom smiles.

"It was alright," I reply less excited than him.

"Miko tripping, the movie is real good! I was telling her that those Chinese mothafuckas are gutta!" he exclaims.

Mom and I share giggles at his enthusiasm.

"Key, the food is good! You did a good job!"

"Thank you," Key replies dryly.

"Damn, what's wrong? That was a compliment," Dad laughs at his own humor.

"She got a fucking attitude because she had to come in. But she better fix it before she get her shit split," Mom answers for Key with a bigger attitude.

"You will see the kids tomorrow. It's not that big of a deal, Key." Dad tries to make Key feel better.

Key just doesn't respond. I know as soon as she finishes, she's going right up to her room.

Mom continues, "All she ever wants to do is go outside and go over Patricia and Porsha's house."

"What's over there, anyway?" my dad questions in a curious way.

"They parents let them do whatever they want to do." Mom takes a wild guess while eating and rolling her eyes.

"Right, they probably do. They over there deep as hell, too," Dad adds.

"Yeah, they living over there with Dona's mama, Betty." Mom continues to eat.

"They probably over there driving her crazy." Dad giggles, shaking his head.

"She stays in her room most of the time," I add, joining the gossip.

"I'm sure she does," Dads giggles.

"Big Mama stays in her room, too," Key comes out of nowhere joining the conversation, trying to be funny.

"Yeah, she does, but Lora doesn't have a husband and four to five kids running around," Dad responds quickly.

"She has kids, though, and they live with her, same difference," Key continues, not afraid to challenge my dad.

"But it's not the same. You're bringing up Big Mama's household as if they're the same circumstances," Mom buts in, shutting Key up.

CHAPTER **TWENTY-THREE**

"I KNOW YOU was irritated downstairs," I smile starting the conversation.

"Girl, I hate both of them," she frowns and then continues. "They always try to make it seem like they better than somebody else. You know damn well Big Mama's house is the same as Betty's. Small, crowded with people, and junky," she proves her point.

"Yup, less people at Big Mama's house but same difference."

"Matter of fact, Betty's house is way bigger than Big Mama's house," she continues.

"Then mama trying to take up for him. But let you take up for him, she would be ready to snap your neck," I instigate.

"Right, if I was to ever fix my lips to take up for him, she would have a fucking fit," she rolls her eyes and continues.

"And they wonder why I like being over there. Tez and Dona keeps it real! If somebody has something to say, they can say it, and it is over with. None of that secret shit goes on or holding grudges forever shit." She brags as if that makes them so perfect of a family.

"If Dona has something to say to Tez, she's going to say it. She's not going to sit back like a coward waiting on him to say something or making one of the kids say something," Key speaks passionately.

I like talking about our parents to each other because Key's the only person I feel comfortable talking about it to. I was surprised when Key told Cory, Patricia, and Porsha about the argument that happened the other day. I didn't realize she opens up to them about what happens in our household. I mean, we do spend a lot of time with them, but I never hear them expressing how they feel about their parents to us. I'm sure everybody has something they don't like about their parents, but Patricia and Porsha never express it to us, or maybe just not to me. Key is around them and their family way more than I am.

After gossiping about our parents, I decide to go downstairs to see what my parents are doing.

"I mean, that's what she wakes up in the morning thinking is fine to do. She don't even be having her teeth brushed or hair done, and her first question is 'Can I go across the street?'" Mom mimics Key in a jokey way.

"You say she don't even say good morning, huh?" Dad jokes along with her.

"Hell no. Ain't that right, Miko?" Mom smiles, looking at me.

"Yeah, she does always want to go over there. I mean, I like going over there sometimes, too, but…"

Mom cuts me off "Miko goes over there sometimes, but that's not all she eat, sleep, and live."

"But what, Mik? Why you only like going over there sometimes?" Dad tries to get more information out of me.

"Because it's so junky over there," I confess.

"Oh, it's nasty over there, huh?" Dad confirms.

"Yeah, I don't even be wanting to take my shoes off, low key." I sit down in the big chair.

They share laughs at my comment.

"And Key just love, love, loves it," my mom makes a disgusting facial expression.

"She probably like their brother," Dad assumes.

"She better not!" Mom looks at Dad and me with the most

serious face.

"Yeah, they probably have a crush on each other," Dad eggs it on.

"Miko, do they like each other?" Mom asks quickly.

"I don't know," I shrug my shoulders hoping they believe my poker face.

"Well, she got another thing coming if she does like him. I will cut that shit the FUCK off," Mom continues with a stern voice.

Damn, what's the big deal if she has a little crush? She is a teenager for Pete's sake!

Of course, I know that they like each other. Why wouldn't I know, I'm around all the time. I would never tell my mom that Key and Cory go together or that they even have a crush on each other. She obviously disapproves it, so I'm not about to get Key in trouble. If my mom found out that Key and Cory are boyfriend and girlfriend, she would literally probably keep Key in the house until she turns eighteen years old. I don't know exactly how my dad would react, but I don't think he's in love with the idea of them together either.

After chilling downstairs with my parents gets old, I head back upstairs to see what Key is doing.

"You went downstairs?" Key asks as soon as I walk into her room.

"Yeah."

"What were they talking about?" Key asks, knowing I'm going to spill all the beans.

"Mama was still going on and on about you liking to go outside and across the street too much," I explain.

"So... nobody wants to stay in this depressing ass house," Key responds.

"Then Daddy said that you and Cory might have a crush on each other, and Mom almost caught on fire from how hot she was," I exaggerate with seriousness.

"What... she got mad?" Key looks surprised.

"Yes! She didn't even like the thought of that."

"That's crazy because she's always so nice to him. She always compliments his looks and everything," Key looks a little sad.

"Girl, she said if you like him you better think again because she will cut it the FUCK off," I try to mimic her attitude and her body language.

"So, what do she expect me to do? Not to like boys or something?" Key asks like I know the answer.

"I don't know, I just know she doesn't want y'all together," I confirm.

"That's bullshit. What was my daddy saying?" Key is focused like she's taking an exam.

"He didn't say anything about her not liking you and Cory being together."

"He probably feel the same way," she takes a guess.

"Yup," I nod my head.

"Because if he didn't, he would have questioned her or said something. You know how he is," Key puts two and two together.

"Right," I agree.

"That's exactly why she doesn't know anything about me. She can't handle the truth. Just because she was wild when she was younger doesn't mean I'm going to be like that," Key expresses in an angry tone of voice.

"Let her tell it, she knows everything about you," I giggle.

"Yeah, fucking right. But it doesn't matter, me and Cory are gone be together regardless, so," Key shrugs her shoulders.

"Mik Mik! Wake up" Dad taps me several times.

"Come on, get up so you can get dressed," he talks as I wake up slowly but surely.

"Where we about to go?" I ask, yawning.

"The family reunion is today," he responds. "Come on, boo," he rushes me.

"Okay... okay..." I mutter in my morning voice.

"Yo' mama picking out yo' outfit," he adds, brushing his hair.

As I walk out of my parent's room, I see Mom in my room picking out my hair accessories to match my outfit.

She can't wait to tare my head up! I roll my eyes at my own thought. Then I quickly peak in Key's room, and it looks like she's in a bad mood.

She probably mad we have to go," I giggle.

These are our last two days of summer break. After tomorrow, Monday will be knocking at the front door. Back to waking up early as hell, I'm not looking forward to it, but I can't wait to see my friends from school.

I wonder if Samantha, Trisha, and Will are coming back to Lathrup Village. After brushing my teeth I take a nice hot shower. Waiting for me in my room is mommy dearest.

"What are these clothes for?" I asks because they are separated from the outfit I'm wearing today.

"Y'all are spending the night over Big Mama's house after the family reunion," Mom replies.

"Oh, okay." I did a quick Michael Jackson spin to express my excitement.

While mom finishes sorting my clothes, I begin getting dressed and mentally preparing for getting my hair done. About thirty minutes later, everybody is ready to leave. The only thing we have to do is get my hair done. As I sit on the floor between Mom's legs, I ask as she combs my hair "Can you do a ponytail at the top and a ponytail at the bottom?"

"Yeah," she responds quickly as if that wasn't her initial plan.

I'm jumping for joy inside because two ponytails shouldn't take long at all. I'm also happy we'll be seeing the whole family today at the park.

This is our last weekend before school starts tomorrow and honestly, I'm going to miss hanging out all day with everybody. Our last performance with the dance team was a success and so much fun. I wonder if Diamond and Shalissa will keep in touch. They were really cool girls. I wonder if I'll ever see my play Mom, Jasmine, again. I'm going to miss her and her nice grandma. As I daydream during church, Big Mama is standing while clapping her hands and rocking to the church music coming from the choir. Key and Evin are nodding off, trying not to fall asleep. The Twins are singing in the choir looking like they're about to die. Bryon and April are entertaining themselves, sneaking hits to each other trying not to get caught by Big Mama. Kyler and Tae are sleep. I guess they're the only two that's allowed to sleep in church since they're the babies. All of our other cousins are spread out throughout the chapel with their immediate families.

"GRRR!" I feel my stomach vibrate.
I'm sure if this music wasn't so loud, I could have heard my stomach growling. I'm starving! I can't wait until we go downstairs to eat. Then after some good food, we'll be heading to the door. Then I'll be that much closer to peeling these freaking stockings off my legs.

Service is finally over, and everyone heads downstairs to eat Sunday dinner. Everyone is laughing, joking, and talking smack to each other. As I eat, I overhear a couple of people asking Big Mama about where my dad is.

"Where is Jihod ugly butt?" cousin Angela asks.
"I don't know; I haven't seen him since yesterday," Big Mama responds just as confused as Angela is.

"Probably somewhere up to no good," Aunt Lora cuts in the conversation.

She always got something smart to say about somebody," I think to myself as I stuff Big Mama's tasty collard greens in my mouth.

But I like her, she sits back and watches cartoons and children's movies with me all the time. Evin disrupts my thoughts when he asks Bryon a question from across the table

"Bryon, you hungry, huh?" Evin laughs, making everybody else who's sitting near us laugh.
"Shut up!" Bryon responds with a smirk as he inhales his food.
"This macaroni and cheese is hitting, though!" I add, taking up for Bryon chowing down on his food.
"It's hitting hitting!" April bites into her chicken.
"Aye, Bryon, when do y'all start school?" I ask.
"We started last week."
"Dang, we don't start until tomorrow," April adds.
"I wonder why y'all started early," Key adds aloud.
Uncle Nutty probably made him go early, I keep my sassy joke to myself. Uncle Nutty just seems so mean and strict most of the times.

After everybody finishes eating and cleaning up, everyone parts ways until next Sunday. It's so funny because I don't see any of the family I see at church until a family reunion or at church. We rarely visit our extended cousins' houses that are not part of Big Mama's grandchildren, but we for sure see them at church.

My parents didn't wait too late to come pick us up since we have school in the morning. Bryon and Kyler got picked up first, then our parents came, and Evin and April are the last to leave. The twins and Tae live with Big Mama. I'm excited to see who's coming back this school semester and I can't wait to see who my 3rd-grade teacher is going to be.

"THERE WILL BE <u>NO</u> GOING TO THE BATHROOM ALONE AFTER LUNCH BREAKS. When you need to ask a question at ALL times, raise your HAND to speak. When WE do take a bathroom break, we will walk inside of the squares on the floor to create a perfectly straight line, with your heads facing forward. While walking to the bathroom, there will be absolutely NO talking. If you're caught talking, you will be forced to walk with your hand covering your mouth until we return to the CLASSROOM. Again, my name is Ms. Jenkins. Welcome to third grade!" Ms. Jenkins sits down at her desk after her announcement.

"Damn, are we in class or boot camp?" An unfamiliar boy sitting next to me leans over to whisper.

I giggle quietly. "I know, right? What type of shit is this?"

"Ugh, Ms. Jenkins! I don't like her!" I express to Samantha during lunchtime.

"Right, her ugly fat black self. Did you see that huge gap in the center of her teeth?" Samantha asks.

I burst into laughter. "How could I miss it with her big ol' mouth?" I bite into my sandwich.

"At ALL times," Samantha mimics her mouth movement.

"That's exactly how she look, too," I laugh. "Man, this year is going to be tough."

Samantha rolls her eyes. "I wish I could have been in Ms. Rogers' class."

"Right, me too," I agree.

"I'm going to see if I can transfer," Samantha adds with confidence.

The day goes by so slowly, but it's finally over. I'm surprised that I didn't see Trisha at lunch or in any other 3rd grade classes. Her parents must have put her in another school this year. As the end of the day approaches, I see a lot of the same people from last year. Surprisingly, my mom is waiting for us at school before we let out.

"Where is your sister?" Mom asks.

"I don't know. I didn't see her when class let out."

"How was your first day?"

"It was okay. I saw a lot of the same people from last year."

"Oh, okay, what about your teacher? Is she nice?" Mom continues with the conversation.

"Her name is Ms. Jenkins. I do not like her, and she's nowhere near nice," I add in a serious tone.

"Why you don't like her?" She giggles.

"She is so mean, nobody like her." I roll my eyes.

"What was she saying?" Mom turns around to look at me.

"She was going over all of these crazy rules. Talking about how many times we're going to be able to go to the bathroom. And if we have to use the bathroom any other time before or after we go as a class, we're not allowed to go at all or by ourselves," I explain.

"What? That sounds crazy!" Mom shouts out. "If you need to go to the bathroom, you go. I don't care if you have to walk out of the class, you hear me?" She says firmly.

"Yeah," I'm soaking in every word.

"Because that doesn't make any sense to me," she turns around as Key gets in the car.

"What's wrong?" Key asks.

"Miko was just telling me about her new teacher and how she thinks it's okay to make them go to the bathroom at certain times of the day. Not when they have to use it," Mom explains.

"She don't let y'all go to the bathroom?" Key throws her book bag in the back seat with me.

"Not alone and not before or after we already been as a class," I add with certainty.

"I told her she better go to the bathroom if she has to pee," Mom adds again.

"Yeah, that's stupid," Key smacks her lips.

"Samantha said she's going to try to transfer out of her class," I continue.

"Oh, Samantha came back, huh"? Mom asks with a smirk on her face.

"Yeah, but we won't be in the same class for long. Trisha didn't come back, though."

"Little off-beat Samantha?" Mom jokes.

"Right," Key laughs.

"Samantha was dancing like she was doing karate at Miko's basement birthday party last year, wasn't she?" Mom giggles.

"Yes, she was!" Key is cracking up.

"She was punching and kicking down the soul train line," I add to the joke.

Now mom is cracking up. "Poor little Samantha, she is too cute, though."

"I don't really care for my teacher this year either," Key adds.

"What's wrong with your teacher?" Mom asks.

"Nothing so far, I just don't care for her." Key looks out of the passenger window.

The small talk in the car made the ride shorter than usual. When we arrive home, no one is outside yet. Which is good, we didn't have to feel left out this time. I don't see my dad's car outside either. That means he's not home, which is not surprising. Ms. Jenkins gave us a packet of homework with all kinds of academic subjects included. I know if I wait too long to do my homework, I will get in trouble. Thank god it's not due tomorrow. The packet is due this coming Friday. I plan on doing half of the packet today, so I won't have that much to do for the rest of the week.

After I undress, I take my homework downstairs to start it in the dining room.

"You have homework?" Mom asks from the kitchen.

"Yeah, a huge packet of it," I add with a fake attitude.

"Oh, she wasn't playing with y'all?" Mom giggles.

"We didn't even learn this much today," I flip through the packet.

"The packet is probably a 2nd-grade packet. Full of stuff you should already know," Mom sounds sure.

Yeah, whatever. I sit down at the dining room table.

"Let me know if you need any help," Mom yells from the living room.

"Yeah, that's not going to happen," I whisper to myself while starting the first page of my homework. I do not like asking my parents for help with my homework. They don't have any patience. I'll be on my way to getting a whopping before learning how to understand and comprehend my homework, messing around with them. I'd rather just get the question marked down when the teacher grades it.

CHAPTER **TWENTY-FOUR**

"JIHOD IS NEVER home!" Mom shakes her head.
Here we go again! I try to keep a straight face.
"I know, he might as well not even live here," Key instigates.
The honest to god truth is NO ONE CARES! At least not me or Key! She's looking for sympathy from the wrong people. No one feels like sitting around talking about my dad all fucking day! And she wonders why Key always wants to go outside. Anywhere, to be away from her ass! Ugh, she just gets on my last nerve. I'm so happy I'm the youngest, and she's not expecting much feedback from an eight-year-old. She shouldn't be expecting much from a thirteen-year-old either, but she does.

"I know, I should put all of his shit right outside and change the locks," Mom stuffs macaroni and cheese in her mouth then continues. "I mean, he doesn't even call and let anybody know if he's fine or not," she continues with a mouth full of food.
"Yeah, like that one time he went missing and came back home talking about all of these karate moves he learned in jail," Key jokes, making everybody laugh because it's true.
"That was funny," I comment to myself.
After dinner, Key washes the dishes and mom sits at the bar watching Key while prepping her for the next altercation with my dad. I

don't feel like hearing the bullshit, so I go up to my room. About ten minutes later, I hear Key go into her room. As I get up from playing with my dolls to go into Key's room, the doorbell rings.

"I wonder who that is?" I asks Key.
Key is sitting by her window looking at everybody outside like a sad puppy.
"It was Porsha," she confirms.
"Did you see if you could go outside?" I ask already knowing the answer.
"Yeah, the stupid bitch said no. Like always."
"Oh, she love that answer," I roll my eyes.
"Man, I swear, when both of them get old, they better not ask me or need me for shit. I will happily put both of them in a home, I promise," Key expresses her favorite line about my parents.

She is so heartbroken that she can't go outside. She knows how my mom is. I think it embarrasses Key that our mom is so strict. It doesn't make it any better that all of our friend's parents aren't strict, so it makes us look like we're the only kids who can't simply go out in front of the house. It's not like we're doing anything in here. We're not doing anything educational. It's not chore day or anything, so I don't see what the big deal is. She can be such a bitch most of the times.

"Miko!"
"She rings." I look at Key sarcastically "Huh?"
"Bring your ass here!" She yells louder.
I jog to her room.
"Say 'huh' to me again, watch you get the shit beat out of you!" she yanks my arm like she wants to pull it out of the socket.
"Go and get your grease so I can oil your scalp," she orders.

I walk across the hall and grab the grease we bought from Mr. John's and a comb. When I get back to her room, she is sitting on the edge of the bed waiting for me to come sit down. I hand her the grease and comb, then turn around to sit on the floor in between her legs. I usually hate when her hands are in my head, but getting my scalp oiled feels so good. As she parts down the middle to divide my long hair, she wraps one side up in a ball, then starts on the loose side, parting small sections and rubbing her finger directly into my scalp with grease. The grease is a little colder than room temperature, so that makes it feel even better.

"If your dad comes home tonight, ask him to take y'all to school in the morning," she orders.
"Why?" I ask confused, forgetting who I'm talking to.
She yanks my hair tightly grabbing it in a ball then hits my head with the comb. "Because I said so!"

The room goes silent for a few minutes, as tears fall quietly from my eyes.

"Now, if he says no, you make sure you say 'If Rock asked you, you would say yes,'" she demands.
"Okay," I sniffle quickly.
Why can't you say the shit? My eight-year-old attitude snaps back in my head.

About fifteen minutes later, she is finally done and I speed to my room so she won't think of anything else stupid to say to me.

"That's why nobody wants to be around her ass now," I confess to myself in my room. "Ooo... I can't wait until I get older," I continue while I put my dolls away. "I would beat her the fuck up!" I roll my eyes while putting the last of my toys in my toy bin.

Instead of crying myself to sleep, I decide to read a chapter of my Josefina book. As the night goes on, I decide to sleep in my own bed.

I just want to be alone! I hate living here! I wish things could be normal around here. This can't be normal. People are always looking at me and the way I'm dressed and think my life is all good and perfect. But it sucks to be me. I don't like my mom, and my dad isn't here half of the time. Maybe Key is right. Maybe if my dad was here more often and had a regular job, things wouldn't be this way.

I hope my dad doesn't come home tonight so I won't have to say anything to him.

I fall asleep as I drown in my own tears.

"Miko, wake up." Mom taps me continuously.

Once I'm finally up, I head to the bathroom. I walk past my parent's room, taking a quick glance to see if dad is laying down in the bed, and he is.

"Damn" I whisper to myself.
"Every time I don't want this nigga' to be here, he is right fucking here! When I want to see him, he's nowhere in sight!" I land my face in both of my hands as I stand in front of the bathroom mirror.

After I'm done getting dressed, I noticed my mom is already downstairs.

"She's probably making our lunches," I whisper to myself.

I'm hoping they had a good night's sleep and she doesn't want me to ask him anything. I head downstairs once I notice Key is finished getting dressed. Once I approach the dining room, I see Key sitting at the bar, well dressed with her yellow and brown uniform on. I'm wearing the exact same uniform as well. Yellow collared shirt with a yellow and brown plaid skirt, topped with a matching plaid tie for girls. As soon as Mom notice me in the dining room, she say "Miko, come here," she signals her pointer finger.

PRETTY CAN BE UGLY

I walk over less excited. "Jihod is upstairs still sleeping. You remember what I told you to say, right?" she looks stern.

"Yeah," I answer dryly.

"Okay, go ahead," she shoos me away.

I hate when she makes me do stuff like this! I scream in my head.

"Here goes nothing," I whisper looking at my dad sleeping like a baby.

"Da!" I tap him several times trying to wake him.

"What?" his growling morning voice slips through.

"Can you take us to school?" I ask.

"Nah, ya' mama gone do it," he answers slowly.

"If Rock asked, you would say yes," I quickly say what I was told and leave the room.

I walk back downstairs, and my mom instantly questions me.

"What did he say?"

"He said no, and that you were going to do it."

"Did you say what I told you afterwards?" she asks with more concern.

"Yeah."

"What did he say?"

"Nothing."

Mom huffs. "That's fucking ridiculous," she shakes her head.

About five minutes later, after Mom finishes packing our lunches, we hear Dad coming down the stairs.

"And you don't tell me what the fuck I will and won't do!" he points his finger directly at me with a challenging voice and a slight frown.

"Come on, are y'all ready?" he asks.

"Yeah, they ready." Mom hands us our lunches.

Now this bitch want to speak up. Ugly ass hoe!

On the way to school, my dad has some bomb music on again. This morning, a song by Eminem called Kill You is playing through the loud speakers. This song is going so hard! Eminem is one of my favorite rappers and he's from Detroit. He is so lyrically inclined and smart. Sometimes his lyrics go over my head and I have to rewind the track to listen again.

"Did y'all hear what he just said?" Dad asks in an ecstatic tone of voice.

"No, what did he say?" I'm excited to hear what I missed.

"That nigga' just said '*I don't even believe in breathing! I'm leaving air in your lungs, just to hear you keep screaming for me to seep it!*' NIGGA! THIS NIGGA IS A BEAST!" he laughs, rewinding the track, waving his hand in the air, while Key and I are cracking up at his reaction to Eminem's metaphors.

He is so goofy sometimes. I wish I could stay in this car and listen to bomb music with him all day. I wish my mom didn't hate him so much, and I could hang out with him more. Too bad he probably won't pick us up from school or won't be home when we get home from school. I just miss him so much! And I love how he's not mad at me anymore. If I say anything, attempting to disagree with my mom, she would be mad forever. My dad is completely opposite. I made him mad earlier and he's over it already.

In no time, we arrived at school. It seems like every time we're in the car with him the travel is much faster.

"Alright, y'all have a good day," he waves us goodbye. As he drives off, we can hear his music in his car just as loud as the car engine driving off.

"See, that's why I fuck with him," I add.

"Why? Because he likes all of the sweet music?" Key giggles.

"Well, that's one reason. But when I said that smart comment to him upstairs that Joyce made me say, he clearly got mad, but he got over it as well," I explain.

"Right, he doesn't hold grudges like mama do," Key agrees.

"Yeah, he was annoyed with me because I got smart, so he checked me and life goes on. Mama would've checked me, beat the crap out of me, then still been mad at me afterwards." I roll my eyes.

"Yeah, she would have been mad for like a full week and some change," Key giggles as we part ways to go to our classes.

"Kimiko, Devin said do you want to be his girlfriend?" Patrick runs behind me with dingy braids in his hair and more missing teeth than teeth in his mouth.

"No, I don't," I answer less excited than him.

"She said she don't like you!" Patrick's loud mouth yells to Devin who is about five lockers down from me.

"She said you ugly as hell, boy!" Patrick continues to instigate the situation then Samantha walks up to me.

"Who is he talking about?" she giggles.

"He told me Devin wanted to go with me. I said I didn't want to go with him. Now he sitting there making up a whole bunch of stuff I didn't say," I giggle.

"Trying to be funny, he so irritating," Samantha laughs.

"Right," I giggle. "Did you finish your packet?"

"No, I started it. I'm almost finished, though."

"Same here, I started yesterday. I just wanted to get it over with," I complain.

"Have you seen your boyfriend yet?" Samantha smiles while sitting at her desk next to me.

"My boyfriend?" I ask confused.

"Yeah, Will," she responds quickly, unable to hold her laugh in.

"Girl, bye. He is not my boyfriend." I smile at her sarcastic joke.

"I bet y'all spoke over the summer," she challenges me.

"So, what if we did, what does that mean?" I challenge back.

"Oh my god! Y'all really talked over the summer? Oh yeah, that's your boo for real!" she claps her hands.

"Samantha!" Ms. Jenkins yells out of nowhere, scaring the whole class.

"Sit over here," she demands.

"Why?" Samantha challenges her.

"Because I said so, now bring it!" she points at a desk on the other side of the room.

"Huuuh..." Samantha huffs, puffs and smacks her lips to the other side of the classroom.

The day continues with orders, demands, and a lot of yelling. Thank God lunch is finally here. After I find the spot where I want to sit, I see Will's class come in the lunchroom soon after us.

"Man, this bitch Ms. Jenkins is going to drive me crazy," Samantha sits down next to me.

"She yelled at you this morning for no reason," I roll my eyes.

"I should have my mom come up here and whop her ass," she opens her lunch box.

I giggle. "Now that would be funny."

"I told my mom that she told us we could only go to the bathroom at certain times of the day and she told me I better go to the bathroom whenever I feel like I have to pee," Samantha explains.

"Me too, and my mom said the same thing!" I laugh.

"What's up, Kimiko?" Will sits down across from me.

"Dang, that's the only person you see?" Samantha looks him dead in the face.

"Hey, Samantha," he speaks, less excited.

"How is it in Ms. Allen's class?" I wonder.

"It's fun, Ms. Allen is cool as hell. She kind of remind me of Mrs. Johnson."

"I don't think Mrs. Johnson work here anymore," Patrick butts in the conversation.

"She died, fool," Samantha snaps.

"What? You lying," Patrick's mouth is open out of shock.

"Why would I lie about that?" Samantha looks at him like he's stupid.

"Nah, she's telling the truth man," Will confirm.

"Damn, that's so bold," Patrick shakes his head.

"I know, right? She was my favorite teacher," I express sadly at the thought of never seeing her again.

"How you like your new teacher?" Will ask, knowing the answer to the question.

"I don't like her at all! She is so mean," I reply first.

"Yeah, I'm thinking about transferring to your class." Samantha bites into her sandwich.

"Kimiko, you should too," Will suggests.

"Yeah, I should." I nod still thinking about how nice Ms. Johnson used to be.

CHAPTER **TWENTY-FIVE**

"KIMIKO, COME HERE!" Brittany yells from down the hallway.

"What's up, Brittany?"

"Let me play in your hair!" she touches my long ponytail.

"I don't like people playing in my hair." I pull back.

"Why?" she frowns.

"Because it's aggravating." I shrug my shoulders.

"My cousin has really long hair like that too."

"Oh, okay," I respond dryly.

"You like any of the boys in our class?" Brittany continues with small talk.

"No," I answer quickly. "I will see you later." I walk away not interested in kicking it with her.

Brittany is annoying and very nosy. I know her from last year, and she's known for spreading rumors. She's a pretty, caramel-skinned girl, tall for a third grader, with two naturally curly ponytails. She's sort of a tomboy, but she keeps her a boyfriend. She goes with anybody to me, which is so nasty.

She probably be kissing on every boy she go with. Nasty ass little girl. My body cringes from the thought of it.

I don't even like to eat after people. I can't imagine sticking my tongue down somebody's throat and tasting their spit.

I gag at the thought of it. Finally, my mom's car interrupts my disgusting thoughts. When Key and I get inside of the car, "Lovely Day" by Bill Withers is playing.

"Hey, y'all," Mom speaks quickly, then rushes to catch the lyrics to the song as if it's her first time hearing it. I know this is the beginning of the song because Mom plays it so much. I like her old school music, but sometimes I get tired of it. Last time I tried to hold that popular "dayyyy" note, I started to gasp for air. Bill Withers holds the word day for a really long time. That's what makes the song so unique. That's probably why she likes it so much.

The ride home went smoothly. Even though we listened to her old school music the entire time, it's better than listening to her sob stories. Entering the house, we hear the phone ringing. I assume it probably is our grandparents, so I stick around downstairs instead of running upstairs to my room.

"Hey ma," Mom responds quickly, then a few seconds later her eyes get bigger in a shocking way.
"What?" her mouth opens, and I look at Key nervously.
"How did he die?" she continues.
"Who found him?" she shakes her head at the devastating news.
Now Mom got our full attention.
"Damn! That is so sad!" Mom adds sincerely.
"So y'all coming up here for the funeral?"
Yes, granny and granddaddy will be here, I get happy for two seconds.
"Okay, so the funeral is next week?" Mom confirms.
"Wow, I know Uncle German is sick to his stomach about this," Mom looks off.
Me and Key look at each other at the same time probably thinking the same thing.
"Mars," Key whispers.

"Yeah, it probably is Mars," I agree quietly, then Mom signals for us to be quiet.

Damn, we can't do anything in this house!

About five minutes later, Mom gets off the phone to share the bad news.

"What happened?" Key beat me to the question.

"They found Mars dead in the bathroom tub last night?" mom sits down sorrowfully.

"In whose tub?" Key continues.

"Uncle German and Aunt Peggy's tub, at home," Mom explains.

"So he died inside the house? In the upstairs bathroom?" I ask in disbelief.

"Yeah, Granny just said Aunt Peggy found him." Mom looks like she's about to cry, I've never seen her cry before.

"He drowned in the tub?" Key asks again looking confused.

"Yeah, that's what Mama said."

"Dang, that's so bold," Key looks sad.

"I know," Mom shakes her head. "Damn Mars."

"I don't ever want to go back over their house again," I add.

"Granny and Granddaddy flying up here?" Key double checks, ignoring my comment.

"Yeah, they're going to come up next week. The funeral is next weekend."

Everyone is dressed in all black inside of the church. Key, my parents, and I are sitting next to my grandparents. All of us are seated towards the front of the church. For some reason, I don't want to see Mars' body in the casket. The viewing was yesterday, and I touched his cold hands. He didn't look like the same Mars to me. It's sad how a person can be here today and gone tomorrow.

A woman takes the stand and asks for a few loved ones to speak

PRETTY CAN BE UGLY

some kind words about Mars. The first person to go up is Aston, his youngest sister. Aston is similar to Mars mentally, minus the stuttering issue. If you don't know her well enough, one would assume she's a little slow. While she is talking, I notice my mom's face turning red slowly but surely. It doesn't take much for her face to turn red because of her pale skin tone. She's trying to hold back from laughing at Aston. Then I look at my dad, and he's looking at my mom like she's stupid for thinking it's funny.

After about four more people speak after Aston, a gospel song by Yolanda Adams begins to slowly play as they close the casket. I don't know the name of this song, but I've heard it several times. Anybody who knows Yolanda Adams knows she has a very powerful voice. As her godly tone takes the room, it brings chills down my small body. I didn't know Mars that well, but I know he was a good person and, after all, he was family. The thought of him actually dying and being gone forever makes me cry. Once the casket closed, Aunt Peggy fell to the floor drowning in tears and sorrow. I can't imagine how she feels about losing her one and only son. Usually, you see children burying their parents. Unfortunately, things don't always go as they should. Cher and Aston are crying uncontrollably as they try to help their mom. This is probably one of the saddest funerals I've ever been to. I can't believe Mars is dead, like I've known him all my life. I'm going to miss his random pop-ups at the house. He was a nice person and made sure he kept in touch with his family.

The next stop is the cemetery, where everyone watches Mars' casket be buried in the ground. More gospel songs are being sung. Besides the singing, the only thing you can hear are sobs and sniffles from people crying nearby. Once Mars is completely buried, everyone met at a church to eat and grieve.

"Y'all notice German doesn't have much to say?" granny sparks a conversation.

"He's probably in disbelief," Mom adds.

"The man is devastated, Mary." granddaddy frowns at granny.

"Well, I'm just saying," granny says softly as she continues to eat.

"I probably wouldn't have much to say if I lost my child either," granddaddy continues with his point.

You need to calm down, I take up for granny in my head.

Granny doesn't respond to his remark, giving him the upper hand as usual. I don't see how she puts up with his smart-ass mouth. I don't understand why he's so grumpy towards her anyways. She's so nice and soft hearted, it would be hard for me to be mean to her all of the time.

"This ain't the right one," I blurt out to Key with giggles making an inside joke.

"Ain't?" granddaddy frowns, looking at me.

"What?" I'm confused.

"Ain't is not a word," granddaddy corrects me.

I ignore him like granny just did.

"You're supposed to be a straight-A student, right?" he continues in his natural baritone voice.

"Yeah," I answer quickly, less interested in his conversation.

"Straight-A students don't talk like that," he smirks.

He knows every word and sentence that comes out of his mouth is not spoken super proper. Ever since they moved down south, he's been spending more time with his white friends. He's been speaking more proper and correcting Key and me every time he can. My grandparents have a lot of White friends. I know more of his white friends than his Black friends, and he was born and raised here in Detroit. I believe he knows his White friends from work. My dad always says he tries to act White. Dad also likes to tease my granddaddy when he's not around and quote him in funny voices.

If it's not White, it's not right! Dad would poke his chest out trying to mimic granddaddy.

PRETTY CAN BE UGLY

I laugh every time he does it. I've personally never heard my granddaddy say those words, but I know my dad was just picking at his character. White people aren't my dad's favorite race of people, and he makes it clear every time the discussion is brought up. I don't necessarily like or dislike White people. I don't know any White kids or White people. I only see random White people when I'm at school. They're mainly teachers or, if I'm out and about, I'll see White people working at businesses. My dad has been living longer than me, so his life experiences have shaped his opinion about White people. Mom never really expresses how she feels about White people.

Shortly after dinner, everybody is mingling with family I hardly ever see. I notice my parents getting ready to leave.

"Granny, can I come with y'all?" I ask.

"Yeah, boo, did you ask Joyce?"

"Not yet," I look in my mom's direction.

"Oh, Mae Jo, this is your grandbaby?" an old woman with two gold teeth in the front yells with a southern accent.

"Yeah," granny smiles.

"Oh my! She is a doll! And look at all of this hair! This is Joyce's daughter?"

"Yeah, this is Mickey," granny introduces me.

"Hey, Mickey, I'm Auntie Lola Bell," she shakes my hand very sternly. "I'm your auntie!" she continues in a loud voice.

"Yeah, she's my mother's twin sister," granny explains.

"Oh, okay, hey," I smile.

"Alright, Mae Jo, I'm heading out of here," Uncle Tedrick comes out of nowhere.

"Alright, y'all be safe. Are y'all driving back to Lansing tonight?" Granny asks.

"Yup, we're getting ready to get on the road." Uncle Tedrick puts his hands in his pocket.

Granny's side of the family is originally from Alabama, so almost everybody is very country. Instead of calling her Mary Jo, they call her Mae Jo, which is so funny to me. Uncle Tedrick is another one of granny's brothers. He's really tall and bald in the center of his head. The rest of his hair proceeds on the sides of his head. He has a really thick southern accent as well. Supposedly he has a son around Key's age that he never brings around. Uncle Tedrick is like the scholar out of my granny's brothers. He graduated from high school and has a few degrees in psychology. I believe he's a psychologist. He comes off very quirky and sort of weird to me.

"Well hi there... little miss Mickey," Uncle Tedrick smiles widely.

"Hey, Uncle Tedrick."

"How are ya'?" he kneels down.

"I'm doing good."

"I wish I would have brought your cousin Jake. He's out of town right now hanging out with his cousins on his mom side," he explains.

"Oh, how is Jake? He's a big boy now, I bet," granny smiles.

"Yeah, he's about my height already. He's a very smart boy, and he says he wants to be a scientist. I always ask him 'well, what kind of scientist Jake?' He doesn't know yet," Tedrick goes on and on.

"Tedrick, what you over here talking about? Jake?" Uncle Brother cuts into the conversation.

"Aye, where the hell is Jake any damn way?" Uncle Brother continues in his country accent.

"Brother, be quiet," granny pats him on the shoulder in a playful way, giggling at his truthful comment because it's obvious Jake is never around.

Uncle Brother is another one of granny's brothers. He's really cool and funny, and one would think he was the youngest of them all. Uncle Brother tells it like it is and doesn't think twice.

"Hey, Uncle Brother!" I wave more comfortably because I know him better than Uncle Tedrick.

"What's up, Mickey!" he put his hand out for me to give him a five.

PRETTY CAN BE UGLY

"Come on, Mik, we about to go." Mom hands me my coat.

"Joyce!!" Uncle Brother hugs my mom.

"Hey, Uncle Brother. Where y'all about to go?" Mom asks.

"German said he wants everybody to come over to his house."

"Oh, okay, ma, y'all going over there?"

"Yeah, I guess," granny shrugs.

"Can I ride with granny and granddaddy?" I pop my question in.

"Yeah," she squints her eyes at me regretfully.

"We will see y'all over there then." Mom walks away, hiding her small attitude.

"Miko! You coming?" Key yells from a short distance.

"I'm riding with granny and granddaddy," I brag.

Key runs to me. "You going with them?"

"Yeah."

"Me too!" Key smiles, hopping on the bandwagon.

"Key, look at you getting taller every time I see you!"

"Hey, Uncle Brother," Key giggles at his energy.

"Key, you riding with us too, boo?" granny asks.

"Yeah," Key nods her head.

"Okay, we're getting ready to leave as well and head over to German's." Granny grabs her coat.

"Come on, Key!" Mom yells.

"She's coming with us too!" granny responds before Key could say anything.

"Okay!"

We leave about ten minutes after my parents left. The drive to Uncle German's house is sort of longer than I expected. Of course, my granddaddy is driving. My granny hardly ever drives; she drives around the resort that they live in down south. Besides that, I never see her behind the wheel.

"Granny, why you never drive?" I question her from the back seat.

"I don't like driving."

"She doesn't know how to drive," granddaddy giggles at his own joke.

"I do know how to drive, Jim," granny responds in a passive-aggressive way.

"I just feel like driving and cars in general are deathtraps," she continues.

"Deathtraps?" I double check if I heard her correctly.

"Yeah, people die in car accidents every day."

"That's just stupid, Mary," granddaddy disagrees sternly.

"It's true," granny defends herself.

"People die doing all kinds of things every day," granddaddy responds quickly.

"People die in cars every day. Several times a day," granny stands her ground.

"Yeah, well people die every day walking or doing something random on foot too," he responds in a clever, sarcastic way. "What now, you're not going to walk anywhere either?" he giggles.

"No, that's not what I mean," Granny gives up.

"Well, it's basically the same thing," granddaddy adds.

Instead of jumping into their petty back-and-forth conversation, I just sit back in my seat as "Keep on Movin" by Soul II Soul is playing on the radio.

Once we get to our destination, I see a lot of the same faces from the funeral. The families that are here at the house are more familiar, which makes me more comfortable. Everybody is everywhere throughout the house. The kids are mainly in the basement, and the adults are everywhere. I'm annoyed that my mom is in the basement. I can just sense that she's getting too drunk. The drunk shit gets on my last nerve, and it's the most embarrassing thing. In the middle of playing with Aston's dolls, I have to use the bathroom. On the way to the bathroom, I see my mom slumped over with her eyes rolling to the back of her head, and it looks like she spilt something on her shirt. What's more embarrassing to me is the fact that no one else's parents or no other adults are as drunk as she is. She's always the only one looking dumb. One would think she would want to stop embarrassing herself. I just walk by disgusted, continuing to the bathroom. Usually, I would go upstairs to the nicer bathroom, but Mars just died in that bathroom upstairs, which is scary to me. Thank God, there is another bathroom in the basement. I'm just thankful my dad is here this time, so I feel safe, and I know that even if my dad is drinking, he never gets as hammered as she does. He always keeps his composure, even when I know he's high off weed, he's still himself and seems normal and under control.

CHAPTER **TWENTY-SIX**

"WHO THE FUCK told you, you could go with your grandparents?" Mom slaps Key in her face.

Key holds her face while crying. "I thought since Miko could go, I could too."

"Miko asked. You didn't. Don't ever think you can go anywhere without asking me first! I don't care who it's with." Mom tries to stay quiet, looking Key in her eyes as if she wants to kill her.

"You are lucky your grandparents are here or else you would be getting your fucking ass beat! Get the fuck out of my face and don't ask to do shit else today." Mom pushes Key.

Key goes to my room, since my grandparents are staying in her room. I wanted to follow her, but instead, I just continue to watch the rest of "Young and the Restless" Mom recorded for us. I'm so happy my grandparents are here too. I hate listening to Key get in trouble.

Mom is still frustrated, "Because I know that was going to be the next thing that comes out of her mouth. "Can I go across the street? Can I go outside? Fuck no."

She is so fucking mean! It's pathetic! I think to myself, laying across my parent's bed.

I feel like that was uncalled for. I'm surprised my mom even remembers something that small from yesterday after how drunk she got last night. That's what Key and I be talking about when we say it seems as if she likes yelling and hitting on us. She doesn't miss any given moment to punish us. It doesn't matter how small the reason is. I want to tell my grandparents so bad about the way she treats us, but I'll just make it even worse for myself. She'll say whatever she has to say in front of them. They will eventually have to go back home to North Carolina, then I'll get my ass beat for talking too much for nothing. Why put myself through so much trouble for no change? So I'm going to stay quiet for now.

My grandparents and dad are downstairs. Granny is whipping up something in the kitchen. Dad and granddaddy are in the living room watching TV "acting" like they're friends. Lord knows they hate each other, but it's cool that they can respect each other for the family's sake. After I get finished watching "Young and the Restless", "Bold and the Beautiful", and "As the World Turns", I go to check on Key.

"What you doing?" I ask as if I can't see.

"I'm playing the game, fool," Key smiles.

"Granny and Granddaddy saved your ass today," I try to hide my stinginess. I low key feel some kind of way about her playing on my Xbox.

"Man, fuck her," Key frowns.

"That was so bold. She gets mad at the smallest stuff," I roll my eyes.

"Right, like, girl, we are all going to the same fucking place. She act like I left with Ran or a family friend or something," Key makes her point.

"Or she acting like we left before them and they were looking for you or something," I add my example.

"Right, now that would have been something to get mad at" Key agrees.

"But it's still not that big of a deal to get slapped over," Key continues.

"Then she talking about 'I know the next thing that was going to come out of her mouth was, 'Can I go across the street?'" I gossip.

"Yeah, because nobody like being over here with her miserable ass," Key rolls her eyes still focusing on the game.

"Key! Mickey! The food is ready!" Granny yells from downstairs.

Granny and granddaddy left a few days after the funeral. It's always sad to see them leave. I think Mom might let us go visit them for the summer this year. I hope she does. I don't think Key is going to want to go, but hopefully that doesn't change Mom's mind about letting us go.

Mom is still giving Key the cold shoulder. She never gets over anything. She's so good at holding grudges. It's unbelievable how a person can stay mad at somebody for something so small for so long.

But that's how she is, a grudge-holding bitch, my second mind admits.

It's already the middle of the week, and I can't wait until the weekend. Today, school is going by pretty slow, with my best friend Samantha not being in my class anymore, that makes it even slower. She said she was going to transfer and she did. She must have told her mom about the bathroom incident and her mom took her out of this class. We have a spelling test today, and I'm pretty sure I'm going to pass it. Spelling and math tests are my favorite kinds of test. I struggle with social studies and science. But overall, I'm an honor student.

I wonder if I do good on my next report card marking, will my grandparents buy me the American Girl Doll named Kit? I look out the window as I wait for everyone else to finish with the test.

"Kimiko, you're done with your test?" Ms. Jenkins questions from her desk.

"Yes."

"Alright, well collect everybody's test as they finish and bring them to me."

I'm used to doing little tasks like this for Mrs. Johnson from last year. I was her pet, so she always had me doing something. That use to make the day go by faster, too; I miss Mrs. Johnson. I still can't believe she passed away. All of the kids used to get so jealous because they knew I was the teacher's pet. Mrs. Johnson was bad at hiding her favoritism towards me. I don't think Ms. Jenkins has a teacher's pet. I think she hates all of us. She's just having me collect the papers because her fat ass doesn't feel like getting up.

After I collect everybody's test, I hand the papers over to her.

"Thank you. Okay, everybody, be prepared for tomorrow and have your homework complete by the morning. Have a nice day." Ms. Jenkins dismisses us.

I walk out to my locker, and I see Will across the hall. I guess he saw me first because he's walking towards me.

"Y'all just now getting out?"

"Yeah. I don't like her." I roll my eyes.

"I wonder why she be letting y'all out so late."

"We had a spelling test today, and everybody was taking all day to spell those easy ass words." I giggle.

"I hate when that happen. We had one on Monday," he laughs.

"I'm surprised she doesn't make us all line up and walk each person to their fucking cars," I joke.

"Right, what's up with that line shit anyway?" Will continues to laugh at our class rules.

"I don't know," I shake my head.

"She must of came from the military or some shit," Will jokes.

"Right! That's what I said when I first met her."

"Kimiko and Will, sitting in the tree. K.I.S.S.I.N.G," Kelsey sings from behind us.

"Kelsey, shut up. I'm surprised you don't have herpes from all the boys you be kissing on," Will jokes, and I can't help but to laugh.

"First of all, I don't be kissing on a whole bunch of boys," she puts her hand on her hip.

"Yeah, that's not what I heard," Will fix his glasses.

"Ugh, and what's herpes anyway? That shit sounds nasty as fuck." I look at Will directly in his eyes.

"Something he probably got," Kelsey answers before Will.

"It's something nasty you can catch, and you have to take medicine for it," Will explains.

"Well, how do..." in the middle of Kelsey question a boy walks by and hits her booty and run. Then she runs after him.

"She so annoying," Will shake his heads.

"I think she like you," I smile.

"She like everybody," he ignores my comment.

"I'ma hook y'all up," I continue to joke.

"Stop fucking playing, dog," he giggles.

"What? Kelsey is pretty," I act clueless.

"She 'aight. She not you, but..." Will adds under his breath.

"Miko! Come on!" Key yells.

"See you later," I ignore his flirtatious comment and run towards the car.

I hope Mom didn't see me talking to Will. She might kill me.

"What's up, y'all?" Mom speaks.

"Nothing, it's nice out today," I add, trying to make conversation.

"Yeah, it is," Mom agrees.

"It was a fight today." Key expresses.

"A girl fight or a boy fight?" Mom looks interested.

"It was some boys fighting."

"Did you know the boys?" I come towards the front seat.

"Sit back," Mom cuts me off.

"Yeah, I know both of them. One boy's name is James, and the other one name is Tony. Tony was kind of bullying James. He made a joke about his shoes and had the whole class rolling! Then James got up and said, "I'll take your shoes from off your feet!" Then Tony said, "How much you want to bet, you won't!" James walked over to Tony, and they started fighting," Key explains enthusiastically.

"Where was the teacher?" Mom asks.

"She stepped out for a minute."

"Who won?" I ask.

"I think it was a tie. Everybody is trying to say that Tony won because he's more popular, but James for sure held his own!" Key continues to chew on her gum.

The next day of school is more like half a day. We just came back from lunch, and, surprisingly, my mom is waiting for us in the office.

"I wonder what's going on," I speak quietly to myself.

She never comes to pick us up early. When I get to the front office, Key is already there, and her eyes are red as if she's been crying.

"Come on," my mom gestures for us to leave, and she looks pissed off.

Aww damn! I hope we're not getting in trouble! I bite hard into my nails.

As soon as we get inside of the car the music starts and it's not coming from the radio.

"Oh, so you think you grown huh?" Mom yells.

"No," Key mutters.

"Yes, you do! I'ma show you grown! Mom starts the car and drives off.

Key doesn't have much to say, just tears and sniffles.

"Where the fuck did you get the cigarettes from anyway?" Mom continues to yell.

"My friend," Key cries.

Damnnn! She is about to get it, I think to myself, feeling sorry for her.

The ride home seemed like it took two minutes. When we pull up to the house, my dad's car is outside. Plus, all of our friends are outside too.

CHAPTER **TWENTY-SEVEN**

"GO TO YOUR room and take off all of your clothes," Mom orders as she pulls into the driveway.

When we get out of the car, everybody is in the street. I try not to look, but I couldn't help but take a quick glance, and everybody is staring at us walk in the house.

I wonder if they can tell something is wrong, I think to myself as I follow Key and Mom.

As soon as we step into the house, my dad is at Key's neck.

"Now how the hell did you think you weren't going to get caught smoking a nasty ass smelling cigarettes in school?" Dad questions Key before she gets up the stairs.
Key didn't answer his question, so Mom hits her on the back of her head. "Answer the god damn question!"
"I don't know." Key continues to cry but much louder.
"And they said she was the ringleader?" Dad asks Mom.
"Yeah, all of her friends said SHE brought the cigarettes," Mom explains.
"Then you hanging around some tattle-telling motherfuckas! Get

yo' ass upstairs!" Dad yells, pointing towards the stairs.

At this point, I don't know what to do or where I should be. Whether I should stay down here or if I should just go in my room.
"You knew she smoked cigarettes?" Dad questioned me out of nowhere.
"No," I shake my head fast. I damn near know everything about Key, but I'm not going to tell them anything. Little do he know Key is the one who stole his weed when it went missing.

I don't want to be questioned about Key's doings. I know she smokes cigarettes but why would I tell on her? They should have known I wasn't going to snitch. So much for the "friends" she has at school. Once I get in my room, I close the door so Key's cries and screams would sound farther away. Her dumb ass should have never got caught. She's pretty good at being sneaky, she hardly ever gets caught doing things she's not supposed to do. Then her stupid ass friends ratted her out. That's what's making it worse.

About twenty minutes went by, and Key still hadn't gotten a whooping yet. I hope she's not getting one anymore. I mean, what she did was bad, but maybe she can be on punishment or something instead of getting a beating. Then a few minutes later I hear my dad yelling.

"Cigarettes will kill you!" he hits Key once with the belt.
Then I hear my mom talking, but I can't hear the words clearly.
"Why are both of them in her room?" I ask myself.
"If I hear about you smoking a cigarette again," he hits her again with a belt, "You're going to get it worse than this!" he lashes her a third time, then that's it. I hear nothing but crying.
"That's it? Umm... he needs to be around more often when we get in trouble," I speak to myself in my room.

Key's 8th grade graduation ceremony was a success. The third graders performed for the event and I feel like I did a pretty good job. This will most likely be our last year here attending Academy of Lathrup Village since this school' highest grade level is middle school. Mom prefers for us to go to the same school so there can be a single drop off and pick up location. My grandparents are in town, too, so I'm really geeked up. After everyone gets dressed to impress, we head to the ceremony.

After Key says her goodbyes to her friends and takes pictures, it's finally time to go eat. The trip to the Boat Club is sort of lengthy, so I just chill in the back seat with my legs up and ride out to "No One's Gonna' Love You" by S.O.S Band as it plays smoothly through the speakers. I like the old school music my grandparents play. It sounds a little older than the old school music Mom listens to. It's always so relaxing and calming when they're here. Granted, they have their times when they call themselves getting in small arguments, but my Granny rarely ever put up a fight, so the arguments don't usually last long, which is the complete opposite of my parents. When my parents argue, it's an all-night fight, then it's hostility in the air after the fight for days. Most of the time, I hate being home with my family. I love going over other people's houses and being around other families because it gives me time to be away from the drama my family keeps.

When we arrive at The Boat Club, Uncle Sunny and Aunt Joan are there before us. Their daughter, Sheen, and her daughter, Brooklyn, are here as well. I didn't know that they would be here, but I could have taken a wild guess. The Boat Club is my Uncle Sunny's favorite spot. He and his family are always here.

I know what my dad is thinking in his head, I giggle to myself. I know he is probably ready to go, and we just got here.

"What's up Puddin'?" Uncle Sunny hugs Granddaddy.
"Hey, Sheen," Mom speaks.
"So, Key, you getting ready for high school, huh?" Aunt Joan asks with a big smile.
"Yeah," Key returns the smiles.
"Yup, Key about to be a high school kid!" Dad adds in a funny way.
"I remember when she was a little baby, running around over there on Indiana," Aunt Joan reminisces.
"Right, she was so cute and small," granny adds.

Aunt Joan reminds me of Granny a lot. Not her looks so much but her mannerism and the way she carries herself. She's very soft-spoken and pretty for an older woman, and she dresses nicely as well.

"Mickey performed at the graduation as well," Granddaddy adds, not leaving me out.
"You performed, Mickey?" Uncle Sunny asks enthusiastically.
"Yeah," I smile.
"She showed all of those little kids out?" Granddaddy brags.
"Yeah, it seemed like the kids were following her lead," Mom nods her head.
"The rest of the kids was everywhere," Dad giggles.
"Yeah, she was the leader of the pack," Granddaddy continues.
"What kind of performance was it?" Aunt Joan asks.
"It was like a dance performance. They did a dance routine to 'Flashlights,'" Granny explains.
"Everybody had their flashlights, shining it on everybody," Mom laughs.
"Flashlights! Neon lights!" Uncle Sunny sings.
"Yeah, she did a good job!" Granddaddy continues with confidence.

"My best friend was mad because she messed up," I giggle.

"All those little kids were messing up," Mom giggles.

"That's what I told her! Then she got jealous, talking about 'Did you?'"

"Got jealous?" Granny adds in disbelief.

"Yeah," I laugh at Granny.

"What did you say?" Granddaddy asks.

"I told her no. I didn't mess up. That dance was easy to me." I drink my Sprite as everybody laughs.

"Mik, Mik…" Dad holds his hand out for me to give him a five.

I'm feeling confident in Mr. Jackson's class playing with my barrettes that's hanging to the middle of my back, waiting for him to pass the test out. Fourth grade is easy for me at Cherry Hill Performing Arts. Cherry Hill grade ranges from kindergarten to twelfth grade. After Key graduated from the eighth grade, Mom wanted Key and me to go to the same school, so we'll probably be here until Key finishes high school. I've made the honor roll every report card, and I receive rewards for it from my grandparents every time. I'm still obsessed with American Girl Dolls, so every time I receive a good report card, I get one. That alone encourages me to perform well in school.

"Line up, shortest to tallest, girls first, boys last," Mr. Jackson proclaims.

He makes us get into these accurate lines for bathroom breaks so we won't be able to talk to our friends. It doesn't bother me because I'm used to this stuff from my strict third-grade teacher, Ms. Jenkins. Mr. Jackson never let us talk on the trip to the bathroom, which is very annoying. Approaching the bathroom, we pass Mrs. Beek's class, another fourth-grade class, and they are walking in a very stern, precisely straight line with their arms folded and their index fingers on their mouths.

"I'm happy I'm not in her class," I whisper in Danielle's ear as we walk past.

Appreciating the classroom that chose me and minding my own business, Mr. Jackson lets three to five people inside the bathroom at a time. Washing my hands, Raeshawn and I have a short conversation.

"How you think you did on the test?" say Raeshawn.
"I think I did ok," I shrug my shoulders.
"I know I didn't pass. I didn't study," Raeshawn giggles.
"Hurry up, girls," Mr. Jackson yells halfway in the entrance of the girls bathroom, banging his stick on the floor.
"He might as well just come inside of the bathroom," I frown while walking out.
Raeshawn laughs while walking behind me.

On the way back to the classroom, we pass another fourth-grade class, the class that I dream about all the time. I'd die to be in Mr. Reed's class, and on top of that, he is so fine. He always smiles at me in a very friendly way. I tell him I want to be in his class all the time. His class always seems to be having so much fun and the whole class seem like they get along so well like a big family. Mr. Reed is much cooler than Mr. Jackson. Mr. Reed is a shorter man, brown-skinned with nice teeth and swag out of this world. Mr. Jackson is a light-skinned man with a peanut bald held and a perky booty. When he walks, he sort of switches his booty like a girl.

"Look at his booty. It sit up, and his stomach sit down," I whisper to Raeshawn.
"Yeah, he's probably gay," Raeshawn giggles.
"Funny looking ass." I giggle as we find our seats in the classroom.

Raeshawn is a cool girl. She's sort of a light brown skin complexion with short hair, and her front tooth is slightly chipped. She really doesn't communicate with a lot of people. Sometimes I wonder why she's so nice to me. I was happy to get back to class so I could sit next to my best friend, Shazlyn. Shazlyn is a dark-skinned girl with naturally curly hair. She usually wears her hair in a curly ponytail. I wish my mom would let me wear my naturally curly texture. Key and I only wear our hair bone straight.

"I like your hair!" I complement Shazlyn.
"I like yours, it's so long! Your mom do your hair every morning?" she asks.
"Yeah, it's so irritating." I roll my eyes.
"Why? You don't like getting your hair done? Shazlyn laughs.
"Not by my mom, she's heavy-handed as fuck."
"Sometimes I wish I could wear different hairstyles," she rubs her hair.
"Your sister Yozlyn have curly hair like you too?" I ask.
"Yeah, all of us do. I have three sisters, Joslyn, Roslyn, Yozlyn, and me, Shazlyn," she explains.
"Oh, okay, I only have one big sister. Everybody calls her Key. Our names are Japanese."
"Are y'all mixed with Japanese?"
"No, but people always ask me if I'm mixed," I giggle.
"That's because you look mixed and you have a Japanese name," she giggles, looking at me like I'm crazy.
"Do your other sisters go here?" I play with my pencil.
"Roslyn and Yozlyn do, Joslyn is older. She's not in school anymore," Shazlyn explains.
"Kimiko. Take this attendance sheet to the front office for me." Mr. Jackson lays the paper on my desk.
"Can I go with her?" Shazlyn raises her hand.
"No," he answers with no hesitation.

I get up quickly so he wouldn't change his mind about me going to the office. The office runs are so fun here because this school is big.

I have to go down a few different hallways to get to the front office. Of course, I'm taking the long way through the high school side. I might run into Key or somebody I ride the bus with.

"What's up, little Key Key?" a cute boy that Key must know speaks to me.

"Hey," I smile, walking like I'm a popular kid on the high school side.

It looks bigger over here. The hallway looks wider, and they have more lockers in the hallways. Every time I come over here, I feel like a celebrity.

"Hey, Brandon!" I wave.

Brandon runs over to me and gives me a hug like he didn't see me this morning on the school bus. Brandon is Key's friend, Joanna's little brother. I think he might be in 6th or 7th grade, but I'm not sure. He's a dark-skinned cute boy with a ton of feminine ways. He may be gay, but I never asked him. All I know is he's cool as hell, and he's my friend.

"Kimiko! Hey, what you doing on this side?" Brandon smiles.

"I'm dropping this paper off to the front office."

"Oh, you must be a teacher's pet or something. You know the students teachers don't like don't ever get to run the errands," Brandon laughs at his own comment.

"I don't think I am. But he do have me run errands sometimes," I giggle.

"You saw Key and them?" I look around.

"Nah, where they at?"

"They down that hallway. Let me show you," he leads the way.

When we approach the crowd of high school kids. Key instantly notices Brandon and me.

"Look at my little sister, y'all!" she points down at me like she's proud.

"Hey, little Key," Tia waves.

"Hey."

Tia is one of Key's best friends. She's a lot shorter than Key, very pretty and skinny with braces.

"Key this is not your little sister," a tall light-skinned chubby boy jokes.

"Yes, the fuck she is, Cartier," she giggles.

"She is so pretty!" a brown-skinned girl I don't recognize reaches for my hair.

"Then why she look way better than you?" Cartier laughs.

"The same reason yo' daddy look better than you!" everybody laughs at Key's come back.

"You on your way to class?" Key asks.

"Nah, I have to take this attendance sheet to the front office," I explain.

"Brandon, you going with her?" Joanna asks.

"I can, anything to stay out of class longer," he shrugs.

Joanna is one of Key's good friends. I'm not sure if she claims her as a best friend, but they're really tight. Joanna is dark-skinned like her brother, a little shorter than Key with noticeably pretty white teeth.

"Yeah, go with her. Make sure none of these pervert little boys try anything," Key demands.

"Alright, you already know I'm not about to let nobody mess with her," Brandon rolls his eyes in a feminine way.

"Alright, Brandon, come on, we out!" I leave without saying bye.

"Dang, bye, little Key Key!" Tyrece yells.

"Bye, y'all!" I wave as Brandon and I proceed.

Every time I see Key on this side, she's around a whole bunch of people, girls and boys. Sometimes I recognize some faces, and other times I don't. It seems like so much fun on the high school side!

I can't wait until I get older! I think to myself.

As Brandon and I walk down another hallway to get to the front office, we bump into Jazz.

"Little sister!" she hugs me.

"Hey, Jazz!"

"Where you about to go?" Jazz asks with a big smile on her face.

"To the office then back to class," I explain.

"Haven't nobody been messing with you have they?" Jazz double checks.

"Nah, I have to drop this attendance sheet off," I giggle.

"Oh! Cause I was about to say!" She laughs.

"Where you about to go?" Brandon asks Jazz.

"To Ms. Smith class, I heard they had a substitute." She smiles in a sneaky way.

"For real! Oh, okay, yeah, you will fasho' see me in there too!" he laughs.

"Alright, see y'all," Jazz waves and walks off.

Jazz rides our school bus as well. I don't remember in detail how we started being cool, but that's my dog now. Jazz is older than me, too, but not as old as Key. She might be in the same grade as Brandon. Jazz is caramel-skinned, sort of tall with a really pretty big smile. She has a small gap in her top row teeth just like me and speaks in a very distinct raspy tone of voice.

"Alright, the office right down there," Brandon points.

"Okay."

"You know how to get back to your classroom from here?"

"Yeah, I'ma just take the elementary side because it's faster," I add knowing I need to hurry and get back to class.

"Alright, see you later," we split ways.

CHAPTER **TWENTY-EIGHT**

SHAZLYN LEANS AND whispers "Damn, where you go?"
"I took a long time?" I ask feeling guilty.
"Yeah," Shazlyn admits.
"I took the long way to the front office, through the high school side," I giggle bashfully.
"Dang, I wish I could have went," she smacks her lips.
"Did he say something about me being gone for too long?" I get a little nervous.
"No, but if it would have been anybody else, he would have had something to say," Shazlyn looks at me side-eye.
"Are you trying to say I'm a teacher's pet?" I look at her crazy.
"You know you're his pet," Shazlyn continues.
"I don't think so. I think he likes Angelice way better than me," I use my serious voice, unconvinced.

Twenty minutes later, the bell ring and school is over.

"Where yo' mama come and pick you up from?" Shazlyn ask.
"I ride the bus. You live out here?"
"Yeah, I don't live that far from here."
"Well, the buses this way. I'll see you later." I walk towards the door and Shazlyn and I part ways.

As I walk out the doors, I notice this dark-skinned nappy headed girl with a big stomach eyeing me, so I look back.

What the fuck is she looking at? I think to myself with a slight attitude.

"Kimiko, you catch the bus?" Angelice gasps for air like she was running around.

"Yeah, do you?"

"Yeah, I ride A20. Which one you ride?"

"I ride D13." I fix my backpack.

"Oh, okay, see ya!" She runs off laughing while a boy chases her.

Angelice is a high yellow heavy-set little girl with short ponytails. She's really nice and really smart. She's Mr. Jackson teacher's pet to me.

Why Shazlyn always thinking I'm the pet? I think to myself as I watch Angelice and a little boy play fight from a distance.

The buses usually wait for about ten to fifteen minutes until all the kids get out of class, so if you're playing for too long, you might get left, especially messing around with our bus driver Roy. He is mean as hell. He barely wants us talking on the bus as if the bus is a classroom or something. He's a tall straggly looking man and you never see him cracking a smile or being nice.

"That's why yo' teeth the biggest thing on yo' fucking face," Demetrius teases Reginald on the bus.

"Boy, shut yo' fat ass up!" Reginald comes back quick.

"Yeah, fat boy! Bite! Bite! Big Boy! Cheeseburger!" Reginald burst out loud enough for the whole bus to hear him.

The entire bus is laughing, as Key and Joanna is hyping it all up.

"Bite! Bite! Big Boy! Cheeseburger!" Key and Joanna sing together like it's a song as everybody cracks up in laughter.

"Aye, Key, you retarded!" Larry turns around crying laughing.

"Right, his fat ass always talking shit." Brandon rolls his eyes.

"Always trying to talk about somebody. Trying to bully Reginald because he's older than him," Joanna agrees.

"He tried to bully Reggie and he came back on his ass!" Key expresses and makes everybody laugh even harder.

Reginald is in the same grade as me, but he's not in my class. He's in the meanest fourth-grade teacher's class. Her name is Mrs. Beek. So many people have transferred from her class. The school stopped letting people transfer because she wouldn't have a class to teach. Demetrius is the fattest boy that rides the bus and always talking shit about somebody else. His primary people to pick with are usually younger than him, and he's in middle school.

"I would slap the shit out of him if he was talking to my little brother or sister like that," Jazz looks serious.

"You wouldn't do nothing," Dennis grabs her to play fight, and they begin to tussle.

"They are so cute," I smile and stare from the other side of the bus.

"Right," Key smiles at Jazz and Dennis obvious puppy love.

"I'm trying to get like that with you," Darnell smiles and licks his lips at Key.

Key giggles. "Like what?"

Darnell smacks his lips. "When you gone stop acting scared of me, girl?"

"Boy, ain't nobody scared of you!" Key laughs as she opens her Flaming Hot Cheetos.

Dennis and Darnell are brothers. Dennis is the oldest; he's light-skinned, very cute with an unusually thick unibrow. Darnell is light-skinned as well and cute, but a different kind of cute than his brother. If you didn't know them, you wouldn't think they were brothers because they don't resemble each other at all.

"Let me have some?" Darnell asks sitting right next to Key.
"Put your hand out, fool!" Key orders.
"I don't want the chips," Darnell corrects her.
"What you want?" Key asks confused.
"Some gum."
"Oh, I had this from earlier."
"Let me have the one you chewing on," Darnell smirks.
"Here," Key hands the gum over and he eats it.

I damn near puke in my mouth and died after being sick.

"Ugh, Darnell! That's disgusting!" I frown.
"What? That's my baby," he shoos me off.
"That's my SISTER, and I don't eat off of her," I continue.
Joanna laughs at my serious reaction.
"Dang, Key, is there something we should know about you. Your own sister don't even eat off of you," Larry teases.
"She don't eat off of nobody," Key rolls her eyes. "She thinks she's too good to eat off people. She don't eat off of my parents or nothing," Key explains.
"That don't mean she think she is too good because she don't like to eat off of people! That eating off people shit is nasty. I don't eat off of people either, Miko!" Joanna takes up for me.
"Thank you!" I feel relieved that somebody in the world understands.
"Girl, you telling me you don't eat off Brandon?" Key challenges her.
"Hell, nah!" Joanna expresses.
"Girl, bye!" Key eats her chips, unconvinced.
"Larry, am I lying?" Joanna leans forward.
"Nope!" Larry looks serious.
"Brandon, am I lying?" Joanna turns around.
"Well, both of y'all funny acting as hell then." Key stands her ground.

Joanna giggles. "Girl, you retarded for trying to make her feel bad about that!" Joanna remains on my side.

I don't get why my family tries to make me feel like an outcast because I don't like to eat off people.

That shit is nasty to me! Point. Blank. Period. I shrug my shoulders nonchalantly.

About twenty minutes later, we arrive at our bus stop location, and everybody's parents are waiting. Our bus stop is right off of 8 Mile and Mendota. My mom is always here before we arrive. Most people's parents usually are, but there are some kids who walk from the bus stop to their homes and others who just have late parents. Not my mom. She's always on time for everything. Especially for important things, she's an on-time, wake up in the morning to get a head start type of parent.

"Hey, Auntie Joyce!" Jazz, Dennis, and Darnell speak at the same time.

"Hey, y'all," Mom yells from the car window with a big smile.

Jazz walks towards a car, and Dennis and Darnell come to talk to my mom.

"Sons! How y'all doing?" Mom looks happy to see them.

"We doing good," Dennis giggles.

"Man, our bus driver is so mean!" Darnell expresses.

"Yes, he is!" Key agrees as she gets in the front seat.

"He tried to get me to sit down, and I wasn't even standing up!" Darnell jokes.

"He be tripping! Talking about how he gone make us sit down!" Key shakes her head.

"Oh, yeah, he did say that!" Dennis laughs.

"I wish that, nigga!" Darnell pauses. "I'm sorry, Auntie," Darnell stops himself and apologizes quickly for cursing.

"It's okay," Mom laughs it off.

"Alright, come on. See y'all," Dennis hints it's time to go to Darnell.

"Y'all mama here?" Mom asks.

"Nah, we walking home," Dennis scratches his head.

"Y'all live far?" Mom continues.

"Not by car," Darnell butts in, getting straight to the point.

"It's not that far, but it's not super close to walk to," Dennis explains in more detail, showing his big brother maturity.

"Get in, I'ma drop y'all off today." Mom starts the car, and they didn't think twice about jumping in.

It's so obvious my mom likes them. She probably secretly wishes they were her sons. She never forgets to periodically remind us how much she wanted all boys, and she got all girls. Just like with my Auntie Cynthia's sons, Dante and Donovan. She loves the crap out of them! Now don't get me wrong, she loves her daughters, Shanae and Shannon too, but she most definitely shows favoritism between the two in my eyes. Maybe the girls don't notice it, but Key and I know for a fact how she feels about boys. In no time we are in front of Dennis and Darnell's house. They live in a neighborhood that's a little rougher than ours, but I've seen worse.

"Thank you, Auntie!" Darnell yells while getting out of the car.

"Yeah, we appreciate it," Dennis confirms while closing the car door.

"See y'all tomorrow," Key waves.

"Those are my babies!" Mom smiles.

Yea, only if you knew what your baby Dennis wanted to do to Key. I roll my eyes in the backseat.

"You like Darnell, don't you?" I call Key's bluff.

"No..." Key giggles.

"Yes, you do, I mean, he is cute!" I admit hoping that would make her confess.

"Yeah, he is, but he's too young for me. If he was my age, Cory might have some competition," Key laughs.

"Right!" I giggle.

"Nah, he just my little boo. I just be playing with him," Key adds.

"Umm hmm!" I leave her awkward crush conversation alone. "Mama a dick sucker!"

Key hits the bed while laughing. "Exactly, she over like them, man!"

"For no reason, it's not like she know their mom or something," I continue.

"Right, she wish they were her sons so bad!" Key looks me dead in my eyes.

"That's the same thing I was thinking in the car!" I confess.

"You got some homework?" I change the topic.

"Yeah, but I'm probably going to do it Sunday." Key shrugs her shoulder.

"You know she gone ask you if you did your homework," I remind her.

"I'm just going to tell her I don't have any. It's just an easy math sheet," Key explains.

"Oh, okay, I'm about to go watch the stories." I get up to leave Key's room.

"You think she will let us go outside?" Key asks before I leave.

"I don't know, I mean it is Friday. I hope so."

"You should ask this time." Key suggests.

"I will ask after I'm done watching the stories." I continue for the door.

I thought Mom was in her room, but she's downstairs.

"Ma, you recorded the stories today?" I yell from the upstairs hallway.

"Yeah, y'all ready to watch them?" she gets up from the couch.

"Yup!" I yell.

"It was deep today!" Mom is coming up the stairs with her jug of water in her hand.

"Yesss! I can't wait!" I clap out of excitement.

After watching Bold and the Beautiful, Young and the Restless, and As the World Turn, it's noticeable to me that Key is waiting for me to ask to go outside.

"Ma, can we go outside?" I get it over with.

"Yeah, y'all can," she answers as she put the tapes back under the TV.

I follow Key to her room. "Aye, since I did you a favor, you owe me a favor," I demand.

"What you want?" Key looks confused.

"I got a bad grade on this Social Studies homework from last week that I'm supposed to have mama sign. Can you sign it?"

"Yeah, where is it?" Key responds without hesitation.

"In my bookbag, let me grab it real quick." I run to my room.

This is not Key's first time signing my mom's name on my homework. Last time I brought home a bad grade I got the shit beat out of me, so I made that the first and last time I let her see my bad grades. What's crazy is that I don't get bad grades often, hardly ever. I guess she thinks whooping us will help us understand the schoolwork. The last report card marking Key got one D, and she got a beating. She couldn't come up with anything better but to put her hands on somebody. When she told my grandparents, they ordered her the "Hooked on Phonics" program. I don't recall my mom ever helping her with using it.

"Key Wee!" Cory yells in a joking tone using my dad's nickname for Key.

Everybody is so happy to see each other because we're not allowed to come outside during the week.

"Y'all missed it the other day!" Porsha starts the gossip.

"What happened?" Key asks super interested.

"Man, that nigga' Jimbo got into a fight with this older man," Cory cuts in ecstatically.

"What older man?" Key asks in shock.

"This man he was working for," Cory explains.

"Did he win?" I ask.

"Barely!" Patricia adds her two cents, and everybody starts laughing.

"That nigga' Jimbo was swinging slow as hell!" Porsha demonstrates the fight.

"But the older man was swinging stupid as shit too!" Cory scratches his head.

"It was the weakest fight I ever saw!" Patricia sums it up.

"Right, the two little boys from the down street fight was hyper than that fight," Porsha jokes. "Cyrus and Marcus go head up stronger than that weak ass fight."

"Next time Jimbo calls his self talking shit. I'ma just say 'I'ma get little Cyrus to whoop yo ass!'" Cory jokes while everyone cracks up.

"Damn… I wish I could've seen it!" Key expresses.

"It was the funniest shit in the world!" Patricia continues to laugh.

"Who else was there?" Key asks.

"Girl, everybody and their mama!" Patricia brags, knowing Key probably feels left out.

We can't help that our mom is strict. I think in the back of my mind.

"Right, them niggas was looking retarded as hell!" Ron agrees after catching his breath from laughing so hard.

"You know if Ron was there, everybody was there!" Jena adds.

"Y'all know I be over my people's and them house sometimes!" Ron takes up for himself.

"Why yo' other brothers and sisters don't live with y'all grandparents?" Patricia asks.

"I don't know." Ron shrugs his shoulders nonchalantly.

He know he just don't want all of us knowing.

The day continues with more gossip, laughs, and trips to the corner store. Before we could notice, the streetlights are on.

"Key!" Mom calls from the front door.
"Damn, she probably about to tell us to come in," Key whispers to everyone.
"See if we can spend the night," Porsha adds while Key is walking away.
"What you think she gone say?" Porsha ask me.
"The same thing she always say," Patricia answers for me in a smart way.

About five minutes went by, and Key is running back outside.

"She just called me to see what shoes went better with her outfit." Key smiles.
"Oh, she about to go out?" Patricia asks.
"Yeah,"
"Did you see if we could come over?" Porsha asks.
"Yeah, she said y'all can spend the night." Key jumps for joy.
"We all can spend the night, she won't be there," Cory jokes.
"Shut up!" Key laughs.

CHAPTER TWENTY-NINE

"ALRIGHT Y'ALL, I'LL be back." Mom grabs her Gucci purse smelling and looking good.

"Bye, Auntie Joyce," Patricia and Porsha waves.

"Now y'all don't open the door for anybody! And don't be eating up all the food," Mom orders.

"Okay, we not." Key walks her to the door.

"Make sure you put the alarm on," Mom reminds Key.

"My mama gone! My mama gone! Work it! Work it!" I stand up, popping my booty while Patricia and Porsha laughs.

"Y'all tryna' smoke?" Key closes the door.

"Yo' daddy got some more weed?" Patricia asks excitedly.

"Yeah, girl! I went to go check earlier when my mama was getting ready," Key giggles.

Key runs downstairs to go get the weed and the papers. She's back in less than a minute. We all sit in the dining room where we usually eat and watch Key roll the weed up.

"How you learn how to roll a blunt?" Porsha asks.

"I'm a natural, the shit is just easy," Key continue to lick the paper.

"Cory taught me," Patricia adds.

"Aww... he didn't even teach me!" Porsha frowns.

"Porsha dumb butt, been and had all the weed on the floor!" Patricia teases.

"Fucking up the blunt!" I instigate.

"Right, didn't even get a chance to fuck up the rotation!" Patricia cracks up.

It took Key a little while to roll the blunt, but she finally got it. We all go out to the backyard so the smell wouldn't be in the house. Key takes the first hit like she's born to do this.

"Damn, this nigga' a pro!" Porsha hypes it up as Key passes the blunt to Patricia.

When Patricia is smoking the blunt, she makes the smoke come out of her nose. Once the blunt gets to Porsha, she hit it so hard she begins to cough.

"Damn, Porsha! Don't hit it so hard." Patricia hits Porsha on the back trying to help her catch her breath.

"Damn, bitch, don't hit ME so hard!" Porsha moves away from Patricia as Key and I are crying laughing.

"She making the shit worse," Porsha continues to smoke.

"Oh, my bad!" Patricia laughs.

"So, y'all remember that time when..." Porsha begins a new conversation.

"Puff puff give nigga'! I haven't even hit the blunt yet!" I cut Porsha off while everybody is laughing.

"Oh yeah, my bad, Mik Mik!" Porsha laughs.

"It's Friday! We ain't got no job. And we ain't got shit to do!" I joke, reciting the lines from the classic movie *Friday*.

After we finish the blunt, Porsha blurts out of nowhere.

"Y'all, what if Mr. Tate and them see us out here smoking?"

"Right, come on y'all, let's go in." Out of paranoia, Key runs into the house first and all of us rush in after her.

"Put that Eminem CD on!" I request as Key walks to the stereo.

"Which Song?" Key asks.

"Superman."

"Good lordy-wody, you must be gone off that water bottle!" Porsha blurts out with laughter, then everybody sings in their soft voices with the music.

"I think I love you, baby."
"I think I love you, too."
"I'm here to save you, girl, come be in Shady's world."
"I wanna' grow together. Let's let our love unfurl."
"You know you want me, baby."
"You know I want you, too."
"They call me Superman. I'm here to rescue you."
"I wanna' see you, girl, come be in Shady's world."
"Oh boy, you drive me crazy."

"BITCH, YOU MAKE ME HURL!" we all cry laugh at Eminem harsh lyrics.

"Yo' that shit was so fun!" Porsha reminisces dramatically about our sleepover.

"So, where y'all get the weed from?" Ron asks excitedly like he was there.

"From my daddy stash," Key giggles.

"Yeah, he be having garbage bags of weed," I add.

"Y'all gotta' bring some over to my house," Jena requests.

"Yeah, but I have to be careful. One time he noticed. Remember, Miko?" Key looks at me quickly.

"Yeah, I remember." I giggle.

"He noticed?" Patricia looks surprised.

"Yeah, he thought my mama stole some, and they got into it." Key laughs.

"Damn, how did he notice out of so much weed? All you be

grabbing is one blunt of weed, right?" Patricia looks amazed.

"That nigga' Jihod know how much is in those garbage bags," Cory adds confidently.

"Shiddd, would've fooled me," Joe laughs.

"Right!" Porsha seconds his comment.

After chit-chatting outside for a few hours, Mom calls us in early because we have school tomorrow. Usually, I would go to my room, but today I decided to stick around.

"I just got off the phone with Granny," Mom mentions as she's in the kitchen cooking.

"Oh, what was she talking about?" Key looks concerned.

"They're going to buy y'all plane tickets for next summer."

"Aww, man, I don't want to go down there. Why can't they just fly up here?" Key pouts.

"You don't want to do nothing but go across the damn street! Plus, they always fly up here." Mom catches a slight attitude.

"I want to go!" I'm sure to add my two cents in.

"Y'all won't be staying for the entire summer anyways," Mom continues.

"*I'm sure we won't,*" I respond in my head.

"It's so boring down there," Key continues to complain.

I do understand why Key feels like it's boring down there. It's not many kids in the neighborhood, especially not any black kids. I don't think I've ever seen black people down there in the area they live in. All of my grandparent's friends are white, and we don't have any other family down there. On the other hand, it's so peaceful, and I love their house. It's so modern, pretty, and clean. Granny keeps it spotless and comfy. The windows are big, and the ceilings are high. I love it out there. The resort is pretty, and the neighborhoods are much nicer than out here in the city of Detroit.

Today for recess, Mr. Jackson finally takes us outside. Every other class gets to go outside for recess every day. I don't know why he doesn't want to enjoy the last of our warmer days in late September. Shazlyn didn't come to school today, so I'm trying to see who else I want to play with.

"What's up, Kimiko!" Angelice speaks, next to her stands a tall brown-skinned boy I've seen around.
"Hey, Angelice!"
"This is my best friend, Pierre," Angelice introduces us.
"I know her!" Pierre adds.
"Yeah, I always see him, you like the tallest boy in your class." I giggle.
"Right, you are tall as hell for a fourth-grader," Angelice laughs.
"I know, my dad is really tall, too," Pierre confesses.
"You just got out here?" Pierre changes the subject quickly.
"Yeah, Mr. Jackson lame-ass finally let us out." I turn to look out at the sunny field.
"He be having y'all locked up like cage animals," Pierre laughs.
"Chill on Mr. Jackson, yo'!" Angelice takes up for her favorite teacher.
"Yeah, whatever, teacher's pet!" I tease.
"I'm not-" Angelice tries to defend herself, but I cut her off.
"Don't even lie!" I give her the side eye.
"You got it all over your face!" Pierre teases as Angelice share small laughs.
"That's why she taking up for him now," I laugh. "I wish I was in Mr. Reed's class so bad." I find Mr. Reed on the field just to stare at him.
"Why?" Angelice looks confused.

"Because he cool as hell!" Pierre answers for me.

"Exactly, and he is so cute!" I continue to stargaze at him from a distance.

"Ugh... his short self?" Angelice disagrees.

"How old are you?" Pierre asks, changing the subject.

"I'm eight. I'll be nine in November," I answer quickly.

"You still eight years old? I'm nine already," Angelice adds.

"I'm nine, too," Pierre giggles.

"You got double promoted?" Angelice asks.

"Nah, my birthday is just later in the year." I explain.

"Oh, okay..." Angelice says as if she's still confused.

"Look at Sydney and Gary." I point in their direction near the trees.

"I think they like each other." Pierre observes Gary and Sydney's playful energy.

"They go together! Y'all late!" Angelice laughs.

"You know his best friend Deontae like you!" Angelice continues to gossip.

"Oh, really, I didn't know that."

"Do you like him?" Angelice asks, noisily drooling for the answer.

"No." I give her the straight face.

"I don't know how you didn't know. Everybody know he like you." Angelice puts me on front.

"You know all the gossip, huh?" Pierre jokes giving Angelice the side eye.

"Right, she hip to all the gossip and business!" I pony off of Pierre's comment.

"Nah, y'all just late on everything," Angelice takes up for herself while grabbing a ball to play with.

"Ooo, let me see." I motion for Angelice to pass the ball to me.

"Y'all ever played 'Claps'?" I catch the ball quickly.

"No," both of them answer at the same time.

"Okay, so we usually go up to ten because no one can ever get higher than that. So, you start with one clap. Throw the ball up and clap once before you catch it. If you don't catch it, you lose. If you do catch it, you go up a number until somebody messes up." I demonstrate as I explain.

"Even if you get your claps and don't catch the ball, you lose?" Pierre asks.

"Right, if you clap five times and don't catch the ball you're out. You have to catch the ball to finish," I explain.

We aren't able to get past six because recess is over, and it is time for everybody to get back to class. As we line back up to head to class, out of nowhere, Raeshawn and Page are hardcore fist fighting in the field. Raeshawn is a little smaller than Page, but she is holding it down. Mr. Jackson and Mr. Reed break the fight up and split the girls up so they won't be near each other.

"Damn, Raeshwan, what happened?" I ask quietly so she's the only person who can hear me.

"That bitch called me ugly." Raeshawn is out of breath.

At this point, Mr. Jackson is pissed off. His entire face is red from yelling and getting the girls off of each other. His entire head looks like a red Sour Head. When we get to the classroom, everybody is unusually quiet.

"This fucking fighting will NOT be tolerated!" Mr. Jackson yells while everybody is seated.

I almost peed on myself after his outburst. I'm trying so hard to hold my laugh in. My stomach feels heavy, and my head is in my arm to hide my face. He is mad as hell, and it's so funny to me. The quiet laughs are always the funniest and the worst to hold in. My eyes are starting to tear up because I'm laughing so hard.

"Now pull out your math books!" Mr. Jackson demands.

Before we could start the lesson, Raeshawn grabs her math book and launches it at Page, and round 2 is live and in effect. They are going so hard this time all of the desk and chairs are moving on their own. Mr. Jackson can't even handle both girls at once, so he leaves to go get Mr. Reed for assistance. Less than a minute later, Mr. Jackson has Raeshawn and Mr. Reed has Page.

"Take her to your classroom until her parent gets here! I'm calling both of their god damn parents!" Mr. Jackson sounds fed up.

After the fight, everyone is grabbing their desk and chairs and placing them back in order. Deontae makes sure he places his desk and chair next to me. He thinks he is being slick, but it's so noticeable now that I know he has a crush on me.

"Dang, I didn't even know they didn't like each other," he whispers, trying to start a conversation.
"Raeshawn told me that Page called her ugly outside," I whisper.
"I know Page big ass not calling nobody ugly," Deontae giggles.
"Right," I laugh quietly.
"That was a good one on one. I don't know who won. It was a tie to me," he smiles.
"I'm happy didn't nobody get jumped or nothing because..." he stops me in the middle of my sentence.
"Because what? You would've jumped in?" he cuts me off.
"Yeah, if Raeshawn would've got jumped, I would've helped her," I continue with a straight face.
"Oh, that's your friend?" he looks confused.
"Not really, but she's cool though. I know her better than Page big self." As I fix my books on my desk trying to ignore him staring at me, he still doesn't budge. I look him dead in his face. "What?"
He giggles looking goofy. "Nothing."
Weirdo, sitting right next to me just staring. I think to myself.

PRETTY CAN BE UGLY

Now that I know he has a crush on me, everything he does is going to be weird. Even though I don't like him back, I'm not going to be mean to him. I'm used to boys having crushes on me, especially boys that I don't like. As long as they don't disrespect me or be rude, I don't see why I should be mean. Most of the little girls that are my age are mean to the boys they don't like, but that's not my personality.

CHAPTER **THIRTY**

"KIMIKO, SIT NEXT to me," Cheryl yells from the front of the bus.

"Sis, you know you don't have to sit up there with her if you don't want to," Jazz adds in a protective way.

"Yeah, I know." I let my nice side get the best of me as I walk towards the front of the bus.

"Why you sit up here?" I ask, placing my book bag in the seat.

"I don't know." She smiles happily as I sit down.

"Oh, I like sitting in the back," I confirm so she won't be surprised when I say no next time.

"Do you like being in Mr. Jackson's class?"

"It's alright. I wish I was in Mr. Reed's class, though."

"Yeah, me too! He is so cute!" She eats her chips.

"Yes, he is!" I smile at the thought of his face.

Not too long after our small talk, I could smell a light scent of pee. It has to be Cheryl because it's most definitely not me. Making sure it wasn't coming from behind me or from the other side. I turn towards the aisle where Demetrius and Reginald are talking smack and joking.

"Why you sitting up here?" Demetrius ask out of nowhere.

"Because I can," I challenge him, knowing he was going to have something smart to say.

"You need to go back to the back of the bus, Rosa Parks," he laughs at his own joke.

"You need to stop talking to me, Fat Joe." I turn from towards him.

"Ha! Fat Joe!" Reginald instigates.

"Shut up, big teeth!" Demetrius aims his jokes at Reginald.

"Shut up, Fat Joe! That's why you look like a Sloppy Joe!" Reginald jokes back.

"That's all they do is talk shit up here," I confess to Cheryl.

"All Demetrius do is pick on people younger than him." Cheryl rolls her eyes.

"What? I know you not over there talking!" Demetrius calls Cheryl out.

"Boy, shut up, ain't nobody talking to you!" Cheryl yells.

So yes, this pee smell is most definitely Cheryl. I wonder if she smells it. I mean, there's no way she can't smell it. I'm surprised I've never heard the boys joking about it because they don't have any filters. Smelling like this, I'm shocked that she even sits up here next to them.

"That's why Reggie be baking his fat ass now," she continues in a softer voice.

"Yeah, Reggie do be getting back with him." I giggle.

"I think he's cute," she smiles sneakily.

"Who?" I'm confused.

"Reggie," she confesses.

"You like him?" I ask surprisingly.

"Yeah," she blushes.

"Oh… so that's why you be sitting up here." I give her the side-eye. She giggles. "Shhh… Be quiet…"

The bus is finally at our destination, and my mom beats us here as usual. Sometimes I wish she would be a little late so we can lollygag.

When we get into the car, Fire and Desire by Rick James ft Teena Marie is playing. Even though this is old school music, I really like this song. Key likes this song, too. This Teena Marie lady can really sing! We all know the words to the duet. I know it's the beginning of the song because Rick James is confessing his wrongs. Then after his intro confession, he breaks down.

> "Remember when I used to. Looooove them and leave them."
> "That's what I used to do. Used them and abuse them."
> "Then I laid eyes on you. It was pain before pleasure."
> "That was my claim to fame. With every measure, baby."

Everybody laughs and sings.

"I wonder, was he really like that?" I ask from the back seat.

"Yes, Rick James was a mess back in the day! Him and Teena Marie used to date in real life," Mom explains like she was there.

"Really?" Key sounds surprised.

"Yup, Rick James was a freaking womanizer! He had all of the women back then." Mom shakes her head.

After our small conversation, the song is back on Rick James talking softly and confessing about how he used to be a dog. That's the queue that Teena Marie's part is up next, which is my favorite part. Teena Marie is hitting so many high-pitch notes on this song. It's almost unbelievable, and the fact that I know that they used to date just made the song that much better. In no time, shortly after the song goes off, I realize the route we are taking is not in the direction of our home.

"She can sing!" Key smiles.

"I know! Teena Marie is one of my favorite artists! People used to say we looked alike back in the day when I used to dance." Mom returns a smile.

"Oh, she's a super high yellow woman?" Key asks.

"No, she's a white woman," Mom giggles.

"You don't look white," I add from the backseat.

"That's what they used to say. It may have been my style, too. She's not a blonde hair blue-eyed white lady. She has big curly hair and everything like a mixed woman," Mom explains.

I've never seen my mom's natural texture hair because she has a perm, so I'm assuming her hair is nappy. Especially judging off my hair and how thick it is. Key has a perm, too. I think I need a perm based on how much it hurts when I'm getting my hair done. I think if I had a softer texture hair like my dad or even like my best friend, Shazlyn. I wouldn't need to get my hair straightened all the time.

I guess with all the talk about Teena Marie, my mom is in the mood to listen to Teena Marie. After Fire and Desire goes off, she changes the song to Lovergirl by Teena Marie. I've heard this one before, too. I know a lot of old school music between my mom and grandparents. I don't have much of a choice. When we ride out with my dad, though, he likes to play the new school music and the rappers that are hot now in the year 2002. We're still not at our destination, so the old school music continues. I must admit, I'd rather listen to old school music instead of her complaining. Now she's slowing the music down with Lenny Williams 'Cause I love You' playing through the speakers. This song is so funny to me. First off, it sounds like he is stuttering and singing at the same time. My mom loves this song, especially the parts when he's stuttering. But I guess that's what makes the song unique and catchy.

"Oh Oh Oh Oh Oh Oh Oh Oh Oh Oh," Mom sings. "See, he's expressing how much love he has for his lady. Y'all music express the complete opposite, nowadays!" Mom preaches, and Key finds it so funny.

"That Rick James and Teena Marie's song is not a love song!" Key defends our generation.

"It's not a love song, but it's not degrading either. And Rick James was the first person from back in the day to start that kind of sexual type of music. Promoting being a player pimp," Mom continues.

"So, who's degrading?" Key asks, already knowing the answer.

"What? I don't think I have enough hours in the day to complete that list of artist. One is Too Short, another is Lil' Jon and them. Ummm, whose else, Trick Daddy, and Trina, all of them fools! Come on now!" Mom waves her hand at Key in a playful way.

"Lil Jon is a hype artist with really good beats," Key explains.

"Whatever. To the windows to walls! To the sweat, drop down my balls! All these bitches crawl!" Mom reiterates the song while Key and I try to hold back our laughs but aren't successful. "Straight bullshit!" she continues as Key and I cry laughing.

We continue to drive towards another city, and then in no time I recognize the area. I can always tell when we're in another city because the atmosphere and the scenery changes drastically. The trees even look nicer out here, and we're not that far from Detroit. We're in Hassel Park on the way to Farmer Jack's. I think it's so stupid that we pass so many other grocery stores just to come out to this specific one.

"Now, when we get in here, don't ask for shit and don't touch shit," Mom's eyes get big, so we know her level of seriousness.

Why even bring us then, stupid bitch? I snap in my head.

"Can I stay in the car?" I ask, hoping she says yes this time.

"No." She opens her door to get out.

Ugly ass! I roll my eyes getting out of the car.

If Mom sees me pouting, that will give her a reason to whoop me into being happy. She tells us all the time to stop looking mad or take that frown off of our face, as if we're not allowed to feel any type of way outside of how she wants us to feel. Sometimes I wonder why she is so mean; her mom is not mean to her. My granny is as sweet as pie. She could have been different when Mom was younger, but I doubt it. Mom never shares stories about my granny being mean when she was a kid. Maybe Mom gets her mean ways from my granddaddy. Because he can definitely be mean when he wants to.

"Girl, did you hear about the fight?" I gossip to Shazlyn as she sits down on the grass.

"Nah, who fought?" her eyes get big out of excitement.

"Girl! Raeshawn and Page had this whole classroom rearranged yesterday. That's how hard they were going."

"Why did they fight?"

"Raeshawn said Page called her ugly during recess."

"So, they fought outside, too?"

"Yes, girl, it started outside and finished in the classroom," I giggle.

"Damn... who won?" Shazlyn gets to the point.

"They didn't fight for that long outside because Mr. Jackson and Mr. Reed broke it up. But they was rumbling in the classroom. I think it was a tie." I shrug my shoulders.

"Oh, Mr. Jackson weak ass couldn't break it up by himself, huh?" Shazlyn laughs.

"Girl, no! He had to go get Mr. Reed from his classroom next door," I laugh.

"Oh my god!" Shazlyn claps her hands out of disbelief.

"Mr. Jackson was pissed the fuck off, it was so funny! I was laughing so hard! I was crying, trying to stay quiet." I laugh from the thought of it.

"He was yelling at the classroom?"

"Yeah, like everybody was fighting or something," I explain. "Then, once it was time to get the classroom back together, Deontae made sure he put his desk next to mines." I roll my eyes.

"I noticed that! I thought Mr. Jackson had changed people's desks around. You know Deontae loves him some Kimiko," she smiles.

"Well, I just found out yesterday. How did you know?" I ask quickly.

"Girl, everybody know!" Shazlyn laughs at me.

"I swear I didn't have a clue," I laugh at myself.

"He always be looking at you and everything. You just don't be paying him no attention."

"Right, I guess I didn't notice because I'm never looking back at him!" Shazlyn and I share laughs.

"He ugly as hell," Shazlyn confesses.

"I don't think he 'Ugly as hell,' but he not cute either." I change the topic. "Look at Sydney and Gary sitting by they love tree."

"K.I.S.S.I.N.G," Shazlyn laughs, finishing my sentence.

"Every time recess comes, they are all in each other's faces," I gossip while looking at them play. Then Sydney notices and begins jogging towards us. Sydney has a light brown-skin complexion with long hair and really pretty teeth.

"What y'all over here doing?" Sydney gasps for air.

"Nothing, chilling," I respond.

"Y'all should come play with us," Sydney suggests.

"What y'all playing?" Shazlyn asks.

"Boys against girls," she smiles. "You know Deontae wants you to come play too." Sydney cheeses from ear to ear.

"I'll pass..." I fake smile back.

"Come on! Deontae is cool peoples!" Sydney tries to talk me into playing.

"You only want them to go together because you and Gary go together!" Shazlyn calls her bluff.

"Right! Gary probably told you to come over here for Deontae." I side-eye Sydney.

Sydney giggles, "Noooooo."

"Yessss!" I laugh. "I'ma play with y'all next time. Why he don't want to go with Morgan? You know, since that's your best friend. It would be like friends going with friends," I suggest.

"He don't like Morgan. She too much of a tomboy for him, she probably would beat him up!" Sydney laughs at her own joke.

CHAPTER **THIRTY-ONE**

"SO, YOU'RE NOT going to ask what's wrong?" Mom grabs Key by the collar.

"I didn't know it was something wrong," Key stutters.

What a bitch! I yell in my head.

"So, Jihod is home, and he's talking about..." Mom begins.

As she talks, I literally try to catch every car that's passing to distract me from listening to her. When she talks about my dad, it just itches my skin from the inside creeping slowly through my nails. I have a really bad feeling it's going to be a huge argument today, and I'm not looking forward to it at all.

When we pull up to the house, my dad's car is in the driveway as expected. When we get out of the car, Porsha yells from across the street, "Hey, Auntie Joyce, can Key and Miko come outside?"

"Hey, boo! Not today... they will see y'all later," Mom waves, using her fake nice voice.

Ugh, she gets on my motherfucking nerves!

As soon as I walk into the house, I speak to my dad since he's sitting right on the couch near the front door. After speaking to him, I feel guilty. I'm praying I don't get in trouble for saying "hi" since my mom likes to make it seem like when she's mad at him, everybody has to be mad at him, like it's all the girls against him. That's probably why he doesn't like being here now, and, honestly, I don't blame him. In no time, I hear my dad raise his voice at Key.

Poor Key, I feel so bad for her having to get involved in their adult problems. I try to ignore all of the noise by playing with my dolls for a few hours, but I can't concentrate with all of the chaos. I don't understand why they have to scream at the top of their lungs to get the point across. But that's my mom hyping everything up. I try to get in my own bed as it gets later in the day to take a nap or to get a head start on sleep, but that doesn't work. I can't sleep through this madness if my life depended on it.

"Maybe I can listen to some music," I say to myself.

Reaching for the open button on my stereo system. I see that my CDs aren't in the CD player.
"Damn, they must be downstairs! I am not trying to go down there," I admit aloud.

After a few minutes of contemplating, I decide to gather up all of my nerves and just run downstairs to grab the CDs. As I walk towards the stair railing, peeking downstairs to see where everybody is, they are still screaming like cats and dogs over nothing. The sun has gone down, and it's getting late. Taking a deep breath, I jog down the stairs and go straight for the stereo. I noticed that, when I got downstairs, my dad kind of lowered his voice. Immediately that made me feel a little more comfortable. It makes me think maybe he's not as mad as he sounds. Because when he gets mad, he can get really crazy and physical. He's told us plenty of stories of things he's done. And it doesn't take much to tick him off. Instead of going straight upstairs, I stop to get a glass of water in the kitchen. As soon as I begin to fill my glass with water from the refrigerator, I hear the argument getting more intense. The shattering of glass scared the shit out of me! Instead of going to see what happened, I run for the side door where I'm closest to.

"That's why I can't wait until I grow up!" tears fall slowly down my cheeks.

It is so cold outside, and it doesn't make it any better that I have on my cheetah print velvet pajama set. The top has sleeves, but the bottoms are shorts. Above the knee shorts, so my legs are out. I don't have socks or shoes, either. Hopefully, somebody notices I'm out here, and they call me in and chill out for the rest of the night. From out here, it still sounds like their going at it hardcore.

"Oh shit," I whisper.

Ron is outside playing basketball in his backyard by himself. I'm happy we have the Chain link fence that you can't see through. If we didn't, then he would see me looking dumb in my pajamas and crying in the cold.

About an hour and a half goes by, and the noise in my house is still at the same level it was at around three o clock this afternoon when we first got out of school, if not worse. Nobody probably noticed me run outside. I'm probably going to be out here all night. I really need something on my feet to help me warm up a little bit. I'm embarrassed to ask Ron for a pair of socks because I don't want him to see me like this, but I'm freezing.

Putting all of my pride aside, I yell, "Ron!"
He's looking around, but he doesn't see me. "Over here... behind the fence," I wave him down.
Ron walks toward the fence, and I meet him at the edge of the back porch.

"Why you out here?" Ron asks looking over the fence.

"My parents are arguing real bad. Do you have a pair of socks?" I answer quickly.

"Yeah, hold on."

In less than 5 minutes, he comes back out with a pair of long white socks, then he tosses them over the fence.

"Thank you!" I have never been so happy to see a pair of socks in my life.

"How long you been out here?" Ron giggles.

"It feel like all fucking night. It's been some hours now, though."

"They don't know you out here?"

"I don't know." I shrug my shoulders.

"Damn... I can hear them from over here!" Ron looks surprised.

"I know, so fucking irritating." I roll my eyes.

"So, you just gone stand out here?" Ron looks confused.

"I guess." I look off.

"You should come over my house," Ron suggests.

"Mr. and Mrs. Tate will let me come in?" I'm shocked because his grandparents aren't that friendly.

"Yeah, especially if you don't want to go back home," Ron assures.

"Okay, cool, because I don't feel like being in there." I begin climbing the fence.

While I'm climbing, I feel so stupid with these pajamas on but better to be somewhere warm and quiet than standing in the cold. Once I get half way over the fence, my shorts get stuck in between the wires on the top of the fence, which is so awkward because one leg is on Ron's side of the fence, and the other one is in the air. After wiggling my leg around for a few minutes, my velvet shorts are still stuck. Before I could even notice, my other leg slips, and I almost fall, but Ron catches me.

"My bad," I laugh.
"Damn, you never jumped a fence before?" Ron giggles.
"Yeah, but not with socks and pajamas on." I fix my shorts.

When we get inside the house, the aroma throughout the house smell just like how Ron smells when he comes outside. It's a very distinct, indescribable smell that smells pretty good. I've never smelled this specific scent, but Ron always says he doesn't smell the scent. It's very clean inside of Ron's house, and Mr. Tate is waiting for us in the living room. I'm very surprised that Mr. and Mrs. Tate would even let me come in. They seem to be more on the "boujee" side of the fence.

"Hey, Mr. Tate," I wave.
"Hey, young lady," he looks at me over his glasses he's wearing.
"Hey, Miko, you want something to drink?" Mrs. Tate comes from upstairs.
"Yes." I sit down on the couch.
"So, what's going on?" Mr. Tate puts down his newspaper.
"My parents are having a really bad argument." I speak softly.
"Do they argue a lot?"
"Sometimes when my dad is home, but this time it sounds like they probably got into a fight," I explain.
"Did you see anybody get hit or hurt?" Mr. Tate continues to interrogate me, showing his detective side.
"No, but I heard some glass break, and that's when I ran outside. I didn't see what happened."
"Have you ever seen one of your parents hit one another?" he continues.
"No."
"Maybe something fell," Mr. Tate seems less worried.
"I don't know, all I know is every time they argue, it's always super bad, and it lasts all night. It's so annoying and scary," I explain, shivering from being cold for hours.

"Here you go, sweetie." Mrs. Tate hands me a glass of water.

"Well, it shouldn't take them that long to notice you're not in the house." Mr. Tate picks his paper back up and continues to read.

I don't feel uncomfortable over Mr. and Mrs. Tate's house, but I'm hoping he's right. I don't want to spend the night over here or be over here for hours, it's already late.

"Yeah, if they take too long, I'll go over and let them know you're over here." Mrs. Tate assures in a warming tone of voice.

She seems really nice, and this is probably my first time actually seeing her face to face. I hardly ever see her entering or leaving the house when we're all outside. It's always Mr. Tate that I see leaving for work and coming home. Almost an hour goes by, and the doorbell rings. Mr. Tate goes to answer it, and I can hear my dad's voice from outside.

"Miko, your dad is here!" Mr. Tate calls for me.

"See you later." I wave Ron goodbye.

"Alright, now! Thanks again, Mr. Tate!" Dad waves Mr. Tate goodbye.

"Sneak-ko, why did you come over here?" Dad giggles, which isn't surprising he finds it funny.

"I was tired of standing outside," I respond dryly.

"Well, you could've came back into the house," he suggest sarcastically.

"I know, y'all scared me, I didn't know what happened," I continue as we walk back into the house and I noticed that one of the glass squares in the walkway door is broken.

"Where was she at?" Mom asks, looking like she got a problem.

"Over Mr. Tate and them house," Dad giggles.

"What? You was over there telling them all of our business?" Mom scolds me.

"No," I answer nervously.

No other questions were asked, and I didn't see Key in sight, so I figured the coast was clear for me to go to my safe place. I guess Mom is finished instigating Key and Dad's argument, so I run upstairs to my room. I started to go into Key's room to gossip, but it's already late and I'm tired. I'll get all of the gossip tomorrow.

CHAPTER **THIRTY-TWO**

"KIMIKO, SIT NEXT to me," Cheryl smiles, patting the seat.

Without even thinking, I sit down next to her, and as soon as I sit down, I smell a really strong pee scent again. It smells like she took a bath in a tub full of urine. I mean, one would think since it's the morning, the smell wouldn't be that bad. It's like she slept in a pissy bed and then put on her uniform and came to school. The smell is so bad I have to say something.

"You smell that?" I ask her, not wanting to be too blunt.
"Nah, I don't smell anything." She sniffs trying to smell what's closest to her.
"It smells like pee," I continue.

As we're talking about her body smell, Reginald and his older sister gets on the bus. Reginald sits in the seat directly across from Cheryl and me.

"Ugh! It smell like piss!" Reginald blurts out.
"Dog, you already know who it is," Demetrius giggles in the seat behind us.
"Man, that shit is ridiculous! She need to WASH... THE... FUCK...

UP..." Reginald over enunciates.

"Hey, quiet down!" Joe the bus driver yells from the driver seat.

"Shit, it's seven o' clock in the morning. A nigga' don't feel like smelling nothing!" Reggie continues in a lower voice.

Cheryl doesn't say anything, so I'm assuming she doesn't get that everybody is talking about her. I'm pretty sure if she thought anybody was talking about her, she would take up for herself. After about fifteen minutes goes by, we take off for Inkster. When I look towards the back of the bus, I notice Dennis and Darnell aren't here. Once we get to the end of the block, I see Dennis and Darnell cutting the corner, trying to wave the bus down before he turns down the street.

"There go Dennis and Darnell!" I stand up so the bus driver can hear me.

"Stop the bus!" Jasmine yells from the back of the bus.

Joe doesn't respond to either of our comments, as he slows the bus down and eventually comes to a stop.

"If you're not at the bus stop by 7:40 am or earlier, I can't pick you up. This is not the bus stop," he explains in an aggressive tone of voice as he closes the bus doors.

Dennis or Darnell didn't have anything to say to him; they just walked past him very quickly. But I'm sure they will have something to say once they get to the back of the bus.

"He acting like he picked them up from off the freeway or something," I comment.

"He is so irritating, mean ass," Cheryl adds.

"Damn! I had homework last night," I remember out of nowhere.

"You better copy off of somebody," Cheryl suggests.

"Shit! And nobody in my class rides this bus," I think aloud, looking around.

"I'm going to try to get as much as I can get done now." I pull my homework out of my book bag.

Of course, since I'm busy, we get to school in no time. I didn't get all of my homework done, so hopefully somebody will let me copy the rest. The first person I look for when I get to my locker is Shazlyn. Usually, she's here before me; hopefully she comes today.

"Aye, Sydney! Did you do the homework?" I yell down the hall.
"Some of it." Sydney giggles.
"Damn, me too."
"I'ma see if Morgan did hers. If she did, I'll let you copy after I'm done copying," Sydney suggests.
"Alright, cool." I feel a little relief.

About two minutes later, I see Shazlyn open her locker.

"Hey, girl, did you do your homework?" I ask in a hurry.
"Yeah,"
"Can I copy? I did most of it. I just didn't get to finish it," I explain.
"Yea, but you better hurry up. You know Mr. Jackson like to collect the homework at the beginning of class," Shazlyn warns me.
"I know, I'ma copy it out here so he won't see me." I grab the small packet from her quickly.

I hurry to my locker to copy the homework. It feel like we are dealing with drugs or something and trying not to get caught by the cops. I only have two pages to copy. I really need to hurry up because if Mr. Jackson catches me copying, both of us are in trouble.

"Come on, guys! Class is about to begin!" Mr. Jackson sticks his head out of the classroom.
"Damn," I whisper as I put both packets in between my books.
"Are you finished?" Shazlyn whispers as we walk into the class.

"Almost," I whisper back.

When we sit down, Mr. Jackson goes straight to the back of the class where his desk is. I sit down quickly to finish the end of the last page.

"Hurry up," Shazlyn whispers.

Usually, when he's at his desk, he's doing something, so I know he's not paying attention. I also know that he's getting prepared to come to the front of the class, so I try to beat him to it. My attempt is accomplished, but before I hand Shazlyn her packet, I turn around very slowly to make sure Mr. Jackson isn't looking. Shazlyn snatches the packet back quickly to put it in her folder.

We have music class today, which I'm sort of excited about. Music class is relaxing, unlike the other elective classes we have during the week. Being that Cherry Hill is a performing arts school, a lot of our other elective classes require us to bring a change of clothes or take off our shoes. I don't usually feel like doing all of that, which is why I prefer music class. The teacher has the instruments and books, and we can stay in our uniforms. On top of that, the class is mad easy.

"Kinko! NO!" I run upstairs as fast as I can. Luckily the bathroom door is the first door to the left coming up the stairs.

Running in the bathroom to lock the door for safety so that our new dog Kinko can't get in got my adrenaline rushing. We literally just got this dog, and he's already too comfortable. Who would have known a little Yorkie Terrier would be so fast and feisty. I didn't even have a clue we were going to get a dog. We just randomly pulled up to a house and bought his cute little self.

"Mik! Why you acting scared of the dog? It's a small dog!" Dad knocks on the door trying to reason with me.

"He snapped at me!" I defend myself.

"He was just trying to play with you. Stop being scary!" I can hear him walk away from the door.

I don't like it when dogs bark and chase me. It makes me feel like they want to attack me. Just like those big dogs down the street near Jena's house, always barking and growling at us like they want us for dinner.

My mom had been talking about wanting a dog for a while. I guess getting the dog around Valentine's Day was the perfect gift. As the day continue, I become more comfortable with Kinko, he's not so bad after all.

"Miko, you got a Valentine?" Key smirks, asking me in front of my dad.

"No, but I know you do, and I bet I can guess what his name is too." I size Key up and she gives me this *why the fuck would you say that* look.

Shouldn't have ever started that game! I think to myself unapologetically.

"I know you got a little boyfriend. What's his name?" Dad smiles at me

"I don't have a boyfriend," I express in a more serious tone.

"It's not a big deal if you do," he shrugs his shoulders then drops the conversation.

I'm just as confused as Key's facial expression. My mom's point of view about boys is the complete opposite. It's so weird to hear him say this. You would think my mom would be more understanding about the topic because she's a girl. *This family is so backwards*.

I'm curious to know how this conversation would've gone if mom heard him say it's not a big deal for me to have a boyfriend. Key knows not to bring up boys when my mom is around. Honestly, I don't like any boys in my class or in other classes, so I just chill and mind my own.

Mr. Jackson is letting us have a Valentine's Day party, and everybody brought their gifts for their Valentines and snacks for the party. We also have pizza, so I'm really happy. My family has ordered pizza plenty of times, but it's always extra exciting when we have it in school.

"Mr. Jackson, can we listen to the radio?" Tina asks.
"No," Mr. Jackson stuffs a piece of candy in his mouth.
"I bet Mr. Reed's class over there listening to music." Shazlyn squints her eyes.
"I know they having fun over there," I add secretly jealous.
When I look to my left and see Deontae approaching me. "Happy Valentine's Day." He hands me a huge basket of stuff.
"This is for me?" my eyes get big.
"Yeah, girl, why you think he handing it to you?" Shazlyn giggles.
"Thank you!" I blush.

Included in the bag is a big teddy bear, with two balloons tied to it, a card, some candy, a huge bag of Hot Cheetos, and a Little Bow Wow poster. I mean, I know he has a crush on me, but I wasn't expecting him to get me anything for Valentine's Day.

"Aww, he really likes you!" Shazlyn rubs it all in my face.
"Girl!" I roll my eyes, hinting for her to shut up.
"Are you going to dance with him at the dance?" Shazlyn smiles.
"I don't know," I answer quickly.

The dance is going to be so fun. Maybe I will dance with Deontae to show some gratitude for my gifts. It was nice for him to bring me something.

"Oooo, you got a gift too!" Sydney walks over slowly with her gift in her hand.

"Yeah," I giggle.

"What you get? Girl, he got you a lot of stuff!" Sydney scrambles through my basket.

"OOOO! Hot Cheetos! When you popping these boys open?" Sydney grabs the bag of Hot Cheetos.

"Not now!" I snatch the bag from her hungry hands.

"Dang stingy… okay," Sydney frowns.

"What you get?" Shazlyn asks Sydney.

"Gary bought me candy and a teddy bear," she smiles like she's on cloud nine.

A few people exchanged gifts in the class. After eating candy, gossiping, and eating pizza, it was time to go to the dance. I feel sort of under pressure because I'm trying to figure out if Deontae is going to try and dance with me or not. Shazlyn isn't making matters any better by telling me what she would do. I mean, his gift is nice, but I still don't like him in that way. He's cool. I'll talk to him and be friends, but I don't want him to be my boyfriend.

"I hope the big kids are in there!" I add as I open a piece of candy.

"You always want to hang around the big kids! Where is the dance supposed to be?" Shazlyn mumbles with a mouth full of candy.

"I know, it's because I'm used to hanging around older people and I think the gym," I explain.

Shazlyn is right. I do love hanging around kids that are a lot older than. It makes me feel cool and overall like the man of the year. Having an older sister compliments that urge. Once we get to the gym, I only see little kids. It's kind of a disappointment, but whatever. The oldest people in here are the fifth graders. When we walk into the gym, "Work It" by Missy Elliott is playing. Not too long after we post up, Shazlyn's older sister, Yozlyn, who's in the fifth grade, finds us.

"What y'all over here doing?" Yozlyn questions us.
"Just chilling," Shazlyn answers quickly.
"You bet not be dancing with no little boys," Yozlyn jokes.
"Shut up! YOU bet not be dancing with no boys!" Shazlyn defends herself.
"Yeah, whatever, I'ma tell mama!" Yozlyn continues.
"Aye look, that's the girl who was staring hard the other day." I point at the dark-skinned chubby-built girl.
"Yup, that is her ugly ass!" Shazlyn adds.
"What? Somebody was messing with y'all?" Yozlyn frowns.
"Nah, but that girl was looking at us crazy a few days ago like there was a problem." Shazlyn points as she explains.
"I'll be back." Yozlyn immediately jogs to the girl and her two friends.
"I wonder what she's going to say." We stare at the girls from a distance.
"I don't know, but if they try to jump my sister I'm running over there." Shazlyn moves side to side.
"And I'll be right behind you!" I look a Shazlyn dead in her eyes.

Yozlyn spent no more than five minutes talking to the girls then jogs back over to us.

"What you say?" Shazlyn asks in a rush as if she can't wait to hear.
"I asked her if she had a problem with y'all, and she said no."
"She didn't ask why you asked her that?" Shazlyn continues.
"Nope, I told her y'all are my little sisters and if there was to be a problem to let me know. Y'all younger and way smaller than her big ass!" Yozlyn explains standing taller than us.

"And that was it? She didn't say anything else?" Shazlyn seems surprised.

"Basically. She was talking about if there was a problem I would know and trying to get smart. I told her, 'Like I motherfucking said!'" Yozlyn laughs, making us laugh.

"Just gimme' the light! Just gimme' the light..." Sean Paul's voice sings through the big speakers.

"Ooooo, I like this song!" I begin to dance.

"You like this Jamaican song?" Shazlyn frowns as Yozlyn giggles.

"Yes! Did y'all see the video? Those girls be fooling! They dance so good!" I look at them like they're crazy.

"They was doing African dances?" Yozlyn asks.

"No, they were doing all kinds of sweet dance moves! Y'all gotta' see it! It comes on 106 and Park all the time!" I continue to brag about the Jamaican song.

"Oh, it's on the countdown?" Shazlyn double checks.

"Yeah, girl, this is the shit! Y'all tripping!" I continue to dance a little.

We didn't stay at the dance for long. By the time we get back to class, the end of the day is approaching.

CHAPTER **THIRTY-THREE**

"MIK, WHAT'S ALL of this?" Dad giggles as he digs in my Valentines basket.

He just had to be here for this shit! I try my hardest not to roll my eyes.

"Who gave this to you?" Mom asks, grabbing the card.

"This boy in my class," I nonchalantly walk off.

Mom opens the card and reads, "To my sweetheart, I hope you enjoy your gift as much as I enjoyed giving it to you."

"Aww, how sweet is this!" Mom is smiling from ear to ear. "And he wrote his own personal note at the bottom. Miko, who is this little boy?" Mom asks while closing the card.

"Just a boy in my class, I didn't even know he was getting me anything." I sit down on the couch less excited than everybody else.

"Look at this poster! It got tape on it already!" Key poses with the poster while laughing.

"Like he took it off his own wall to give it to Miko!" Mom laughs.

"Can I have some Hot Cheetos?" Key grabs the bag.

They so irritating!

"No... I haven't even opened them yet!" I frown, grabbing them from her.

"Stingy self!" Key rolls her eyes.

Yo' mama!

After everyone is done teasing me, I gather all of my things and take them to my room.

"Damn, they get on my fucking nerves," I whisper to myself once I get to my room.

I put my teddy bear on my shelf. I stick my poster of Little Bow Wow on my wall, and pop my Hot Cheetos bag open. Coincidentally, my parents are under the same roof and are not fighting. After eating my snacks and finishing my homework, I run downstairs to see what everybody is doing and why it seemed so peaceful in this broken home.

"Don't hate me! Don't hate me!" Dad does his signature dance, and that immediately warms my heart.

"Mik, come play! Key getting whopped, so it's your turn!" Dad jokes.

"Nah, it's her turn next!" Key corrects him.

"The loser gotta' give up their controller next round!" Dad announces seeming overly excited.

While Key and Dad are in the living room playing the PlayStation, Mom is sitting on the couch drinking on her White Zinfandel.

"Come here, boo, sit next to me," Mom pats the seat.

I really don't want to sit next to her because I can tell by how she looks that she's drunk and, judging from the bottle, it looks like she's only had a half of a glass. It doesn't take much for her to get drunk at all. Everybody in this house knows that, but I don't have a choice. I'm not trying to get cussed out or whooped once my dad leaves. It's weird when she acts affectionate towards me; I'm not used to it. I can accept other family members being affectionate, like Aunt Deanna or even our cousin Gwen. Every time I see them, they're hugging and kissing on me and telling me they love me. My mom never says she loves us, most of the time doesn't act like it either. My dad hardly ever says it either, but he has said it before, and he's way better at showing it than my mom.

Luckily, I don't have to sit under her for too long because daddy just beat Key in no time.

"Say it again! Say it again!" he yells as his character K.Os Key's character and wins the round.

"I'm next!" I jump up fast grabbing the controller from Key.

"Yeah, don't get too comfortable," Dad continues to talk junk.

"Whatever"

We play up to two rounds, and we're tied up. I won the first round, Dad wins the second round and whoever wins the third round keeps their controller. The night continues with fun and games and surprisingly no drama. My mom is obviously drunk off of wine and looking so stupid. She's slurring her words and moving her hands in slow motion.

Ugh, she makes me sick! I frown.

I hate when she gets drunk, but I'm happy we're not out in public. It's not that bad since we're at home and nobody can see her. I never hear my dad complain about how she acts when she's drinking. I wonder if he thinks it's cute. Or if he just doesn't care, maybe he tells her about herself in a casual way. I don't know, but if I were him, I would tell her that she needs to stop drinking, but maybe he does, and she just doesn't give a fuck. As her child, it embarrasses me, so I would think, as her husband, it would be even more embarrassing.

After we finish playing the board game "Clue", Key and I head for bed. I think my parents are coming to bed too, but I'm going to sleep with Key tonight. As I get ready to get in Key's bed, I overhear Mom coming up the stairs, yelling, "I need some dick!"

Then I hear Key burst out laughing, lying next to me.

"I thought you were asleep," I giggle.

"I was about to be," Key giggle.

"Me too. They get on my nerves, and she drunk as hell," I express with an attitude.

"She told me that they don't have a lot of sex." Key turns on her back looking at the ceiling.

"She told you that?" I double check if I heard her clearly.

"Yeah, like I give two fucks." Key giggles.

"Right. Did you give her marriage advice?" I ask sarcastically.

Key laughs, "I just be sitting there listening, looking at her like she dumb."

"I'm so happy she don't be saying stupid shit like that to me. I don't know what she expect you to say or do." I add, aggravated.

"I don't know, all I know is neither one of those motherfuckas better not call me when they get old and needy. I promise you!" Key says confidently as she rolls back over to fall asleep.

"Did Ron tell y'all how Miko snuck over to his house?" Key giggles.

"Nah! What happened?" Patricia looks overly interested.

Damn, Ron didn't even say nothing yet. Bigmouth ass!

"My parents got into a big argument, and Miko decided to leave out of nowhere to go next door," Key explains.

"Didn't nobody see you?" Porsha asks.

"No, because I left out of the back door and jumped the fence," I decide to speak for myself.

"They didn't see you go out the back either?" Patricia giggles.

"Nope," Key and I answer at the same time while Patricia and Porsha share laughs.

"And she was over there for a long ass time too!" Key exaggerates.

Girl, you don't even know how long I was over for. I decide to hold my tongue so I won't seem like I'm acting funny style.

"Was Uncle Jihod and Auntie Joyce mad?" Porsha asks.

"I don't know," I shrug my shoulders.

Then Key hops in. "Nah, they wasn't mad, but they noticed she wasn't in her room after they decided to stop arguing. Then my dad started calling her name throughout the house," Key giggles.

"That is so funny!" Patricia continues to laugh.

After Key ran her mouth about me going over Ron's house, it sort of annoyed me, so I decide to go in the house and watch a movie or something.

"You about to go in?" Porsha asks.

"Yeah, my stomach is feeling weird," I lie.

"Alright. See you tomorrow! And don't be trying to stay in the house tomorrow either!" Porsha jokes.

"Girl, you act like I'm always in the house!" I giggle.

"Sometimes you are," Patricia butts in.

"Most of the time I come outside though," I defend myself.

"Yeah, whatever!" Porsha gives me the side-eye as I walk towards my house.

I'm sure Key wants her alone time with her best friends anyways, I roll my eyes as I walk upstairs to my room. She literally tells them all of our family business. She couldn't even wait for me to tell them that story. I'm the one who left. Ron hadn't even run his mouth about it yet. Maybe he hadn't been outside though, I know sometimes Mr. and Mrs. Tate be acting strict about him coming outside too. But I get it, she really likes them and their family. She feels really comfortable with talking to them. I'm just hoping my mom leaves me alone while Key is outside because her lonely ass gets on my motherfucking nerves as well.

When I get to my room, I decide to watch a Mary-Kate and Ashley movie called "Billboard Dad." By the time the movie is over, I hear Key and Mom talking downstairs. They're probably gossiping about my dad as usual. I decide to be nosy and prove myself right, so I go downstairs.

"Yeah, they were acting crazy!" Key laughs
"Those are my babies!" Mom smiles.
"And Patricia had on these shoes called Melissa's. I want a pair too!" Key adds.
"Melissa's?" Mom frowns.
"Yeah! They look like a see-through kind of shoe with a really short heel in the back," Key describes with excitement.
"Oh, you just trying to follow Patricia," Mom adds with an attitude, totally shooting Key's request down the drain.

Key didn't even say anything after Mom's mean comment. Friends wear the same stuff all the time. Maybe Mom doesn't know that because she doesn't have any friends.
"You should ask Daddy to buy you some," I butt in trying to even the tone out.
"Yeah…" Key sounds less excited by Mom's energy.
"Before you ask him for anything, you ask me first," Mom bucks her eyes at Key.
"Can I ask him?" Key gives her a straight face because of how petty my mom is.
Mom pauses for a minute as if she has to think about it. Eventually, she decides to respond to Key's question. "Yeah, you can," she waves her hand up like she doesn't want to talk to us anymore.

After Mom made a normal conversation awkward, Key decides to leave and go upstairs to her room, and I follow.

"And they wonder why I always stay in my room." Key sits on her bed.
"I don't see how that's being a follower just because you want the same shoes as your friend." I shrug my shoulders.

"Girl, she's a fucking bitch, then want somebody to ask her first." Key frowns.

"Right, remember when she was doing that when my grandparents was here?" I ask.

"Yeah, I don't know where the fuck she get that shit from. I mean, the shit is ridiculous!" Key shakes her head out of frustration.

After having another "Hate your Parents" discussion, I decide to go back to my room. Instead of playing with my dolls, I decide to watch another Mary-Kate and Ashley movie called "Holiday in the Sun." I have so many of their movies. I can literally sit back and watch all of their movies over and over again. I just love how most of their movies are family orientated. They're more than likely loved by their parents or some sort of family member. I love their sisterly bond and, overall, the storylines are good. All of their movies have happy endings. Sometimes it gives me hope that my childhood life story will end happily. As the movie comes on, I just mesmerize over Mary-Kate and Ashley's portrayed lifestyle. I sit back in my bed, stargazing at the television, wishing and imagining how it would be to be them or one of their siblings.

"Rich, happy, carefree, and not a worry in the world," I say to myself.

"Y'all come take y'all vitamins before bed!" Mom yells from her room, messing up my daydream.

CHAPTER **THIRTY-FOUR**

"SIT, KINKO. SIT!" I point to the floor as he continues wagging his tail.

After trying to get Kinko to listen, I give up and let him follow me around. He's not quite trained yet. I reach for the cabinet to pick out what kind of cereal I want. I have three options: Honeycombs, Frosted Flakes, or Fruit Loops.

"Ummm, I want Frosted Flakes!" I quickly grab the cereal box.

Noticing the box hadn't been open yet, I remember getting cussed out about opening several boxes of cereal at once. Checking all three boxes, I see that the Fruit Loops are open.

"Damn," I whisper.

I have to eat Fruit Loops since this box is open already. The last time I opened a new box of cereal while another one was open, I damn near got the shit smacked out of me. I grab a bowl from another cabinet and made me a bowl of Fruit Loops with a slight attitude. As soon as I sit down, Kinko sits right next to me, wagging his tail.

"What, Kinko? Are you hungry?" I ask as if he's going to respond.

Instantly getting tired of his begging, I drop a couple of Fruit Loops on the floor. As soon as the small cereal hits the floor, Kinko devours them.

"Dang, Kinko! You want some dog food?" I giggle at his energy.

"Come on, let's put some dog food in your bowl." I guide him to his doggy bowl and pour him a fresh bowl of dog food with water on the side. Once I finish, he continues to watch me as if I poured the dog food for myself.

"So you don't want your food, you want my food, huh?" I giggle at Kinko's little personality.

"Yeah, that dog likes table food." Mom comes downstairs out of nowhere.

I put the dog food bag down and continue to eat my breakfast.

"Don't be giving him table food, though. I don't know why he likes table food so much," Mom continues.

Instead of telling her I already gave him some of my cereal, I decide to keep it between Kinko and me.

"It's about time for y'all to be getting y'all hair done again. You know Mr. John's will be closing," Mom scrambles around the kitchen.

"Really? Why?" I'm shocked by the news.

"I don't know, so we going to have to find y'all a new hairdresser," Mom explains.

Damn, somebody new.

"Maybe Ran can do y'all hair temporarily," Mom suggests.

"Do she hurt?" I ask.

"No, but you're tender-headed, so she might hurt to you," she smirks.

I really don't like getting my hair done because it hurts so bad, especially when I have to get my hair blow-dried. I pray our new hairstylist knows how to blow dry thick long hair.

The morning swings by, and as soon as Key wakes up, she eats, get dressed to go outside, and I'm right behind her. No one but the bright shiny sun is outside, so Key and I walk across the street to see what Patricia and Porsha are up to.

"Look at the twins! Kekoshow and Kemishe!" Tez, Patricia, and Porsha's dad teases our Japanese names.

"We do not look alike, talking about 'twins'," Key jokes back.

"Y'all both got Asian names, and y'all always dressed to impress. That's as much alike as I need!" Tez laughs, closing the door.

"What's up, Dona!" Key taps Dona on the shoulder as she comfortably goes upstairs.

"Hey, Key! Where you going? To bother my son?" Dona jokes.

"You already know she is! You know C got that on lock!" Tez brags to Dona.

Surprisingly, Betty's room door isn't closed, so I make sure I speak to her as I walk past to Patricia and Porsha's room.

"Hey, Betty," I wave.

"Hey, Miko, how you doing?" Betty asks as she sits on the edge of her bed.

"I'm doing fine," I respond.

"That's good," Betty smiles.

"Miko peeko bobeko banana fana, sike nah!" Porsha sings as I walk into the room, reminding me of her dad.

I laugh "Girl, you and, yo' daddy just alike. He just made a joke to me and Key about our names when he answered the door!"

"Where is Key?" Patricia sounds confused.

"She went into Cory's room." I sit on the bed.

"Mhmm." Patricia attitude changes instantly.

"She been going in his room a lot lately," Porsha adds with a slight attitude.

"That shit low key annoying." Patricia rolls her eyes.

Instead of taking up for Key, I choose not to say anything because I'm not over here as much as she is. What they're saying is probably true. I don't know where their attitude or funny acting ways are coming from, and I honestly don't care.

"Joyce... your girls are so beautiful!" Ran expresses in a dramatic way.
"Thank you!" Mom gives this fake smile that Key and I can only see.
"But this one right here! Got a head full of hair! Okay!" Ran bucks her eyes in a serious but joking way, pointing at me.
"Yes, Joyce, they are gorgeous, and that little one has so much pretty hair!" another woman who doesn't look familiar adds, sitting under the dryer agrees.
"Miko is Jihod twin!" Ran continues.
"Yeah, she do look just like her daddy," Mom smiles.
And I'm happy about it!

My mom is physically pretty, but the way she treats us behind closed doors makes her ugly in my eyes, so I just love it when people tell me I look just like my daddy. Ran is married to my mom's first cousin, Poochie. Poochie is my mom's cousin on my Granny's side of the family.

"Cousin Joyce! What y'all doing here?" Poochie hugs my mom after coming from upstairs.
"Getting our hair done, getting styled and profiled!" Mom jokes and seems a bit happier to see Poochie.
"Using me as sloppy seconds!" Ran butts in, giggling.

"Nah, Ran, you know it's not like that!" Mom smiles.

"Look at baby cousins Key and Miko. Hey, y'all!" Poochie waves with a big smile on his face.

"Pooch, where you headed?" Ran asks.

"To the liquor store. You want something?" Poochie turns back around.

Ran looks concerned before she starts naming her snack list, "hmm, bring me back a strawberry juice and Lays chips."

"Okay, cool. Y'all want something?" Poochie ask Key and me.

"I'll get they stuff. I'ma ride with you!" Mom hops up before Poochie leaves.

I notice Ran giving the side-eye to both of them like she knows what they're up to. A little after Mom and Poochie left, it was time for me to get in the chair. Ran is pretty good with my hair. She doesn't hurt me too badly. Ran isn't working at a salon at the moment, but she has everything she needs set up in her basement. After Ran takes forever to do my hair, I'm finally free at last, no one touching my head. She started Key's hair first, so once she was done, Key just waited on my mom to come back with the snacks, but that took longer than expected.

"Ran, can I go play with London?" I kindly ask.

"Yeah, y'all can go upstairs! Y'all don't have to ask, y'all family!" Ran assures, winking her eye.

That's nice of her to say I don't have to ask because, in my house, my mom makes us ask for every little thing. London is a couple of years younger than me, which is weird because I'm so used to being the youngest out of the crowd. She's still fun to play with, though, and Paris is her older brother. He's a couple of years older than me, and he is super fun to play with too. He always got so much energy, and he's funny as hell to me. Sometimes, London and Paris get into arguments, and it makes me feel like I have to choose whom I want to play with.

I always try to work my way around that and play with both of them.

Key came up to kick it with one of the oldest brothers, Ralph, but he's super quiet, so she eventually went back downstairs in the basement with Ran.

I know she is ready to go home! I giggle to myself.
I hope we stay over here all night, and I really hope my mom doesn't come back drunk as a skunk.

After a few hours pass by, I hear Poochie call my name from the basement. When I get to the stairs, my mom is leaning on the bottom of the staircase with a huge wet pee stain on the back of her light grey jogging pants. I can't believe this bitch peed on herself! I walk down the stairs, slowly noticing Key's straight face as London follows me.

"What's up, Miko? I think y'all getting ready to head out, pretty girl," Poochie adds, sounding sober. He doesn't sound or look drunk. I can smell the alcohol on him, but he looks fine.
Why does my mom always have to be the only one hoeing herself all the fucking time! I begin to feel the embarrassment.
"Auntie Joyce, can Miko spend the night, or can I come over y'all house?" London asks.
"Not tonight, boo, not tonight! Next time, Lay, okay," Ran answers for my mom.

I'm scared to death to get in the car with her behind the wheel. I hope somebody speaks up and drive us home. Times like these, I hate being her child. I wish my daddy was here.

CHAPTER THIRTY-FIVE

"JOYCE, YOU GONE be okay driving home?" Poochie asks.

Umm, does it look like she's okay? Am I the only one that can SEE her right now? I snap in my head.

"Yeah, Pooch, I'm good. I just need something to eat." Mom slurs her words.

"Well, you know White Castle is right around the corner," Poochie suggest.

"Yeah, I know, I'ma stop by there. We don't live that far from here anyways." Everybody is just looking at her looking dumb.

"Y'all ready?" she blinks slowly.

"Yeah, everybody waiting on you," Poochie responds softly.

As we walk out to the car, my heart is beating so fast. I'm literally scared for my life. I hope we don't get into a car accident and one of us passes away. Key is not saying anything, but I know she's scared too. Mom can barely walk straight, let alone drive a vehicle, but no one is saying anything about her obviously drunken behavior.

"Okay, y'all let me know when y'all get home," Poochie demands from the outside of the car window.

"Alright," Mom adds quickly, as she rolls the window up.

"You alright?" Key asks nervously.
"YEAH! DUMMY!" Mom yells at Key for no reason.

Now, she wouldn't have ever said that to Key if somebody else was in this car.
Fucking bitch, I hate her!

When she starts the car, she presses on the gas very lightly, so the car is moving very slowly down the street. Once we get to the corner, she stops for way longer than needed, then turns the car towards the left. The White Castle is literally around the corner from Poochie and Ran's house. We get there in no time and, most importantly, safely. Thank God!

Mom rolls down the window to try and order but becomes confused out of nowhere.

"You can start when you're ready," a woman's voice comes through the speaker loudly.

"Okay, hold on!" Mom slurs, still having trouble rolling down the window.

"I want..." Key starts to talk but immediately gets cut off.

"Shut the fuck up, Key! Stop fucking with me!" Mom points her finger in Key's face.

This lady is fucking crazy!

Mom got us out here in the hood at three o'clock in the morning, taking all day at White Castles drive thru like she's never been here before and acting like she can't press the button for the window to slide down automatically.

"Hello?" the woman speaks again.

This time my mom didn't respond. From the back seat of the car, it looks like she's reading the menu. But when she didn't respond to the woman, Key leans over to see what she's looking at while her head is turned away from Key and Mom is passed out.

"Girl, she is sleep!" Key looks nervous.

"Really?" I lean up to the front seat to see for myself. "I'm happy nobody is behind us," I add.

"Right," Key agrees.

"All of these weird ass people keep walking by though." I continue to look outside through the window at the unfamiliar neighborhood.

"I know, now, if we get kidnapped, then what?" Key has an attitude.

Key continues to tap my mom's arm really hard, trying to wake her up, but Mom isn't budging. Ten minutes in the drive-thru turned into an hour. Once the workers in White Castles notice the person in the car is not responding, the manager comes outside in his uniform, and Key gets out of the car.

"What's going on out here?" the younger black man asks in a concerned way.

"My mom is asleep and won't wake up," Key explains without telling the whole truth.

"Are you sure she's sleeping?" the guy looks nervous.

"Yeah, she's still breathing," Key assures him.

"Does she usually sleep this hard?" the guy continues.

"No, she's drunk," Key gives in.

"Oh, okay, that explains everything. I'm going to try to wake her up." The guy walks over to the driver's window.

The guy taps and shakes my mom, and about five minutes later, another car pulls up.

"Yeah, she's not waking up, and we can't leave this car in our drive-thru because of other customers, so I'm going to have to call the police. Hopefully, by the time they get here, she will be sobered up. Y'all know how the police are. It will be a while before they show up. But y'all will be fine. We will be watching y'all through the cameras until they get here." the guy sounds confident.

"Okay, thank you," Key nods her head.

"No problem." The guy walks away and signals for the car behind us to go around our car.

The daylight is peeking through and Mom is still slumped at the White Castle drive-thru. Ever since we've been here, Mom hasn't moved a little bit. Key keeps checking her nose to see if she feels her breathing.

Another hour goes by, and when I try tapping Mom, she pulls away, as if she wants me to leave her alone. When she yanked from me, it made Key and me jump because she hadn't moved all night. Time went by and by, and finally, the police pulls up. When they pull into the parking lot, they park right next to us. Both of the officers are black men, so that's comforting. One goes to the passenger's window to talk to Key, and the other officer walks to the driver window to try to wake my mom up.

The officer on Key's side speaks first. "Are you okay?"

"Yeah," Key answers quickly.

"Ma'am, wake up, this is Officer Bryant speaking!" he flashes a flashlight in her face.

Mom's head moves to the other side, and her eyes open slowly but surely.

"Ma'am! What's her name?" the officer asks Key.

"Joyce Lewis."

"Mrs. Lewis, wake up!" he continues to flash the light in her face.

Mom is still passed out sleep.

"Does she do this often?" the other officer asks Key.

"No, this is the first time," Key tells half of the truth. This is the first time she's fallen asleep at a restaurant drive-thru. It's not the first time she's fallen asleep behind the wheel.

After about thirty minutes of interrogating, the police called the ambulance for my mom since she's not waking up and they had Key call my dad.

I hope she's okay. I mean I don't like her but I would hate to see something bad happen to her.

It took my dad no time to get to the White Castle. When my dad gets out of the car it looks like he's been up. It's early in the morning and he's doesn't look sleepy at all.

"Hello sir, are you Jihod Lewis?" the officer aggressively asks.

"Yes sir, I am" Dad reply confidently.

"And your wife is Joyce Lewis, these are your daughter correct?" the officer confirms.

"Correct" Dad stands tall as he listens.

"Your wife fell asleep at the wheel about four am this morning in the parking lot," the officer explains.

"What?" Dad sounds disappointed.

"Yes, were you aware of the amount of alcohol intake she had last night?" the officer asks.

"I sure didn't officer. I wouldn't had let her drive under those conditions if I had known" Dad speaks clearly.

"Right now she's still extremely intoxicated. She won't wake up, so were going to have to take her to the hospital."

Dad takes a deep breath "Okay, which hospital are y'all going to be taking her to?"

"She'll be going up to Sinai Grace Hospital"

"Alright, well thank you officer. Come on y'all." Dad cuts the conversation short. I know how much he hates the police.

After dad signs a couple of forms the ambulance people gave to him, I can tell he is ready to go.

"You should try getting her signed into a program, this isn't a good look." The officer adds.

"Yea, okay, thanks!" Dad walks us off quickly.

"Fuck you." Dad says sternly so only Key and I can hear as we get into the car.

Key and I are cracking up at my dad side comment he made at the police.

Dad giggles "What's funny?"

"You" Key laughs

"Fuck the police. Hoe ass motherfuckas, suggesting some shit. Talking about 'it's not a good look', nigga I know how it look. I'm the one married to the motherfucka!" Dad goes on as we continue to laugh.

"I can't believe she didn't wake up," I shake my head in the back seat.

"Me either, that shit is ridiculous," Dad changes his tone of voice for assurance.

"We thought she was just playing at first." Key giggles.

Dad buss out laughing "Y'all thought she was playing?"

"I didn't. I was hoping she wasn't dead," I add.

Now Dad is laughing so hard nothing but silence is coming out of his mouth.

"I thought she was reading the menu that whole time." Key continues to laugh at daddy laughter.

After dad wipes his tears from his face from laughing so hard he adds, "Y'all crazy man. I'm just happy nothing happened to y'all. She had y'all over here in this rough ass neighborhood late as hell."

"We was over Poochie and Ran house yesterday. We wasn't far from they house," Key explains.

"I'm surprised they let her leave like that." Dad shakes his head.

"Everybody always do! Like y'all don't see that she can barely walk, let alone, drive. I mean she had pee on the back of her pants for Christ sake," I show my frustration because I know my dad is cool.

Dad can't hold his laugh in from my comment.

"Right, I was low key scared. It was crack heads and people walking past. I was happy when the White Castle manager said they would watch us on the cameras," Key giggles.

"Yea, but Joyce gotta do better. We all grown, that shit not safe for her to be out here like that with y'all," Dad admits.

I wonder if he's going to talk to her. Probably not, and if he does, she most likely won't listen because he's no angel himself. I overthink as I look out the window.

CHAPTER **THIRTY-SIX**

"I DON'T CARE!" Dovonna yells at Ms. Walker.

"Well, I don't either!" Ms. Walker yells back standing in front of the class.

Dovonna gets out of her seat and walks out of the classroom as normal.

She is always so bad in school. I've never seen her parents come to talk with Ms. Walker. I wonder, does she have parents or maybe I just haven't seen them come in yet.

"I don't know what to do with a child who is barely here and when she is, she's acting disrespectful and rude," Ms. Walker speaks aloud so the whole class can hear.

Ms. Walker is my fifth-grade teacher. She's tall, light-skinned with short hair. She's nice for the most part, especially to her favorite students — she's one to show extreme favoritism, and it's hard for her to hide it. It's so obvious who her favorite students are. I wonder if the other students feel bad or unequally treated. I notice because I'm used to being a teacher's pet, but I don't think I'm in Ms. Walker's favorite pick. If so, I think I'm at the end of her list. Ms. Walker's favorite students are Pierre, Angelice, Nessa, Javonte, and maybe I come last.

It's weird because I'm close friends with all of them, so maybe that's why I feel like I'm in her favorite group, but I know I don't come before them. It doesn't bother me though or make me jealous of my friends. She likes Nessa and Angelice so much that their desk sits in the back of the classroom next to hers, overseeing the entire classroom, while everybody else's desks are facing toward the board. I call those seats the "Golden Seats." My best friend Shazlyn from fourth grade didn't end up coming back to Cherry Hill Performing Arts for fifth grade. I'm glad I made other friends outside of her, so I would know other people this year.

Every Friday, we have recess after Social Studies, and everybody goes into their own friend groups. Usually, it's me, Javonte, Pierre, Nessa, Angelice, and sometimes Patrice.

"That little girl is so ugly!" Javonte jokes.
"And bad as hell!" Pierre adds.
"Shit, if I acted like that in school my mama would be whooping my ass from Monday all the way through Sunday," I joke, in a serious way.
"Right! Girl, my ass would've been sore as hell, I wouldn't of been able to walk," Patrice laughs.
"Her mama probably don't care about her. She be coming to school looking raggedy as hell," Angelice giggles, which makes everybody else laugh except for me.

I didn't express how I feel about her comment since everybody thought it was funny. But in my mind, no one knows what she goes through at home or if she even has a home. People think I have the best life and that I'm so spoiled because my mom keeps Key and me nicely groomed. But what they don't know is what happens behind closed doors. How I hate going home and how much I hate being around my own mom 90 percent of the time, how my family is mentally fucked up and how often I wish I was another person other than myself.

Instead of laughing with the crowd, I change the subject.

"Y'all know Spirit Week is coming up. Do y'all know what y'all wearing?"

"Girl, I don't! You know what you wearing?" Nessa asks.

"I've been trying to plan it. I know there is pajama day, twin day, jersey day, and two other days," I explain.

"Pierre, you want to be my twin on Twin Day?" Angelice asks.

"Yeah, I don't care," he shrugs his shoulders.

"How is he going to be your twin?" Javonte asks.

"He doesn't have to wear anything girly. We can wear the same colors or something," Angelice explains.

"Oooo, Kimiko, you should be my twin!" Nessa suggests.

"Okay, that's cool!" I agree.

"I wanted her to be my twin!" Javonte gives me a flirty smile.

"No, you didn't," I smack my lips.

"Yes, I did, you can get some straight back braids like me and everything," Javonte continues as everyone cracks up at his joke.

"My mama braid too tight! I am not letting her braid my hair!" the thought of my mom's braiding makes me shiver.

"I can tell my mama to do your hair. All I have to say is 'Ma braid my girlfriend's hair.' She would do it too," he smiles confidently.

"He is lying!" Nessa calls his bluff.

"Right, his mama would probably be like, 'What girlfriend?'" Angelice bursts out in laughter.

"No, she wouldn't, she would be like 'Aww, she is so pretty. Okay, I'll do it!" Javonte tries to sound like a girl.

"His mama do look young, though!" Patrice laughs.

"She is... I'm telling y'all," Javonte giggles, sticking to his story.

After the small talk, recess is over, and not too long after, the end of the day is finally here. As I get my stuff out of my locker, I see Nessa coming towards me.

"Girl, so do you go with Javonte?"

"No, why?" I play with my hair.

"Because he did call you his girlfriend earlier and you didn't say you weren't his girlfriend. You know he likes you!" Nessa continues.

"Yeah, I know... he is cute too! That's why I didn't say anything," I giggle. "Had to let it sit."

"Yeah, girl, y'all should go together! You want me to tell him you like him too?" Nessa asks.

"No!" I giggle.

"Why not?" Nessa looks confused.

"Because... he probably already know!" I make up something real quick trying to ignore my shy side.

"But you never told him before," Nessa laughs.

"I will... I will... it's not a rush. He will be here tomorrow," I rush the topic, hoping Nessa drops the pressure ball.

"Well, you better hurry up before one of those other girls from another class tries to get him." Nessa looks me dead in the eyes.

"Girl, I'm not worried. If so, then whatever, I don't care." I roll my eyes as we walk outside to the yellow buses.

Today I'm sitting in the back with the big dogs. Key and all of her friends are conversing, being loud and cracking jokes. It's hot on the bus today, so almost all of the windows are down.

"Can I have a bag of Hot Cheetos?" I ask Key because I see she bought four for a dollar.

"No..." Key frowns and swooshes me away.

"Girl, why you so mean to her?" Joanna hops in. "Here you go, Miko, you can have one of mine."

"Thank you," I give her a light smile.

"Do you want some juice?" Larry offers.

"Yeah, thanks!"

"You're welcome." Larry turns back around from in front of me.

I like Larry; he is cool as hell. He's kind of on the quiet side but, still be in the mix as well. After I'm done with my chips and juice, I finish off my snack feast with a Snickers bar. I just love chocolate bars; they do something good to my soul. When I finish, I didn't have anywhere to put my trash, so I dump it all out of the window, like usual. This time wasn't the best time to litter because a police car is literally the next car behind the school bus. As soon as the litter flies from the window, the police immediately pulls the school bus over. My heart feels like it's thumping a hundred miles per hours. I'm all the way in the back of the bus, so I can't hear the conversation the police and Joe are having. They didn't talk for long before the bus driver, Joe speaks.

"I don't know who littered on this freeway, but I know somebody know who did it! Whoever threw all of that trash out of the window come to the front of the bus right now!" Joe yells so everybody on the bus can hear him.

I scoot down in my seat quickly. "It wasn't me."

Everybody who's sitting in the back knows it was me who littered, but no one snitched on me. After about ten minutes of no one confessing, Joe speaks again.

"If somebody don't confess, we're going to sit here all damn day, and y'all parents will have to come to pick y'all up from this freeway!" Joe yells again as all of the kids sigh and complain.

After about thirty minutes went by, Joe goes to talk to the policeman for a short moment then comes back to speak.

"Matter of fact, y'all parents won't need to come pick y'all up from this freeway. They will have to pick y'all up from the jail cell!" Joe looks as serious as a heart attack.

"Aww, man! I'm not trying to go to jail! Who did it?" Reginald cries out from the front of the bus.

After he said the jail thing, it made me get a little nervous. Plus, we've been sitting here for almost forty-five minutes to an hour now, which made me believe they were really going to keep us. I know I'm going to get in trouble, but my mom will be even madder if she has to come pick us up from jail. As I contemplate and shiver with fear, I gather everything that's in me and raise my hand very slowly from the back of the bus.

"Come to the front!" Joe yells.

When I peek at the aisle towards the front of the bus, it resembles a movie I've seen before. Where everyone is waiting and staring quietly. Everyone's head is turned towards the back of the bus trying to see who caused all of the drama. I didn't think we would be here for this long. I thought the police would probably give the bus driver a ticket or something and let us leave. It feels like we've spent the entire day here already.

I look around, scared out of my mind. I don't know if I'm going to jail or what's going to happen. No one around me is consoling me or making me feel like everything will be okay. Instead, everybody is looking at me like they feel sorry for me, which is making all of the matter ten times worse. I begin walking toward the front of the bus very slowly. If you couldn't see my feet, you would have thought that they were chained together like a prisoner. When I finally get to the front of the bus, the white policeman kneels down to talk to me.

"Now, Ms. Lady, did you know littering is against the law and that you could have gotten the bus driver a ticket?" the policeman speaks clearly.

I just shake my head.

"What took you so long to come up here?" Joe asks with an attitude.

"I was scared."

"Well, you're not going to jail, but you have to promise me you won't litter again," the policeman smiles.

"Okay, I promise." I speak in a lower tone voice.

"Alright, Mr. Joe, thank you for your cooperation." The policeman pokes his hand out at Joe for a handshake.

"No problem, officer." Joe shakes his hand.

Once the policeman leaves the bus, Joe sits back down in the driver seat to start the yellow bus.

"You know I'm telling yo' mama, right?" Joe assures. "You can go sit back down now."

Damn, I'm going to get in trouble! I should of known his hating ass would tell.

We get to our destination faster than usual, and everybody's parents are here. I've never seen so many cars here at once.

I should try to sneak past him.

When all the bigger kids got up, I try to maneuver behind and between them to hide myself. As we get closer to the front, Joe notices me.

"Hey, Miko! Sit down." He signals at me.

So I stop and do as I'm told. Once everybody is off the bus, Joe goes to talk to my mom. I feel like I want to piss on myself. I'm so scared shitless, I just want to run away for the night. He was only outside talking to her for less than five minutes, and then he calls me off the bus.

"I'm sorry, Joe, this won't be happening again," Mom apologizes to Joe politely.

"Come on." Mom changes her voice tone towards me.

When we get in the car, Mom doesn't speak to Key, and she doesn't say much to me.

"When we get to the house, go to your room and take off all of your clothes," Mom orders looking me dead in my eyes.

The drive home was as quick as a snap of a finger. My room feels cold and unfamiliar as I wait for mommy dearest to come in with her belt and big eyes.

"That's why I don't like her ugly ass now," I speak quietly to myself as tears fall slowly down my face and my naked body trembles.

Mom storms in the room out of nowhere and orders me to lie on my stomach. I thought about running, but I changed my mind quickly out of straight fear. Once I lay on my stomach, she begins to lash my butt over and over again. After several whips on the butt, she moves to my legs as I squirm and scream for my life.

"Stop fucking moving!" Mom screams as she continues with the lashing.

CHAPTER **THIRTY-SEVEN**

"AND GUESS WHAT the motherfucka said?" Mom asks Key overly animated.

"What?" Key asks less excited.

"By who? As if we're not married!" Mom is hyped up.

"Really?" she got Key's attention now.

"Yes! Can you believe that shit!" Mom bites into her apple.

"What did you say?" Key slightly giggles.

"By YOU! Dumbass!" Mom rolls her eyes.

"Miko, you're not going to be the youngest anymore!" Key teases.

"Damn, I wanted to tell her!" Mom catches a quick attitude.

"Oh, my bad." Key pauses, looking a little embarrassed.

"Y'all having another baby?" I take a quick guess.

"Yup, you're going to have a little brother," Mom smiles like she's in heaven at the thought of a little boy being in the family.

"Oh, it's a boy?" I jump for joy.

"It's too early to know, but I'm praying for a boy." Mom crosses her fingers.

Yeah, I'm sure you are.

It's not surprising that she hopes she's pregnant with a boy. Mom makes it her business to tell us frequently that she wishes we were boys and how she always wanted all boys. Sometimes she even goes on to tell us what her dream boy names are. That's probably a big part of the reason she's so mean to us. I decide to leave the dining room after she made that annoying comment about the baby being a boy. It would be fun to have a little brother, but I honestly don't care what the gender of the baby is. A few minutes after I get to my room, I see Key go into her room.

"She kills me with the boy talk," I start the conversation.
"Yeah, she talking about if it's a boy she's going to name him Kelli," Key adds.
"Good for fucking her." I do a fake round of applause.
"I still don't understand why she has to tell me everything they talk about," Key frowns.
"Right, she was telling you what my daddy said too?" I ask.
"Yeah, she said when she told him she was pregnant, he asked her by who," Key giggles.
"Wow, that's crazy! She was mad?" I laugh.
"Yeah, she was wondering why he would say that," Key explains.
"Probably because he's barely here." I laugh at my own comment. "What you want it to be?" I smirk.
"I really don't give two fucks," Key scratches her head.
"The way they argue, I wonder when they find time to fuck."
Key burst out in laughter. "Probably that time when she was yelling, "I NEED SOME DICK," Key continues to laugh.
"Key!" Mom calls from downstairs.
"Huhhh… she gets on my fucking nerve. Damn," Key complains to me right before going downstairs to see what Mom wants

I'm really surprised that my parents are having another child. More than half of the time, they act like they hate each other. I'm about to be ten years old, and they're about to have another baby. This baby is about to be way younger than us. I'm already five years younger than Key. If I was any younger, I probably wouldn't be able to hang with the big kids, and that would hurt me to the core.

After playing with my American Girl Dolls and reading their books, I notice Key hadn't been back upstairs to her room, so I go downstairs to see what she is doing. When I get downstairs, nobody is there, but I hear voices coming from the basement. I walk to the basement, and there they are talking and doing each other's nails. My mom has her own nail collection. She used to work in a nail shop, so she has her own personal booth. The nail booth has lights and wheels on it, and all of the nail utensils one needs to professionally get the nail job done. She also has nail accessories and anything you can think of dealing with nails and nail equipment. Mom has naturally long nails, sometimes she goes to the nail shop, but most of the time, she'll sit back and do them herself or coach Key through the process because Key likes doing hair and nails.

"Can I have some acrylic on my nails?" I ask nicely, walking down the basement stairs.
"Nah, not yet, Mik. When you get to middle school, you can," Mom answers while doing Key's nails.
"Okay, cool, that's just next year. I'll be in the 6th grade!" I did a little dance to express my happiness.

After mom is done doing Key's nails, I'm up next. Even though I can't get acrylic, I still enjoy getting my nails filed, polished, and painted a pretty color.
Ring... Ring...
"Key grab the phone real quick! If it's your grandparents, don't tell them about what we discussed earlier," Mom reminds Key.

Mom makes it clear not to tell people our business all the time. I guess she doesn't think we caught on by now. She gets so mad at the smallest things; it makes me paranoid to say anything to anybody about our business. Once Key is done talking on the phone, she hands it over to me.

"Hey," I speak into the phone.

"Hey, boo, how are you?" Granny speaks softly.

"I'm good. What you doing?" I ask sitting in the nail chair.

"Just finished dinner and dessert. What are you doing?"

Dang I wish I was over her house. I think to myself. "Waiting to get my nails done." I look at Mom monitoring every word I speak.

"Okay, what color are you going to get?" Granny asks.

"Umm, maybe a shiny pink or I don't know whatever color my mom has," I explain.

"She has a lot of colors, doesn't she?" Granny giggles.

"Yeah. For the next report card marking, if I get a 4.0, can you buy me another American Doll?" I ask, changing the topic.

"How many do you have already, Mickey?" Granny asks, sounding a little annoyed by my American Doll obsession.

"Only four."

"ONLY?" Granddaddy yells from the background. "Mickey, four is a lot, you don't think so?" Granny asks.

"Well, there's like ten of them altogether. I wanted Molly next for getting a good report card." I emphasize the report card part.

"Okay, well, if you get all A's, you can get Molly," Granny replies before being interrupted by Granddaddy. "Here go, Granddaddy." I hear Granny give Granddaddy the phone.

"Mickey?" Granddaddy's baritone voice sizzle through the phone.

"Huh?" I answer dryly, feeling like he was about to say something smart.

"Do you know those American Girl Dolls cost two to three hundred dollars a piece?" Granddaddy asks sarcastically. "Plus, those accessories you like and extra outfits cost like fifty to a hundred dollars."

"Yeah, that's why I ask for one as a reward, if I get all A's on my next report card," I explain again.

"Well, I guess if you get a perfect report card, we can get the American Girl Doll for you," Granddaddy gives in.

"Okay, I'm going to do my best to get a 4.0." I get excited.

"Okay, honey, what y'all over there doing?" Granddaddy asks.

"Doing nails."

"Joyce doing y'all nails?"

"Yeah."

"Alright, well, call us back later." Granddaddy ends the conversation.

"Okay."

"Love you," Granddaddy adds before hanging up.

"Love you too... bye." I hang up.

"They didn't ask to speak to me?" Mom looks bothered.

"Nope." I put the basement phone back on the charger.

Mom squints her eyes but tries to hide it by continuing with doing Key's nails.

Out of nowhere, we hear the side door open, and everybody automatically knows it's my dad. Instantly, the vibe and mood in the basement switches. It's only awkward because my mom makes it awkward between everybody.

"What's up, y'all?" Dad walks downstairs with a large black garbage bag.

"Hey," Key speaks quickly.

"Hey, Da!" I smile, but Mom doesn't speak at all.

"What y'all doing?" Dad sits down.

"I'm getting my nails polished yellow." As I engage in the conversation, Mom yanks my finger, probably signaling for me to shut up.

"Ooo, that should be pretty!" Dad replies.

By Mom yanking my finger, I assume that mean, stop being so nice. I can't help that I miss my daddy. Since she calls herself having an attitude with him, we have to be mad at him too. It just gets on my fucking nerve! It makes me just want to seclude myself from this entire family. Always having to say something to somebody, always having to look this way and go that way and be on the hush. It's so aggravating, that's why I don't like being here now! Every chance I get to spend the night over somebody's house, I take it and run with it. I miss being able to go over my grandparent's house. Thank god we still have Big Mama's house to go over.

Surprisingly, Key went upstairs a little after Dad walked through the door. I say surprisingly because usually she would be ordered to stick around and start an argument with him. Soon after Mom is done with my nails, I head upstairs to see what Key is doing because I don't want to have to referee WWE between Mom and Dad either.

When I walk into Key's room, she has Aaliyah playing through her speakers.
"What you in here doing?"
"Trying to stay as far away from them as possible." Key picks at her face in the mirror.
"Right, Mom got mad when I was talking to Daddy," I giggle.
"What she do?"
"I was just having small talk with him when she was finishing my nails, and she yanked my hand while I was talking."
"Were you moving?" Key tries to rationalize for Mom.
"No, I wasn't turned around or anything. She's just a jealous bitch. She don't want anybody to talk to him because she mad. Like, girl, get the fuck over it." I express my frustration to Key per usual.
"She lucky I didn't tell him she beat me for littering," I continue.
"She told you not to tell him you got a whooping?" Key asks.
"Yeah, she threatened me about it. Talking about if I tell him she's going to fuck me up,"
"I can't believe you got a whooping for that anyway. Okay, what you did far as getting the school bus pulled over by the police was bad, but she could of put you on punishment or something for that," Key explains.
"Right, it's not like she doesn't litter. Everybody litters sometimes; I just didn't notice the cops were right behind us," I defend myself.
"And I don't see how you didn't catch the cops were behind us. You were sitting in, like, the last row on the bus by the big window."

Key giggles.

"I know… so stupid!" I shake my head.

"But she still overdid it with the whooping shit," Key confesses.

"Yeah, every little chance she get, she take advantage of putting her hands on us." I gaze off in deep thought.

"She know that was bold, that's why she told you not to tell him," Key adds.

"It's almost like she hate us. That's why I can't wait until I get older." I daydream about me as an adult.

"Girl, neither one of those motherfuckas better not ask me for shit when I get older," Key looks me dead in my eyes to show her seriousness.

"If my dad knew how she treated us he would probably defend us," I add.

"He wouldn't do shit. And if he did say something, they would get into an argument. He would leave for days, and you would be getting your ass beat to next week." Key shrugs her shoulders. "No problems solved," Key continues as if she's certain of her assumption.

"Yeah, you probably right. You want to watch a movie?"

"Yeah, but I don't feel like watching Mary-Kate and Ashley," Key laughs.

"Me either, I'm in the mood to watch Menace II Society," I smirk knowing she would want to watch it.

"Ooo, yeah that's a good one! I'm down!" Key smiles

I love my Mary-Kate and Ashley movies but I also love my hood movies too. I feel like I can relate to both kinds of movies in different ways. After watching *Menace II Society* and *Next Friday*, I decide to go to my favorite territory, my room. There's just so much to do in here. I don't know if I want to play with my Barbie dolls, play with my American Girl Dolls, read my American Girl Doll books, play my Xbox, play other games, or just watch a movie. While I decide on what I want to do. I hear Kinko scratching at my bedroom door.

"Hey, Kinko!" I rub on his head.

Kinko doesn't scare me anymore. It took me a while to get used to him because he has so much energy. I think that's what scared me at first, his hyper personality. Anytime somebody knocks on the door, he's barking ready to get in protection mode. He's a small Yorky Terrier, but his energy and protective personality is as tough as a Pit Bull. It's funny because Kinko actually likes playing around with our girl Pit Bull, Keila, in the backyard. Keila is a light brown Pit Bull. She has eyes to match her top fur and a white stomach. She's our outside dog, aka watchdog. Daddy brought her home a few weeks ago, and she's a pretty chill dog. Instead of playing with my toys in my room, I decide to show Kinko some attention and play with him instead.

CHAPTER **THIRTY- EIGHT**

"HEY, JOYCE BOO!" Uncle Bomma speaks in his country accent.

"What's up, Uncle Bomma! How you doing?" Mom returns a smile.

"Nothing much, just got off work. Need to ease my mind, you know how life can get." Uncle Bomma sits on the couch. Uncle Bomma is one of my Granny's brothers out of the four.

106 & Park is on, so my full attention is on the television. I didn't even turn around to speak to Uncle Bomma, but I could tell it's him by his distinct country accent. Mom and Uncle Bomma are having a conversation then out of nowhere, an awkward, quick silent pause comes about, and I hear some plastic being passed. They're behind me so I can't see exactly what happened, but I'm sure my mom probably passed him a bag of weed. Uncle Bomma comes over every now and then to grab a bag from my mom. It seems like she gets a tinkle of joy in her eyes when she gets to do stuff like that. It probably reminds her of the days when she didn't have children and could do whatever she wanted—the old times when she could run the streets with my dad.

Meanwhile, I'm amazed at the Beenie Man video King of the Dancehall. The way these women are dancing and rolling their bodies to this reggae beat makes me want to get up and mimic them. The video is in black and white, and they're having a dance competition during the entire video. All of the women are dressed differently and doing all kinds of moves I've never seen before. I low key love these kinds of songs with the Jamaican vibes. When a song like this makes the countdown or is popular enough to get some radio play, I have to suck it in. Reggae music is not a very popular kind of genre here in Detroit, but I have a strong liking to it when I hear it. I love dancing; I love watching people dance and dancing seems to be a big thing in the Jamaican culture. I wish I had more personal access to the culture, but unfortunately, I don't.

When Uncle Bomma leaves, it's more than obvious that Mom is in a good mood, so she starts a conversation with Key about when she was younger. Thank God Key is in the kitchen area because I wouldn't be able to watch my music videos in peace. Only about ten minutes goes by, and Key navigates her way to the living room where I'm watching T.V.

"Damn!" I think instantly. I can easily go upstairs and watch T.V in my parents' room, but the experience is different down here. Watching T.V on the huge T.V screen makes the videos look better.

"But yeah, Trevor used to be my favorite cousin!" Mom smiles.
"Whose son is he again?" Key asks.
"That's Uncle Chi's son," Mom responds.
"Oh, why we don't ever see Trevor around?" Key continues.
"Remember I told you he passed away a long time ago? He got murdered," Mom explains.
"Oh yeah, did the killer ever get caught?" Key asks.
"Nope, not that anybody knows of." Mom looks kind of sad.
"Dang, you always be talking about him. I know that hurt your feelings when he died," Key continues.
"Yeah, I still hurt to this day. It's fucked up. He was a good guy, you know," Mom speaks softly.

Who gives a mother fuck! Y'all need to go back to the other room, shit! I can't even hear the song! I cuss both of them out in my head.

"Y'all used to be doing everything together?" Key continues.

"Yeah, outside of being family, he was like my best friend. It's hard losing a best friend at a young age," Mom continues.

Why the fuck is Key acting so interested in this conversation? Damn! Stop asking her questions! Stop prolonging the conversation!

"Yup, that's the way the cookie crumbled." Mom moves around in her seat awkwardly.

"Look at R. Kelly looking smooth," Key giggles at the video on T.V.

"And you already know that! He's the ladies man of the century," Mom adds.

"Now, look at Mr. Biggz' old self still making music," I joke.

"You know they did this as a continuation for those Kelly Price songs Mr. Biggz featured in?" Mom explains.

"Yeah, Mr. Biggz played Kelly Price god daddy or uncle or something and R. Kelly was her cheating boyfriend," Key explains.

"That was pretty neat how they did that with the whole storyline thing," Mom bobs her head to the song.

"See, that's why he said, 'Don't I know you from somewhere a long time ago?'" I laugh.

"Right, and R. Kelly talking about 'Nah Nah, I don't think so.'" Mom giggles.

"Now I think y'all better leave this place..." Mom sings.

"Cause I'm about to catch a case..." Key and I join in.

Recess is so fun today. Ms. Walker has been gone for more than a few minutes, and everybody is joking around and playing.

"That's why yo' ponytails as long as my pinky fingers!" Denzel points his pinky up as the class roars in laughter.

"Boy, shut yo' Arthur-looking ass up!" Angelice claps back.

"Girl, you shut yo' fat ass up!" Denzel fixes his glasses.

"Boy, shut the fuck up before I knock your glasses off your face!" Angelice laughs with everybody else.

Right before Denzel responded back, Ms. Walker walks back into a classroom of 5th graders that are crowded around each other.

"Do it, BITCH!" Denzel gets mad.

"WHAT YOU CALL ME?" Angelice steps back and hits him in his face, and they are fighting for no more than a few seconds because people are getting in between them. Ms. Walker is pulling them away from each other. Javontae is getting roughed up in the middle of the fight, trying to break it up. Then the fight is finally over.

"I LEAVE FOR 4 FUCKING MINUTES, AND THIS IS WHAT Y'ALL ARE DOING?" Ms. Walker yells to the top of her lungs.

"She was!" Denzel tries to talk in between his tears.

"SHUT UP!" Ms. Walker cuts him off, then she inhales and exhales to calm herself down.

"Now you should know better than to be hitting on a girl!" Ms. Walker continues.

"SHE HIT ME FIRST!" Denzel defends himself.

"I don't care!" Ms. Walker hits the desk.

"Right, you hitting on a girl. I should," Javontae jumps in the conversation like the troublemaker he can be at times.

"Javontae, please!" Ms. Walker stops him in his tracks.

"You two come with me. I'm taking y'all to the front office!" Ms. Walker guides them out of the classroom door.

"And everybody stay in your seats until I get back! Don't walk, don't talk, don't do anything until I get back!" Ms. Walker speaks firmly as she walks out of the door.

As soon as she leaves, everybody starts to gossip quietly.

"Damn, I can't believe a roasting session just got real," I gossip to Patrice.

"I know, Angelice beat him up," Patrice giggles.

"If he would've put his hands on you, I would've put this move down on him." Javontae demonstrates a karate move he learned in karate class.

"Boy, sit down." Patrice laughs.

"I'm for real!" Javontae looks me dead in my eyes.

"He just happy about his karate class," I whisper to Patrice.

"What just happened?" Nessa runs over to my desk and leans down because her desk is by the teacher's desk.

"Girl, you didn't see the fight?" I laugh aloud.

"Girl, barely!" Nessa jogs back to her seat because she hears Ms. Walker's heels clapping against the hallway floor.

When Ms. Walker gets back to the classroom, she seems to be stressed out. The class gets quiet as soon as she steps through the door. When she gets to her desk, she lays her head on her desk as if she isn't feeling good.

"Everybody take your math books out and start on chapter five," Ms. Walker demands in a lower tone voice.

About ten minutes into chapter five, I hear whispers from the back of the classroom. Ms. Walker is talking to Nessa and Pierre in the back. That's nothing new, though, Ms. Walker always talks privately with her favorite students, which is irritating to me, but I can't control whom she favors. I just wish I knew what they are talking about. Their mumbling behind my back is itching at my skin. I want to know what they're talking about so bad, but I'm too prideful to ask Pierre or Nessa about the gossip. I don't want them to think I care.

Today, everybody is scrambling around for the baby shower. There are so many games, decorations, and people at once. One thing I am happy to see we have is hella' food. On top of that, I'm geeked up because my grandparents are in town. That's the only time my parents act like they have some sense. Things are always better when they are in town. And of course, my Granny did most of the cooking, so the food is about to be so good!

I've never seen so much pink at once in my life! Pink is everywhere from the front door to the back of the hall. Mom wasn't too stoked about the gender of the baby. But hey, what can we say. Girls rule the world over here. Mom decided the baby's name is going to be Keoako (Kee-oak-ko), another Japanese name. My dad was very vocal about him wanting a chance to name one of us, but Mom didn't let it happen. She didn't even let him put in on the middle name, which I don't understand because she swears she hates girls. One would think she would have let him name all of us. I never got a chance to hear what his suggestion was. We would probably have ghetto names if it were up to him. Maybe it was a good idea for her to control our names.

My mom has so much help with the shower, so I'm just walking around, acting like I'm busy. After the men carried the heavy stuff in, all of the men leave soon after.

"Granddaddy, where you going?" I ask, staring up at his extremely tall face.

"Probably over Sunny's until the shower is over. I'll be back."

"Why you not staying?"

"Because men don't go to baby showers, it's just for the women." He giggles.

"Is my dad staying?" I ask, confused.

"I don't know, he may." Granddaddy sounds as confused as me.

"I'ma go ask him." I jog off to find Dad quickly while everyone is setting up.

"Da! You leaving too?"

"I don't know. I probably should, though," he smiles.

"Because all the other men are," I add.

He giggles. "I know... I forgot they only invited women. I don't know if I want to be here with a whole bunch of women." He looks around like he's just realizing where he is.

"Yo' granddaddy leaving too?" He asks quickly.

"Yeah," I nod my head.

After having a short conversation with Dad, I sit back and admire the decorations and the work everybody put in. I see familiar faces walking through the door, so I'm guessing the baby shower is about start.

"Mickey!" Granny calls.
"Huh?" I look towards her direction.
"Bring your mama's hat over!"
"Where is it?" I look around.
"Behind you!" Granny points in the direction the hat is in.

Behind me, I see a huge hat with all kinds of things on it. There are bows, ribbons, letters, glitter, sequins, and just a lot of other bouncy gadgets flopping and popping out. I pick it up like it's a creature I've never seen before.

"Come on, Mickey!" Granny rushes me.

I run to Granny with this ridiculous hat in my hand.

"Don't flip it like that, you're going to make the eyeballs come off!" Granny grabs the hat from me. After Granny makes sure everything is on the hat. She places it on my mom's head. My mom is already tall, and this tall hat with all this crap on it is making her even taller. She's already big and pregnant. What a way to make her feel and look better.

"Oh my god! I know I look crazy!" Mom laughs at herself as everyone is surrounding her.

"No, you don't, Joyce! You look gorg, just gorg!" Shalonda tries to make Mom feel better.

"Why do she have to wear that hat?" I'm still confused.

"Because she's the pregnant lady, and the pregnant lady has to wear the silly hat," Irene teases, doing a silly dance.

"Shut up, Irene!" Mom jumps in.

"What? I'm just answering the pretty girl's question!" Irene burst out in laughter.

In about fifteen to twenty minutes, people are rolling in. The food is hot and ready, and the games are about to begin. My dad ended up staying and sitting next to my mom towards the front of the hall, while Tina and Shalonda host the baby shower. Granny and Aunt Joan are helping with serving food and snacks. Our other friends and family like Aunt Lora, Aunt Deana, Aunt Von, and Irene are helping with games and fun. I'm sitting with Raven and Micha, Tina's daughters. Key is over there sitting with cousins her age, Breana, and Amanda. The first game we play is a tissue game. The object of the game is to take an estimated guess of how big my mom's belly is by measuring it with the tissue. And whoever's tissue length comes closest to her exact bump size wins a prize. Ran ended up winning this game and received some candles and a gift card.

We play more games as the late people arrive with gifts and try to catch up with the flow. Towards the end of the shower, we open gifts and cards to give thanks to people who showed love for baby Keoako. The shower seems like it's lasting forever. By the time we get home, it is dark outside. Uncle Tedrick and his wife Sandy are here visiting since my grandparents are in town. After Uncle Tedrick help with bringing gifts and decorations in with the guys, they head back to Lansing. We literally only see them when my grandparents come to town. Once they leave, everybody is helping with putting stuff together and cleaning up. Granddaddy is building the crib they bought. It looks like it's going to be a nice big wooden crib.

Once Granddaddy finally takes a break, he sits on the couch to relax, then I flop next to him and begin to play with his earlobe.

"Mickey, what's wrong with you?" he sounds a little aggravated which is hilarious to me.

"What?" I giggle acting oblivious to what he's talking about.

"You want to play with my ears, and you see I'm trying to put this crib together," he frowns as he complains.

"But you taking a break. I wanted to play with Granny's arms, but I think she's cleaning up," I try to reason with him.

"Play with her arms?" he sounds agitated.

"Yeah, to squeeze her arm fat." I smile as I continue to play with his earlobe fat.

"Her fat?" he chuckles.

"She has a fat fetish!" Mom jokes.

"A fat fetish! You like fat people?" Granddaddy laughs at me.

"No!" I answer quickly without thinking.

"Yes, she do! Her first boyfriend was a little chubby boy in pre-school!" Key teases.

"Boyfriend?" Granddaddy says the word "boyfriend" like it's a foreign word.

Mom plays off Key's joke. "Little Nicholas Mendoza. He was too cute with his long pretty ponytail," Mom giggles.

"Why don't you go play with somebody else's ears? Key got some fat earlobes, doesn't she?" Granddaddy giggles.

"No! She can't play with my ears!" Key shut that suggestion down quickly.

I try to change the subject because they are irritating me. "I think my tooth is loose." I put my other hand in my mouth.

"Really? Finally! Y'all kids lose teeth late around here!" Mom expresses.

"I think you started losing teeth around five years old, Joyce," Granny adds.

"Right, that's when you suppose to start losing teeth. Key didn't start losing her teeth until she was like nine years old. Miko is ten years old and just now about to lose her first tooth," Mom explains.

"And I'm still pulling teeth out. That is so annoying!" Key rolls her eyes.

"Right, and you about to be sixteen years old. Damn!" Dad comes out of nowhere, making everybody laugh.

Family bonding is the best time! Everybody is chilling, relaxing, and kicking it—no one arguing over unnecessary things that don't matter. Granddaddy is not being mean to Granny for no apparent reason. Everybody is just enjoying everybody's company. I love this feeling with the family. I feel at home; I feel love, happiness, and joy, which is not a usual feeling, so I have to soak it up while it last.

CHAPTER **THIRTY-NINE**

AFTER A FEW yanks and pulls, my other front tooth is finally out. I look so silly with my two front teeth missing. *I wonder if Javontae will still like me,* I think to myself as I drop both teeth in a small plastic bag and place it under my pillow. Key's long legs are taking up damn near my entire twin bed. She sleeps in my room when my Grandparents are in town, and they sleep in her room. I'm low key embarrassed to go to school snaggletooth like this.

"What? Why you acting like that?" Key notices something is wrong.

"You real big in this bed, for one." I catch a small attitude since she wants to be nosy.

Key interrupts my sentence with laughter.

"And for two, they about to fry me at school for being snagga' tooth." I cover my face in both of my hands.

"Girl, all the little kids are snagga' tooth. Who you think is going to say something about you?" Key flops her head up from her pillow.

"I don't know, Reggie, Demetrius, people in my class, people in other classes," I stutter, throwing out random names.

"Girl, Reggie big teeth butt better not say anything. Demetrius with his fat bite bite big boy cheeseburger looking ass. The people in your class, teeth are probably big as hell too. Trust me, it's not that big of a deal." Key lay back down, and we both fall eventually asleep.

The next morning comes so fast, and I'm excited to see how much the "Tooth Fairy" left me for two teeth. Under my pillow is fifteen dollars. "Yes," I whisper to myself. Key is already up getting ready for school, which is weird because I'm always the first to get dressed in the morning for school. Granny is up too. I can tell from the sweet aroma coming from the kitchen. Granny always cooks us breakfast in the morning, no matter if we have school or if it's the weekend.

Key comes in my room with her red jersey on and jeans.

"Oh yeah, I forgot this week is spirit week!" I play with my money in the bed.

"Yeah, girl, today is jersey day!" Key poses.

"Mama already picked out your jersey outfit." Key grabs my outfit from my closet to show me.

"Oh, this is cute!" I check out my blue and silver jersey from my bed.

"You got some money last night?" Key asks.

"Yup, fifteen dollaaasss." I pop my booty with too much energy in a playful doggy style position.

"Girl!" Key laughs.

"And you know they gone come in here talking about a "Tooth Fairy" in a minute." I give Key a fake serious look.

She burst out with laughter "Right."

I don't believe in the "Tooth Fairy," but I never tell my parents or my grandparents. I don't believe in any of the mythical characters like Santa Clause and The Easter Bunny. I don't ever make a big deal out of it because it's not a big deal to me. Plus, I don't' want to take the fun out of it for them.

I'm praying my mom listens to my hairstyle request this morning. I just want a simple side ponytail. After I'm done with brushing my teeth and taking a shower, it is time to face reality.

"Ma, can I have a side ponytail today?" I ask desperately.

"Yeah, and that blue and silver hat goes good with your outfit too!" Mom is still accessorizing my outfit.

"Good, I want to take all the attention off of my mouth," I confess.

Mom burst out with laughter, "Why, boo?"

"Because I don't have any teeth in the front of my mouth," I add in an "obviously" tone of voice.

"Well, how much did the Tooth Fairy leave you?" Granny comes downstairs.

"Fifteen dollars," I answer the question they already know the answer to.

"Oh… that's good!" Mom tries to geek it up.

"I'm just going to try to say as less as possible today in school," I add before Key cuts me off.

"She still talking about being snagga' tooth." Key walks in the dining room.

"Yeah," Mom giggles.

"All little kids lose their teeth, Mickey. It's normal." Granny tries to make me feel better.

"What's wrong?" Granddaddy comes out of nowhere.

Aww shit, I huff and puff. *Here he go.*

"Mickey is embarrassed about her teeth being missing," Granny explains.

"Well, your adult teeth have to grow in somehow." Granddaddy frowns at me.

"I know," I respond with a straight face.

"Well, what is there to be embarrassed about?" Granddaddy snaps back.

Oh my god… who asked you to join the conversation? I hold back my smart comment. *He so motherfucking irritating. I'm the one with the missing teeth.* I just ignore his last question.

After everybody put their five cents in about my missing teeth, breakfast is finally ready, and everybody is getting ready to eat before Dad drops us off at the bus stop. This type of stuff is so fun to me. I don't think my mom has ever cooked a full breakfast for us this early in the morning.

"Miko, why you chewing like that?" Dad asks, but I just stay quiet. "What's wrong?" he asks again

"She said she's trying to say less as possible today," Granny intrudes.

"Why? Because of her teeth?" Dad laughs.

"Yeah," I whisper.

"She said she think people are going to talk about her at school," Key adds.

See, I'ma start laying her shit out on the table too!

"And if they do, just say something about them." Dad shrugs his shoulders.

"Right, that's what I said," Key agrees.

"I mean, little kids be ugly as hell!" Dad bites his bacon as Granddaddy snickers at his joke.

"No one is going to talk about you at school, Miko," Granddaddy adds in a serious tone as if he's for sure.

And how do you know?

As everybody goes on and on about my teeth, I just sit back and block everybody out. At this point, everybody seated at this table is getting on my last nerve. Soon after, the small talk is over, the early breakfast is finished, and it is time for us to go to school.

"Alright, y'all ready?" Dad puts his shoes on.

"Yeah," I answer, less excited.

"Yeah, been ready!" Key adds with a huge smile on her face.

"Oh, y'all ready with y'all jerseys on for jersey day!" Dad sings jokingly.

"Let me take a picture of y'all on the stairs real quick!" Mom grabs her disposable camera.

"Joyce, you're gonna make them late!" Granddaddy adds as if it's the end of the world.

"Come on y'all real quick, real quick." Mom shoo us towards the stairs ignoring Granddaddy's comment.

Key takes like three solo pictures. Then I take about three solo pictures. Then Key and I take some pictures together and pose differently as the camera flashes like the paparazzi. After pictures, we finally head towards the car. On the way to the bus stop, Dad turns down the music.

"Aye, Miko, if kids tease you at school about your teeth, just look at their ugly ass face and pick something to joke about." Key is cracking up in the front seat.

"I'm for real. You can talk about their big ass nose, their big ass teeth, their nappy ass hair. Anything!" Dad giggles as he preaches.

"I'm serious, Mik, don't let them motherfuckas talk about you. You crack on they ass back! They used to try and talk about me when I was younger. Talk about how small and skinny I was. I used to have to tell them motherfuckas off! Like if you don't get yo' dweedle dumb-looking ass from out my face!" Dad goes on as Key and I die laughing.

"Better shut that hot tamale breath the fuck up before you kill us all!" Dad continues with his rant.

Dad tells the funniest stories about his childhood and stories in general. He always expresses himself so boldly and honestly. He never starts his story off like "once upon a time," but he captures your attention as if he's about to tell a fictional story. That's what makes his stories interesting because they're true, real-life stories.

From what my dad explains, he had it pretty rough after his father died. They went from not wanting anything to growing out of clothes they still had to wear. It was hard for Big Mama to raise three children on her own with one income, especially when she was used to having support from her drug-dealing husband. My dad told us how one time, his shoes got too small for his feet to fit and how he had to walk on the back of them like flip flops. And people would tease him, which lead to baking competitions and, eventually, fights. Then he confessed how, as he got older and the humiliation became unbearable, he turned to the streets at a young age and started getting money the fast way and was able to buy himself better clothes and shoes and was able to help Big Mama with bills.

These kinds of stories humble me and make me feel so thankful that I don't have to go through stuff like that. After the storytelling, we arrive at the bus stop sooner than expected.

"Alright, y'all have a good day!" Dad turns towards us as we get out of the car.

"Snagga' tooth snagga' tooth!" Dilaneo sticks his tongue out.
"Shut up, big teeth boy!" I tease in return.
"At least I got teeth," Dilaneo smiles big and wide.
"At least I got teeth, ha ha," I mimic him. "At least I'm not ugly!" I let him finish his remarks to my hand as I walk away.

It's weird because he usually doesn't even talk to me. Out of all people, I wouldn't have ever thought he would be the one to say something about my teeth. Angelice and Denzel are back from suspension, and everything is back to normal. Almost everybody in my class has their jerseys on today. Even Ms. Walker has her jersey on. I'm surprised to see her with a jersey on because she seems to be a real girly girl. I didn't think she would celebrate this day for spirit week. There are a few people who didn't wear jerseys today. I'm guessing because they forgot about it or because they didn't have jerseys to wear.

Once recess comes around, Nessa, Angelice, Patrice, Pierre, Javontae, and I gather around Ms. Walker's desk for some gossiping.

"Did I win the fight?" Angelice asks in a low tone of voice.

"Girl, yes!" Patrice burst out in laughter.

"I didn't see the fight, but when I walked in, I saw you pounding his face." Ms. Walker giggles.

"You really think we would've sat back and let that nerd beat you up?" Javontae gives Angelice this funny stare.

"It was so many people in the way I couldn't even see." Nessa smacks her lips.

"Girl, you retarded." I laugh at Nessa.

"I'm glad you whooped his butt. He needed to learn how to talk to people. They told me what happened," Ms. Walker continues.

"Yeah, he just out of the blue got mad over some jokes." Angelice shrugs her shoulders.

"Has he said anything to you today?" I ask.

"No," Angelice frowns.

"He better not say anything to her," Pierre adds with a straight face.

"This time he gone get jumped," Patrice jokes, making everybody laugh.

The end of the day finally comes and Pierre stops me out of nowhere by my locker.

"Here you go." He hands me a piece of paper that's nicely folded. "Read it later." He didn't wait for me to respond or ask any questions. He just continues to walk towards the yellow school buses.

Not really thinking about it too hard, I throw the piece of paper in my book bag.

"Where we about to go?" I ask from the back seat of the car.

"To the grocery store," Mom responds.

"Can you drop me off with Granny and Granddaddy?" I ask, knowing the answer.

"No! Don't ask me that dumb shit no more!" Mom's eyes get big.

Ugly ass hoe! I roll my eyes discreetly.

When we get to the grocery store, we follow Mom around the store without saying anything. We're not allowed to ask for nothing, so I decide to read Pierre's letter.

"What's that?" Key asks.

"A letter Pierre gave me after school."

"Is he gay?" Key asks.

"No," I answer quickly.

"How do you know?" Key challenges me.

"Because he's my friend! Plus, I think he might have a crush on me on the low." I shrug my shoulders.

"What make you think he like you?" Key looks at me not convinced at all.

"I don't know. It's just that weird feeling that you get when you know somebody might like you." I block her out as I begin to read this full-page letter.

"Dang, that's a whole page!" Key goes out of her way to look at the letter.

Kimiko,

So, I know we've been best friends for like two years now, but I think I like you more than just a friend. It's weird writing this because I have never had a crush on one of my friends and especially my best friend. I've been keeping this to myself for so long because I don't know how you feel about me, and I don't want to make things weird. I don't want to lose you as a friend, either. I know you and Javontae have a thing for each other, and he's my best friend too. I don't want to seem like I'm trying to come in between y'all or between y'all relationship. I just was tired of holding this in...

"See! I told you he like me!" I clap my hands once for confirmation. "I freaking knew it!"

"That's a love letter?" Key giggles.

"Yeah."

"Let me read it!" Key snatches the paper with no hesitation.

"Dang, thirsty!" I frown.

"Awww!" Key over exaggerates as she reads the letter.

"What?" Mom notices our excitement behind her.

Aww shit, what is this bitch about to say?

"Pierre wrote Miko a love letter!" Key explains in a playful way because she knows Mom is not as hard on me about the boyfriend thing.

"Who?" Mom frowns.

"You know Pierre, my friend Passion's little brother." Key tries to help her remember.

"Oh, he's in your class, right?" Mom asks looking at me with comforting eyes.

"Yeah."

"Maybe little Pierre not gay after all." Key adds.

"Why would you think he was gay?" Mom giggles.

"He's just a little feminine, that's all." Key shrugs her shoulders.

"Well, he has an older sister, and his mom is probably raising them by herself. So that's two women in the household and no father figure. But I'm just assuming. I don't know. That could be a general reason for his feminine ways. You know Bruce was feminine growing up, and everybody used to think he was going to be gay, but he's not," Mom voices her opinion.

"Right, he's married with children and everything." Key nods her head as if Mom made a good point.

"And him and Paulette have all boys. And they get in their asses too!" Mom laughs at the thought of Bruce and Paulette strict parenting.

PRETTY CAN BE UGLY

"Right, I be feeling bad for them," I add, thinking about how hard I've seen them be on the boys.

"But they all bad though!" Key giggles.

"Yeah, they are bad as hell, but they are my boys. I love Lanz and them!" Mom admits with a huge smile on her face.

She be so quick to express her love for somebody else's children, especially somebody else's sons. She wanted baby Koko to be a boy so bad. That's what she get for being so mean to us. Boom! Another girl for your ass! Happy fucking Birthday!

After going down a few more cold aisles, we have finally finished grocery shopping. When we get to the lines, every single line is long, and everybody's shopping cart is full of food.

"Your daughters are so beautiful!" a random woman walking past compliments Key and me.

"Thank you!" Mom smiles.

People are always telling us how pretty we are. It doesn't matter where we are. When we're around family, our relatives are always complimenting us. When we're out in public, strangers compliment us as well. It doesn't make me feel good or happy because it's just something I'm used to hearing all of the time.

CHAPTER **FORTY**

"SO, YOU DON'T know what a dick is?" I'm looking at Nessa like she's been sleeping under a rock for her whole ten years of life. Ignorant to the fact that everybody doesn't hang around older people in their neighborhood like me.

"No…" she looks clueless.

"Oh my god, you are so lame! You don't ever cuss or nothing. Say bitch," I challenge Nessa.

"Why?" Nessa giggles.

"Just say it, man." I smack my lips.

"Bitch." Nessa shrugs her shoulders.

"Okay, good job, welcome to first grade." I give her a silent round of applause. "How you gone be my twin on twin day and never even cuss before?" I continue to tease.

"Girl, it's not even that big of a deal," Nessa laughs.

"How about Pierre wrote me a love letter," I whisper changing the subject.

"What?" Nessa yells in her outside voice.

"Shsssh!" I calm her down.

"Oh, my bad," Nessa whispers. "What did it say?" I got Nessa's full attention.

"It was a full-page letter. It said a whole bunch of stuff." I make a long story short.

"Let me read it." Nessa smiles holding her hand out.

"I left it at home."

"So, what he say? He told you he like you, didn't he?" Nessa continues to dig for more details.

"Yeah, basically, and he was saying how he didn't want to mess up me and Javontae's relationship because that is his best friend too," I explain.

"Right… that's crazy… Javontae would probably be so mad if y'all went together. His crush and his best friend," Nessa begins speculating.

"Yeah, but I don't like him in that way." I put an end to her assumptions.

"So, what you gone say to him?" Nessa pressures me.

"I don't know…"

"Aye, did you see that new boy in Ms. Darget's class?" Nessa changes the topic.

"Nah, what's his name?" I ask.

"I don't know, but he is fine as hell, girl!" Nessa claps her hands out of excitement.

I giggle. "How do he look?"

"He is high yellow, tall, with light brown hair and light brown eyes," Nessa describes the young boy.

"Are y'all talking about my brother?" Alontae's nosy self butts in out of nowhere.

"Nah, I don't think so." Nessa looks at him up and down like it's a problem.

Alontae is the new boy in our class. He's tall, high yellow with jet-black naturally curly hair and kind of funny looking.

"Does he have a straight to the back curly ponytail like mine?" Alontae turns around to show his perfect black curls that his black ponytail holder is keeping together.

"Yeah, but he doesn't look like you." Nessa looks confused.

"Yeah, I know, he's my twin brother though!" Alontae has a goofy smile on his face showing his buckteeth loud and proud.

"His name is Davontae, and it rhymes with my name Alontae,"

"So, y'all are twins that don't look alike?" Nessa asks as if it's clicking now.

"Yeah, we're fraternal twins." Alontae bobs his head.

"That means we are fraternal twins today then, bitch!" Nessa yells, and we burst out in laughter while Alontae looks confused.

The school day goes by sort of fast. I'm so happy Pierre didn't ask me about the letter. He's not acting strange or anything which makes me happy. I was hoping that he wouldn't be awkward today. I'm nervous to tell him that I don't like him in that way because I don't want to hurt his feelings. Hopefully, he gets the picture if I never act like I like him and just eventually bury it in the dirt.

Sitting here in this cold hospital room is so annoying. My granddaddy is knocked out, and I don't see how he can sleep in this uncomfortable room. We've been here all day. I'm ready to go.

"Granddaddy," I tap him several times trying to wake him up.

"Huh?" a snore comes through his nose as he pops up.

"Can I have some change for a candy bar?" I ask politely.

"A candy bar?" Granddaddy frowns like he's never heard of a candy bar before.

"Yeah."

"What kind of candy bar?" he reaches in his pants pockets for change.

"A Snickers." I stand up with my hand out.

"Here," he pours more than enough silver change in my hands.

When I get to the vending machine to insert my change, Granddaddy yells "Get me one too!"

"You want a Snickers?" I confirm so I won't get cussed out for getting the wrong thing.

"Yeah, a Snickers bar." Granddaddy takes off his hat.

Soon as I get back to our seats, I hand Granddaddy his Snickers and Granny comes into the waiting room filled with joy.

"She's here! Baby Keoako is here!" Granny smiles from ear to ear.

"Well shh… finally!" Granddaddy chuckles after stopping himself from saying the word "shit," which is pretty funny every time he does it.

"Right, it feels like we've been out here forever!" I complain with Granddaddy.

"Key cut the umbilical cord," Granny adds as we walk to the room to meet the baby.

"Where is Jihod?" Granddaddy frowns but more so in a serious way. Not his friendly frown.

"I don't know, we tried to get in touch with him. I think Key paged him," Granny explains.

"That's ridiculous, can't even make it to his own child birthday. I don't know why Joyce deal with his sorry ass in the first place." Granddaddy looks fed up.

"Okay, Jim," Granny tries to calm him down in a nice way.

When we get inside the room, Mom looks crazier than ever. Her hair is everywhere. She looks like she just jumped out of a tornado storm. At the same time, she looks filled with joy as she stares into baby Keoako eyes.

"Meet baby Keoako," Granny smiles.

"Keoako… (KE-OAK-KO)" Granddaddy repeats the name with a warm smile across his face. "She looks like a little Asian baby, doesn't she?" Granddaddy chuckle as he observes the baby.

Yeah, her nickname can be Koko. "Mom smiles warmly."

"She look just like Mickey when she was a newborn." Granny gets teary eyed.

"Mickey, look at your baby sister." Granddaddy moves his tall body out of the way so I can see her.

"You see her?" Mom asks looking like she's going to shed a tear too.

I smile and nod "Yeah. She so small."

"You have to be a good big sister and watch over her." Mom looks at me.

"Alright," I touch baby Koko's hand.

Baby Koko isn't even a month old yet, and Mom is already drunk as a skunk. It's like she couldn't wait to tilt that bottle over. Of course, she's drinking her Sutter Home White Zinfandel. She let us taste the wine before, and it tastes very sweet to me. I don't see how she gets so drunk off something that's not even that strong. Plus, the amount that she's been drinking is so little, but I can tell she's way past her limit.

My Grandparents left to go back to North Carolina a few weeks ago. They know how she gets when she's drinking too, but I've never seen or heard about them saying anything about her low tolerance. It's like no one says anything about it as if it's okay or normal. Anytime we're at a family get together and the adults are drinking, no one ever gets as drunk as she gets. I have never seen any other adults blinking slowly, can't walk, laid out on the ground, or just being sloppy drunk. Both of my Grandparents' sides of the family like to drink, but they don't get like her. I'm happy we're at home today though, but I still hate it when she gets like this.

Koko is screaming to the top of her lungs. Her cry is so loud that she makes me nervous. Granny said she has a strong pair of lungs. I mean, her cry is so piercing, I wouldn't be surprised if people from outside can hear her.

PRETTY CAN BE UGLY

"Shut up! Shut the!" Mom walks over to Koko's bouncy and pinches her arm a few times making her scream even louder.

As soon as she walks away from Koko's bouncy, I go to pick Koko up to comfort her. Koko is screaming to the top of her lungs from the pain now, so I take her upstairs away from my mom and try to calm her down. I walk back and forth slowly, from my room to Key's room, acting as Koko's human rocking chair.

"Shhh... it's okay... we will get away from that mean bitch one of these days," I whisper to Koko as if she can understand me.

Watching my mom pinch baby Koko hurt my feelings to the core. It makes me want to slap the shit out of my mom when she's mean to Koko. This is not the first time she has pinched Koko because of her crying. She didn't do it because she's drunk. She's pinched Koko several times sober too. That's what babies do, they cry. Unfortunately, it is the first time I've seen her pinch her so many times at once. It's so weird because she tries to find the smallest reasons to be abusive towards us. But I can bet a million dollars she's probably only gotten a hand full of whippings from my Grandparents as a child. It's not like my grandparents used to be super mean or strict to her. All of the stories I hear from her and other people. It seems like she had it pretty easy, and she was spoiled rotten. I don't know why her anger and jealousy towards us is so strong, but Koko is just a baby. It seems like she gains pleasure from causing us pain, then she wonders why we don't like being around her ass.

The night passes very slowly and dreadful, but finally, my mom is passed out on the couch. Not talking, not being aggressive and leaving us the fuck alone. She's laid out on the couch with her head hanging from the armrest of the couch. One leg is hanging from off the couch, and the other one is spread across the other side of the couch. Her eyes are rolled in the back of her head while her eyelids are open wide enough to see the white part of her eyeballs. That's normal for her eyes to do this though. Every time she's sleeping, her eyes lids are open enough to see the white part of the eyeball.

Sometimes I want to tell my Grandparents and my dad how she treats us, but I don't know if it would change anything. I'm scared that things might get worst if I do tell. Then she will torture me even more, and no one will be able to save me. My dad will still be gone a lot, and my Grandparents are all the way in North Carolina. I just hate being here with her. I want to go over somebody else's house and be around other people's family or some of my other family members. This is exactly why Key is so close to Patricia and Porsha and their family. I'm getting so fed up with this shit, and it feels like I'm about to explode.

Morning creeps through, and Koko is up before me. She is looking so pretty with her smooth high yellow skin complexion and her soft straight black hair. Koko's hair hasn't even curled yet, and she's a little over a month old now. Mom never knows how to do her hair because it's so straight, so she just put cute headbands around her head. I'm so happy Koko is not crying. She's just cooing and waiting for somebody to play with her. Koko and I fell asleep in my parents' room. I made sure that I put a pillow on the other side of her so she wouldn't fall off the bed like I see everybody else do.

"Koko…" I use an overly high pitch tone of voice as Koko gets excited. "What you doing, baby girl? Huh? Huh?" I tickle Koko.

Koko laughs so hard at my talking and tickling, her mouth full of gums begins drooling. Then seconds later, a waft of a funky smell lingers for just too long.

"Ugh girl… you could of warned somebody before you let loose!"

I squeeze my nose close from the smell of her stinky diaper.

I check her heavy diaper expecting a huge load of poop, but instead, it's just a diaper full of pee. Usually, when she poops, she tears, so you know what she's doing. But she's just sitting here smiling right now. Looks like she just passed gas, but she smells like she might have a case of diarrhea.

"You a tinky whittle girl! A tinky tinky girl!" I tickle Koko making her laugh some more.

In a matter of seconds, Mom walks in the room looking so stupid.

"What the fuck you looking at?" she frowns at me like I did something to her.
I wish I wasn't looking at yo' ass! I get smart right back with her in my head.

Damn, she gets on my last nerve! She just woke up mad as hell. Nobody said anything to her, and she has an attitude for no reason. I'm not the one who got you drunk yesterday and made us miss school. I wish I was at school right now. Anytime I can use to be away from her miserable ass, I try to take full advantage of it. I mean, if she hates us so much, she should just let us live with our grandparents. Or she shouldn't have ever had children in the first place. Just like her biological mother did with her. She didn't want her, so she gave her up for adoption. She didn't walk around telling her how much she wishes she was a boy. Or acting as if she hates her. She gave her up to a family who may treat her nicely, people who actually want her. I wish Mom would just let my grandparents adopt us like they adopted her. I mean, I must admit, it is pretty boring in Sunset Beach, N.C., but I'm sure if we moved down there, we would meet people and it wouldn't be as boring as it seems.

My mom told Key once before the reason she so strict and doesn't let us go anywhere is because she was adopted. What that truly means I don't know. What does Key going over her friend's house from school for a couple of hours have anything to do with her being adopted? She literally doesn't let Key do anything but go outside. Sometimes, she's even strict about us going outside. We can't even go down the street or around the corner without permission. Usually, the answer to those questions is no. She wants us under her all the time, but she's so mean to us eighty percent of the time.

Man, I just miss my daddy and my grandparents! I think to myself as I look into Koko's innocent eyes.

CHAPTER **FORTY-ONE**

KEY'S SWEET 16 birthday party is today, and everybody is running around everywhere trying to get everything together. My grandparents are in town, so you know I'm in a great mood. I don't know who's in charge of what, but I know that Key is having her party at a hall. There will be food, music, and dessert. Key always have big parties for her birthday. Every time my birthday comes around, they just throw me a basic basement party. I did have a hotel party for my last birthday, and that was fun. I must admit, my parents know how to throw a party. Anytime they throw a party, it's always a good turnout. All of the family and friends come out and show love.

    Thank god it's not snowing this year on Key's birthday, but it is cold as fuck. You never know what kind of weather you're going to get in the city of Detroit in April.

    The DJ beat us to the hall, and he's setting up his station toward the back of the hall. We didn't have to buy tables and chairs because it is included in the hall. While everybody is bringing stuff in for the party, my duty is to watch after Koko. She's one year old going on two, and she's already walking and talking some. My mom has her dressed so cute. She has a light purple suede jogging suit on with light purple and pink gym shoes. Her pacifier latch even matches her outfit with her two curly ponytails at the top of her head like Mickey Mouse. Of course, Mom had Koko's gold rings custom made for her small baby fingers. I just pray Koko doesn't get in trouble if one falls off. She's only a baby, and she doesn't even know what's on her fingers. To compliment her gold rings, her diamond stud earrings shine easily, matching her gold bracelet.

"Go, Koko! Go Koko," I cheer her on as the DJ tests his music.

Koko already feels the nature of dancing because that's all she sees us doing. It's so funny because she's so young and has so much rhythm. She's always on beat to every song that comes on.
Everybody is looking nice. My grandparents are always dressed to impress, dripping in gold jewelry. I'm guessing that's where my mom gets her love for gold. Key looks really pretty, covered in name brand clothing to the socks. I have a Baby Phat jean dress on, and my hair isn't in a complicated hairstyle today, thank God. Mom just brushed half of the front of my hair in a ponytail and let the rest in the back hang while leaving two pieces in the front out. Mom and Dad are Coogi and Gucci down as usual.

It's so annoying to see my mom already getting drunk before the party is even started. I'm sure everybody notices, but this time Granny is the only person who decides to say something.

"Joyce, don't you think you should slow down?" Granny suggests in a polite way.
"I'm straight!" Mom frowns as if Granny is overreacting.

Everybody know when alcohol gets in Joyce's body, she acts a fool. Even I know that, and I'm only ten years old, I'll be eleven this year in November. After ignoring my Granny's request, Mom refills her glass with this clear drink.
It's about to be a hell of a night! I shake my head and continue to tend to Koko.

PRETTY CAN BE UGLY

When the DJ starts to mix in the Gel-n-Weave mix song, all of Key's friends from high school, from the neighborhood, and the rest of the kids run to the dance floor to dance. At this point, my mom is drunk as hell and damn near want to be on the dance floor with the kids.

Mom is in the middle of the floor, trying to get the cousins and friends who comes over our house often to do the footwork dance. Once she gets everybody from the neighborhood and our cousins together, we all laugh and dance doing the footwork as she hypes everybody up. Soon after, Key's friends join in because the dance goes well with the song. I can tell she's getting on Key's last nerves, but she's trying not to let her ruin her time with her friends. I know Key is happy that her friends from school showed up because she can't ever go to their parties. She can't even go to the school events if they're not during school hours. That's why Key is so sneaky now. She can't do anything but go outside and hang in front of the house.

I'm not sure if the other kids notice how drunk my mom is, but they act like they like her so much. I mean, it's cool sometimes for her to be the hype man, but she needs to go sit her ass the fuck down with the other adults at this point.

The night continues with good music, good food, and good vibes. After a while, I sense the tension between my parents. I have a bad feeling that this night is not going to end well. I know how my parents are, and on top of that, Mom is drunk as a drunken master.

"Man, I want to go over somebody else house when it's time to go," I speak to myself for only me to hear.

Out of nowhere, the photographer moves very quickly to grab Koko, Key, my parents and me for a family photo. The photo took less than three minutes to print. After the photo printed, the photographer framed it in a pretty white cardboard kind of material frame, then he tries to hand it to my mom.

"I don't want that bullshit!" Mom waves her hand in the air and walks away.
"Joyce..." Granny calls her name out of embarrassment, but Mom continues to walk away, ignoring her.

Once Granny see the photographer looking lost because he didn't know who to give the picture to since my dad wasn't in sight, Granny walks over and apologizes for my mom's rude behavior and takes the picture. Then Granny walks over to Granddaddy to converse.

"Joyce is way too drunk now, this is ridiculous." Granny looks fed up.
"I know she's been dancing all crazy, talking loud, acting like she can't control herself. She's acting like she's at the club or something. This is Key's Sweet Sixteen birthday party." Granddaddy looks disappointed.
"That's probably why a lot of the kids whose parents stayed decided to leave earlier, because she's acting a damn fool," Granny frowns.
Granny hardly ever uses curse words, so when she uses profanity, it means she's serious.
"Yeah, well, you know what, I'm sick of it." Granddaddy looks like he's on his last straw with my mom.

Overhearing my grandparents' conversation about my mom has me trembling inside. I walk over to my grandparents, instead of continuing to eavesdrop.

"Miko, does your mom act like this all the time?" Granny asks.
"Yeah, especially when she drunk," I respond quickly as my heart begin to race because I know my mom wouldn't approve of that answer.
"See, now that's just crazy!" Granny shakes her head while doing

some cleaning up in the area.

"I always get scared when she starts drinking," I confess nervously.

"Scared?" Granddaddy looks surprised.

Yeah, motherfucka! Shit is fucked up around here!

"Scared of what, Mickey?" Granny sounds concerned.

"Scared of how the night is going to end. She acts so crazy when she gets drunk." I try to stay away from full details to avoid getting in more trouble I'm probably already in.

"She got a goddamn problem! She might as well let the girls come stay with us if she needs help." Granddaddy gives my mom a mean look from where he's sitting.

"Yeah, that would make sense. She knows we wouldn't mind keeping them until she got herself together," Granny agrees.

I'm hoping I didn't say too much or anything wrong. I am not trying to get a beating once everybody leaves. At the same time, I really wish they knew the full details of how she treats us. If they knew, maybe they would try to help us or let us live with them. If it were up to me, I would tell my grandparents and my dad about how she abuses us. Hopefully, they would stand up for us, and that would make her change. But that seems too simple for this difficult, dysfunctional ass family. I know Mom wouldn't punish us in front of my daddy or my grandparents. That's why I know half of the time; the reason she punishes us is based on some bullshit because it's always a secret. Like when Key got in trouble for smoking cigarettes at school, everybody knew about it. That was worth actually getting in trouble for. She knows if she whoops us while the family is around, they will ask questions like "What I did or what happened" and the honest-to-god truth would be nothing or nothing big enough for a beating.

The party is finally over, and I am not ready to face the music tonight. Mom is mad and drunk. My grandparents are angry and disappointed, and Dad, I'm sure, is somewhere pissed at Mom. Everyone is pissed at my mom tonight. I guess everybody is fed up with her not being able to control her liquor. Wilding out at Key's Sweet Sixteen birthday party in front of family, friends, and strangers is just doing too much. In my opinion, I feel like somebody should have talked to her about her drinking a long time ago. It's quite obvious she can't handle a sip of alcohol. If I know this at ten years old, I know everybody and their mama knows and have known for a while now.

The party is over, and a couple of the family members like Big Mama, Aunt Lora, and Aunt Joan stayed after a little bit to help clean up. Mom is laid out on the chair, chewing on something looking like an oversized baby. Times like these, I hate that she's my mom. I know everybody be talking about her once they get home. I don't see how it doesn't embarrass my dad. I'm sure her friends have a mouthful to say about her. She doesn't have many friends, but I know I couldn't be her friend if I was an adult. I would have to reject all of her invites dealing with hanging out and drinks. I wouldn't have time to be dragging her out of the party every time we go out.

Once we get home, the tension breaks through in full force.

"Joyce, sit the hell down! I'm tired of you!" Dad raises his voice.

"I don't give a fuck what you tired of! Shit! You can get the fuck on!" Mom yells.

"You know, Joyce, you shouldn't be drinking the way you do," Granny adds with a slight attitude.

"What? Drinking the way I drink! Y'all drink like motherfucking fishes! Mom shoots back with no remorse.

"We not talking about us! We talking about you! We're not the ones who were acting like a fool at Key's Sweet Sixteen!" Granddaddy jumps in taking up for Granny.

"And how many nights have I seen you act a fucking fool from being drunk?" Mom challenges Granddaddy.

"You don't use that kind of language with your mother or me!" Granddaddy steps to my mom.

"She's not my mother and y'all not my real parents anyway! Y'all can get the fuck on too!" Mom doesn't back down.

"What?" Dad yells out of disbelief.

"You heard what the fuck I said! All of you motherfuckas can step out of my house!" Mom sits down on the stool, unable to keep her balance.

"YOUR HOUSE?" Granddaddy is furious now.

"Out of all of the things we've done for you, that's how you treat us?" Granny sheds a few tears.

"Come on, Jim, let's go. We can't help nobody who doesn't want our help." Granny wipes her face and heads upstairs to pack their things.

"Just remember, there would be no house, no car if it wasn't for us!" Granddaddy follows Granny upstairs.

"Yeah fucking right!" Mom looks sober now.

"You a sad case, man." Dad shakes his head while leaving out the door.

"Yeah, go ahead and leave, that's what you're best at doing!" Mom flicks him off with both middle fingers as the door slams.

Not too long after my dad left, I hear my Grandparents coming down the stairs with their suitcases and luggage. I want to pack my bags and leave with them so bad. Them leaving makes tears fall down my eyes. Once Granny see me crying, she immediately comes to me.

"It's okay, Mickey, everything is going to be fine. We'll be seeing you soon." Granny hugs and kisses me on the cheek, then heads over to Key to say goodbye before walking out of the door.

"Shiiid! Oh no you won't be seeing MY children! Over my dead body will you be seeing MY KIDS!" Mom goes on with her ignorant comments.

Granddaddy proceeds to do the same thing by kissing us goodbye and sending "I love you's." Granny leaves without even looking at my mom. Granddaddy says his peace before heading for the door.

"You're pathetic, and I hope you seek help." Granddaddy heads for the door.
"Bye! And I don't ever have to see you again!" Mom says those words as if she meant them from the bottom of her heart.

More tears begin to run down my face.

"And wipe those ugly ass tears off your fucking face!" Mom looks at me with disgust.

I do as I'm told and wipe my tears away with my hands. Key looks as if she can't believe what just happened. My parents arguing and fighting is normal, but we've never witnessed my mom and grandparents get into this bad of an argument. Mom has shared stories about our grandparents and her differences with them, like any other child and parents' relationship. The hate I'm feeling in this house right now is like no other. I know one thing about my mom, she is a woman of her word. Nine times out of ten, she means what she says. She hardly ever changes her mind or thoughts about anything. Even if she is in the wrong, she will never apologize or admit she's wrong. She didn't graduate with her high school diploma, but she's most definitely a scholar at holding grudges. She doesn't forgive or forget. She's cold hearted.

"I can't believe them motherfuckas! Can you?" she asks Key, pacing from the dining room to the kitchen.
"Taking Jihod's side over mine! They don't even like him!" she continues more sober than earlier.
"Then daddy wants to say 'I wouldn't have anything without them.' Mom opens the refrigerator to grab the gallon of water.
And he's telling the truth! Everybody and they mama know that they spoil you rotten! You don't have shit! I think as she speaks.

"That's cool, though! Watch I get the fuck up out of this house and lose that car!" she drinks her glass of water to the head after the mouth full of words.

"Where we going?" she grabs Key's attention with that one.

"I don't know yet, but I'll figure it out. They not about to be holding shit over my head for the rest of my life," Mom continues.

"When are we leaving?" Key sounds sad.

"It will be sometime after school is out, so don't worry, you will have a few months to spend with your *Patricia and Porsha*," Mom adds in a sarcastic way, noticing Key's all of a sudden interest in one of her venting moments.

Oh my god, she isn't saying anything about my dad being included with this moving deal.

"And Jihod, fuck him! I wouldn't give a damn if I didn't cross paths with his sorry ass either!" she frowns, looking off in a daze.

"So, he's not coming with us when we leave?" Key asks the question I'm dying for the answer to.

"Nope! I might not even tell his ass till this bitch is packed up and empty. Nothing left but his couple items," Mom contemplates as she pours another glass of water.

They want to look down on me because I got a little drunk. I wonder who I got it from! That's all I saw growing up! Them drinking throughout all times of the damn day, and getting fucked up! Huh! It's cool, though!" Mom lowers her voice. "Since them motherfuckas want to put all of the blame on me and leave me, I will show all of them how to leave correctly!" Mom has nothing but pure hate in her eyes.

CHAPTER **FORTY-TWO**

EVER SINCE THE big argument between my mom and grandparents, Mom has been ignoring all of their calls. Two months have passed and she's still mad at them for telling her the truth about herself. She did make it very clear that she doesn't mind not seeing them ever again. I know sometimes people say things out of anger, but I couldn't imagine not ever seeing my grandparents again. The thought of it makes me feel nauseous. I don't understand how she can be so evil. My grandparents have done so much for her and for all of us as a family. They have always had her back and ours twice as much. With them being her parents and being pretty well off, she doesn't have much to say or show about things she's done without out them, besides getting pregnant with Key while in high school. I think she went to go get her GED, but I've never seen it. She had a really bad accident at a young age and is able to collect disability checks. I believe she had minor jobs in between like working at a nail salon. She then married a straight hustler from the streets.

With all of these poor decisions being made, my grandparents still didn't show tough love towards her. They supported her, helped her with getting houses and cars so she could live a half decent normal lifestyle. That's why I'm so confused about where all of this hatred and anger comes from. I know she was adopted and my grandparents aren't her biological parents, but they're the only parents she knows. They adopted her when she was a newborn baby. I do remember her trying to reach out to her biological mother a few years back. That didn't go as planned, apparently, after twenty to thirty years went by. Her biological mother, Margaret, still isn't interested in building a relationship with her. I think what doesn't make sense to my mom is the fact that she's her biological mother's middle child of three. My mom is the only child that was put up for adoption. She never talks about how that affects her, if it affects her at all. She's pretty vocal about her opinion to us about almost everything, but she sort of skipped that sentiment.

Right now, she's coaching and manipulating Key in her bedroom. I bet Key is going to ask to go outside right after their talk is over. As I'm in my room entertaining Koko, all of a sudden, the phone rings. Mom let the phone ring, so I'm assuming it is my grandparents calling again. It makes me so sad that I haven't talked to my grandparents in months. Last time my dad was home, he asked me if I talked to them and I lied because Mom made me. She doesn't want him to know that we haven't talked to them since Key's Sweet Sixteen. That also makes me feel pitiful knowing that he has no clue about what's going on.

"That's why I can't wait until I get older," I whine to myself, feeling the tears gathering in my eyeballs slowly forming from the thoughts of everything.

Feeling kind of blue, I turn on "My Immortal" by Evanescence to mirror my mood. I don't remember how I found out about this group because my parents don't listen to this kind of music. All I know is this lady who's singing on this song has a voice that touches my soul. I can tell she's a White woman by the way she sounds. She's also a great singer! Hearing the intro of the song starting off with the piano matches my depressing mood. I'm tired of being here, and I'm ready to leave. I just want to be with my dad or my grandparents. I'm so sick of her being so mean and evil to us, and I'm fed up with her being mean to everybody close to us that shows us love she hardly ever shows. I'm tired of her controlling us and making us feel like shit, getting us involved in the adult business that we don't care about and shouldn't know about.

Koko is still in my room, sitting on my bed, studying me as I cry. I've never seen her two-year-old body become so attentive. It's as if she knows I'm sad and the reason why I'm crying.

"I'm okay, Koko." I smile at her, wiping my tears as she continues to keep her eyes buried on my face.

Once I notice Koko's full attention is still on me, I go to turn off the sad song. I don't want to scare the baby. After I calm down, I take a deep breath while looking at my reflection through my dresser mirror.

"There has to be a way out," I mumble to myself.

About ten minutes goes by, and I hear Key close her bedroom door, which means she's out of Mom's mental counseling session. I was going to go straight into her room to be nosy, but I decide to wait until Mom goes downstairs, so it won't seem so obvious.

"What was y'all talking about?" I ask as I walk through the door.
"The basic bullshit, talking about Granny and Granddaddy and how she can't believe they betrayed her. The same stuff about Daddy, how he not ever here and how she can't wait to leave him." Key didn't hold back one thing.
"And nothing is ever her fault, huh?" I ask in a sarcastic manner.
"Right, then she wants me to give my input. But she doesn't want to hear how I really feel. She just wants me to listen and agree with everything she says. Then she doesn't want me to go outside. Like, bitch, do me a favor. I just sat back and listen to you for three hours straight." Key frowns.
"Right, I remember she said something about them being

alcoholics, but they don't act like her. They have way more control," I explain.

"Exactly everything, not for everybody. I get that's what she saw growing up, but it's been too many big mistakes on her part. That's well-needed wake-up calls for her to stop drinking," Key agrees.

"She said you couldn't go outside too?"

"She said I could after we eat." Key doesn't sound satisfied.

"Did she say anything about us moving?" I slowly sit down on her bed waiting for the scary news.

"Yeah, she said we will be moving sometime next month. She makes me sick. Like, what the fuck are we moving for? If she wants to get a divorce, I'm sure he wouldn't mind just leaving. He's never here anyway. What's the point of us packing up all of our stuff to move?" Key continues looking like she's fed up.

"Did you ask her why do we have to move?"

"Yeah, she said 'Fuck all of them,' and that she doesn't want Granny, Granddaddy, or my daddy to be able to contact us." Key looks down at her hands.

"What?" I'm confused and nervous.

"Yeah, she doesn't want them to know where we live no more, or she doesn't want them to have our number." Key sounds a little sad passing the news.

"That's fucked up." I frown out of disbelief and anger.

"She's fucking retarded. It's not like she has her own money. She's never even been on her own before," Key continues nonchalantly as if she doesn't care anymore.

"So, how are you going to see Cory?" I ask in a nosy way.

"I don't know. I guess I'm going to have to tell her that I'm having sex with him and that he's my boyfriend one of these days, because the Patricia and Porsha thing is getting old." Key plays with her fingernails.

"Aww, shit, you don't think you're going to get in trouble?" my eyes open wider for her next response.

"I don't think so, I mean, she had me at eighteen years old." Key shrugs her shoulders.

"Damn, I'm scared for you," I shake my head.

"If she gets mad, then she gets mad. It's not like she never got mad at me before. I need to start taking birth control anyway," Key continues.

"Right, before you end up like her," I agree. "But damn, girl, I would be terrified if I was you," I continue in disbelief. "The woman doesn't even want you having a boyfriend, let alone having sex."

"It's whatever. I'm over it." Key turns on her music.

Monday comes pretty quickly. Ever since I found out that we would be moving soon, it seems like the days have been flying by. The end of the school year is already here, and I know if we're moving that I won't be coming back to Cherry Hill Performing Arts for middle school, which is so disappointing because I have so many close friends at Cherry Hill.

Key walks into my room. "Let me wear that DKNY sweater."

"What DKNY sweater?" I ask dryly already knowing what she's talking about.

"The red one," she reminds me.

"Nooo... you not about to stretch my sweater out," I catch a quick attitude.

"You so fucking stingy!" Key rolls her eyes and storms out of my room.

"And I don't care! Bye, girl." I roll my eyes back at her.

On the way to school, Mom controlled the radio this morning. She has 'Cause I Love You' by Lenny Williams playing through the speakers.

"See, this is the song I was telling y'all Twista copied off of. He remixed this song," Mom continues as if she's educating us about something so important.

"Yeah, the beginning of the Twista song sounds just like this song with the violins," I add from the back seat as the music plays.

Key didn't join the conversation. From the front seat of the car, she looks like she's in her own world.

She probably still has an attitude at me for not letting her wear my sweater.

It's one of those hot, muggy mornings. Stepping out of the car to head to the bus made me feel like I want to take another shower before going to school. I hate when the humidity is so high. It makes my skin feel moist and sticky.

"Come here, sis, sit with me!" Jazz pats the seat next to hers.

"Dennis not sitting here today?" I ask, placing my book bag in front of me.

"Nah, he not coming today." Jazz fixes her hair.

"You have a perm?" Jazz looks at my hair.

"Nope, never had one,"

"I'm surprised your hair stay straight with all of this humidity." Jazz runs her fingers through one of my long ponytails. Usually, that would annoy me, but for some reason, it didn't this time.

"My mama always tells me not to let people play in my hair or it will fall out." I roll my eyes to show my disbelief.

"My mama tell me and my sister the same thing," Jazz giggles.

After a small talk with Jazz, I stare out the window getting lost in my thoughts about this coming summer, and how my life is about to change with my parents getting a divorce and us moving out of the neighborhood we grew up in. The thought almost brings tears to my eyes. I'm going to miss everybody in the neighborhood. God only knows how much I miss my grandparents. We haven't talked to them in months, but it feels like forever. We've never gone this long without speaking to them. I hate how my mom is so bad at forgiving people. She doesn't know how to let things go. The big argument they had happened in April, it's June now. I hope that they are doing well. I know they miss us just as much as we miss them.

We're down to our last days of the school year. We did a little bit of work in class and went over all of the procedures and do's and don'ts for the 5th-grade graduation. I can't believe the end of the year came so fast. I hate that I'm not coming back next year for middle school.

"School almost out and my birthday is next week!" Pierre announces to our small group of friends.
"Oh, what you doing for your birthday?" Angelice asks.
"I think we going to Jeepers. I'ma have a party up there," Pierre explains.
"Oooo, Jeepers sound fun!" Nessa smiles.
"Yeah, y'all should come!" Pierre invites everybody.
"Is that what you're doing for sure?" Javontae double checks.
"Yeah, I'll call y'all next week and let y'all know for sure for sure," Pierre ensures.
"Okay, cool! My mama most likely will let me come," Patrice adds.
"I already know my mama will bring me," Javontae sounds confident.
"Kimiko, will you be able to come?" Pierre asks as the group wait for my answer.
"I'll have to ask, just let me know." I play it off cool. Secretly, I know my mama is not going to let me do anything. If she doesn't let my sixteen-year-old sister jump off the porch, I don't have a chance.
"I'll be there!" Angelice looks like she wouldn't miss it for the world.
"Yeah, Jeepers be so fun. I love that roller coaster ride they have!" Nessa sparks up Jeepers conversation, and everybody is excited

talking about their favorite games and rides.

Damn, I'm going to miss all of my friends and Ms. Walker. The ride on the bus went the fastest it's ever gone since the beginning of the school year. I think I actually saw the bus driver Joe crack a smile today. He's probably happy he won't have to be driving us for the summer. He acts like he hates this job and everybody around it.

"So, if your dad comes home today or tomorrow, don't tell him that we're leaving tomorrow. I'm going to have somebody come get the furniture sometime this week and put it in the storage," Mom goes on and on about our moving plan.

She doesn't want my dad to know where we're going to be living. I want to ask her so bad how or when are we going to see him. I know she would get an attitude about me wanting to see my dad, so I just hold it in. I can't believe she's going to disappear on him like this.

"I mean, he doesn't give a fuck about us. He's never here any fucking way, so I don't see why I need to tell him what I'm doing. If he cared, he would keep his ass home sometimes, then he would know what was going on around here," Mom continues with her manipulation and reasoning.

She just wants to take us away from everybody!

I wish somebody would take us away from her crazy ass. All she does is try to make us hate everybody she's mad at. She doesn't let us express ourselves in any way, shape, or form. She drags us through long lectures about bullshit, especially Key, then she doesn't want us to say anything that goes against anything she has to say. She punishes us for the smallest things. I still can't believe she whooped Key for wearing my red sweater that one time. I mean, I didn't want her to wear it, but I wasn't that mad about it. Just at any given time, she takes advantage of abusing us. Overall, she's just a mean ass person in my eyes. I know she gets on Key's nerves, but I really don't like her. Sometimes I feel like she doesn't love us. She's never said it, and she most definitely doesn't act like it.

"Damn, I hate my life. Why do I have to be going through this?" I speak to myself in the comfort of my room that won't be my room for much longer.

The front door closing to the house never felt scarier. My heart drops to the floor at the sound. I know that's my dad coming in and I know he's going to come in here talking to me. My hands are sweating at the thought of it. I'm trembling inside, and I don't know what to do. I feel like I should do something, but I'm scared shitless. Mom, Key, and Koko are downstairs, and I can hear them talking a little bit. Then about five minutes go by, and I can hear someone coming up the stairs. Dad's loud rapping helps me confirm that it is him. I thought he would come to speak to me as soon as he came up, but he went inside their room first.

My heart is beating so fast, and I feel like I should make a move, take a risk. I usually abide by everything that comes out of my mom's mouth, but this time just feels different. I don't know if I'm ever going to be able to see my dad again after tomorrow. I wouldn't be able to live with myself, knowing that all I had to do was speak up to see my dad or my grandparents. What's scary is that I don't know if speaking up is going to make things better or worst.

Since I haven't been speaking up, I decide to do something I've never done before, as I stand before my dad.

CHAPTER **FORTY-THREE**

"HEY, DA," I wave, walking in my parents' room more scared than I've ever been.

"What's up, Mik Mik!" Dad smiles as if he's in a good mood.

"Umm, I have to tell you something," I say in a low tone voice almost feeling numb inside.

Dad notices my body language and energy, so he sits down. "What's wrong boo?" Dad looks concerned.

"We are moving out of here tomorrow." I cut to the chase as if I'm in a hurry.

Dad doesn't seem worried. "Where y'all going?"

"I don't know, but Mom told us not to tell you. She does this all the time. She tells us not to tell you stuff. She threatens us, she makes us say certain things to you and if we don't listen, she beats us when you leave," I explain quickly as my heart feels like it's pounding out of my chest.

"Whhaat?" Dad looks like he can't believe the words that are coming out of my mouth.

"Yeah, every time you and Key get into an argument, it's because she's behind it. She forces Key to argue with you and say certain things to you every time," I continue with no hesitation, feeling a little relieved.

"Well, ain't that about a bitch." Dad looks off into deep thought.

"She does it to me too, but not as much since I'm younger. Just like when I made that comment to you about Rock. She made me say it and told me if I didn't say it that I would get a whooping when you leave."

"I can't believe this shit." Dad shakes his head in total shock.

"I hate being here with her. She always tells us not to go with you. If you ask, she makes us say no to you," I feel like a fifty pound weight is being lifted from my shoulders as I continue to spill the beans.

"I wonder why Key never said anything." Dad frowns a little bit.

"Because she's scared she's going to get in trouble," I defend Key.

"Well, she's getting in trouble anyway, right?" Dad asks to confirm he's hearing everything clearly.

"Yeah, she picks at the smallest stuff to punish us for," I confirm.

"You want to come with me?" Dad asks.

"Yeah, but..." Dad cuts me off.

"Come on, y'all coming with me. Y'all don't have to deal with this shit." Dad gets up and walks me to my room to get clothes and shoes.

I feel relief yet and still terrified at what's about to happen. I don't know how either one of my parents are about to react from this news, but I don't have a good feeling about it. After we pack a small bag for me, we head back to my parents' room to pack Koko's small bag. I can't believe what I just did. I don't want them to get into a fight or for my dad to go to jail. He doesn't seem like he's too pissed off, so that's making me feel a little better, but he does look like he has a bit of an attitude. I'm so scared to walk downstairs and see Mom and Key's face when Koko and I leave with my dad.

Walking down the stairs feel like I'm walking into a prison cell for a life sentence, even though I'm happy deep inside to be able to go with my dad, at the same time, I know my mom is going to be heated at the fact that I'm not rejecting it.

"They are coming with me," Dad picks Koko up.

Mom frowns. "Where y'all going?"

"It doesn't matter. These are my motherfuckin kids too. They're coming with me." Dad, Koko, and I walk out of the front door easier than I expected.

I wasn't expecting Key to come or speak up because of the fear of my mom, but her face looks like she's in awe.

"We haven't even spoken to Granny and Granddaddy," I continue.

"You lying!" Dad is still tripping off of all of this information he's being smothered with.

"So, why can't y'all talk to y'all grandparents?" Aunt Lora asks in a confusing way.

"Because she got into a big argument with them for Key's Sweet Sixteen birthday party, so since she's mad at them, we have to be mad at them too," I explain how my mom operates.

"Well, if she cut her own parents off, you know she won't hesitate to do it to you, Jihod," Big Mama adds with her cigarette in between her pointer and middle fingers.

"Right!" Dad agrees as he chews on some candy.

"And we really don't have a chance!" Aunt Lora giggles, trying to lighten up the conversation.

"I really can't believe Joyce," Dad continues to smack on his candy and looks in a daze as if he doesn't know what he's gotten himself into.

"Where Key at?" Aunt Lora asks.

"With my mama," I respond.

"She didn't want to come?" Big Mama asks.

"She probably wanted to stay with Joyce ass," Dad answers the question for me.

"No, she probably did want to come, but she was scared. I know she was. My mom whoops her for every little thing," I correct my dad.

"It ain't that much fear in the world! You still spoke up and said something! She sixteen years old! If Joyce been controlling y'all and beating on y'all all this time, she should have spoken up!" Dad sounds confident in his opinion.

"It takes for a ten, eleven-year-old to speak up and be brave?" Dad doesn't sound convinced.

"So, what you gone do when she comes over here looking for the kids?" Big Mama asks Dad.

"I'm not giving her shit. These are my kids too!" Dad adds with assurance and a slight attitude.

"Well, I'm sure she's not that stupid just to come over alone. She'll probably come with the police or something." Aunt Lora helps my Dad think a little more clearly.

"Well, she can bring whoever she wants over here. They're my kids too!" Dad continues with the same alibi.

"You know she'll probably tell them you sell drugs and that you in the streets." Big Mama takes a puff of her cigarette.

"Well, I can say stuff about her too. She not an angel! She has a drinking problem, and Miko just said she abuses them." Dad looks like he's thinking now.

"You'll probably have to get child protective services involved," Big Mama adds.

"Yeah, and start some kind of claim. And the kids would have to speak up too, your word against hers." Aunt Lora lights her cigarette.

The cigarette smoke stinks so badly. As much as we come over here, one would think I would be used to the smell, but I'm not.

"Can we watch Little Rascals?" I ask once I notice the hectic conversation start to calm down.

"Yeah, let me go find it." Aunt Lora gets up from relaxing out on the couch.

"Do Tae be watching the Little Rascals movie?" I ask Big Mama out of curiosity.

"Nah, not that I know of." Big Mama sounds pretty confident.

I didn't think so. I think to myself sort of agitated at how the movie

349

is lost every time I come over here.

I mean, I know I'm not the only kid who comes over here. But I'm almost sure out of all of the cousins and kids, I'm the only one who ever wants to watch the Little Rascals all of the time. The only person I could think of that probably watches it when I'm not here is Aunt Lora.

Once Aunt Lora finally finds the movie, she pops it in Big Mama's VCR since Tae and Koko are playing in her room. I was hoping the movie would take my mind off of everything that's actually happening, but it didn't. I'm scared as shit for tomorrow to come. If I have to go back with my mom, only the lord knows what she'll do to me. I know she is beyond furious that I walked out of our house with my dad. The look on her face was just screaming, "THE NEXT TIME I SEE YOU, YOU BETTER RUN."

I can't believe I actually left with my dad tonight. *I just want this to be over.*

"You want to call your grandparents tomorrow so you can talk to them?" Big Mama asks as she sits on her bed.

"Yeah," I feel a splash of happiness.

I know my grandparents' number by heart. We used to talk to them every day after they moved to North Carolina. I wonder what they're going to say or do once I catch them up on everything. I'm hoping they fly up here and just rescue us from this madness. I'm honestly scared to wake up tomorrow. I know my mom and Key are going to be waiting on us bright and early tomorrow.

Once I get to the middle of the movie, Big Mama is knocked out on the bed as Dad walks into the room.

"Come on, Mik, we about to go." Dad has Koko in his hands.

"Where we about to go?" I get up slowly.

"We about to go over my friend house."

I put my shoes on and gather my things to follow Koko and Dad to the car.

The house that we pull up to is in a very raggedy neighborhood. It's dark outside and there isn't a street light in sight. I can't see the other houses, but in my view, it doesn't look like there are many houses on this block. I'm guessing we're spending the night over here because he brought all of our things.

Once we get inside the house, Koko is sleeping. Dad lays her down on the couch temporarily as he gets settled in. Five minutes later, this tall, high yellow woman walks down the stairs. She approaches me as if she already knows me.

"Hey, Miko baby, how are you?" the woman hugs me softly.

"Hi." I speak dryly because I don't know her and I'm not feeling the vibe.

"Ha, look at Koko. She's knocked out!" the woman giggles.

"Miko, this is Selena. She's been knowing you since you were little," Dad introduces us very casually.

"Oh." I speak quickly, sensing some bullshit is going on here.

It's been about a week since Koko and I have been with my dad. We've basically been hiding out at this Selena lady's house. The Selena lady is low key a really nice woman. She has been very helpful. She's been giving my dad advice on how to go about getting full custody of us. She wrote down her number on a small piece of paper and told me to always keep it. She seems as if she really cares about us, my dad, and our whole situation. Even after all of her help and assistance, I still don't like her. I feel some type of way about her. I feel like she's been sleeping with my dad, knowing that he was married to my mom. Then they want me to be all in and acting friendly, but I don't like that shit. I'm young, but I'm far from stupid. I know he's been over here playing house with her. He probably was over here with her those days and nights he wasn't home with us. And they think I can't put two and two together. That's exactly why I've been standoffish with her the entire time.

Big Mama told us that my mom came over to her house by herself and threatened to get the police involved if he doesn't bring us back to Big Mama's house. She's planning on coming to get us this weekend. When Big Mama delivered the message, Dad opened up a Child Protective Service case on her.

"Yeah, there has been plenty of times she's got drunk and fell asleep at the wheel for hours," I explain to Selena and Dad.

"You're going to have to tell the Social Worker that," Selena nods her head with confidence.

"And didn't you say she's abusive?" Dad asks, looking very focused.

"Yeah, especially when she's drunk. But even when she's not drunk, she whoops us for the smallest things. She pinches on Koko all the time when she cries. Key just recently got a whooping for wearing my red sweater," I continue as I eat my food.

"Yeah, she can report that. And being that she's so young, it will be valuable information," Selena speaks in her proper voice.

"I mean, I know she's going to say I sell drugs, but I can always get a job and just say I got a job." Dad paces around the living room.

I'm supposed to talk to the Social Worker tomorrow. I'm a little nervous, but I'm just hoping this will help us be able to live with my dad legally. When I spoke with my grandparents, they encouraged me to talk to the Social Worker too. They believe something is mentally wrong with my mother. Granny was so happy to hear from me;

she cried on the phone as soon as she heard my voice. I told them everything. From how the way my mom treats us to the way she acts in front of people, everybody is so surprised to hear about the real her. I feel so scared to go back with her, but at the same time, I feel relieved that the truth is finally coming to light. Maybe once my mom sees that everybody knows the truth about her, she will lower her high horse.

CHAPTER **FORTY-FOUR**

"SIR, YOU DON'T have full custody of these two children," a White cop speaks sternly outside of Big Mama's house.

"She doesn't have full custody, either!" Dad challenges the cop with no fear in his eyes.

"Yes, well that's why this needs to be settled in court," the cop continues.

"Well, until it is, my kids can stay with me," Dad continues with his attitude.

"Now I'm not a judge, Sir. Your wife has exposed me to your drug use and dealing. I can easily find any excuse to take you into custody, but all I'm asking, since your wife have contacted the police first, is that you give the kids over until you guys settle things in court." The cop looks less patient.

"Did she tell you about her drinking problem?" Dad switches the bomb on her.

"Come on, Miko!" Mom orders as Dad and the cop go back and forth while Key goes to grab Koko from Big Mama's lap as they sit on the porch.

In no time, Koko and I are back with my mom and Key. Mom is giving me the silent treatment. I wonder if she has a can of whoopass waiting for me. Key isn't really speaking to me either. I wonder where we're heading. I hope it's home. I really do miss my room, but I doubt we're going back home though because that would just be too simple for my mom's complicated ass.

"What did you tell him?" Mom asks sternly as she drives.
"Nothing," I lie just as good as she's taught me all this time.
"So, he didn't ask you anything about us moving? Or where to?" Mom continues to interrogate me.
I forgot about us moving. I wonder where we're going right now. "No," I answer quickly.
"You better not be fucking lying to me, little girl. I don't know what made you go with him any fucking ways," she goes on a mini rant.
I left with him because you act like you want to keep us away from him and the rest of my family"
As she continues to fuss, I continue to respond to her bullshit in my mind. I'm too fearful of what may happen if I go against anything she says.
Don't nobody want to be here with your mean ass any fucking way. You not letting us talk to our grandparents. I'm not even sure when the next time I will be able to see my dad.
The thought of not seeing my dad makes my stomach drop. Tears want to fall so bad that my eyes are starting to burn. I notice Koko staring at me again with her cute fat cheeks. Her stares help me try to get it together. I hate it when she catches me in a bad mood. It's as if she knows something is wrong and she wants to talk to me, but she's too young to have a full conversation. Poor baby doesn't know what's going on. She is just sitting pretty with her two curly pigtails that Aunt Lora did earlier.

We shouldn't have ever gone back over Big Mama's house! I roll my eyes in the back seat of the car.

Mom is finally done talking shit. Little does she know, I didn't hear a word she just said. I really fucking hate her and her evil ways.

We're finally at our destination, and this neighborhood doesn't look familiar at all. Then out of nowhere, I see our cousin Dante come outside with a huge smile on his face. When I see him, I instantly feel a little joy. This must be Aunt Cynthia's new place.

"Hey, Auntie Joyce!" Dante hugs my mom like he hasn't seen her in years and she returns the love.

Key and I happily pass them up to approach the rest of the family inside of the duplex house. I'm surprised everybody not outside sitting on the porch on this nice summer day. As soon as we approach the house, I hear Aunt Cynthia's hyper personality.

"Heyyy, nieces!" she sits her glass of wine down before coming to give us hugs and kisses.

The house is fairly empty with a few pieces of furniture here and there. No wonder I didn't recognize this neighborhood. Every time we come see Auntie Cynthia and them, they live in a different neighborhood. But every time we visit, they make us feel very welcomed. We cook, play games, dance, and Aunt Cynthia and Mom will talk about the "Good Old Days" as they sip on their drinks.

As the day goes on, Shanae and Shannon introduces us to their "fake" neighborhood friends. It's so funny because before we came down the street, Shannon was talking mad shit about the girls we're talking to right now. As Shanae, Key, and I are sitting back, cracking up, Dante and Donovan are play fighting and cracking jokes with the boys in the street.

Once it starts getting dark, everybody head back to the house. Mom and Auntie Cynthia are sitting on the porch with Koko. I know they been gossiping about our situation and the drama all day. I could bet a million dollars that Mom is sitting up there lying her ass off.

"When I say my niece Keoako is so so so beautiful!" Auntie Cynthia picks Koko up in a playful way.

"Thank you!" Mom smiles.

"Y'all wanna play Questions?" I smile in a daring way.

"Who?" Donovan ask sarcastically.

Shanae burst out in laughter, "Bro, stop acting scary!"

"Last time we played that game, I was constipated for days!" Dante blurts out.

Everybody is laughing at Dante's confession. "Stop lying, Dante!" Shannon calls his bluff.

"If anything, the game made you, Go to the bathroom! I think Joyce added olive juice in the drink. That's what did it!" Aunt Cynthia laughs

"Right! That drink cleaned us out!" Shanae laughs while giving her mom a high five.

From the outside looking in, it seems like Shanae and Aunt Cynthia's has a super close mother/daughter relationship. I say "from the outside looking in" because I know better not to judge a book by its cover. I know better than to assume certain things about people's lives, when unaware of the full story. People do it to me all of the time, so I try not to do it to others. People assume our lives are so perfect because we present ourselves well, but they have no idea.

But Shanae and Aunt Cynthia's mother/daughter relationship doesn't seem forced or fake like Mom and Key's. I think my mom wants Key and her to be close like that, but she doesn't know how to let it happen naturally. Instead, Mom forces herself on Key and Mom doesn't listen to her, which results in Key distancing herself from Mom. There's so much my mom doesn't know about Key or me that it's ridiculous. But let her tell it, she knows every little thing.

Sitting back, watching everybody laugh and having a good time brings me a little joy. I wonder if Key ever opens up to Shanae and tells her the real deal and how everything really is. Key and Shanae are closer in age, and Shannon and I are closer in age. The boys fall in between all of us. It's always fun and love shown when we're around them. I'm wondering where we're going after this. From the sound of it, it doesn't sound like we're going back on 7 Mile and Manor to our old neighborhood. I haven't gotten a chance to kick it with Key to get filled in on the bullshit or to fill her in on my leave with dad.

As Donovan takes his shot of a cup full of milk, orange juice, ketchup, mustard, and pepper, Shannon taps me.

"Y'all should see if y'all can spend the night."

"Okay, I think my mama mad at me, though. I'll see if Key wants to ask."

"I don't think so. It doesn't seem like she mad." Shannon takes a double look at my mom for confirmation.

"Girl, she's hard to read. You will never know how she really feels unless you know, know," I whisper under everybody loud voices. "You feel me?" I ask, knowing the answer.

Shannon burst out in laughter "Yeah, dog, I feel you," she mimics my same tone of voice.

"I love Kimiko dog!" Shannon expresses aloud as the game continues.

It's so weird, but they're the only cousins that call all of us by our full names as if we just met or something. After the game is over, everybody is gossiping, sitting around listening to music.

"It look like we might not have to ask to spend the night. Look at her." I point at Mom dozing off in the chair.

"Bbbbtttt!" Shannon makes an ongoing fart noise from her mouth before laughing at Mom.

"Her eyes roll to the back of her head when she sleep. You can see the white part of her eyeball," Shannon states the obvious.

"I know, it's because she's crazy," I giggle, and Shannon laughs at my joke.

"Come on, let's go up upstairs." Shannon leads, and I follow.

Shannon bursts into the room that Key and Shanae are listening to music in.

"Damn, Shannon! I'm behind the door!" Shanae catches a quick attitude.

Shannon walks in, ignoring her. "Kimiko talking about the reason Auntie Joyce's eyes roll behind her head when she sleeping is because she crazy!"

Shannon, Shanae, and Key burst out in laughter.

"That is not the reason, Kimiko!" Shanae laughs, continuing to hip-roll in the mirror behind the door.

"Y'all don't know her like we know her. That bitch is nuts!" Key seconds my comment as we all join in the laughter.

The morning comes quicker than usual, and before we know it, we are saying our goodbyes to Aunt Cynthia, Shanae, Dante, Donovan, and Shannon. I know in my head that we won't be seeing them anytime soon. That's just how it is with them. I've never asked my mom why we don't see them more often. We all have so much fun when we do unite.

"Auntie Joyce, when the next time y'all coming over?" Dante ask leaning outside the front door with only his shorts on.

"We'll be back soon, nephew. Maybe sometime next weekend." Mom turns around to walk towards the car.

"*That's all she do is lie.*" I roll my eyes as I carry Koko to her car seat.

After putting Koko in her car seat, I notice a whole bunch of black garbage bags filled with stuff in the trunk.

"Shanae asked about Kinko last night. She was like 'where y'all little dog at?'" Key smiles.

"You told her he died?" Mom asks from the driver's seat.

"Yeah, she couldn't believe it. I told her he got hit by a car." Key shakes her head from the thought of it.

"Dang, I miss Kinko so much," I confess.

"His bad but always used to go visit his girlfriend around the corner," Key adds.

"Right, we tried patching up those holes at the bottom of the gate that he used to always dig through, but he kept digging new ones." Mom explains.

"Yup, he just kept getting out." I look out of the window, wondering where we're going next.

"So, we going to drive out to Browns Town and try to see if Uncle German will let us stay with him for a few months." Mom explains to Key, answering the question that was just in my head.

"Browns Town?" Key asks as if she didn't hear her clearly.

"Yeah, that's where he lives," Mom confirms.

Key knows not to even question her any further. I don't know why she bothers to tell us anything if she doesn't want a response or doesn't care what we think.

After we get finished eating, we head to Browns Town. Thank God my mom didn't put on her old school music. I'm just not feeling that right now. Instead, she just let the radio play. Donell Jones' smooth voice is playing through the speakers, talking about how he wants to leave the girl he's with.

"Miko, wake up!" Mom taps me sort of hard.

When I wake up, we are in an average looking apartment complex. I can tell we're not in Detroit anymore. The atmosphere is just different.

"Now, when we get in here, y'all let me do the talking. Just follow my lead. If he asks you anything, just listen to what I say and repeat it." Mom looks as serious as a judge in a courtroom.

"Hey, boo!" Uncle German opens the front door with a huge smile on his face.

"Hey, Unc!" Mom returns the energy.

"Y'all want something to drink?" Uncle German heads to the kitchen.

"Do you have lemonade?" Key asks as she sits on the couch.

"Nope, I have water and grapefruit juice." Uncle German looks in the refrigerator.

"Grapefruit juice? Don't nobody drink grapefruit juice, Unc." Mom giggles at him.

"Right, I barely even like the actual fruit," I comment sitting next to Key.

"I'll take some water," Mom suggests.

"You want some too, boo?" he asks Key.

"Nah, I'm fine."

"So, what's going on, Joyce?" Uncle German cracks a beer open for himself.

"To be honest, it's too much going on right now. You know I left Jihod, and it's been crazy. You know how divorces go. He is trying to get the kids from me like he can take care of them better than me. You know he in the streets. The kids don't need to be around that mess," Mom explains.

"The kids don't need to be around none of this mess," Uncle German cuts her off.

"I know, and right now, I need to get out of dodge, and we really don't have anywhere to go." Mom starts her guilt trip.

Yes, the fuck we do have somewhere to go! You just want us to suffer here with you! Stupid bitch! Her words just itch my skin.

"It don't sound like you have it all the way together, either, Joyce. If you don't have anywhere to stay, it probably will be easier for you to navigate without the kids," Uncle German speaks in his southern accent.

"So, where would the kids go?" Mom looks at him like he's stupid.

I know the answer to that fucking question. I roll my eyes because nobody can see me.

"Well, you know May Jo and Puddin' wouldn't mind helping you with the kids," Uncle German suggests.

"I haven't talked to my parents in a while now. I don't think that would be a good idea. They don't respect my wishes, so I don't think they should have my kids." Mom sounds like her mind is made up.

What wishes? That's a fucking lie! Selfish bitch! She can't think past her own ass! Now I'm fuming.

"I don't know anything about that, but I know that May Jo and Puddin' love those kids to death. You know they in those kids' best interest. They would be well taken care of until you get on your feet," Uncle German continues to make his point.

Right, Uncle German! Now that's the truth!

"Well, I'm tired of their help. They've helped me enough in life. It's time for me to do my own thing. I'm a grown woman, and I need to figure it out by myself, so I'm asking you, can you look out for your nieces for a few months until I can pull something together?"

Uncle German takes a deep breath as if what's about to come out of his mouth is hard to say.

"Okay, Joyce, y'all can stay for a few months." He gulps down the rest of his beer that he just opened five minutes ago.

Aww, shit! The two 'drunken masters' under the same roof? Now, where are we going to sleep? This is only a one-bedroom apartment! This is some bullshit! I yell at my mom in my head.

CHAPTER **FORTY-FIVE**

IT'S DECEMBER ALREADY, and I've never been so bored and aggravated in my life. Several inches of snow is covering the pavement, and it's below 0 degrees. I can't catch a break around here because Mom hasn't enrolled us in school out here in the city of Browns Town. In between Uncle German, all of his girlfriends, and my mom, I can't pick which one is the worst. I do catch a break from Uncle German during the week because he has a job. But when the weekend comes, I don't know which girlfriend I'm going to meet. And my mom is just sickening. She sits around whooping and pinching on Koko all day. When she's not waiting on Koko to do one thing wrong, she's trying her hardest to manipulate Key and me about family bullshit. I still haven't seen or talked to my grandparents since I got back with my mom. She keeps telling us she will let us call them "one of these days." She has a new cell phone, and no one has the number. She acts like not talking to them doesn't faze her one bit. Words can't explain how much I miss them. I want to ask to call them all the time, but I know she's not going to allow it.

I'm so tired of sleeping on these dumb ass couches. I can't wait until we get our own place. I wish she would hurry up and enroll us in school so I can get away from here for a few hours. I mean, I guess it is nice that he's letting us stay here since we don't have anywhere else to go, but she can stay here with him and let us go live with our grandparents until she gets everything together. That's what a responsible parent would do. They would do what's best for the kids, but nope, not my mother. That's what's making me so fucking mad. Why would she put us through all of this if we don't have to be here? Some people don't have any help or anybody to lean on, but that's not her life. She has well-established parents who are ready and willing to help with anything at any time. Instead, she has us sitting here struggling with her dumb ass. Plus, everything she's mad at is so old! Like, girl, get over it and move on!

As I sit here watching "Which Way Is Up" starring Richard Pryor, I overhear knocking on the walls and moaning coming from Uncle German's room. Mom and Key went to grab some McDonalds. They've been gone for about ten to fifteen minutes. Today he has this older lady around his age named Mary over.

Nasty ass old people! I speak aloud only for myself to hear.

Even though I'm only ten years old, I know exactly what they're doing in there. I've snuck and watched pornos over Patricia and Porsha's house before. I've found sex cards in my parents' dresser drawers, and just hanging around older kids on the block enlightened me on a lot of stuff I probably shouldn't know about. *I wonder what my mom would say if she heard them having sex right now.*

Trying to block out Uncle German's noise in the next room, I decide to try sneaking and calling my grandparents on Uncle German's landline. When I dial the number the first time, I get no answer.

"Damn, they probably think I'm Uncle German." I smack my teeth.

Feeling a rush, I try calling one more time and Granny answers on the second ring. We didn't stay on the phone for too long because I told her Key and Mama only went to go get food and that I was sneaking to call them. Granny sound like she was happy to hear from me. She kept saying she's happy we're safe. I also told her that I don't think we're going to be here at Uncle German's for too long. She made sure to confirm that I can always call at any time I get a chance before we got off the phone. About fifteen minutes later, Uncle German and his girlfriend walks out of the room looking crazy.

"Hey, baby..." the lady Mary smiles and waves at me.
"Hi," I respond with a straight face showing I don't want to be bothered.
"Mickey, we will be right back." Uncle German grabs both of their coats.
Bye! Don't trip on your way out! I jump for joy.
"Okay," I answer quickly.
"You're going to leave her here by herself?" Mary asks like she's concerned.
"Yeah, her mama just went up the street for some food," Uncle German responds with confidence.
"How do you know where she went?" Mary doesn't give up.
"Boo, ya' mama went to go get food, right?" Uncle German asks.
"Yeah," I nod my head.
"See, I told you, come on, Nah. Her mama don't have a job. She ain't gone that far." Uncle German and Mary finally walk out the front door.

Now that I'm home alone, I feel some sort of happiness. Everybody is out of my hair for a little minute, and I have the apartment to myself. "Which Way Is Up" is going off, so I look through the huge stack of old movies. As I scramble through the large collection, I skim past a movie with a sexual type of cover. It doesn't look like a porno, but it looks like it might be some freaky stuff on here. To spice my life up, I dare to cut the movie on to see what it is.

The movie comes on like a regular movie, so I press the fast forward button because Mom and Key should be back sooner than later. About ten minutes in the movie, I get to a nasty scene with a man and a woman in the living room. Watching the sex scene makes me laugh a little and gets my adrenaline rushing because I know I'm not supposed to be watching this movie. The sex scene didn't last long and right before I press the fast forward button to search for another sex scene. I hear a car door close from outside. Instead of checking to see who it is, I assume it's Mom or Uncle German and immediately press the eject button. I pop the DVD back in the case and continue my search for another movie I'm actually allowed to watch.

Thank god my assumption was right, as Mom, Key, and Koko come through the door brushing the snow off of their boots.

"Uncle German left, Miko?" Mom asks.

"Yeah, I just got finished watching "Which Way Is Up." I didn't know that Richard Pryor guy was so funny." I giggle as I skim through movies trying to be cool.

"Oh, yeah! Richard Pryor is a legend! He's one of the funniest!" Mom confirms.

"Which movie?" Key asks while biting her Big Mac.

"Which Way Is Up," Mom answers before me.

"Oh, I think I seen that one," Key mumbles with food in her mouth.

"Yeah, that's a good one." Mom stuffs her Big Mac in her mouth.

"Miko, yo' chicken nuggets over here."

"I was telling Key in the car that we will be moving out of here at the end of the month," Mom fills me in.

"Where we going?" I ask.

"We are going to stay with cousin Monica for a while," Mom responds.

"Who?" Cousin Monica doesn't sound familiar to me.

"Our cousin on Granny side of the family," Mom explains.

Great! Not our own place yet!

"Oh," I answer less excitedly while grabbing the McDonalds bag from Key.

We've already been staying here for basically the whole summer, fall, and now we are about to move with somebody else. That is so fucking aggravating. All she has to do is ask my grandparents for some help because she obviously can't handle doing this on her own. She'd rather ask all of these other people we barely even see or talk to for help instead of her own parents. That shit is stupid as fuck to me.

"Do you remember what I told you to say when you call?" Mom confirms with Key.
Oh, that's what took them so long to come back. She was giving Key another lying lesson. That's all she do is lie. And that's all she wants us to do is lie, lie, lie.

Christmas day is here, and it's feeling like a regular ol' day. My mom or Uncle German didn't even put a tree up. I know this apartment is small, but they didn't put in any kind of effort to share the holiday spirit. My grandparents have been calling all day, and she keeps ignoring their calls. Since there's no tree, of course, there are no gifts. The only thing I got was a dry ass "Merry Christmas" from my mom and Uncle German. My dad has been calling too. Last time she let us talk to him, he told her that he's going through the courts to get some type of papers to see us.

MacDowell still looks the same from when I was going here in first grade. It feels so weird being back in my old neighborhood. It seems like it's been forever. No one knows we're back in the city, and my mom is going to do everything in her power to keep it that way. I hate being the new girl, especially when it's basically in the middle of the school year and everybody already knows each other. The last time I've been to this school was for Key's 6th-grade graduation. My parents got her a limo, and she invited five or six of her friends to go with her to see the water and have some fun. Now I'm a 6th grader just sitting here looking stupid, waiting on somebody to talk to me. Everybody is looking at me like they have never seen a new person before. It's making me feel like I might have something on my face.

I wish I had a small mirror to check myself. I think quickly at my desk.

"Hey, girl," a pretty brown-skin girl sitting right next to me speaks friendly.

"Hey," I return the smile.

"What school you come from?" she asks.

"Dang, everybody looking at me. That's so annoying," I confess trying to avoid the question because I haven't been in school since school started.

She laughs. "I know all the boys probably like you."

"I don't have anything on my face, do I?" I ask sarcastically.

"No," she continues to laugh.

"What's your name?" I ask.

"I'm Shatay, but all my friends call me Tay Tay. You can just call me Tay Tay."

"Okay, cool, my name is Kimiko, but you can call me Miko." I fix my hair.

"I was just about to ask you to repeat that. Miko is way easier to remember. Is that all your hair?" Tay Tay stares at my long ponytail.

"Yeah," I answer, expecting that question was going to come up sooner or later.

"Damn, girl, what you mixed with?"

"Nothing, I just have long hair," I giggle.

"Girl, you have to be mixed with something. I mean, I have a little Indian in me, and my hair is not as long as yours," Tay Tay is convinced.

"I can tell, with that pretty natural curly ponytail. I could never wear my hair natural like that. My hair is too much and too nappy," I giggle.

"Yeah, right! With all of that baby hair in the front of your head! Do you have a perm or something?" Tay Tay asks.

"Nah, I've never had a perm before."

"Right, so that mean your hair is not that nappy. Your mama probably think it's easier to do your hair while it's straight because you do have a lot of hair." Tay Tay explains

"I don't know. All I know is when I get my hair washed or when I wet my hair, it's not as curly as yours." I switch the conversation back to her hair. "You have hair like my god sisters' Patricia and Porsha. They wear their hair naturally curly all the time too." I gaze at her pretty, slick soft texture.

"I have cousins named Patricia and Porsha," Tay Tay eyebrows pop up.

"Really? Is Patricia light-skinned and Porsha brown-skinned?" I ask quickly.

"Yeah! They mama and daddy name Dona and Tez?" Tay Tay asks in shock.

"Yup!" I laugh out of excitement.

"Bitch, we cousins!" Tay Tay flops her hand out for a high five as I lean over to hit her hand. Both of us share laughs and a connection.

I knew right then and there, Tay Tay was about to be my home-girl.

"You know they live right around the corner from here," I add

"Nah, I didn't know that. I haven't seen them in a minute," Tay Tay smiles.

"You know exactly where they live?" Tay Tay asks.

"Yeah, we used to live right across the street from them," I explain.

"We should walk over there one day," Tay Tay suggests.

"Yeah, that would be fun! Their house is literally a couple of blocks over." I get excited.

After our small talk, the teacher got the class' attention, and we start on an assignment. Now, this is another reason why I hate being new. Everybody knows what's going on in the lesson while I have to play catch up.

The end of the day comes pretty fast, and I'm kind of annoyed about it. I don't like living with Monica and her family. Her older daughter, Tasha, is really nice, but I can tell something is not right with her. And her younger son, Felix, is bad as fuck! He's only like seven, and he runs the entire house. He doesn't listen to anybody, and never gets punished for his bad behavior.

"How was your first day?" Mom asks.
"It was straight." I take my book bag off.
"Do you like your teacher?" Mom asks, seeming to be in a good mood.
"Yeah, she seems like a cool little White lady." I look out the window at people talking and playing with their friends.

Monica doesn't live far from MacDowell, so the ride home is very quick. Key is already in the car when I get out of school. I don't even know what school she's going to. I hate that we haven't been able to gossip like we used to when we had our own rooms. Since we don't have our own space, my mom is right there all the fucking time.

Since Monica lives in a smaller house, Mom, Key, and I are staying in the basement. It's always cold down here, but it is clean and set up nicely. It's carpet down here and a big-screen television with a nice dining room table and chairs set in the corner. We sleep on the couches, and the rest of the basement is covered with black garbage bags full of our stuff.

Key seems a little distance today. She's probably tired of my mom making her lie all of the time. I'm sure she's missing the heck out of Cory, Patricia, and Porsha. Especially Cory, that's her love, and she went from seeing him every day to not seeing him at all.

Today, the vibe in the house is awkward because Big Felix is here. He's a tall, light-skinned man with silky hair and a grim face. When he comes around, everybody gets so tense. Monica has less to say, and Tasha stays in her room. Little Felix is the only one that seems to be happy to see his dad. Big Felix is not Tasha's biological father. Key told me that Tasha said he's very mean to her, so that's probably why she tries to stay away from him. About an hour goes by with Big Felix being here, and I hear little Felix crying. Everybody acts like when his bad ass starts to cry that it's the end of the world. I take my focus off of my homework and tune into the loud yelling upstairs.

"What's wrong?" Big Felix asks.
"Tasha hit me!" Little Felix cries.
"Why did you hit my son?" Big Felix storms into Tasha's room yelling, like it's the end of the world.
"Because he cut up my clothes! Look at this!" Tasha yells back.
"I don't give a fuck what he did! You don't put your hands on him!" Big Felix screams.
"Wait, wait, what's going on now?" Monica joins the argument.
"This not the first time I've told her not to touch Felix, and she continues to put her hands on him! Now, how about I put my hands on you!" Big Felix slams something on the ground.
"Now, why would you hit him?" Monica asks Tasha in a you-know-better tone of voice.
"Look at my clothes he cut up! He is not a baby!" Tasha defends herself.
"You know who else is not a baby? You! So, since you want to discipline around here like you're grown, I'm going to show you grown!" Felix stumps around the house as if he's looking for something.
"Mama!" Tasha cries out to her mother.
"Felix, calm down!" Monica tries to calm Big Felix down, but it doesn't sound like it's working.

"Where is that extension cord?" Big Felix yells.

About five minutes later, I hear Big Felix storm into Tasha's room, and all I can hear is screaming and crying. It sounds like Big Felix is whooping Tasha with an extension cord.
"That's so bold," Key breaks the silence in the basement.
"Yeah, Little Felix is bad as hell. He's the one that needs his ass whooped." Mom flicks through the TV channels.
"Right, he cut her clothes up," I shake my head.
"I wish he would come down here cutting up anything in these bags," Mom frowns.
"You and Big Felix would have to get into it," Key giggles.
"I wish that motherfucka' would lay a hand on me or y'all," Mom sounds confident.
"That is so bold." I add feeling sorry for Tasha.
"I don't see how Monica put up with his ass. How is he just going to come up in here whopping people for no reason? And his ass hasn't been here for days at a time," Mom starts venting for Monica.
"I know his hits hurt," I admit listening to Tasha's cries.
"It sound like he made her take her clothes off too," Key adds.
"And Little Felix doesn't get touched at all. That's just so bold." I continue
"That's why he act the way he act now. Bad, hard-headed, and disrespectful as fuck. And she getting her ass beat for nothing. That's not right at all. We won't be here for long either." Mom continues to eat her chips watching TV.
I hope that doesn't mean I'm going to be going to another new school.

It seems like Tasha has been getting a whopping for about twenty minutes straight. That is so wrong that her parents show favoritism towards her younger brother. I don't know if it's because she's a girl and he's a boy, or if it's because little Felix is his biological child and Tasha isn't. Maybe it's because of their age difference because she is a lot older than him. All I know is that he's bad as hell and needs some kind of discipline in his life. If somebody doesn't straighten him up, he seems like the type that will grow up and become a woman beater or something. I say that because he hit on his mom and sister now and never gets in trouble for it because he knows his daddy will run to his defense.

Ring, ring, ring

"This is your grandparents. Remember what I told you. Don't tell them what school you're going to and..." mom gives Key a brief talk before answering the phone for my grandparents.
"Hello?" Key answers the phone.

I want to talk to them so badly but not under my mom's supervision, monitoring everything I say. It just doesn't seem normal. My grandparents know that she's up to no good anyway.

I'm surprised she didn't put them on speaker to hear what they're saying on the other end. I roll my eyes at my homework sheet.

The way she's staring at Key and watching her talk on the phone is making me not even want to talk to them at all.

CHAPTER FORTY-SIX

"YOU WANT TO play bloody knuckles?" Kelly asks as she stands about four inches taller than me with a high yellow skin complexion and wavy hair.

"Yeah," my response looks like it surprised her.

We take turns hitting our fists against each other's knuckles until somebody gives in from the pain. I was trying so hard not to give in as my knuckles turn red because she's known to be so "tough." I didn't want to seem like I was weak, but the pain is getting too excruciating, and I give up.

"Dang, you must play this a lot!" I shake my hand as if I have water on it.

"Yeah, sometimes." Kelly looks at her red hand.

"That's probably why your knuckles so dark," I giggle, low key throwing shade.

"Yeah, and from boxing," she balls her fist up.

"Oh, you take boxing classes?" I ask as the blood in my hand feels like it's flowing again.

"Yeah, me and all of my sisters."

"Oh, okay, you want to play again?" I ask, feeling confident about this round.

"Yeah," she smiles.

We hit each other's knuckles faster this time as we stand in line in the hallway. This round, I'm not backing down. Kelly's pace is slowing down from the pain. Right before she was looking like she was about to quit, the teacher interrupts our game.

"Okay, class, let's go!" Ms. Laughton leads the way.
"Shit! That hurts!" Kelly holds her hand.
"I know, right?" I laugh as I follow the person in front of me.

Today is a nice day, the sun is shining, and everybody is happy that school is out. I'm not too excited about going home, but there's nothing I can do about it. I don't know where Tay Tay went, but when I got my coat out of the locker, her coat was already gone. Once I get outside, surprisingly, my mom is not here yet. She usually doesn't keep me waiting because she doesn't have anything else to do around this time. After not seeing my mom's car in sight, I see Tay Tay talking to Porsha.

I rush over to Porsha because it feels like I haven't seen her in forever.

"Porsha!" I scream with my arms out for a hug.
Porsha basically jumps on top of me. "Miko, baby!"
"Y'all stupid." Tay Tay laughs at our excitement.
"Damn, I miss you so much!" Porsha kisses me on my cheek.
"Right, I miss y'all too! It feel like we haven't seen each other in decades," I exaggerate.
"Bitch, it feel like it's been centuries! I didn't know you go here! Ain't nobody been messing with y'all, have they?" Porsha asks Tay Tay and me.
"Nah," Tay Tay and I laugh at Porsha's overprotective question.
"Alright, well, y'all let me know if I have to come up here and put that work on ANYBODY!" Porsha balls her fist up hugging both of us

as we share laughs.

"Girl, everything has been so crazy after my parents' divorce." I complain.

"I'm sure it has. Cory miss Key so much. His ass cry about her every night, looking stupid!" Porsha makes a puppy dog facial expression.

"My mama let her call him sometimes, right?" I ask.

"Nah, less than sometimes. And every time he call Auntie Joyce's phone, she doesn't answer, or she will forward him to voicemail," Porsha explains.

"That's bold." I shake my head.

"She just dismissed us from her life," Porsha adds in a funny way, but I know there's some seriousness in her humor.

"Girl, y'all not the only ones," I add, trying not to say too much.

"For real? Who else has she cut off? I know she trying to keep y'all away from y'all daddy," Porsha asks as my mom pulls right up.

"See you later, Tay Tay." I fix my book bag and walk over to the car as Porsha follows.

Before Porsha could speak to my mom, Key hops out of the car and tackles Porsha.

"I miss y'all so much!" Key kisses Porsha on her entire face.

"I can't tell! Every time you call it be for Cory!" Porsha smiles.

"Girl, my mama be acting stingy with her stupid ass phone," Key whispers so my mom won't hear from the car.

"Auntie Joyce mean as hell low key, huh?" Porsha giggles using the same level voice as Key.

"Come on, y'all, we gotta' go!" Mom yells from the driver's side of the car.

"We don't have to go nowhere," I add for only Key and Porsha to hear before getting in the car.

"Okay, I'ma talk to you later." Key hugs Porsha one last time before getting in the car.

"Miko, you call me too!" Porsha waves.

I roll down the back-seat window. "Alright! I got you, my dog!" I give her a wink.

"Hey, Auntie Joyce," Porsha waves, noticing Mom didn't even say hi to her.

"Hey, boo!" Mom waves from inside of the car.

Once we get down the street, Mom starts her interrogation.

"You told her where we live?" Mom looks at me with her deadly eyes.

"No"

"Yeah, don't be telling people where the fuck we live or any of our business." Mom looks me directly in my eyes through the rearview mirror.

Like you haven't said this a million times! Shut the fuck up already! I scream at her in my head as she continues to sing the same old song.

Uncle Chi's house is very small and cluttered. This is a two-bedroom house, so Mom, Key, Koko and I sleep together in the second bedroom. I'm dreading being up under them every freaking second. The only time I get to be by myself or have my own space is when I go to school. I had a strong feeling after my mom learned that Porsha knew I was going to school right around the corner from our old neighborhood that she was going to switch my school. Mom made it seem like she switched my school because of the move, but I noticed the way her energy changed when we saw Porsha. She wasn't happy about her knowing how close I was in range. The way Key jumped out of the car when she saw Porsha made her skin curl. She hates how much Key loves Cory's family, so she made sure she got me out of MacDowell ASAP.

"Come here, girl, let me show you how to peel a potato," Uncle

Chi stands in the kitchen with a small knife.

I look back at my mom sitting in the living for reassurance because she's always trying to control every little thing we do. She looks confused, so I quickly decided to head to the kitchen. Uncle Chi hands me a knife similar to his and demonstrates before letting me try. At first, I wasn't too excited to learn how to peel a potato, but after a few minutes, surprisingly, I was starting to have fun. Just when I was starting to get the hang of it, Mom walks her yellow ass in the kitchen.

"Uncle Chi, she's too young to be cutting potatoes," Mom pops her hand on her hip.

"No, she's not, how old are you?" Uncle Chi looks at me.

"I'm eleven years old," I speak clearly and confidently.

"I started cooking when I was a young boy too. It's better when they start young." Uncle Chi ignores Mom's comment.

"Nah, she's too young to be peeling potatoes with sharp knives like that. Come on, Miko, come back in here." Mom signals for me to leave the kitchen.

"You gotta' stop babying those kids," Uncle Chi continues as we walk out of the kitchen.

Mom throws her hand up as if what he says doesn't matter to her. Just when I was starting to have a little bit of fun away from her ass, she has to come and ruin it. There's literally nothing else for me to do around here but play with Koko, but she's sleeping. It's so boring and small in here. It's times like these when I think about how much I miss my dad and grandparents. My grandparents don't call as much as they used to. I guess they're realizing that she really doesn't want to have anything to do with them. I wish she would stop being so stubborn and talk to them so they can help us get our own place, then we will be able to live normally again. That's what breaks my balls so much about this living situation. We don't even have to be living like this. We don't have to be homeless. This is Mom, being selfish and making stupid decisions.

"Can I go outside?" Key breaks the silence in the living room.

"Why?" Mom seems annoyed by the question.

Because you're the only one watching this dumb ass show!

"I don't know, just to do something," Key shrugs her shoulders.

"Go ahead," Mom shoos Key away with an attitude.

"You want to come, Miko?" Key asks.

"Yeah" *You don't have to ask me twice!* I get up and put my shoes and coat on.

"I don't know why she got an attitude!" I start the conversation standing on the sidewalk.

"Right, like can a nigga' get some fresh air? Shit!" Key frowns.

I giggle at her facial expression. "Exactly! She want somebody to sit up under her all fucking day!"

"Talking about 'Why?' Like, bitch, why fucking not?" Key talks slowly.

"She the only one watching that stupid ass show on TV anyway!" I bend down to tie my shoe.

"Acting like she watching it!" Key laughs.

"Right, the TV only got four fucking channels on it," I joke.

Key laughs as I continue. "He doesn't even have basic cable, god damn!"

"He need to get that bootleg cable or something!" Key continues to laugh.

"Aye, you noticed that picture of the little boy on the wall?" I change the subject.

"Yeah, that's like the first thing you see when you walk in the house. That's his son, Trevor. The one my mama always used to be talking about," Key explains as we walk back and forth on the sidewalk.

"Oh, the one that passed away?" I ask almost sure of the answer.

"Yeah," Key confirms.

"Did you notice he look a lot like you?" I look at her in a confusing way.

Key grins. "Yeah, I noticed. My daddy told me that he's my

biological father."

"What? Trevor?" my mouth drops to the floor.

"Yup," Key bobs her head.

"So that would make Uncle Chi your biological grandfather?" My words are coming out as shocked as I am.

"Uh-huh," Key confirms.

"So that would mean that you're blood related to granddaddy." I'm still in shock.

"Yeah, because Uncle Chi and Granddaddy are like first or second cousins," Key explains.

"Wooooww. So now I get why she wouldn't want you or anybody to know who your biological father is. Because she's embarrassed to say that she was sleeping around with her adopted cousin," I piece everything together aloud.

"Yeah, her adopted cousin. Not her blood cousin," Key cuts me off.

"But it's still probably embarrassing," I stick to my story.

"I mean, but he passed away. And she told my dad so it must not be that embarrassing." Key shrugs her shoulders.

"I wonder if my grandparents know." I'm still caught by surprise.

"Probably not, because they don't know a lot of stuff about her already, you know," Key tries to reason.

"That's true, but that little boy on that picture looks exactly like your baby pictures." I can't believe it.

"Yeah, he does!" Key stares off into the sky.

CHAPTER **FORTY-SEVEN**

"GIRL, I DO not like her!" Micha points out this tall high yellow chick I have never seen before.

"Why not?" I ask as we post up on the playground.

"Because that bitch lame as hell to me. And she always following after Trisha and them." Micha frowns, pointing at her so she can see.

"Oh, she a dick sucker, huh?" I giggle.

"Dick sucking hard as hell. Scary ass!" Micha rolls her eyes.

Bagley sort of reminds me of MacDowell. The inside of the schools looks the same, and we wear the same blue and white uniform colors. I don't have many friends here, but I don't feel like I need too many friends because my cousin, Micha, is making sure everybody knows we are cousins and best friends. Surprisingly, my mom doesn't mind Tina, Raven, Micha, and Breana knowing where we go to school. It's probably because Tina doesn't really have any connection to the family. Tina is like a long-distance sister to Mom. They don't talk much, but often enough. Even though my mom is the only child. I've overheard them saying things about Tina and her sisters having some kind of relations with my mom's biological family, so we just claim each other as family. All of us resemble each other in a general kind of way. People assume we're blood related all the time.

PRETTY CAN BE UGLY

Micha lives right around the corner from Bagley, so she walks home every day. Today my mom told me I could walk home with Micha and that she would pick me up from their house, so today should be kind of fun. Since it's Friday, I'm hoping she doesn't come until later tonight, but I doubt she will do that. She'll probably beat us to Micha's house, knowing her ready ass.

Thank God Micha and I are not in the same class because we would probably get in trouble too much. I don't think Tina is as hard on them as my mom is on us. My mom doesn't play, so I don't have time to be getting in trouble over stupid stuff. The end of the day comes pretty quickly, and my teacher, Mrs. Patterson, makes sure she loads us with hella' homework this weekend. Mrs. Patterson looks like she's in her late 40s, early 50s, tall and brown-skinned with a short haircut and doesn't mind cussing a kid out.

"So, make sure your packets are complete by Monday," Mrs. Patterson speaks firmly.
"The whole packet?" Devin asks with his hand up.
"Yes, the entire packet." Mrs. Patterson doesn't show any sympathy.
"This bitch doesn't let up," Chrisstana leans over and speaks softly.
"Does she give out homework every weekend?" I frown.
"Basically," Chrisstana looks agitated.
"Man, that's so bold." I shake my head as everybody gets ready to go home.

It didn't take long for me to find Micha after class. She was already in the hallway, ready to go when my class let out.

"You ready?" Micha asks with her book bag on her back.
"Yeah, let me grab my jacket and my book bag." I open my locker.
"Did you get homework for the weekend?" I ask curiously.
"No, I don't think so. I ended up getting kicked out of class today because this ugly ass little boy kept playing with me," Micha frowns.

"What happened?" I close my locker and we head downstairs.

"He kept touching my hair and tapping me on my shoulder, so I got up and slapped him in his face. Then the teacher told me to go downstairs to the front office to call my mom. Like that was what I was really going to do," Micha giggles.

I burst out in laughter. "What you end up doing?"

"I just roamed the hallway for a minute and hid in the bathrooms." Micha shrugs her shoulders.

"Hecky naw, that's crazy! Do that little boy like you?"

"I don't know, but I don't like his crooked teeth ass. He play too much!" Micha frowns as I crack up at her.

"And they think they so cute." Micha looks at Trisha and Eric walking in the same direction in front of us.

"Stop hating! They really do make a cute couple," I smack my lips.

"Everybody think he is so fine! I don't think he is that cute. He okay to me," Micha expresses her opinion.

"I think he is really cute. He's a little short, but he still has a nice cute face, and his hair stay cut and clean," I smile, gazing at just Eric from a distance.

"A little short? Girl, he is way too short!" Micha continues to show her jealous side.

"Trisha short too! I think they look cute together." I stand my own ground, disagreeing with Micha.

"Girl, you tripping." Micha shakes her head at my comment.

Surprisingly when we get to the house, my mom isn't here yet, which makes me very happy. Once we settle in, I notice Micha starts acting a little distance. She isn't acting as nice as she usually does. "I'm assuming she's mad because I didn't hop on her "hater train" on the way home about Trisha and Eric. Even though I notice her change of attitude, my stubborn ways stopped me from asking her what is wrong. Instead, I go to see what her older sister Raven is doing.

When I get to Micha and Raven's room, Raven is dancing in the mirror. She is hitting a move to every beat in the song. I love watching people dance, so I make myself comfortable as she continues with her routine. About five minutes after, Micha comes storming in the room.

"Take my top off!" Micha stands by the door.

"Micha, close the door. I'm using the mirror!" Raven yells louder.

"I don't care, and I told you to stop wearing my clothes!" Micha doesn't back down.

"This is not your shirt! This is Mommy's lounge shirt, now get the f.." right before Raven was about to push Micha out of the way, Tina barges in the room.

"Why are y'all yelling in here?"

"She keep stealing my clothes!" Micha yells.

"Girl, don't nobody gotta' steal nothing from you! I'm trying to practice for this audition, and she sitting up here trying to show out in front of Miko!" Raven defends herself.

"Ain't nobody!" Micha sentence gets off by Tina.

"What's the big deal about some clothes?" Tina sounds annoyed.

"Tell her this is your top." Raven pulls the shirt down so both of them can see it.

"Yeah, this is my shirt." Tina takes a good look at it.

"No!" Micha tries to cut Tina off, but Tina beats her to the chase.

"Stop with all of this fucking screaming. Danny is in there sleeping. Micha, go put on another shirt." the doorbell rings as Tina nips their argument in the bud.

"Fuck Danny," Raven says in a soft tone voice after closing the bedroom door and cutting the music back on.

I giggle at her rude comment. "So what team are you trying out for?"

"I'm trying out for the majorette team," Raven continues to the dance.

"This routine is really sweet!" I smile at her creative dance skills.

"Thanks!"

"Did you make it up, or y'all had to learn it?" I ask.

"We had to learn the beginning part, then make up our own ending," Raven explains.

Oh, okay! I wish I knew this routine! It's cute! I bounce and bob my head to the unfamiliar song.

"I can teach you this other routine I know!" Raven gets excited.

"Okay, cool!" I smile, getting ready to dance.

Raven switched the CD, and within a minute or two, the mix song "Bounce and Break Your Back" comes on.

"Okay, so let's start here!" Raven starts doing dance moves.

After about an hour of dancing, sweating, and laughing, Mom calls for me to come downstairs.

"Damn, it's probably time for us to go," I smack my lips.

"You should see if y'all can spend the night," Raven suggests.

"Okay, I'ma see. You think your mom will let me spend the night?"

"Yeah, she don't care," Raven sounds confident.

"Okay, I'ma be right back." I run downstairs to see what Mom wants.

"What you been doing?" Mom asks as she sips on her wine.

"Raven and I was up there dancing." I wipe the sweat from my head.

"Oh, okay, where Micha at?" Mom asks.

"I don't know."

"She's probably downstairs in the basement playing." Tina giggles as she sips on her glass of wine.

"Micha know she will stand alone. That's my girl!" Mom smiles.

"You know she wasn't going to be up there dancing with them," Tina laughs.

"Right, Micha a little tomboy!" Mom giggles.

"Yeah, she a little rough around the edges." Tina rolls her eyes with a smirk on her face.

Key walks in the room with Koko on her hip. "Koko said 'I'm a Gemini.'"

"You asked her what her sign is?" Mom laughs.

"No, she just said it out of nowhere." Key giggles, looking at Koko's pretty face.

"Koko is so beautiful, Joyce!" Tina holds her hands out signaling to hold her, but when Key tries to hand Koko over, Koko moves the opposite way from Tina.

"My baby funny acting," Mom smiles.

"Oh, she doesn't go to people she don't know?" Tina pouts.

"Nope, she only let familiar faces in," Mom explains.

"That's good, though, at least she's not too friendly. You don't have to worry about her running off in public with a stranger," Tina giggles.

"Nah, Koko would be screaming to the top of her lungs if somebody tried to take her. And she know how to scream!" Key adds with laughter.

"Right, think you about to take her if you want to!" I play with her in Key's arms.

"Yeah, she got some lungs on her!" Mom shakes her head.

"Is Breana coming home this weekend?" Key asks Tina because Breana is closest to her age out of all the girls.

"Nah, she's over her grandma's. She's living over there for now," Tina explains.

"Oh, okay, I didn't know that," mom adds.

"Yeah, I said she needs to go stay with her for a minute after I found out she was having sex. Her grandma was way more understanding than me." Tina takes a big gulp of her wine.

"Oh yeah, I remember you told me you took that pretty hard. I feel you, though, Key not having sex yet, I can't even imagine." Mom rolls her eyes as she agrees with Tina.

Nah, she not having sex. She's most definitely making love and everything in between though. And been doing it for a while now. I think to myself as Key exits the room with Koko.

I'm kind of nervous to ask if I can spend the night because I know what the answer is going to be. I'm trying to find the right time to chime in and just ask.

"Is Breana on birth control?" Mom asks.

"Now she is! At first, her dumb ass was just having sex like a fucking dummy." Tina tries not to get too emotional.

"Well, that's good she's on birth control now," mom adds.

"I wouldn't be surprised if she has gotten an abortion before. Out here just having unprotected sex. I mean, it's not like she has a boyfriend." Tina looks depressed at her thoughts.

"Damn, you have to tell her she has to be careful." Mom sounds as if she feels bad for Tina.

"Girl, it's been eating me up inside. But at the end of the day, there's nothing I can do about it." Tina finishes her glass of wine.

"Yeah, that's true. I mean they're not babies no more." mom takes a big gulp of her glass of wine as well.

I hope she doesn't get drunk tonight. I watch every sip she takes.

"I told her daddy and he had the most "humblest" things to say all the way from prison." Tina pours her another glass of wine.

"It's really easy to be humble and have all the right answers when you not there everyday," mom adds with confidence.

"Joyce, that's exactly what I told that fool!" Tina looks as if my mom just read her mind.

"Girl, I know a thing or two about a motherfucka' not being around on the daily, then they want to come around being all nice like everything peachy," Mom frowns. "Shit, at least he's in jail. My ex-husband wasn't even locked up and couldn't keep his ass at home." Mom continues with her thoughts.

"So, the divorce is final?" Tina asks.

"As final as it can get," Mom confirms.

"I'm so sorry to hear that. So, how has everything been? Do y'all have an arrangement with the kids?" Tina asks.

"Girl, everything is pretty much the same. He doesn't see the kids much. But he pays what he needs to pay. As far as time, he's still very selfish when it comes to that," Mom lies through her teeth.

I want to join this conversation so bad. If I was big and brave enough, I would lay her shit out on the floor. That's all she ever does is lie about every fucking thing. NOTHING has been the same since the divorce! We haven't seen or heard from our grandparents because she can't seem to let anything go. My dad literally calls her every day trying to set up a schedule to get us. She's keeping us away from everybody we love the most, and it's the worst feeling in the world. Then on top of that, we don't have our own place. We've been moving like ants ever since she calls herself cutting everybody off. I can't stand to hear her lying all the fucking time. It really gets under my skin the way she makes everybody sound like the bad guy.

This conversation is annoying me so badly. It encourages me to just ask what I came down here to ask.

"Ma, can I spend the night?"
"You don't have any clothes. And you didn't ask Tina if you can stay over," Mom giggles, looking at Tina.
"Raven said she wouldn't care."
"Don't you love when they think they can read your mind," Tina sarcastically adds her comment.
"I know, right?" Mom giggles.
"No, but I don't mind, though. She can spend the night any time!" Tina smiles.
"We can come back tomorrow. That way you can have a bag packed and everything," Mom confirms.
"Okay." I exit the room hoping my mom really means what she just said because she lies most of the time.

CHAPTER **FORTY-EIGHT**

MOM DECIDED TO keep her word for today. She's actually going to let me spend the night over Tina's house. I'm so used to my parents letting me down it's ridiculous. I remember a time when I used to hold onto my parents' and grandparents' words. But nowadays I just expect that they're not going to do what they say to protect my own feelings, and if they come through at the end, then I'll be happy. If not, it won't bother me as much. That way, I won't be expecting anything and won't be let down. It's a great defense mechanism, and it really works for me.

"Can I pack this outfit in my overnight bag?" I ask, reminding her about today's sleepover.

Mom looks at me like she's annoyed. "Yeah," she answers dryly at my excitement.

"*Yes!*" I jump for joy inside.

I'm so happy I'll get a day away from Uncle Chi's house. I hate living here too. At least Monica's house was bigger and cleaner. I thought we were up under each other then. It feels even worst now in this little bitty house.

"Oh, you spending the night over Tina's and them house?" Key asks, looking sort of surprised and desperate at the same time.

"Yeaaah," I sing to express my joy.

"Oh," Key looks at Mom as if she wants to ask if she can come, but it's obvious that Mom barely wants me to go, so she just swallows the thought in her head.

Mom's cellphone starts ringing out of nowhere. From where I'm standing, I can see her flip phone screen ID and it's my dad.

"Miko, come here, it's Jihod. Remember, don't tell him where we live and don't tell him what school you go to." She opens the phone very quickly and places the cellphone to my ear.

"Hello?" I answer the phone less excited than I really am.

"What's up, Mik Mik?" dad's voice changes once he hears my voice.

"Nothing," I answer shortly because I'm being watched like a fucking movie.

"How are you doing, boo? I miss you," Dad asks with concern, and his voice almost makes me tear up, but I resist to the best of my ability.

"I miss you too, and I'm doing good." I swallow my saliva as hard as I can to fight the tears.

"I was calling to let your mother know that I have a court order saying that I can see y'all every weekend," Dad explains.

"Okay," I continue to be short.

"But Joyce act like she can't answer the goddamn phone. Is she sitting right there in front of you?" Dad asks, remembering what I last told him.

"Yes," I answer quickly and nervously, thanking God that she didn't put the phone on speaker before she answered.

"Oh, okay, that's why you're being so short. Well, just know things are going to be changing soon, boo. Stay strong and keep your head up," Dad tries to encourage me, which is only making me feel even more sorry for myself and our situation.

"Okay, I will," my voice cracks a little bit.
"Alright, let me speak to your mom," dad asks politely.

As soon as I hand the cellphone over, I notice Koko giving me that stare again as if she knows something is wrong with me. Mom grabs the phone, and I head to the bathroom to let all my cries out in my hands.

I feel like my life has hit rock bottom. We're moving house to house, and my mom is still keeping us away from everybody. There have been plenty of nights we go without food. My parents are going through this custody battle, which is making me feel like they are playing "Tug o' War" with us. I wish they could just maturely handle things so that everybody can be happy. This divorce has really caused a huge toll on me. At this point, I have no motivation to pay attention in class, do any assignments, or do any homework. I'm usually afraid of doing badly in school or getting bad grades because of the consequences I would have to face at home, but life is just so fucked up right now, and I really don't give a fuck.

"Kimiko, it's your turn to read," Mrs. Patterson calls out.
I pause for a little minute deciding if I was going to listen to her or not.
"Kimiko!" Mrs. Patterson calls again but a little louder.
Staying here and reading aloud for a couple of minutes will probably be better than getting a call home and going home early. God knows I will do anything to stay away from home. I rationalize with myself.
"Okay, I heard you!" I speak loudly with an attitude.

After my turn is up for reading, I go back to not paying attention. For the rest of the day, I just daydream and eventually fall asleep at my desk until the class is over.

"Kimiko, wake up!" Mrs. Patterson taps me on the shoulder.

"You can just call me Miko," I yawn, looking around at the empty class.

"What's going on with you? Are you okay?" Mrs. Patterson looks concerned.

"It's a lot going on at home. I hate going home," I confess.

"Oh my, are you being abused?" Mrs. Patterson looks nervous.

"No, not really. I mean, my mom is pretty mean. She does whoop us over the smallest things, but that's not really the problem," I explain.

"Okay, well, I'm here if you want to talk. I've just noticed a drastic change in your behavior over the last few weeks." Mrs. Patterson sits down at the desk next to me.

"Yeah, it's just that I really miss my dad and my grandparents. My mom is keeping my sisters and me away from them because she's mad at something stupid," I frown.

"Does the reason have anything to do with you guys as kids?" Mrs. Patterson asks.

"No, it's all personal adult stuff that has nothing to do with us, but she still wants to put us in it, by keeping us away from them. We don't have our own house anymore. Our car is broke down. I just hate my life right now." I put my head back down on the desk as tear start to fill my eyes.

"Yeah, that sounds tough. So, your parents are going through a divorce, huh?" Mrs. Patterson's voice sounds softer.

"Yeah, but since my mom doesn't want us to see my dad at all, he's trying to build a case on her to get custody of us. If she would just stop being so mean, all of this wouldn't even be happening."

"So, your dad actually wants to be involved, and she's keeping you guys away from him?" Mrs. Patterson sounds confused.

"Right, and her reasons for keeping us away are because of adult reasons that have nothing to do with us. She's mad at him for her own personal whatever reasons," I wipe my eyes.

"Wow, usually these young black men don't want to take responsibility for their children. That's so sad, and I can tell you really love your dad." Mrs. Patterson rubs my arm.

"I have to sneak and call my dad and grandparents to let them know that we are okay. I have their phone numbers secretly written down. My dad and my grandparents love us so much. They show us more love than she ever has." I wipe my tears with the Kleenex Mrs. Patterson hands to me.

"Damn, what about your grandparents? Are those his or her parents?"

"Her parents, she's not talking to her own parents that's willing to do anything for her at the drop of a dime. We're homeless right now, but we don't even have to be. My grandparents want to help her out, but she doesn't know how to get over anything," I continue with no filter.

"Wow, that's so sad and stubborn of her. A lot of people these days don't have any support at all," Mrs. Patterson admits with a slight frown.

"My dad and grandparents are good people. That's why she's keeping us away from them, to be evil," I continue to cry.

"Well, do you have the piece of paper with their numbers on it now?" Mrs. Patterson asks politely.

"Yeah, I keep it in my sock," I nod my head.

"I'll let you use my cellphone really quick to call them," Mrs. Patterson grins.

My puffy face lights up. "Really? Okay." I dig in my sock to grab the small folded white piece of paper.

"Is your mom waiting on you outside right now?" Mrs. Patterson asks as she grabs her cellphone from her desk.

"No, she usually picks my sister up from school first."

"Okay, hurry up. Here you go." Mrs. Patterson hands me her cell phone.

I dial my dad's number first, and he picks up the phone on the first ring.

"Hello?"

"Hey, daddy! It's Miko," I smile.

"Hey, boo, where you at?" he asks.

"I'm at school using my teacher's cellphone."

He giggles. "What school do you go to now?"

"I go to Bagley, and we're living with Uncle Chi in his small cluttered house."

"You stole your teacher's phone?" he sounds surprised.

I laugh. "No, she's right here. I told her about our situation, and she was nice enough to let me use her phone to call you and my grandparents," I explain.

"Oh, that was really nice! You probably better get outside before your mom comes in. You can call your grandparents tomorrow when I come to pick you up," dad explains.

I inhale out of nervousness, knowing my dad means what he's saying. "Okay, I'm going to go."

"Okay, talk to you later." He hangs up the phone.

After we get off the phone, I thank Mrs. Patterson for letting me use her phone, then rush downstairs to meet my mom in the front of the school. When I get outside, my mom is just pulling up.

"Perfect!" I speak to myself.

I'm so anxious and nervous in class today. I snuck a few extra pairs of panties in my book bag, knowing I would be with my dad for a few days. I still can't believe Mrs. Patterson was nice enough to let me use her phone. She comes off so hard and stern in class, I wouldn't have ever thought she had a heart under the metal suit.

"Okay, class, let's head to the gym!" Mrs. Patterson claps her hands, seeming to be in a good mood.

The gymnasium is downstairs towards the right if you take the staircase closest to my classroom. We get to the gym in no time because Bagley is not that big of a school. Once we get inside the gym, it is obvious our gym teacher is absent today. Mr. Dickson usually greets us at the door, so Mrs. Patterson doesn't even have to come in. Today is different, which means easy gym day.

"Yes! I'm so happy Mr. Dickson isn't here today!" Chrisstana turns around and smile at me.
"I know, we'll probably just get to have free time," I return the smile.

Once Mrs. Patterson leaves, the substitute teacher makes an announcement.

"Hello, young ladies and gentlemen. My names is Ms. Lily, and I'll be your substitute teacher for today and tomorrow. Being that Mr. Dickson called out last minute, I didn't prepare a plan for today. With that being said, you guys will get free time today."

The class begins a soft cheer out of happiness.

"I will need everybody to bring their gym shoes to class tomorrow. I'll have a ton of workout moves and activities for tomorrow's hour. You guys get some rest today and come prepared tomorrow. Free time can begin!" Ms. Lily finishes.

Everybody grabs balls and ropes to play with their best friends. Usually, for recess, I'll try to find my cousin, Micha, when we're outside, but she's not in my class. I don't have a best friend in my class because I haven't been going to this school for that long.

PRETTY CAN BE UGLY

As I'm standing there trying to figure out what I'm going to do, Chrisstana walks up to me. "Hey, you want to see who can hold onto the monkey bar for the longest?"

"Okay" I shrug my shoulders, since I'm not doing anything else.

Out of all the girl stuff we could have done, Chrisstana wants to play a strength game. I'm not surprised because she seems like a tomboy. Even though she's really pretty with naturally long wavy hair, she has a boyish way about herself.

"Okay, so just grab the monkey bars like this and whoever lets go first, loses," Chrisstana explains.

"Alright," I giggle, feeling confident about this one.

As Chrisstana and I hold ourselves up on the money bars, we start to attract a small crowd. Then a few minutes later, Chrisstana lets go.

"Yes!" I let go of the monkey bar to fall down to the gym floor right after her.

"Aye, new girl, what y'all playing?" Matthew walks up to me bouncing a basketball.

"My name is Miko," I correct him.

He exhales hard. "Miko, what y'all playing, man?"

"This monkey bar game. Whoever can hold themselves up the longest wins," I explain.

"Aww, let me see if Tim want to play. Tim!" Matthew runs to go get Tim.

"You got lucky! Let's go again!" Chrisstana challenges me again.

By the time Matthew and Tim comes to play, Chrisstana and I had been holding ourselves for about a minute or more. I take a quick glance at her to the right of me, and her high yellow face is turning bloodshot red.

"Chrisstana's face looks like a cherry!" Matthew jokes aloud, making everybody around us laugh.

"Kimiko Lewis!" Ms. Lily calls.

As soon as she calls, I drop to the floor.

"Damn, cutie, what's your number?" Tim asks as if this is the first time we've seen each other.

I giggle at his joke and continued to jog toward the teacher.

"Your father is here to pick you up," Ms. Lily's words send chills down my spine.

"Okay, he's in the front office?" I ask.

"Yes, so go upstairs and get your belongings." Ms. Lily smiles nicely.

I run upstairs as fast as I can. My adrenaline is rushing as if I'm about to get caught by my mom. The sound of my locker opening causes Mrs. Patterson to come out of the classroom.

"Kimiko, where are you going?" Mrs. Patterson sounds concerned.

"My dad is here to pick me up," I smile, praying she doesn't ask any other questions.

"Okay, are you going to be okay?" She kneels down to look me in my eyes.

"Yeah, I'll be fine! Thank you so much!" I couldn't resist hugging her.

"You're welcome, baby. I pray that your situation gets better by the grace of God. Oh, wait before you leave. Let me grab your report card." Mrs. Patterson pulls my report card from her files really quickly.

"Good luck, baby girl." Mrs. Patterson hands me my report card and waves goodbye.

Running downstairs as fast as possible, I get to the front office in no time.

"Mik Mik!" Dad picks me up and hugs me.

"Hey!" Just seeing him makes my heart warm.

"You ready?" Dad asks in a cheerful spirit.

"Yup!" I giggle, following him out the door.

Even though I know I'm not supposed to leave with my dad, when I'm with him, it just feels safe. I know my dad might be considered a bad guy to the world or to society because he's in the streets, but to me, he's my hero.

"Did your teacher give you your report card before you left?" Dad closes the door to the car.

"Yeah, but I'm scared to look at it," my eyebrows rise to the top of my head.

"Why? You always do good in school," he sounds confused.

"I just haven't been happy. Moving around from here to there, switching schools. It's been hard to concentrate on schoolwork." I admit hoping he let's up on me.

Dad snatches the report card from my hand quickly. "Concentrate my ass! Let's see here."

I hope I don't get in trouble. I close my eyes tightly waiting for his reaction.

"Dang, all of these C's, D's and F's," Dad, says softly.

"For real?" I ask shockingly.

"Yeah," he flips the report card in my direction for me to see.

"I'm surprised it's other letters on here besides the letter F," I add sarcastically, grabbing the piece of paper.

"It's okay, Booka! You will do better next time." Dad puts his seat belt on and starts the car.

What? That's all he gotta' say! See, that's why he's my nigga! I instantly feel better.

"Where we about to go?" I ask while sitting in the front seat.

"Over Selena's Aunt's house."

Ugh, this bitch Selena again." I roll my eyes behind his back. "Why? Let's go over Big Mama's house," I suggest.

"Joyce might come over there with the police again. We have to go to places she don't know about," Dad makes his point.

I don't like this Selena bitch, I think to myself looking out of the window.

"Selena is going to help us get Koko and help me get full custody of y'all since Joyce wants to play hardball." Dad's attitude slightly changes.

CHAPTER **FORTY-NINE**

"YOUR HAIR IS so thick and long. My hair used to be just like that when I was younger." Selena tries hard to make conversation with me while my dad is upstairs.

Yeah fucking right, bitch, you're basically a White woman. I snap back rudely in my head. "Thank you," I respond shortly so it's obvious I don't want to talk to her.

"I know you miss your sister Koko, huh?" Selena still bites.

"Yeah, I miss a lot of my family members. That reminds me, I need to call my grandparents." I get up to go ask my dad for his cellphone. *Sloppy seconds ass hoe.* I roll my eyes as I walk up the stairs.

"Dad, can I see your phone to call my grandparents?" I ask from the doorway.

"Yeah, did Selena tell you the caseworker is coming to talk to us tomorrow in the morning?" Dad asks.

"No," I answer quickly. *She probably was trying to though and I cut the conversation short.* I giggle to myself.

Instead of talking on the phone downstairs in front of Selena, I go outside on the porch for some privacy. The only phone number I know by heart is my grandparents'. I look at them to be my superheroes because I know no matter what, they will always have things under control and have their shit together. Sometimes my dad might try to act like things are under control when they're really not, but my grandparents always have their t's crossed and their i's dotted. I can always, under any circumstance, depend on my grandparents. That's why they hold a special place in my heart. The thought of not being able to talk or see them kills me inside.

    Granny picks up the phone. "Hello."
    "Hey, Granny!" my eyes get watery from hearing her voice.
    "Mickey? Hey boo! Where are you?" Granny sounds relieved.
    "I'm with my daddy right now," I pace around the porch.
    "This is his new number?" Granny sounds confused.
    "I don't know if it's new, but this is his cellphone number."
    "Okay, I'll have to change it in the phone book then. How did you get back with him? Is Koko there too?"
    "Well, my teacher let me call him from her cell phone at school yesterday. Once I told him what school I was going to, he came to pick me up," I explain.
    "So, your mom doesn't know about this?" Granny asks.
    "She will once school let out and she sees I'm not there," I giggle at the thought.
    "I'm guessing the school doesn't notify her when you leave early," Granny adds.
    "Not when it's a parent. I don't think so." I shrug my shoulders.
    "Joyce is going to be pissed about that." Granny sounds more than sure.
    "I know, all of this back and forth is so stressful Granny," I confess.
    "I'm sorry, boo, I know it is. I don't know why they won't let y'all come down here with us until they figure it out." Granny slurps the last of her drink.
    "I know, then my mama got us over there living with Uncle Chi and his cluttered house. I hate it there!"
    "Mary, who is it?" I can hear Granddaddy in the background. "It's Mickey! She's with Jihod right now." In no time, Granddaddy picks up another phone in the house.

"Hello?" Granddaddy speaks a little louder than usual.

"Yes, we can hear you, Jim!" Granny speaks as loud as him.

"Mickey, this is your daddy's new phone number?" Granddaddy sounds like he's frowning, his favorite thing to do.

"Yes," I smile not even wanting to explain.

"He switches numbers like his boxers," granddaddy jokes in a serious way.

"I was telling granny how much I hate living over there with Uncle Chi," I try to catch granddaddy up on the conversation.

"Shh! That's ridiculous! I don't know why she left from Manor!" Granddaddy adds.

"She doesn't want nobody knowing where we live," I roll my eyes.

"But why? What does she think is going to happen? It's not like she can take care of herself. She's leaning on everybody else for help and shelter," Granddaddy sounds convinced.

"I don't like how she's making the kids suffer when they have plenty of places to go," Granny throws her two cents in.

"Exactly, we keep changing schools. We're living out of bags," I lay our business out on the floor.

"Living out of bags?" Granddaddy sounds shocked.

"Yeah, black garbage bags!" I try not to giggle at his temper.

"I told Mickey I don't know why she won't let them come down here with us until she gets her life settled." Granny sounds sad.

"She's still mad at y'all from Key's Sweet Sixteen party." I shake my head.

"She needs to get over herself!" Granddaddy adds sternly.

"I know, then she's always making us lie to everybody about every little thing. She wants everybody to feel so bad for her," I continue.

"That's why she want y'all to stay with her, so people can feel sorry for her," Granny puts two and two together.

"My daddy said the social worker is coming to talk to me tomorrow and she's going to ask me questions about how she treats us," I explain.

"Child Protective Services?" Granddaddy asks.

"Yeah" I confirm.

"Is it that bad?" Granddaddy sounds overwhelmed.

"Yeah, she hasn't been drinking as much as she used to when they were married, but she has done some crazy stuff when she's drunk," I confess.

"Like what?" Granny asks.

"Like fall asleep at the wheel in the drive-thru," I welcomingly give an example.

"Really?" Granny sounds surprised.

"Yeah, and she's done it more than once. Key and I were scared for our lives. The ambulance had to come and pick her up because she was passed out at the wheel. Anything could have happened to us." I try not to get emotional.

"Y'all are little girls, that's true, anything could have happened. Somebody could have tried to rob or kidnap y'all. Take the car, anything," Granddaddy agrees.

"Are you going to tell the social worker?" Granny asks.

"Yup, since she's trying to keep us away from everybody like she's crazy," I answer with confidence.

"She should!" Granddaddy sounds proud.

The session with the social worker was not as bad as I thought it would be. She is a Black woman, so that made me feel comfortable. She didn't ask too many questions or didn't stay for too long. She did tell us the information I provided could be enough to get Koko. I wish Key could come with us too, but I know that's impossible, being that she's not my daddy's biological daughter. I'm sure my mom would use that to her advantage. It kind of makes me sad, but Key is older, so I know she will be doing her own thing a lot sooner than me.

"I know you're happy that's over," Selena tries to start a conversation with me again.

Girl, here you go with these annoying ass comments.

"Yeah," I try to respond as shortly as I can.

"All of this will be over sooner than later, Honey." Selena ignores my attitude and continues with her upbeat, proper usual self.

"I hope so." I look away trying to figure out what I can do to end this conversation.

"Hopefully, Koko will be with us soon too with her pretty self." Selena smiles.

I give her a fake smile then get up to find my dad.

"Where you about to go?" I ask quickly.

"We about to go over Deanna's house. Put your shoes on." Dad walks towards the door while Selena and I get ready to follow.

I'm so happy that we're going over Aunt Deanna's house! I haven't seen Evin, April, or Adrian in so long. The area that we pull into seems to be in the same area that Big Mama lives in.

"Is this near Big Mama's house?" I ask looking out of the window at the familiar area.

"Yeah, Big Mama doesn't live that far from here, but we not going over there anytime soon. I don't want Joyce pulling up with the police," Dad explains.

"Yeah, I remember you told me that."

"Does she know where Deanna lives?" Selena asks.

Who the fuck is talking to you? I motion my lips silently.

"Nah, she doesn't," Dad shakes his head.

"Are you sure?" Selena sounds concerned.

You heard the man! Every word that comes out of her mouth itches me.

"Yeah, I'm sure. Deanna moved a few times since the last place Joyce knows of." Dad turns down a street that has a dead-end.

"Who is it?" A young man's voice slightly comes through the door.

"It's me, punk!" Dad yells, making Selena and me laugh.

"Who is me?" the young man behind the door sounds confused.

"Jihod, fool!" Dad yells louder.

"Oh, Uncle Jihod." Evin opens the door with a goofy smile on his face.

"Open the door, goofball! It's cold out here!" Dad laughs as everybody rushes out of the cold weather.

"Hey, niecey pooh!" Aunt Deanna screams as we walk through the door.

"Hey, Aunt Deanna!" I giggle at her enthusiasm.

"How you doing, baby girl?" Aunt Deanna kisses me on my cheek and forehead.

"I'm doing good."

"We missed you!" Aunt Deanna smiles.

"We thought you were never coming back," Evin giggles.

"Boy, shut up! We did not think that!" Aunt Deanna laughs at Evin.

"Right, he sitting up there saying anything!" Dad jokes.

"Where is April?" I ask, changing the subject off of me.

"Oh, she went outside. She's probably across the street, or something." Aunt Deanna grabs my coat and puts it in the closet.

"So, what's been going on, Deanna?" Selena asks, getting comfortable on the couch.

"Nothing much, just started my new job a few weeks ago." Aunt Deanna sits on the couch.

"You like it?" Selena asks.

"Same old bullshit, different company." Aunt Deanna shrugs her shoulders, giggling at her own comment.

Dad laughs. "Right, aye, Deanna, you got some Kool-Aid?"

"Yeah, you want some?" Aunt Deanna offers without hesitation.

"Yeah, let me get a glass." Dad takes his fitted cap off.

"Y'all want some too?" Aunt Deanna looks at Selena and me.

"Nah, I don't like Kool-Aid," I add.

"You do!" Dad corrects me as if he could persuade me into liking it.

"No, I don't, I never liked Kool-Aid!" I look at him headstrong, sure of myself.

"I'll just have some of Jihod's," Selena adds properly.

"Some of mine?" Dad looks at her with confusion.

"Yeah, silly!" Selena giggles.

"Now, why would you want some of mines when she's asking if you want your own, silly?" Dad asks sarcastically, making everybody else laugh.

"I just want a couple of gulps," Selena adds politely.

"Right, that's what a glass is. A couple of gulps, I just want a couple of gulps as well." Dad stands his ground, laughing at the conversation.

"Okay, I'm just going to get y'all separate glasses!" Aunt Deanna walks to the kitchen.

"You didn't ask me if I wanted some!" Evin yells so Aunt Deanna could hear him from the kitchen.

"Boy, you can come get your own glass of Kool-Aid!" Aunt Deanna laughs at Evin.

"Dang, I ain't never met a Black person who didn't like Kool-Aid," Evin continues with his jokes.

"Right, I don't know what's wrong with her!" Dad looks at me like I'm ill.

"First time for everything." I lean back on the couch, ignoring their sarcasm.

"Here y'all go." Deanna hands the glass of Kool-Aid to Daddy and Selena.

"Good looking," Dad thanks Aunt Deanna.

"Where is Adrian?" I look around.

"He's upstairs, knocked out." Aunt Deanna sips her Kool-Aid.

"Last time I was over here he was knocked out," Dad adds.

"He act like an old man," Evin adds before getting up.

"So, what's up, J! What's going on?" Aunt Deanna flops on the couch.

"Man, going through this bullshit with Joyce." Dad's mood slightly changes.

"She still trying to keep you away from the kids?" Aunt Deanna sounds surprised.

"Yeah, and I'm like damn! What does anything we went through have to do with the kids!" Dad explains.

"Right! Then she trying to keep them away from the family too," Aunt Deanna adds.

"Exactly! What the fuck did anybody else do to you? I just don't understand the shit at all. She making things way more complicated than it has to be." Dad sounds stressed.

"Joyce is crazy," Aunt Deanna tries to lighten the conversation.

"She's crazy as hell, then she keeps changing their schools so I won't know where they are, so now I'm about to play the same game because she doesn't have full custody of them. So, I can do the same thing! They my kids too!" Dad frowns.

"So, what about school? You not gone take her back to the school she go to?" Aunt Deanna asks.

"Nah, I'ma put Miko in another school. What school do April go to?" Dad finishes his Kool-Aid in no time.

"She goes right up here to the YMCA," Aunt Deanna points as if it's super close.

"I'm a bit nervous because I think Joyce knows about the house on Mendota, so I'm sure she'll be coming over with the police, trying to act like she has full custody. And if Miko is there, they will make her go with Joyce," Dad explains.

"Maybe you should let her stay here. She doesn't know where I live," Aunt Deanna suggests.

"Right, until the school year-end or something." Dad looks like he's in deep thought.

"Yeah, and she can just walk to school every day with April. The Y is right up here at the corner," Aunt Deanna continues.

"Okay, cool, that sounds like a plan!" Dad rubs his hands together.

"So, yeah, you would just have to enroll her and go get some uniforms," Aunt Deanna explains.

"Oh, okay, what color uniforms do they wear?" Dad asks.

"Burgundy and pink," Aunt Deanna adds quickly.

"Oooo, I love those uniform colors!" I get excited.

"I don't think I ever seen those uniforms color," Dad looks confused.

"I have, the girls wear like pink plaid skirts, right?" Selena asks.

"Yeah, with the light pink shirts." Aunt Deanna walks to the backroom.

"It look just like the yellow and brown uniforms we used to wear at Cherry Hill," I try to give dad an idea.

"The uniforms look like this," Aunt Deanna brings out April's top and bottom.

"Oh, okay! Yeah, it does look just like the yellow and brown uniform," Dad agrees.

"The pink is way cuter!" I cross my legs, excited at the thought of wearing cute uniforms.

"Yeah, it is!" Selena agrees.

"Okay, so we can go pick up the uniforms today, and we'll go enroll you on Monday," Dad explains.

"Okay!" I'm so happy!

"You want to come with us to go get the uniforms?" Dad asks.

"Nah, can I stay here?" I look at dad with pleading eyes.

"I don't care."

"She's going to be staying here anyway. She can stay!" Aunt Deanna laughs.

CHAPTER **FIFTY**

ANOTHER DAY, ANOTHER school, only this time I'll be going to school with my cousin April. Living with Aunt Deanna and them has been so much fun. Everybody is always joking around and showing affection. There's no tension, no lying, and no attitudes. Everybody, for the most part, are always chilling. Even though I'm not one of Aunt Deanna's children, I don't feel left out. Aunt Deanna never makes me feel like I'm an outcast. She plays with me just as much as her own kids, and if I get out of line, she will cuss me out like one of her own kids as well.

Today is my first day of school at the YMCA, and I'm so freaking nervous. Even though I've been doing this switching school stuff often lately, I still haven't gotten used to being the "New Girl". I hate being the center of attention. Too much attention at once makes me feel so uncomfortable.

"I hate this new girl, shit!" I confess to April as we walk to school.
"How many schools have you been to already?" April giggles.
"This is my third school this year for 6th grade." I roll my eyes.
"Dang, did you even get to make any friends?" April asks.
"Barely, my parents keep switching my school because of this custody battle bullshit. I can't wait until I get older, dog." I start to become aggravated by the thought of everything I've been going through.

"That's crazy, I mean, we move a lot too, which is annoying, but most of the time I get to stay at the same school unless it's too far," April continues to guide the way to school, and in a matter of feet, we're at the school in no time.

"Damn, we here already?" I didn't realize the school is damn near right next door to the house on the other side of the alley.

"Yeah, I told you it was close." April laughs.

"Aww, damn, I'm getting the bubble guts! I wish somebody else was new with me." I hold my stomach.

April laughs even harder. "Miko, you good! It's not that bad!"

When I got to the front office, they were expecting me and acted as if they already knew me. Everybody is very nice, which makes me feel a little bit more comfortable. After grabbing a few pieces of paper, a lady with all black on leads me upstairs to my homeroom class. I take a deep breath while I stand outside of the classroom. The lady and my new teacher are having small talk then my teacher introduces herself to me.

"Hi, my name is Ms. Green. What's yours?" Ms. Green smiles really big.

"I'm Kimiko (Kee-mee-ko)." I try to pronounce my name slowly because everybody always pronounces it wrong.

"Okay, nice to meet you Kimiko." Ms. Green still pronounces my name wrong.

"Okay, come to the front office if you need anything in the future," the lady in the black waves bye as Ms. Green guides me into the classroom.

"Class, everybody meet Kimiko! She's going to be joining us for the remaining of the academic year." Ms. Green takes me to my desk. As we're headed to the back of the classroom, I hear soft giggles.

"Okay, it looks like all of your books are in your desk. Let me know if you have any questions," Ms. Green continues to be very polite.

I feel like everybody is looking at me, which is killing me inside. All I can think of is the end of the day. I can't wait to link up with April after school. A little after Ms. Green goes to her desk, she asks the class to pull out our math books so we can start a lesson. Hopefully, playing catch up won't be too hard, but by the looks of this school and the up keeping, it looks like it might be a challenge. This school, compared to Bagley, is much cleaner and up to date. I haven't even seen the entire school yet, but I can tell by the hallways and the lockers that it's going to be an overall better school.

"Class, don't forget we will be attending an assembly after lunch today, so don't bring anything you are not going to want to carry around," Ms. Green announces.

After Math, Social Studies, and Literature, it was time for Art. Instead of having the class line up and taking us to the Art class, Ms. Green let's us out by ourselves.

"Kimiko, do you want me to show you where the Art class is?" Ms. Green asks loud enough for my classmates to hear.
"I'll show her where it is," a skinny light-skinned girl with really short hair offers out of nowhere.
"Okay, thanks, Kesha! See you guys in a few!" Ms. Green gets back to work at her desk.
"I'm Kesha, what's your name again?" Kesha asks looking confused like she didn't hear it clearly when Ms. Green introduced me.
"It's Kee-mee-ko," I say slowly.
"That's pretty, Kimiko!" Kesha surprisingly pronounces it correctly.
"Oh, wow, you said it right!"
"What do people usually say?" Kesha smiles.
"People usually pronounce it like Kah-mee-ko or Ky-mee-ko. My family just calls me Miko," I explain.
"I don't see what's so hard about the pronunciation." Kesha shrugs her shoulders.

"I know, right? That's what I say all the time." I can tell already Kesha and I are going to be friends.

"So, do you know anybody else here at the school?" Kesha asks.

"Yeah, my cousin April go here too." I point in her direction when I see her in the hallway as other classes start letting out.

"Cousin!" April wraps her arm around me standing about four to five inches taller than me.

"What's up, April?" Kesha speaks as if she knows her already.

"Hey, Kesha! Y'all in the same class?" April asks.

"Yeah," I'm happy at the fact that they already know each other.

"Who class y'all in?" April asks.

"Ms. Green's class, she pretty cool," I add, holding my books.

"Oh yeah, I know her, she nice." April pops her gum.

"So, where is the Art class again?" I ask Kesha.

"Oh, right there!" she points right across the hallway.

"Okay, that's close!"

"Oooo, April, let me get some gum!" a cute brown-skinned guy with a nice haircut walks up to April.

"Boy, nooo, I already told yo' annoying self I don't have anymore!" April laughs.

"You lying, I saw you pass Alexa one just a few minutes ago!" he continues looking silly.

"That was my last one!" April laughs at his funny facial expression.

"Say 'you swear to God,'" he challenges her.

April can't help but to burst in laughter. "I don't say that!"

"See, you lying! It's cool! You want to be stingy! I got you! Hold on, who is this?" he stops in his own sentence.

"Step away, this is my cousin!" April put her hand in between us.

"Heyyy, cousin!" he waves at me with a cute smirk.

"Hey," I giggle at his flirting.

"I'ma see you later." He walks away slowly looking at me in a flirty way.

"Let me get some gum?" I ask jokingly.

"Damn, people be checking for me like I'm the vending

machine. I'm about to start charging niggas." April digs in her pocket discreetly.

Kesha giggles, mimicking April. "Talking about, 'I'm about to start charging niggas!'"

"Thanks! And who was that anyway?"

"That's Ernest, and girl he's nobody. So y'all about to go to Art class?" April asks quickly.

"Yeah, it's right here."

"Alright, well, my class is all the way downstairs. I'ma see you at the end of the day." April walks and talks at the same time as she jogs down the stairs to make it to class on time.

"Come on." Kesha walks ahead of me to the class, and we sit next to each other.

I notice this high yellow girl on the other side of Kesha looking like she kind of has an attitude. I don't know her name yet, but I'm assuming she and Kesha are friends.

When the end of the day finally arrives, Kesha introduces me to a couple of her friends. The mean looking high yellow girl isn't anywhere around, so I still don't really know who she is.

"You walking home with April?" Kesha asks as she looks for her mom.

"Yeah, have you seen her out here?" I look around.

"No, but I gotta' go. My mama here. See you tomorrow!" Kesha waves and runs to her car.

As I'm walking around, I see the boy, Ernest, from earlier with two other really cute boys.

I wonder what grade they in. I grin at the nice sight.

While I'm being nosy, I accidentally walked into this pretty brown-skinned girl. "My bad! I didn't even see you."

"It's okay, I wasn't paying attention either!" she giggles. "Hey, you the new girl, right?" she points at me.

"Yeah, I'm in Ms. Green's class." I nod my head.

"Oh, okay, me too! I'm Stacey!" she smiles.

"I'm Kimiko." I didn't even bother saying it slowly.

"That's a pretty name! I never heard of that name before," Stacey continues with her bubbly personality.

"Thank you! It's Japanese!" I return the smile.

"You mixed with Japanese?" Stacey asks, looking surprised.

I can't help but laugh. "No, my mom just like Japanese names. My other two sisters have Japanese names too."

"Oh, okay, you look like you could be mixed with Japanese or something. Is this all of your hair too?" Stacey touches my ponytail in disbelief.

"Yeah," I giggle at her energy.

"Girl! Can I borrow some? And you said you not mixed with nothing?" Stacey continues.

"Nope, I'm not mixed."

"Shidd, yes, you are! Even I got a little Indian in me!" Stacey rejects my answer.

"Well, maybe a little Indian and White. But my parents are both Black people." I wiggle my answer a little bit for the first time.

"Yeah, you most definitely mixed with something!" Stacey sticks with her opinion.

"People always say that!" I giggle.

The last time I told my dad that people always think that I'm mixed, he told me that we are. He said that his grandmother, who is my great grandmother, is a full-blooded Indian. I remember her a little bit when the family church was open. But she died when I was younger. Mom, on the other hand, likes to say that we're mixed with White on her side, but she's adopted, so how does she really know? I mean, Mom does have a really pale skin complexion, but Black people come in all skin complexions.

As Stacey and I finish conversing, a high yellow boy with braces runs by and hits Stacey.

"Stop playing, Jay!" Stacey starts to run after him but decided not to.

"Who is that?" I laugh noticing him from earlier.

"That's Jay ugly butt! He play too much!" Stacey smiles.

"Is he friends with Ernest?" I ask, trying to get familiar with everything.

"Yeah, him, Ernest, and Jeremy are like best friends," Stacey explains.

"Oh, okay, do you know April? I been looking for her since I got out here." I glanced around again trying to see if she's outside yet.

"Yeah, I know April. I just saw her not too long ago. She was over there!" Stacey points from where we're standing.

"Oh, there she go right there!" I finally can see her.

"How you know her?" Stacey asks.

"She's my cousin, I'ma see you tomorrow in class!"

As I approach April, I see she's talking to a girl and two boys.

"Oh, there you go! I was looking for you!"

"Girl, I was looking for you!" I continue to walk over towards the small group.

"Damn, April, this yo' cousin?" a short, light-skinned boy smiles really big.

"Boy, shut up!" April laughs.

"Sike! Nah," he adds in a funny tone voice.

"April, you rude, introduce us to yo' cousin!" the other boy adds.

"Introduce yourself!" April snaps in a jokey way.

"Right, she is standing right here!" the other girl takes up for April.

"But that is rude if she already know us, and she already know her. Then she is supposed to introduce us since she's the mutual friend," the first boy takes up for the second boy.

"But you basically spoke to her when you made your little comment. From there, you could have introduced yourself," April chews on her gum.

"Well, I'm Kimiko. Hey, y'all!" I introduce myself to everybody to end the stupid conversation.

"Right, since y'all can't seem to come up with a solution!" the other girl laughs.

"Since April gotta' be rude, I'm Deon, nice to meet you." Deon grabs my hand and kisses it, making all of us crack up laughing.

"Now you see why I didn't want to introduce you, right? Straight ham!" April continue laughing.

"April, don't hate!" Deon smiles like he's the mac of the year.

"Boy, bye, on what?" April smacks her lips.

"I'm Lip, but I'm not gone kiss you on your hand. You might pass out if these lips touch you girl," Lip smiles in a funny way making everybody laugh.

"Okay, Lip! You say you Rico Suave with the lines, huh?" Deon dap Lip up.

"Y'all so irritating. I'm Tish!" Tish waves.

"Yes, this is Tish, my best friend!" April wraps her arm around her.

"Oh, so you can introduce her, but you can't introduce us?" Deon gives April the side-eye.

"That's cause y'all irritating! Come on, Miko, we out!" April starts walking away.

"Alright, see y'all later!" I wave bye.

"Bye, cutie!" one of the boys speak softly, but I can't tell which one.

The walk home is literally like five minutes tops. I can tell I'm going to like this school way better than the last two schools I went to. The uniform colors are prettier, and the kids are cooler. As soon as we get home, April turns on the small television in the kitchen.

"You like the Jamie Foxx show?" April asks while she opens the box of Frosted Flakes.

"Not really, he be trying too hard to me." I reach my hand out for the box of cereal so I can pour me a bowl too.

"You tripping! Jamie Foxx is funny as hell! He be having me rolling!" April laughs at the thought of the show.

"He aight." I'm not convinced.

"It should be coming on in a minute." April pours the milk in the bowl.

"So, what grade is that boy Ernest in? He is cute!" I confess, taking a full spoon of cereal from my bowl.

"Ernest is in the same grade as me. He's in the seventh grade, and he is a hot mess!" April shakes her head.

"Why you say that?" she got my attention now.

"Girl, cause they all some hoes. They all some big fat hoes!" April shrugs her shoulders.

"Really?" I ask in fake disbelief hoping she would elaborate.

"Yeah, him and all of his friends, Jay and Jeremy and them. All they do is walk around flirting with all the girls. Hitting girls on their booties, just being childish," April explains.

"What? Yeah right!"

"I'm serious, every time Jay talks to me, he be staring at my boobs. I know that's probably the only reason they talk to me because I have big boobs," April giggles.

Bursting out in laughter I add, "What you be saying when he be staring at your boobs."

"I be like boy... what the fuck you looking at?"

I crack up laughing "And what he be saying?"

"Sitting there looking stupid with his braces." April chews her Frosted Flakes.

"That's hilarious! These Frosted Flakes are banging right now!" I change the subject.

"I know, right? These my favorite!" April does a silly dance across the table.

"Where Auntie Deanna at?" I ask as the Jamie Foxx show comes on.

"She at work." April's eyes are glued to the TV.

"Oh, okay."

I forgot that other people's parents actually have jobs and that they are gone every day between the same hours. With my mom being disabled and my dad being in the streets, I'm not used to that type of schedule. I'm used to my mom being around every second of the day. It's pretty cool having the house to ourselves every day after school. I'm sure that's the kind of lifestyle my mom had growing up with two working parents. That's probably what allowed her to be so fast in the pants growing up, and why she's so hard on Key when it comes to boys because she's afraid she might be just like her.

CHAPTER **FIFTY-ONE**

"SPISS… SPISS," I hear a hissing sound from behind me.

When I turn around, it's Everett trying to get my attention. He balls up a small piece of paper and throws it at me. I grab the piece of paper off the floor quickly so Ms. Walker won't notice. When I open it, it reads: *"You smell that?"*

I want to laugh aloud, but it's super quiet in the classroom. On top of that, what's making the note even funnier is that it really is a weird aroma coming from the right of me, but I don't know what it is.

I write back on the crumpled paper, *"Yeah! What the fuck is that???"* Then I ball the paper back up. Drop it on the floor and kick it back towards Everett.

"Okay, class, you guys are free to go to lunch!" Ms. Walker announces at her desk.

After gathering a few things, I see Everett approaching me with my peripheral vision.

"That's Mitchel stanky ass!" Everett admits in a blunt way.

I burst in laughter. "Damn, that nigga' need to get it together. It's called soap and water."

"Yeah, I told that nigga' last month that he needed to take a shower." Everett seems annoyed, which is even more hilarious.

"What's up, Kimiko!" Rachel walks up to me in her usual bubbly way.

"What's up, y'all ready to go?" I ask.

"Yeah, we just waiting on Kansas." Rachel points towards her.

It's been a month since I started this school, and I hang with Kesha, Rachel, Tiara, and Kansas. We call ourselves "Triple KRT." I hang with Stacey as well sometimes; she's really cool too. The other girls aren't as close to Stacey like I am, so I kind of just talk to her on my own time. Kansas is the mean looking high yellow girl that was distant towards me when I first started. She's still pretty short with me most of the time. I think she's secretly jealous of how close Kesha and I are becoming. Kesha calls both of us her best friend, and I've been over Kesha's house a few times already. Every time I go over Kesha's house, Kansas is over there. Kesha and Kansas' mothers are close friends, so they're around each other like family all the time. Even though Kansas is weird towards me, Kesha and I don't let it alter our friendship. Kansas doesn't talk to me, and I don't talk to her. I was thinking about trying to be nice to her, but I'm not about to kiss her ass.

On the way to lunch, I see Jeremy talking to a group of people. Oh my god, he is so cute to me! He never ever talks to me. It's so annoying. His best friends, Ernest and Jay, talk and play with me all the time, but he doesn't pay me any attention. I'm almost sure he doesn't have a crush on me. I don't have boobs or a big booty, so I'm probably last on his list. Unfortunately, that's not cutting my huge crush shorter. I feel so stupid having a crush on somebody that doesn't like me back. I wish this feeling could just go away. I haven't told many people about how much I like Jeremy. Of course, April knows since we live together. I've also told Kesha, Tiara, and

Stacey. I haven't physically told Kansas, since we don't talk much, but we do talk to most of the same people, so I'm sure she already knows about my crush. I'm sure Rachel knows already as well, but I haven't told her myself because she has too many other friends. I'm afraid if I tell her, the word might get all the way out. I made everybody promise to God they wouldn't tell him I like him. I just don't think he's feeling me back, so I don't want to face the rejection.

"You see your boo, Jeremy?" Tiara secretly whispers in my ear.
"Nooo, I don't." I try to hide my blushing.
"Yeah, right!" Tiara laughs.

During lunchtime, everyone is talking, joking and chilling with their close friends.

"Do y'all know that song 'Closer to my dreams'?" Rachel takes the floor.
"Oh, yeah! I love that song!" Kesha gets excited.
"Me too! Look, I know how to do the beat!" I hit my fist and knuckles against the lunch table making sounds similar to the song.
"Closer to my dreams..." Kesha sings and bobs her head.
"Feel it in my sleep..." Rachel joins in.

Kesha and Rachel are singing, as everybody else at the table joins in while I'm beating on the table. I'm so happy that everybody can sing to my beat. That gives me confirmation that I'm doing a good job with making the beat sound like the actual song; if I wasn't, everybody would have clowned me for thinking I knew the song.

As soon as lunch was starting to get fun, it was over. I take a glance around the lunchroom to see what Jeremy is doing. I see him flirting with some girls in his grade. These girls look like they've hit puberty already. They have boobs, booty, and everything in between. And I'm sitting over here still shaped like a third grader.

"Guess what I heard." Stacey walks up to me and locks her arm around mine.

"What?" I'm all ears.

"I heard Marcus like you." Stacey smiles really big.

"Who?" The name doesn't ring a bell .

"Marcus, girl! The cute boy with the braids." Stacey sounds excited.

"I don't think I know who he is." I'm still lost.

"I'll show you!" She pulls me in her direction.

"Is he in the seventh grade?"

"No, he in our grade," Stacey continues to guide me upstairs.

Sometimes when I hang out with Stacey, I feel like no one wants to see us hanging out for whatever reason. Her other friends, my friends, everybody seems to be against our friendship. No one has ever said anything to me about it, but I can just feel the vibe.

"Him over there, with the long straight back braids." Stacey points in a discreet way.

Marcus is a little bit taller than me, kind of on the chubby side, about a shade darker than me, with long braids. I'm surprised this is my first time noticing him because he's really cute.

"So, what do you think?" Stacey nudges me.

"I mean… he is cute." I shrug my shoulders.

"I go with his best friend, Nickolas." Stacey smiles.

"Oh, okay, which one is Nickolas?" I ask looking over at them across the hallway.

"Nickolas is the taller brown-skinned one," Stacey points.

"Oh yeah, I see." Marcus looks at me from across the hall.

"So, you want me to tell him you want to go with him?" Stacey jumps right to conclusions.

"No, don't tell him that!" I stop her in her tracks.

"Why not?" Stacey giggles as I guide her back to the class.
"You can tell him I think he's cute too," I correct her.
"Okay, cool, I'll be back." Stacey runs to deliver the message.
"Damn, she can't wait," I speak to myself quietly.

Stacey's speedy response made me get a little nervous, so instead of talking to people in the hallway before class starts, I decide to go to class a little earlier.

"Hey, girl!" I mistakenly speak to Kansas out of nervousness.
"Hey," Kansas responds dryly.
Oh yeah, I forgot we don't really fuck with each other like that for whatever reason. I walk to my seat, sort of anxious, waiting on Stacey.
"Do you know where Stacey is?" Sharee asks.
"Nope," I lie, not feeling like explaining what is going on.

Sharee is Stacey's best friend. She's kind of corny to me. She tries to be nice to me, but she follows after everything Stacey does, so I don't think it's genuine. My heart drops as Stacey walks into the classroom.

"Where you end up going?" Stacey looks confused.
"I came in here," I giggle at myself.
"He said, do you want to go with him?" Stacey smiles.
"Class, everybody find their seats!" Ms. Green walks to the front of the class.
"Tell him yea," I reply quietly as everyone settles in the classroom.

"I saw Jeremy talking to Ciara and Chasity and them today. I'm just looking like, these girls got all of this body. I'm sure he never even think to look my way!" I take another scoop of Frosted Flakes.

"You won't ever know until you find out." April burst out laughing at Jamie Foxx.

"I can tell if a boy like me. He literally never even looks in my direction."

"You want me to ask him tomorrow?" April looks at me.

"Hell, Nah!" I burst out.

April giggles. "See, that's what I'm talking about."

"I found out Marcus likes me today," I change the subject, giving up on Jeremy.

"Aww, little Marcus with the braids?" April smiles.

"Yeah."

"Y'all make a cute couple!" April confesses.

"Girl, Stacey so happy because she go with his best friend, Nickolas," I explain.

"Her sister so wack," April adds out of nowhere.

"Really?"

"Yeah, she got a real bad attitude. She be trying to act so stuck up," April explains.

"Wow, I never noticed. She seems kind of quiet to me. When I went over Stacey's house, she was just chilling," I explain.

"Well, she act completely different in school." April continues to eat her bowl of Frosted Flakes.

"Well, Stacey don't act like that," I confirm.

"I don't know Stacey that well, but her sister." April shakes her head.

"You think Aunt Deanna gone cook today?" I ask.

"Probably something quick if she do. The food stamps don't cut back on until next week," April explains.

"Oh, okay." I finish my bowl of Frosted Flakes.

"Have you talked to your mama or Key?" April ask.

I shake my head "Nope, I haven't."

"You don't be missing them?"

"Yeah, I do, but girl my mama so mean. I be happy to get a break from her ass. I hate that she act like that. She always lying, giving us whipping for no reason, keeping secrets and trying to keep us away from everybody. The shit is stressful"

"Dang, that's crazy. Auntie Joyce never seemed that way to me." April looks like what I'm saying is hard to believe.

"Looks can be deceiving. That's why I never judge a book by the cover. You never know how people really are. And you never know what a person is going through."

"Dang, that's deep but it's true," April look like she's in deep thought.

"Just be thankful you and your mama have a good relationship and that she loves you," I start to feel a little sorry for myself.

I'm guessing my mom still doesn't know what school I go to or where I live. I'm sure if she did, she would have come to get me. I'm honestly not missing her one bit. I do miss Key, and it feels like I haven't seen her in years. I don't get to see Koko often because she's back with my dad for now, and I'm not living with them. On the bright side, I get to call my grandparents whenever I want because my dad is not trying to keep us away from them. I love the school I'm going to. I'm just so happy with my life right now. I hope it can stay this way. My granddaddy said he would help my dad with his own trucking company since that's what he wants to do. That will help my dad financially and add some stability in our lives. It will also be good for him during this custody battle.

By the time we got finished with our homework, it's around the time Aunt Deanna should be coming home from work. When she comes home, she likes for the kitchen and house to be clean, so before we go outside after doing our homework, we make sure we clean the house up so Aunt Deanna won't come in tripping.

"So, you got a crush on Ashley's brother, huh?" I give April the side-eye.

"He got a crush on me," April smiles.

"He's cute! Y'all should go together," I suggest.

"Yeah, he is cute. I don't think Evin like him or the niggas he hang with though," April explains.

"Oh okay, I didn't know he was Evin's age," I add.

"Yeah, I don't know how Evin know his friends because they don't go to the same school, but I overheard stuff. I'm going to try and find out how they know each other."

"Why can't you just ask Evin?" I ask, kind of confused because that's her brother.

"Evin not gone just tell me. I have to find out on my own," April explains.

"APRIL! GET YO ASS IN HERE!" Aunt Deanna screams from the side door.

April and I both jump up, wondering what's wrong.

"This bitch." April looks me dead in my eyes before walking into the house.

"Why isn't the kitchen clean?" Aunt Deanna clearly has an attitude.

"I did clean up! Me and Miko did, you can ask her," April defends herself.

"So, where did all of these dishes come from?" Aunt Deanna is not convinced.

"I don't know! Must of came from Evin and Adrian. When we finished cleaning, it wasn't any dishes in the sink. Why don't you ask Evin to clean up?" April frowns.

"Don't ask me about what I ask him! I'm asking you! Shit!" Aunt Deanna yells louder at April.

Instead of April arguing back and forth with Aunt Deanna, April walks in her room. Aunt Deanna seems too angry, so I just follow April to her room.

"That's the shit I be talking about. She always checking me like I'm the maid around this bitch. Evin comes and goes, but while he's here, he should have to clean up too. Now watch, she don't say shit to him." April vents to me, pacing around the room looking like she's about to shed a tear.

"Right, that is bold." I just listen.

"Then all she do is sit around and baby Adrian. That shit so fucking annoying," April continues.

"Girl, did you hear what happened?" Rachel asks.

"What?" Kesha answers for me.

"So, I heard this past weekend at Nickolas's basement party, Sharee was touching on Marcus stuff," Rachel talks fast.

"Wow," that's all I could say at the moment.

"That bitch is a hoe!" Kesha frowns.

"Who?" Stacey joins the conversation out of nowhere with a grin on her face.

"Your best friend, Sharee!" Kesha looks Stacey dead in her eyes.

"Oh, are y'all talking about that rumor about this weekend?" Stacey tries to lighten the tension.

"Yeah, what happened?" I ask with the same attitude Kesha has.

"Nothing, I think they were just dancing together, then somebody made up a rumor. Talking about she was sucking on his stuff. But I was there, and that did not happen," Stacey explains, sounding pretty sure.

"What?" Rachel burst out in laughter.

"We should beat that bitch ass!" Kesha sounds like she's thinking aloud.

"Right!" Kansas backs her up.

Before any more gossip could go on, it was time for class to start. I'm not even mad about the rumor. I mean Marcus is my boyfriend or whatever, but I was never crazy about him from the start. I just went with him because everybody was acting like we made the cutest couple in the world. I still have a huge crush on Jeremy on the low. Marcus and I have only been going together for a few weeks now. For some reason, I felt unsure about going with him from the beginning, so this is just giving me a reason to break up with him.

When the class gets seated, Sharee decides to sit next to me.

"Oh, no this bitch didn't." Kesha whispers in my ear as I size Sharee up and down.

"Kimiko, I'm so sorry, but all of that stuff you heard about me and Marcus is a lie." Sharee's eyes get watery.

"Girl, don't fucking talk to me." I raise my hand to her face.

"I swear to God." Sharee starts crying.

"So, if nothing happened then why is she crying?" Kesha is still not convinced from the tears.

"Yeah, because she's guilty," Kansas adds sitting on the other side of Kesha.

"I don't even care. Fuck him and her, I'm breaking up with his fat ass after class." I roll my eyes and proceed to take out my assignment.

"I would too if I was you. You know Marcus and Nickolas and them some players anyway." Kansas rolls her eyes.

Once the end of the day comes, I kind of feel nervous. I could just easily tell somebody to tell Marcus I don't want to go with him anymore, but I want to do it myself. Marcus has been avoiding me all day. That's another reason why I know something happened between him and Sharee. Before I try to find Marcus, I have to get my stuff out of my locker. Out of nowhere, Nickolas turns the corner.

"Man, whatever you heard is a lie."

"Whatever, Nickolas. Where is Marcus?" I disregard everything that just came out of his mouth.

"He downstairs," Nickolas folds his arms.

Without saying bye to Nickolas, I rush downstairs to catch Marcus before he leaves. When I get downstairs, he's right by the door.

"Marcus, it's over. You can have Sharee since that's who you want." I walk away before he could say anything.

CHAPTER **FIFTY-TWO**

I CAN'T BELIEVE the last day of school is tomorrow. These last couple of months went by so fast. I'm going to make sure I have everybody's phone number written in my phonebook tomorrow. I'm really going to miss my friends! I've already asked if I could come back to YMCA for seventh grade and my dad said yes. It's pretty fun living with Aunt Deanna, even though she comes home from work tripping sometimes. She's still cool and jokes around with us most of the time. Living here with them and seeing April and Aunt Deanna's mother-daughter relationship makes me wish me and my sister could have a good relationship like that with our mom. The kind of relationship that doesn't hold grudges and isn't filled with jealousy and hate. The kind of relationship that doesn't have to be questioned or feels cold. I would like to think that my mom loves us, but most of the time, it's hard to tell. She barely acts like it, and she never says it.

I'm sure everybody gets mad at their mom and gets into arguments with their parents, but one thing I can say about Aunt Deanna is that she loves her kids. And I love her for that. I'm not even her child and I can see it. Even though she's not my daddy's blood sister, she's been more of an Aunt to me than a lot of my blood Aunts and relatives.

"I know y'all happy tomorrow the last day of school!" Aunt

Deanna smiles with the fan blowing against her body.

"I'ma be happy when you share that fan!" April burst out jokingly.

"Y'all had it all day! Aunt Deanna burst out laughing, play fighting with April.

"I'm really not that happy. I like the Y." I giggle at them fighting with each other.

"You just mad you not gone be able to see Jeremy!" April puts me on blast.

"Ooo! Miko, you got a boyfriend?" Aunt Deanna looks at me with a side-eye.

"No," I laugh.

"Yes, you do!" Aunt Deanna smacks her lips.

"Dang! Hogging the fan, let me and Miko see it!" April comes to sit down by me and places the fan directly in front of us.

"I wish I could go see Big Mama. I heard she not doing so well," I add, less excited.

"I know, yeah, Big Mama not doing good at all. Yo' daddy don't want Joyce to pull up trying to take y'all away again. I don't know why Joyce acting like that towards us." Aunt Deanna seems confused.

"She act like that towards everybody. She don't even want us talking to her own parents," I explain.

"Jihod told me, but why, is the question." Aunt Deanna seems even more confused.

"Just holding grudges. Her and my grandparents got into it at Key's Sweet Sixteen, and she still mad at that."

"Dang! That was a long time ago!" April shakes her head.

"Joyce know she need to cut it out! That's too long to still be mad at anybody, and I know your grandparents didn't do anything that bad. Joyce was the one drunk as hell." Aunt Deanna reminisces about the day of the party.

"They didn't do anything but tell her she was too drunk, and she was!" I explain taking my grandparents side.

"Well, everybody know she has a low tolerance for alcohol," Aunt Deanna admits.

"Right! She act like she the only one that don't know," I add as April and Aunt Deanna giggles at my comment.

"That's bold, she trying to keep y'all away from y'all grandparents too. Y'all got some good grandparents!" April admits.

"James and Mary will do anything for y'all and Joyce! She know she ain't right!" Aunt Deanna looks serious.

"I wish I had grandparents like y'all." April smiles.

"Girl, shut up!" Aunt Deanna laughs.

"Sike, nah, I love my grandma too, though." April picks up a sock to throw it at Aunt Deanna.

The summertime seems like it kicked in early this year. It's so hot outside! I'm surprised my hair hasn't sweated out. Everybody is being so nice to everybody today. I was expecting for it to be a whole bunch of fights, but it's the complete opposite. I guess everybody is going to miss everybody. Today, we're not doing much work, just talking and hanging around the classroom.

"Man, I'ma miss y'all ugly butts!" Everett looks around at all of us.

"We gone miss you too, E!" Kesha smiles.

"Ugh, no, we not!" Kansas smirks.

"Shut up, big head! You think Mama will let me come over for the summer?" Everett asks Kesha.

"Yeah! You know my mama love you!" Kesha sounds sure.

Kesha has like three or four sisters, and they all have a lot of friends. They also know a lot of people from cheerleading and playing sports, so there's always company over her house. Everybody calls Kesha's mom "Mama". She's really cool and is really nice about having company and opening her house doors.

"Hi, ma'am, who are you here for?" Ms. Green speaks from her desk.

"Kimiko Lewis. I'm Kimiko's mother," Mom stands in the doorway.

"That's her mom?" Stacy speaks aloud looking confused because of the lack of resemblance.

I didn't want it to be true, so it took me a few seconds to turn around. But I know from the sound of that fake ass "nice guy" voice that it is for sure my mother, Joyce. Hearing her voice just makes my skin crawl.

How the fuck did she find me? I think to myself. I can't believe this. I literally just want Jesus himself to come down from the heavenly skies and save me. I don't know what to do, and everybody is looking at me weird because it's obvious I'm not too happy to see her.

"Kimiko, come here." Ms. Green can see something is wrong.

When I get to Ms. Green desk, I unfold. "I don't want to go with her. She beats and whoops on me for no reason."

"Okay, calm down, is she your mother?" Ms. Green looks very nervous like she doesn't know what to do.

"Yes." I can feel the tears developing behind my eyeballs.

"Who are you living with as of now?" Ms. Green looks panicked.

"My dad. My parents are going through a divorce and a custody battle right now." I wipe the tear from my right eye before it falls.

"Oh... I see. Okay, we're going to go check your files at the front office." Ms. Green walks my mom and me downstairs to the front office.

Once we get to the front office, we learn that my dad didn't give the school any custody papers or didn't leave any notice stating that she isn't allowed to pick me up, so my mom is free to take me since I'm her daughter.

"Okay, Kimiko, let's go gather your things, and I'll bring you back down." Ms. Green takes my hand.

"Okay, hurry up," my mom adds, looking mean.

"We won't be long ma'am." Ms. Green gives her a fake smile.

As we walk up to the classroom, I feel like my life is going right back down the drain. I'm trying so hard not to cry, but I feel so depressed and sad. My life just changed in a matter of seconds, and I'm just ready for it to be over.

"Now, I'm going to give you my personal phone number. If you feel in danger, you call me. My brother works with child protective services," Ms. Green sounds serious as she writes on a piece of paper.

I say my last goodbyes to everybody. My throat hurts so badly from trying to hold back my cries. I hate for people to see me cry; it makes me feel so weak and vulnerable. Everybody made sure to give me their numbers so we can keep in contact over the summer. On my way to my locker, I see Jeremy coming from the bathroom. I want to speak to him so bad, but I'm so scared. It's extremely awkward between us for no reason. With all the guts I have in me, I gather up the courage to say bye.

"Bye, Jeremy." I wave, feeling awkward because we barely talk.

"Bye," Jeremy smiles.

Oh lord, I think to myself as I get the sweats out of nervousness.

Let me get out of here! I begin to rush downstairs to my mom. When we get to the car, Key and Koko are waiting on us. I instantly feel a little bit at ease when I see Koko. At least we will be together. I prefer for us to be together wherever we are, as opposed to being apart. I mean, she is my baby sister.

"Get yo' ass in the car!" Mom pushes me towards the car as if I wasn't going in the right direction.

"I should beat yo' ass when we get home!" Mom uses her outside voice once we get inside the car.

Home? I remain silent.

"I told you not to go with him in the first fucking place!" Mom continues to drive.

Please don't let us be going back to Uncle Chi's uncomfortable ass house," I think to myself as mom curses me out from the drivers seat.

I'm just ready for my whopping. I'm ready to get it over with. The worst part about a whooping is the anticipation. The wait you have to experience before actually getting whooped is the worst feeling.

Surprisingly, we weren't in the car for too long. The YMCA is on 7 Mile and Lahser, and we just pulled up to a nice house right down the street on 7 Mile and Greenfield. It's only about a five to ten-minute drive from the school. When we pull into the driveway, I see a truck that looks very similar to my grandparents' truck. The thought of my grandparents being in town made me feel overwhelmed with joy. Before I get excited for no reason, I calm down and help Koko from her car seat. Then right before my eyes there she was coming from out the house.

"Granny!" I run to her arms as fast as I can with Koko on my hip.

"Hey, Mickey boo! Don't drop the baby now." Granny walks to the porch steps to meet me.

I can't believe it is Granny and Granddaddy! I'm assuming the few months we were with my daddy, they were able to hash things out with my mama.

"You like your new home?" Granny points to the house behind us.

"This is OUR house?" I ask in disbelief.

"Yes, and you have your own room too," Granny giggles, knowing I hadn't had my own room since our house on Manor.

Looking at the front porch and how wide and big it is. I'm sure the house is spacious as well. It doesn't look like a big house from the front, but judging from the driveway, you can see how far the house goes back. It looks like about four to five cars can park comfortably in the driveway. When we go into the house, I was expecting it to be empty, but it is damn near fully furnished. The first room coming in through the front door is the living room. It has a burnt orange living room sofa set with a fireplace, which is where my Granddaddy is waiting.

"Hey, pretty girls!" Granddaddy looks like he's so happy to see us.
"Hey, Granddaddy!" I run to him with open arms.
"Mickey, you are getting tall!" Granddaddy proclaims.
"Isn't she?" Granny giggles.
"Yeah, she is getting tall," Mom adds.
"And where is that Koko? Huh? Where is she? I can't see her." Granddaddy makes a funny voice as Koko sits on Granny's hip giggling.
"Oh, there she is!" Granddaddy grabs Koko from Granny's arms to kiss her on her cheeks. Koko gets nervous from how far up in the air Granddaddy is bringing her because of his tall height, so she begins to cry.

Koko whining and crying doesn't bother Granddaddy at all. He's just happy to see her and to know that we're okay. Eventually, he hands Koko back to Granny when he realized she's not going to stop crying. She instantly stops crying when she gets lower to the ground in Granny's lap.

"You ain't nothing but a big ol' cry baby anyway," Granddaddy teases Koko from Granny's arms.

First, I walk through the large living room with burnt orange furniture, then into a circular dining room. Finally, I walk into the den, which is much larger than the first two rooms. After seeing the kitchen, a bedroom, bathroom, and basement, we make our way upstairs to our new rooms. The smaller room is mine, and the bigger one is Key's.

Even though my room is smaller, it's also cozier with cream color carpet. The carpet goes out to the hallway, all the way down the stairs. I have a big closet for my clothes and built-in shelves on my wall. Key's room has wooden flooring, and the walls are wooden too. Her room kind of reminds me of a huge attic. She has two walk-in closets, and she also has built-in shelves on one of her walls too.

"Why do our rooms look so different?" I ask.
"Because the old man that used to own this property added the den which is Key's rooms," Granddaddy answers before anybody else could.
"Yeah, he built it separately," Granny confirms.
"They said he died in this house," Key eyes get big.
"Really?" I feel spooked out all of a sudden.
"Look at her scary butt!" Mom giggles.
"Yeah, that's what they said." Granddaddy nods his head for confirmation.
"Where he die at, like in what room?" I ask quickly.
"You mean where did he die, in which room," Granny corrects me as Granddaddy frowns at me.
"Yeah" I add ignoring the both of them.
"I don't know, Miko." I can tell Granddaddy is aggravated from my improper speech.

Key says ever since my grandparents moved down south with their White friends, they like to correct us when we speak improperly. The thing is, I know that I speak improperly most of the time. I know when to turn it on and off. I know how to write a paper and explain myself correctly. I just don't casually talk like I'm writing a paper. This house is really nice inside, despite the bad news I just heard about somebody dying in here.

I must admit, this has all caught me by surprise. I didn't know how long my mom was going to have my grandparents cut off. I know she's really bad at forgiving people, so when several months went past, I didn't know how long it would last. I know we only have this house because my Grandparents came to save the day as usual. That's exactly why I love them so much. They always have our backs and never will leave us drowning in the river. Everybody that's friends with my grandparents, and especially family knows, if my grandparents can help, they will. Not only with us but with friends and family that are in need. So many of my family members owe my grandparents, it's ridiculous. I just feel so thankful, blessed, and special to have them for grandparents. If it weren't for them, my sisters and I would just be left with Jihod and Joyce; two lost souls.

I still don't know how my mom found out about what school I go to, and honestly, it's the least of my worries. I'm just happy she's not beating me right now, and I'm so happy that my grandparents are here.

CHAPTER **FIFTY-THREE**

"MIKO, THIS IS Tiffany and Toya. Key's blood sisters on her daddy's side of the family." Mom smiles.

Another day, another lie! I straight-face both of the girls, showing my lack of interest.

"Hey!" they both speak at the same time as if it was rehearsed.

"Hi," I wave with a noticeably fake smile.

"Don't you think me and Key look just alike?" Toya lays her head on Key's shoulder.

"Nah, I don't see it." I squint my eyes sarcastically but honestly.

"Everybody say they look alike!" Tiffany smiles.

"Who be saying that?" I'm confused because these girls don't even look like they could be our cousins.

"My grandma say it all the time!" Toya giggles like she's so happy to be Key's sister.

Tiffany and Toya don't have a feature that resembles Key's features or even each other's. I later found out that Tiffany is just claimed by Darnell, "Key's biological father." Toya, on the other hand, is Darnell's biological daughter and his twin. She is the spitting image of him. She looks more like him than I do of my dad. Toya is tall for her age, so that's one thing her and Key have in common. She's kind of on the dark-skinned side and just literally the complete opposite of Key.

I might be coming off a little jealous, and I must admit I am, not of these girls but just of the fact that Key get to see her "daddy" and I don't. Even though Key and I know Darnell is not her real dad, it's the principal that's getting to me. It's been about a month and some change since I've seen or heard from my dad. Ever since Mom came and stole me from school, she hasn't been letting me see her phone, so my dad doesn't have a clue where we are again. My mom doesn't let me call him at all. She just wants us to act like he doesn't exist because she's mad at him. It's all about her — her way or the highway.

Listening to Key and her "sisters" talking about their dad, Darnell, is really breaking my heart inside. Before showing my emotions in front of everybody, I go to the bathroom like everything is normal. As soon as the door closes, I make sure the door is locked, and I let the tears pour down my face. I try my hardest not to make any noises of weeping. I don't want anybody to know how sad I am. No one cares anyway. If I want something in my life, I'm realizing I have to go get it myself.

On the other hand, I am happy about having my own room again and being back in contact with my grandparents. So, everything isn't all bad, but I do miss my dad to death, and I know he misses me.

After everybody got acquainted, I learned that Tiffany and Toya are nice girls. As the summer night gets later, Darnell comes over and he seems to be pretty chill. I'm looking at Darnell and my mom, and it's making me sick and chuckle at the same time. Key and my mom would have to be identical twins for Darnell to even consider Key as his daughter. I can't believe that he's buying this bullshit. I wish Patricia and Porsha could see this! This shit is comical! I know Key is going to have a mouthful to say tonight when we come home, and honestly, I can't wait.

Meanwhile, it's starting to get late, so Mom and Darnell decides to go over on the east side to his mama's house. Most people I know never even been on the east of Detroit. My great grandma lives over there, so I'm familiar with the east side. Instead of driving separately, all of us drive with my mom. Darnell left his car in front of our house. On the way to the east side, my mom bangs her mix songs the whole way there, dancing in the driver seat, making everybody laugh. Mom sings along with the song:

"Where my dogs at? Where my hustla's at? Where my playa's at? Where my pimps at?"
"Where my dogs at? On the floor, on the floor."
"Where my hustla's at? On the floor, on the floor."
"Where my playa's at? On the floor, on the floor."
"Where my pimps at? On the floor, on the floor."

Even though that's the only thing the song repeats throughout the whole track, the beat and the overall tempo keeps you on your feet!

Once we get to Darnell's mama's house, the neighborhood and atmosphere changed drastically. Even though its dark outside, I can tell this neighborhood is more ran down than the neighborhood we live in. It doesn't make me feel nervous, though, because it's not my first time being in a raggedy neighborhood. There are raggedy neighborhoods all throughout Detroit.

Once we got inside the house, Darnell's mom is waiting on us in the living room. Judging from the inside of the house, it's obvious it's a very old house. I'm surprised to see Key's baby pictures on the walls with the rest of the kids.

"Hey, Grandma!" Key waves and adds a polite smile on the side.
That's all Joyce right there! I know my mama put her up to that shit!" I scream in my mind.
"Hey, beautiful, come sit down!" the older woman seems happy to see Key.

"Grandma, you got some food?" Toya asks walking to the kitchen.

"I don't know, you gotta' see what's in there," the older woman speaks louder.

"Daddy, can you buy us some pizza?" Tiffany asks.

"Yeah, what y'all want? A meat lover pizza?" Darnell asks.

"Yeah," Tiffany and my mom speak at the same time.

"Are you the same age as Key?" I ask Tiffany.

"I'm a year older than her. You know Toya yo' age, right?" Tiffany adds.

"What! I knew she was younger than y'all, but I thought she was older than me."

Toya has height, boobs, and some booty too. She most definitely doesn't look like she's in middle school. She acts like she's my age though so, I guess it makes sense.

It seems like Darnell's family really loves Key, and they seem to be really excited that Key and my mom are around.

"I'm so happy Mama didn't get fucked up last night. You know how her drunk ass do." I roll my eyes sitting on Key's bed.

"I know, gotta' appreciate those kinds of nights, but they saw her drunk as hell before though. They know she can't handle her liquor," Key explains.

"Can you believe she's pulling this "daddy" shit?" I giggle.

"Girl! Shit is annoying as fuck." Key continues to sew her pants.

"Like Stevie fucking Wonder can see that he is not your dad."

Key burst out in laughter. "Right! And she full of shit too! She be telling me to call Darnell's mama 'grandma' so she can give us money," Key continues.

"Really? I knew she put you up to the grandma thing!"

"Yes, girl," Key looks at me with a straight face.

"Ri-di-cu-lous!" I shake my head.

"She brought his ass around when I asked about Trevor." Key spills the beans.

"Trying to cover the truth up?" I assume.

"Yeah, I just straight up asked her if Trevor was my dad out of nowhere." Key looks serious.

"What did she say?"

"She didn't say anything. She was just sitting there looking dumb." Key continues to sew her jeans.

"So, she didn't say no?" I try to dig deeper.

"Nope, she didn't say yes or no," Key shakes her head.

"Wow, that's crazy! Well that should tell you then because if he wasn't, she would've said no," I put two and two together.

"Right, that's the same thing I said. I don't see what the big fucking deal is. He is dead, so one would think that it would be easier to drop the bomb." Key frowns.

"She's embarrassed," I try to reason for Mom.

"Embarrassed? What she should be embarrassed about is her lack of controlling her motherfucking alcohol intake. She should be embarrassed about not knowing shit but have two good parents. This bitch literally can't survive out here without her parents. And once again, she hasn't learned a God damn thing from their assistance," Key speaks with anger in her blood.

"She still is embarrassed about sleeping with her 'cousin' and having a baby by him too." I stand my ground.

"But one would think since she knows how it feels not to know her biological parents that she would at least have the decency to inform me about my biological father. It's not like I can have a relationship with the man. It's been a secret for sixteen to seventeen years now." Key sounds passionate.

"Yeah, that is very selfish. I mean, it's her 'cousin', but they're not blood cousins anyway," I agree.

"Exactly, everybody know that my mama is adopted. Get the fuck over it. That's one thing I hate about this fucking family. Everybody is so hush hush about every fucking thing! When I'm over there with

Patricia and Porsha and them, they keep it real with each other! If somebody has something to say about something, it's going to be put out on the floor. Somebody is going to argue and the day goes on. My parents look down on Dona and Tez because they don't got shit and they live with Betty, but one thing I can say is that they love each other. And when shit pops off, it happens, and it's over! Nobody's holding lifelong grudges and staying mad for days and years. That's what I love about their family, that's true love!" Key is filled with aggression and anger.

Last night was pretty funny. Mom let Cory come over, and we all chilled, watched movies, and bought a case of White Castle burgers. I still can't believe Mom is accepting Key and Cory's relationship. I mean, they are older now, and mom is starting to change a little bit. I'm still surprised I didn't get a whopping for going with my dad. All she did was threaten me. Which is different because anytime she used to get a chance to put her hands on us, she always took advantage. But recently she hasn't been hitting on us as much. It's probably because child protective services are involved now.

Mom made it crystal clear that I wouldn't be going back to the YMCA, and she meant what she said. So now I'm attending this school called Winship. It's a neighborhood school, and it's literally right around the corner from our house. Back when my parents were married, she despised Detroit public schools. She would never let Key go to the neighborhood schools, and Key actually wanted to go to the public schools because all of our friends from the neighborhood did. Things have clearly changed, and 7th grade at Winship is as wild as a zoo. One of my closest friends at this school is Yalonda. She is Patricia and Porsha's cousin. I've seen her a few times in our old neighborhood back when we stayed on Manor. She used to act like she was jealous of mine and Porsha's friendship, so when I noticed she was in my class, I didn't know if she would want to be my friend or not. But she ended up being cool about it and embraced the fact that we already knew each other.

"You should come over my house this weekend!" Yalonda bites into her sandwich.
"Where you live?" I ask sitting across the lunch table.
"I live like right down the street from here."
"I live right around the corner from here." I giggle.
"Oh, well, you can just walk to my house then," Yalonda suggests.
"Alright, I'ma see and call you to let you know."

This school is pretty easy. The work and homework are pretty easy also. Everybody seems to be cliqued up. There are a few cute boys at this school, but I don't really have a crush on any of them. I still have this ongoing crush on Jeremy from YMCA. I snuck and called him all this past summer, but I kept getting his answering machine. I got his number from Kesha since I was too shy to ask for it when I saw him.

Carthel interrupts my daydream about Jeremy. "Miko, look at that wedgie in Ms. Frost booty."
We both share quiet laughs at the teacher as she writes on the chalkboard. Then about a minute later, Carthel yells out while the class is quiet. "Somebody's booty hunger!" the whole class burst out laughing.
Ms. Frost turns around. "Who said that?"

Everybody knows it was Carthel, but nobody snitches on him.

"Oh, well, since nobody knows, how about all of you write a ten-page packet about this chapter!" Ms. Frost gets an attitude.

Ms. Frost's threat caused small roaring, as mumbles and teeth smacking floats around the classroom.

Yalonda leans over from her desk. "I'm not writing shit. She got me fucked up."

"I know, right?" I giggle.

While everybody is chattering among themselves, my stomach is turning upside down. I feel like I have to boo boo, but I wouldn't dare do the number two in the school bathroom. I'm too afraid somebody might hear my boo boo drop in the toilet. Then whoever happens to be in there is going to tell somebody. I'm not trying to have any rumors about me doing the number two roaming around the school.

As the class begins to quiet down, I feel a fart coming closer to my booty hole. I'm trying so hard to hold back, but it's making my stomach feel even worst. It feels like it's a big one, and I'm so scared that it's going to be loud.

Damn! Why fucking now! Now that the class is getting quiet! I think to myself as the fart is about to cruise out.

Surprisingly, the fart is the complete opposite of what I was expecting. It is a quiet fart, thank God! But you know what they say about quiet farts. They are quiet in sound but loud in smell. About two minutes after I let my fart loose, Roger, who's sitting across the classroom blurts out "Eww, somebody was eating White Castle!"

Fuck! It's the White Castles burgers! I forgot about that last night.

After my second fart, the entire class smells like old White Castle burgers. It is so bad, Ms. Frost even had to say something.

"Okay, whoever got gas, please, go fart in the hallway. This is getting out of hand now," Ms. Frost holds her nose.

As soon as Ms. Frost finished talking, I feel another one coming. Instead of farting in the classroom again, I decide to hold my nuts and confess it's me.

And if anybody wants to tease me then we about to have a roasting battle, flat the fuck out! I hype myself up.

"Okay, y'all, it's me! My bad, I didn't think it was going to be this bad!" I get up from my seat to walk in the hallway.

"Dang, Miko, you ate White Castles last night?" Roger ask.

"Yeah, but I didn't know it gave me gas like this," I confess as everybody laughs

"Duh, everybody know that!" Roger laughs.

I continue to walk out in the hallway to let the third fart go. Surprisingly, nobody had any jokes for me for the rest of the day.

CHAPTER **FIFTY-FOUR**

"HOW WAS SCHOOL today?" Mom asks from the drivers seat.

"Embarrassing," I roll my eyes.

Key turns around from the passenger's side "Why?"

"Because I was farting up a storm and had the classroom smelling like White Castles burgers," I explain in detail as Mom and Key crowd the car with laughter.

"I'm never eating White Castles on a Sunday night again," I shake my head, looking out of the window.

"Oh my God, so everybody knew it was you?" Key asks in between her laughs.

"Yeah, after it got so bad, I just said forget it and told everybody it was me."

"She talking about, after it got so bad!" Mom mocks me as she continues to laugh.

"Oh, you real brave, I wouldn't have said nothing. I would've played it off like 'ughhh, somebody doing too much!'" Key laughs.

"What were the kids saying?" Mom ask.

"Nothing really, they were just laughing. The first time I farted, this boy sitting across the classroom yelled out 'Ugh, somebody was eating White Castles!'" I explain making Mom and Key laugh even harder.

"I can't breathe!" Mom is wiping the tears from her face from laughing so hard.

"Did you have to use the bathroom?" Key ask, still cracking up.

"Yeah! I gotta' go right now, so I hope we not about to go grocery shopping, are we?" I ask as serious as a hear attack.

"Miko, don't boo boo on yourself!" Mom teases.

Thank the Lord our house is just right around the corner because the bathroom is calling my name.

"Miko, I made a mistake and left the side door unlocked so," Mom continues to talk as I jump out of the car to run to the bathroom. After I release myself in the bathroom, I feel like a new woman.

"Wooooow I felt like Popz from *'Next Friday'* when he had to boo boo in the car." I laugh at myself.

Key burst out laughing. "Right! When he ran into Mr. Stanley."

"Get the fuck out of my face, Stanley!" I mimic the movie as Key cracks up laughing.

"Girl, that shit had me rolling!" Key confesses.

I giggle. "So embarrassing," I shake my head.

"But that's good didn't nobody tease you," Key adds.

"Yet, who's to say somebody won't have anything to say about it later?" I overthink.

"I doubt it." Key disagrees.

"What if somebody wants to call me shitty pants or shitty boo boo?" I go on.

"It's not like you boo booed on yourself."

"Shid, it smelled like I did!" I tease myself.

Key burst out in laughter. "Oh my god, that is too funny!"

"But whatever, because as soon as somebody has something to say, I'm on they head. Point. Blank. Period" I admit, changing the subject. "That was nice how Mama let Cory come over yesterday though."

"Yeah, she be letting him come over now, but she won't let Patricia and Porsha come." Key looks annoyed by the thought.

"What? Why not? " I'm lost.

"She's mad because she feels like they should have told her about Cory and me liking each other," Key explains.

"Now, why would they do that?" I'm still lost.

"Right, like they her friends or something," Key frowns.

"So, they haven't been over here at all?"

"Nope, she serious about not letting them come over." Key rolls her eyes.

"That's crazy!" I shake my head.

"Then Saturday she asked him how my pussy feel and told him that that's her pussy. Then she asked me the same question," Key explains.

"She asked with those exact words?" My mouth drops to the floor.

"Yeah, so stupid, right? I told her it feel regular." Key shrugs her shoulder.

"Like what? That bitch is crazy for real, for real!" I'm still in shock.

"I know, I don't know what she got from that or what it was supposed to mean." Key looks confused.

"I think I overheard her saying she was going out this weekend. I'ma sneak and call daddy," I slyly confess.

"Yeah, because she most likely will leave her phone here," Key nods her head agreeing with my thinking.

"Y'all don't answer the door for nobody. I'll be back." Mom walks out of the den to head to her car.

As soon as she leaves, Key calls my dad. They didn't stay on the phone for long.

"Why you didn't let me talk to him?" I catch a quick attitude.

"He about to come over here, that's why." Key looks at me like I'm dumb.

"He about to come over here right now?"

"Yeah, that's what he said. I told him where we live," Key explains.

"Mama will be out all night anyway, huh?" I try to reason with the quick decision that was just made.

"Right, that's what I said," Key agrees.

It didn't take long for my dad to get to our new home. He got here so fast you would have thought he was right around the corner.

"Who would have known y'all was right here on 7 Mile?" Dad shakes his head in the center of our kitchen.

"I know, that's what I said when I first got here," I smile.

"So, y'all grandparents got this for y'all, huh?" Dad asks.

"Yeah, and granddaddy keep saying this house is for all of us," Key explains.

"That's what's up, this house is nice!" Dad looks around.

"Yeah, it's a lot bigger than the house on Manor," Key adds.

"Koko sleeping?" Dad looks around.

"Yeah, she's in the den," I point towards the back of the house.

"Dang, they got it fully furnished for y'all too?" Dad looks surprised.

"Damn near," Key adds.

Dad giggles. "Talking about damn near. This is fully furnished, Key."

"I'm about to check on Koko." I walk back to the den as Key and Daddy go back to the kitchen near the side door.

As soon as I take a quick peep at Koko to make sure she didn't fall off of the pull-out bed, I hear the side door slam. Before I could even hear if my dad left or not, I hear my mom's voice screaming to the top of her lungs. Time instantly starts moving in slow motion. My heart feels like it literally is dropping to my toes. I can't believe my mom came right back. All I can hear is my mom cussing Key out and telling my dad to get the fuck out of her house.

"*She must of forgot something. She came back too fast!*" I make sure I stay in the back with Koko.

"If you want to be with him and sneak him in MY HOUSE, GO with his ass then! I don't want to see your fucking face! LEAVE! You can get THE FUCK OUT!" Mom screams out of rage.

She kicking Key out! I whisper to myself as tears slowly fall.

"STUPID BITCH!" Mom continues to scream as the door slams.

It's been three days since Key got kicked out and we haven't heard anything from her. Mom hasn't checked in on her and, from what mom says, Key hasn't called to try to come back or apologize. Honestly, I'm not surprised Key hasn't called to try to come back. I know I wouldn't be in a rush to come back either. Even though Mom is starting to be a little bit more lenient these days, it's too little too late. Key is about grown now. I'm sure she'd rather be out there doing what she wants with my grandparents' support.

"We're going to be moving from here soon. Probably next week sometime," Mom breaks the silence.

"Where we going?" I'm about fed up with this moving ass bitch.

"I will figure something out." Mom looks off in a daze.

I can't stand her dumb ass! You got a nice ass house FOR FREE and about to throw it away FOR WHAT? People would kill for this kind of blessing!

"This is exactly why I don't like people knowing anything about me. But it's cool, I'm about to cut all this shit short. Watch." Mom looks dead serious.

"So, I'ma have to go to another new school?" I ask, knowing the answer.

"Yup," Mom shrugs her shoulders.

This bitch doesn't have any money. All she has is two kids to look after, and she's not making the best decisions for us. Everything is about her. She doesn't give a fuck about how I feel or anybody else's feelings. As long as Joyce is happy, that's all that matters. At this point, she's not even happy, she just making stupid decisions out of anger.

"Kesha called you earlier when I was talking to Irene," Mom hands me her cellphone.

I take the phone and go upstairs to talk to Kesha in private to help take my mind off the daily bullshit my life consists of.

"Hey, Kesha!"
"Hey, Miko! I miss you, girl!" Kesha sounds sincere.
"I miss you too, man! I'm still pissed my mama won't let me come back to the Y!" I flop on my bed.
"What school you going to now?" Kesha asks.
"I go to Winship. It's right around the corner from my house," I smack my lips.
"You like it?"
"It's alright, but I don't like it better than the Y." I look up to the ceiling reminiscing about YMCA and my old friends.
"Girl, we have so many new people at the Y. Stacey got her a new little clique, so she think she so hard." Kesha sounds annoyed.
"Really? What she be doing?" I'm surprised at the news.
"Talking too fucking much, thinking she can just say anything, but at the same time, she scary-ass fuck. Kansas was about to fight her, but her scared ass basically ran," Kesha explains.
"Y'all was about to jump her?"
"Nah, she had her friends there, and it was me, Kansas, Tiara, and Ashley. Kansas and Stacey were supposed to fight, but Stacey backed down."

"Why they don't like each other?"

"Because Stacey is a hoe and she talk too fucking much."

"Now, how is she a hoe?" I'm not convinced.

"Girl, she won't stop trying to get back with Nickolas, and she know that Kansas and Nickolas are together now. She was even trying to get with Jeremy!" Kesha goes on.

"Really?"

"And she know you used to like him sooo much. I even heard that she had sex with him this past summer," Kesha continues with the gossip.

"Sex with Jeremy?" I frown.

"Yeah! Because you know she lives right down the street from his best friend, Jay?" Kesha backs the rumor up.

"That's crazy… backstabbing ass bitch!" I catch a slight attitude.

"I know, right? She better watch out before I touch her. Her and her best friend, Sharee, are just the same. They some weak ass scared hoes." Kesha sounds sure.

Today is a pretty depressing day. Mom and I have been packing all day. We are leaving the big furniture that my grandparents bought with the house, and all of our belongings are in black garbage bags. It's so annoying because Mom won't tell me where we're going. She's not talking to my grandparents again. She thinks that they knew about my dad and Key's meet up and they didn't tell her. She thinks everybody is against her, that's why she's trying to count everybody out.

By the time we finished packing and loading all of the bags in the car, it's dark outside. Mom has been in her phone calling different people all day, but it seems like nobody is giving her the answers she needs. Instead of wasting more and more gas, not going anywhere, Mom decides to pull into a park's parking lot. After awkward silence went on for about thirty minutes to an hour, Mom decides to say something.

"Well, I guess we'll be sleeping here for the night." Mom reclines her chair back a little.
"Here in the car?" I'm confused and nervous.
"Yes! Do you got a fucking problem with that?" Mom checks me.
Hell yea! Don't you?
"No," I lie, turning my head to look out into the playground.

I can't wait until I get older so I can be confident and brave enough to tell her how I really fucking feel. Do I have a problem? The real question is, do YOU have a fucking problem! We just packed up and left a three-bedroom, fully furnished house with an added den and a huge basement for absolutely NO REASON! This shit doesn't make any kind of sense! Nobody forced her to leave. This is the smartest thing she can come up with! I pray we don't have to sleep at this park tomorrow night.

CHAPTER **FIFTY-FIVE**

SLEEPING IN THE car for weeks straight is the worst. Some days we go without showering. Eating ham sandwiches is getting sickening, and my mom is acting like everything is normal. We literally just sit around watching the birds live free, flying around. I wish I was a bird most of the time. I haven't been able to catch a break or sneak and call anybody since Mom, Koko, and I have been up each other's asses in this small car. The only thing that's been bringing me a little peace around here is the radio. Music is another temporary way out for me, and it brings me joy in the most indescribable way. Mom has been making phones calls every day after she decided she wanted to live out of the car. When she finally got in touch with her childhood friend, Irene, we head to the Holiday Inn.

"Now, when we get in here do not be telling them our business." Mom looks as serious as usual.

"Okay," I say quickly. *What the fuck else is new?*

I know by now to just say what her lying ass says. This Holiday Inn location looks a lot bigger than the Holiday Inns I'm used to seeing. Once the elevator dings, letting us know we're on our desired floor, Mom looks at me.

"Remember what I said."

"Okay," I reply. *Girl, shut the fuck up"* I yell in my head.

"Hey, Joyce!" Irene opens her room door welcoming my mom in with a hug.

"Hey, Irene!" Mom looks like she misses her.

"Y'all come in! Look at the girls! Miko still looking just like Jihod! And look at little Koko! Now, Joyce, she looks more like you!" Irene smiles.

"Where is Amanda?" I ask looking for the kids.

"She's at school. She should be getting out soon. Her and Jordan should be here in a minute," Irene explains.

"So, what's up, Joyce?" Irene cuts to the chase.

"Girl, too much to bear." Mom shakes her head.

"I know getting a divorce is hard!" Irene sympathizes with Mom.

"Yes, it's been ridiculous. Jihod is nowhere to be found as usual. Then when he does decide to pop up, he's trying to get full custody of the kids without a job. My parents are acting like they agree with his ass. I just feel like everybody is against me." Mom puts her head down.

"I thought they didn't like Jihod!" Irene frowns.

"That's what I thought too! That's why I'm like fuck all of them, Irene, for real!" Mom sounds passionate.

"What about Key, where is she?" Irene goes on.

"That bitch think she so grown. She's probably somewhere with her little boyfriend." mom rolls her eyes.

Irene burst out in laughter. "Joyce! Shut up!"

Mom giggles. "I'm serious, Irene, shit is crazy. Now we have to find somewhere to live. I don't know where to go," Mom explains.

"Your parents won't help you?"

"Nope," Mom lies.

"Wow, when did they get so cruel? They've always been there to help you and everybody else," Irene states the truth.

"So now we have to see what to do." Mom ignores her question.

"Y'all should get a room for about a month or two here. That's what we've been doing," Irene suggests.

I didn't know you could book a room for that long at a hotel."

"That's sounding like my only option at this point." Mom looks out of the window.

Sounds better than the fucking car.

"Yeah, then we can be hotel neighbors!" Irene tries to lighten up the mood as everyone laughs at her comment.

"Yeah right!" Mom smiles.

"You know, Kim and her kids been staying here too," Irene adds.

"Kim from back in the day?" Mom looks surprised.

"Yeah, her and her three boys," Irene nods her head.

"Last time I heard from her she was married," Mom adds.

"Yeah, she ended up getting a divorce too. Her husband was whopping her ass. She had to run from him!" Irene pops some ice in her mouth.

"Whaaat?" Mom looks surprised.

From the decisions my mom is making, you would think she is running from an ass whopping too.

After hanging out with Irene and her daughter, Amanda, and her son, Jordan, Mom decides to go downstairs to the lobby and purchase a room for us. I don't know how she got the money for it, and I don't care. I'm just happy to see a bed for Pete's sake!

"Miko, what school you go to?" Amanda asks as she plays on the workout equipment.

"No school," I grab a weight.

Amanda laughs. "Why not?"

"Because my mama is scared my daddy might find us," I honestly explain.

"I thought he didn't want anything to do with y'all. At least that's what Auntie Joyce said," Amanda continues.

I walk towards Amanda. "Look, my mama is a pathological liar. My parents are going through a custody battle. The only reason they're going through a custody battle is because she's trying to keep us away from him," I speak clearly.

"Keep y'all away from who?" Amanda looks confused.

"My dad, my grandparents... everybody! The bitch is sick in the head!" I yell out of frustration.

"Wait, wait, wait, wait hold on. Your mom is trying to keep you away from your grandparents too?" Amanda's eyes are big.

"Yes, because they disagreed with her, so since she can't handle anybody disagreeing with her and not being on her side, it's fuck everybody, even her own daughter. She doesn't give a fuck about nobody but herself."

"She keeping y'all away from Key, too?" Amanda sounds overwhelmed.

"Yes, she doesn't want anything to do with her."

"What did Key do?"

"She got caught sneaking my dad in the house, so my mama kicked her out."

"Oh, because she wasn't supposed to be talking to him?" Amanda sounds like she's getting it now.

"Exactly, but that's our dad and we miss him," I snap my fingers.

"And what exactly did your dad do again?" Amanda continues with the questions.

"Nothing, just trying to be in our lives, so since she's mad at him for whatever they got a divorce over, she keeping us away from him," I explain.

"Damn, that's so bold, he still y'all daddy," Amanda sympathizes for me.

"I know, it's fucked up because I haven't talked to him in months, Key or my grandparents."

"Damn, Miko, everything is going to be fine. But why is Auntie

Joyce lying about everything?" Amanda is still piecing the puzzle together.

"Because that's all she do, girl, is lie!" I roll my eyes.

I must admit, despite not being able to see my dad, grandparents, and Key, it is kind of fun living here in the hotel. I hang out with Amanda and Kim's boys, Daniel, Kiemon, and Manny. They are all older than me, which I personally love. The only one that's my age is Manny.

"Hit it, Daniel!" Amanda hypes Daniel up as he hip roll in the mirror.

"Dang, I wish my hips could move like that!" I watch from the bed.

Daniel is dancing to the new Twista song called "Make a Movie", and his hips are dropping to every beat in the song. Daniel is tall, brown-skinned with a nice smile.

"This nigga' showing out! Let me show y'all who he learned from!" Kiemon gets up from the desk area.

Kiemon pulls his shirt up slowly and places the end of his shirt in his mouth so the shirt won't fall down. Then he pulls his pants up just for them to fall back to where they were. Then he starts rolling his waistline to the beat. Chris Brown sounds so sexy on this song. Kiemon is really good at hip rolling too. Kiemon is tall, dark-skinned with pretty teeth as well.

"Okay, KK, I see you! Amanda laughs at herself for hyping him up.

"Sounding just like Irene!" I smile at Amanda.

"Please don't say that!" Amanda rolls her eyes in a less serious way.

"Go ahead, Amanda, your turn!" I push her to get up.

"I got the next song! I got the next song!" Amanda giggles.

"Okay, Brody, okay!" Kiemon hits Daniel on the back, giving him credit.

"Talking about who you taught! Nigga' I raised you!" Daniel lets his shirt down as everybody cracks up laughing.

"Oooo, this is my song!" Amanda pops up from the bed and head to the mirror to dance.

"What's this?" Manny looks like he's not familiar with this song.

"This that song by The-Dream called Falsetto!" I answer before anybody else can.

"You don't know this song?" Kiemon looks at Manny like he's crazy.

"I don't think so." Manny shrugs his shoulders.

"This nigga' Manny off!" Kiemon teases.

"Just because I'm not no dancing ass nigga' don't mean nothing!" Manny catches a slight attitude.

"Dog, stop boosting in front of Miko!" Daniel laughs.

"Right! That nigga' know he be dancing, acting shy and shit!" Kiemon teases.

"Ain't nobody acting shy! Y'all niggas dance way more than me!" Manny defends himself.

"Yeah, because we better dancers than you, fatty!" Kiemon jokes.

"Y'all want to go downstairs in the lounge/game area?" I change the topic, getting bored.

"Yeah! Let's go tell my mama and them first." Amanda puts her shoes on.

Once we get to Irene and Amanda's room, I can tell my mom is toasted. I don't know what they're drinking on, but I can tell she is hanging on by a loose string. Irene and Kim seem to be fine, maybe a little tipsy, but not half as drunk as my mom.

"Ma, we about to go down to the lounge area." Amanda grabs a room key.

"Alright, y'all don't be down there acting like a bunch of hoodlums!" Irene jokes.

Kim laughs with her drink in her hand. "Yeah, y'all act like y'all have some home training down there."

My mom is too drunk to utter a word, so she just nods her head back and forth. Thank God Koko is sleeping so she won't try to pin her on me. I don't mind watching Koko, especially when my mom is drunk, but I wish my mom knew how to handle herself. That shit is so fucking embarrassing and ugly to me.

The lounge area is pretty big. It includes cute sofas and coffee tables. The light green, burnt orange, and brown interior design makes it really pretty. They also have a pinball machine and a foosball table.

"Dang, I miss our Pinball machine!" I reminisce back when we were a family living together on 7 Mile and Manor.

"Y'all were the only people I knew that actually had a Pinball machine in y'all basement." Amanda giggles.

"Yeah, I never would've thought that I would be saying this, but I miss how everything used to be." I stare off.

"I'm sure you do," Amanda agrees.

"Even though shit wasn't all butterflies and flowers back then, it was still better than this."

Not too longer after we chill and kick it in the lounge. I see Irene getting off of the elevator as if she's in a rush.

"Miko, Amanda told me about Joyce lying this whole time, is that true?" Irene pulls me to the side looking distraught.

"Yeah!" I look her dead in her eyes.

"So, your mom is keeping y'all away from everybody?" Irene sounds like she might not believe me.

"Yup, I haven't talked to my grandparents for a long time. I'm sure they're probably worried about us," I explain.

"Well yeah, I'm sure they are! They know Joyce don't have anything but her small disability check that comes in every month. Man, that's crazy! She know Jim and Mary loves y'all to death!" Irene sounds sympathetic.

"I know!" I cut myself short trying to fight the tears from falling.

"And your daddy looking for y'all too?"

"Yeah, and all he wants to do is be able to see us. But no, if she's mad at somebody, we gotta' suffer the consequences," I look off.

"And she kicked Key out for talking to your daddy?" Irene continues to go down the checklist Amanda gave her.

"Yeah," I shake my head, "and I haven't seen or heard from her since."

"Wow, Miko, that's fucked up! Excuse my language! I don't know why Joyce is acting like this. That is still your sister. Then sitting up there lying about everything. She told me y'all lost the house," Irene continues.

"That's all she do is lie! We LEFT the house. Nobody lost any house. She left a free, fully-furnished house." I over enunciate so Irene can hear me clearly.

Irene mistakenly giggles at my articulation. "See, I told Joyce you were going to be the one to set her straight." Irene looks sure.

"I just wish I could talk to my family." I put my head down.

"You want to call your grandparents from my cellphone and let them know y'all are still alive?" Irene laughs, unable to hide her goofy personality.

"Yeah," I'm instantly filled with excitement.

"Okay, but you can't tell Joyce," Irene looks serious.

"Ahh, duhh," I giggle.

Irene hands me her cellphone and I dial my grandparents' house phone. I spoke with them for about twenty minutes and filled them in on where we were living and how my mom is going about everything.

They were mind-blown and asked a lot of questions. I told them I was not in school at the time and that we are living in a hotel. I also told them before we got to the hotel that we were living out of the car. I could tell those words broke my granny's heart. They feel so sorry for Koko and me. I feel sorry for us too. I still have my daddy's number secretly written down. I'm going to sneak and call him next and get Key's contact information from him.

CHAPTER FIFTY-SIX

AFTER ABOUT TWO months of staying in the room at the hotel, Mom said that we would be living with her friend for a minute. She left out the part that describes him to be a man. A man I don't even know, have never heard of, and never seen before. This guy's name is Stephen. He's tall, light-skinned and has a permanent aggressive look on his face. I personally don't like him, and I barely talk to him. He just comes off so cold, and it seems to me like he really doesn't want us here. He doesn't try to be nice or play with Koko either. He lives in a small two-bedroom house. All of our bags of clothes are in his small basement because his entire upstairs is cluttered. This house reminds me of Uncle Chi's house. It's a little bit cleaner, though. My mom hasn't put me in school yet. Hopefully, that means she doesn't plan on staying here for long.

"How long we staying here?" I ask fighting to get the thought out of my head.

"I don't know yet, but when I find out, you will know," she responds with a smart attitude.

I decide not to continue with the conversation because I can tell she's aggravated.

"It's so cold in here," I shiver.
"Yeah, it is kind of chilly, huh?" Mom rubs her hands together.
"It's always cold in here," I frown uncomfortably.
"I'm going to ask Stephen if he can cut the heat up a little." Mom looks like she really doesn't want to ask him anything.
I wonder where she found this guy. I doubt if he's an old friend from the past because his name would have rung a bell."

When Mom went into his bedroom to ask him about cutting the heat up, I couldn't make out what he said, but it doesn't sound like anything nice. It sounded like he was annoyed with her or like she pinched one of his nerves. I wonder if he's acting mean because he's not getting any sex from her. She sleeps in the room with Koko and me every night.

Mom walks back in our room looking aggravated.
"We won't be here for long either."
Thank God!

"Irene, that was a good service!" Mom smiles.
"I know, the pastor is really good here. Y'all should join the church!"
"Yeah, we just might!" Mom sounds confident.
"Amanda and them did so good on their performance!" I add.
"Amanda has been dancing with the Mine/Praise Team for a while now," Irene smiles proudly.
"And they have a nice daycare here too. Jordan seems to like it a lot," Irene continues.
"It seems like a really nice church," Mom bobs her head.
"Are y'all staying for the second service? I think they might be serving food afterwards," Irene grins.
"Nah, we gone get out of here. I have an appointment," Mom lies.

"Okay, will I see y'all next Sunday?"

"You sure will!" Mom waves as we head to the car.

"Where we about to go?" I ask.

"My good friend D lives right around the corner from here. I'm sure he will hook us up with food and everything." Mom puts Koko in her car seat.

Who the fuck is D? Why can't we just stay here and eat? I try hard not to show my attitude.

On the way to D's house, we pass a lot of abandoned houses and buildings. There's a lot of vacant lots over here, where the grass has grown really tall.

"Is this the east side?"

"Yeah, why?" Mom answers quickly.

I can tell. I clear my throat. "Nothing," I answer quickly.

I figured this was the east side, but this part of the east side doesn't look too familiar to me. I wonder how far away we are from grandma's house. I know my dad used to be over on the east side a lot, I just don't know what part. I'm sure to pay attention to the street signs to familiarize myself with the area, and it reads "Mac and Conners."

I have to remember these streets when I talk to my dad. I also read the street that we turn on, where the house is located, and it reads "El Gaugwen."

D lives in the third house from the corner. His house is raggedy from the outside, so I can only imagine how it looks in the inside. All of these houses on the block look pretty bad from the outside.

When we pull up, D is sitting on the porch enjoying the Spring breeze. He's kind of on the short side, dark-skinned with a chubby belly. As soon as we get out of the car, he comes to greet us as if he missed us.

"Joy... and pain! Sunshine and rain! Joyce! What's up!" D sings the familiar old school song, walking up to my mom with open arms.

Mom giggles. "Hey. D, long time no see!"

"And look at these beautiful soon-to-be models you have here!" D stargazes at Koko and me.

"D, you so silly! This is Miko, and the baby's name is Koko!" Mom introduces us.

"Nice to meet you, young ladies. Ooo, Joyce, even the baby is pretty! I might have to make a model baby with you!" D jokes.

"Boy, stop playing!" Mom giggles, brushing off his flirty joke.

"Y'all come on in! Make y'all self comfortable!" D leads us into his house.

The inside of D's house reminds me of a tornado. It is so junky and dirty in here. Stuff is literally everywhere, and it looks like he hasn't cleaned up in years. To top it off, it stinks in here too. He must be used to the odor because he's walking around singing and shit like he doesn't smell anything. I mean, even the soft breeze coming through the screen door is still not airing out this house out.

"I was sitting outside, enjoying this nice weather. If y'all want, we can go sit on the porch," D suggests in a friendly tone.

I hop up not thinking twice. "Okay, that's cool! Come on, Koko puff!" I grab Koko's hand, taking all advantage of his suggestion to leave.

I can't believe she has us staying in this filthy fucking house. I'm surprised I haven't seen any mice or rats running around. I'm so uncomfortable here. I hate walking around here. I don't even want my socks touching this nasty floor. I'm shocked as fuck, that my mom is acting like everything is cool. I mean, granted, I do like D better than Stephen, but shit, this house is the nastiest house I've ever been in. I've seen junky and cluttered houses before, but this is straight-up filthy! I'm wondering where my mom's neat-freakish ways disappeared to. I mean, this bitch would call me from outside to pick up a piece of lint off of the floor that's sitting right next to her. This is a lady that made us clean up the house every two weeks. Vacuum, wipe down tables and our leather furniture, she even made us clean the windows as well. Now we're living in a fucking dumpster.

On another note, school is pretty cool over here on the eastside of Detroit. There haven't been as many fights as I expected, and, surprisingly, there are a bunch of cute boys at Joy Middle School. I must admit, that keeps me looking forward to every academic day. There are about two cute boys in my class alone. That's just so uncommon for me. I usually have to kill to see one cute boy in the entire school, but to have two in my homeroom class is so much fun.

"Miko, you tried out for the dance team yet?" Lanae asks.
"You sure I can still try out being that it's so late?" I second guess her.
"Yeah, girl! And we at the end of this old routine we been learning too," Lanae smiles.
"I'm nervous," I shyly giggle.
"For what? Ms. King is cool, and she might not even make you try out!" Lanae grabs my hand.
"Where we going?" I stop walking.
"To the dance room, stop being a scare-dee-cat!" Lanae continues to walk with my hand in hers.

Lanae is not the cutest girl in the world. She's short, kind of chubby, dark-skinned with long hair, but she's nice to me, so I'm nice to her. As we race downstairs, we bump into one of the cuties from class.

"Dang, why you holding my girlfriend's hand like that?" Cortez smiles smoothly, looking me dead in my eyes so I know he's referring to me.

"Boy, this is not your girlfriend!" Lanae shoves him out of our way.

"Yeah, not now, but I bet you she will be later!" I smile at Cortez leaving him to wonder as we run down the stairs.

Cortez is so cute! He's light-skinned with soft curly light brown hair and always wears it in a straight back ponytail. His front tooth is chipped, which is very edgy to me. It mirrors his personality.

"Does he have a girlfriend?" I ask quickly.

"He probably got like five. Why? You like him?" Lanae stops in front of the dance room.

"No," I lie, sensing her nose being too nosy.

"MMM-HMM…" Lanae gives me a 'yea right' look.

"Hey, Lanae, who is this?" Ms. King runs into us at the doorway.

"This is Kimi—" Lanae tries to pronounce my whole name.

"Miko. I'm Miko," I correct her.

"Nice to meet you, Miko!" Ms. King smiles warmly.

"Nice to meet you too!" I return the smile.

"Miko wants to join the dance team!" Lanae cut straight to the point.

"Okay, great! You want to sit in today and start tomorrow?" Ms. King nicely asks.

"Okay, I just have to see if my mom is here. If not, I'll call her to tell her to come get me in a hour." I run to the front doors to see if I could see our car and I do.

"I wonder will she just let me stay. It's not like we live far from here," I mumble to myself as I approach our car.

"Ma, the dance teacher just asked if I wanted to be on the dance team. Is it okay for me to stay after for like a hour today?" I ask her through the passenger window.

"For a hour? How long does practice usually last?"

"I'm going to get all of the information today."

"Alright, I'll be back in a hour." Mom rolls the window up a little before pulling off.

That went smoother than I expected.

One thing I can say about my mom is that she is always on time, so when she say she's going to be back in an hour, I know she means right on the dot.

The dance team is pretty good. Before they started practicing on the routine, they stretched first. Lanae might be a little chubby, but the girl can dance! Her spot is right in the front, and she's hitting every move to every beat. I see a couple of girls from my homeroom class as well. Everybody is dressed comfortably, enabling them to move and sway around. I'm happy this is a Hip Hop dance team and not ballet or something.

Looking at the clock, my hour came too fast. Ms. King notices me heading to the front door and yells.

"Don't forget to bring comfortable clothes on Friday, Miko! We're learning a new routine!"

"Okay, I will!" I continue to walk out.

"How was practice?" Mom asks nicely as I get in the car.

"It was cool. I think this will be fun!"

"How long is the practice?

"Two hours on every Thursday and Friday."

"Oh okay, that's not bad. Is it a lot of people on the team?" Mom continues.

"Umm, nah, probably about ten to fifteen girls. Ms. King is the dance teacher. She told me to bring something comfortable to wear on Friday," I explain.

"Okay, did you tell her you used to dance when you were younger?" Mom asks in a confident way.

"Nah, I didn't tell her. But she did say that we are going to be learning a new routine. I'm happy about that too! I feel excited."

"Why?" Mom smiles.

"Because I won't have to play catch up. We can all start fresh on the new routine together," I explain looking out of the window.

CHAPTER FIFTY-SEVEN

LUNCH IS SO packed today. For whatever reason, it seems like it's so many people here. Usually, Lanae finds me in the lunchroom and we sit next to each other, but she didn't come to school today.

"You the new girl, right?" a brown-skinned skinny girl walks up.

"Yeah," I answer quickly.

"I just transferred to your class because I hate Mr. Barn ol' ugly ass," she frowns, making the other girl skinny girl standing next to her laugh.

"Oh, you transferred out of his class before I started?" I ask.

"Yeah, like a week or two before you started. I'm Tanjaneka, and this is my best friend, Erin."

"Tan-ja-nee-ka?" I pronounce slowly.

"Yeah." Tanjaneka and Erin sit down next to me at the lunch table.

Damn that's ghetto as fuck!

"So, y'all been going here since sixth grade?" I spark more conversation.

"Yeah, we been friends since like fourth grade, though." Erin bites into her pizza.

"Oh, okay, that's cool!" I add.

"We been meaning to talk to you but Lanae always in your ass crack," Tanjaneka jokes, making all of us laugh.

"She can be a little clingy." I try not to tease her.

"She don't even know you well enough to be all in like that," Tanjaneka shakes her head.

About ten minutes into our conversation, a fight broke out of nowhere. Two girls are rumbling in the center of the lunchroom. The entire lunchroom runs to surround them to watch the fight. From where we're sitting, all we have to do is stand on top of the lunch table to get a good view. These girls are going at it hardcore, like some bitches in the streets. One of the girls look familiar, I think I've seen her in the hallway before. The other girl doesn't look familiar at all.

"You know those girls?" I ask Tanjaneka, geeked up from the fight.

"Yeah, they been beefing since last year." Tanjaneka moves over to get a better view.

"Damn! Rochell blew her shit out!" Erin instigates.

After a few minutes passed, the fight was broken up. I'm not sure if the men who broke the fight up are teachers or not, but it took about four men to get these two girls off of each of other.

"Ugly ass bitch! You better watch your back, hoe!" one of the girls screams at the other girl as she's escorted out of the lunchroom.

"How long y'all think they will be suspended for?" I ask as we sit back down like nothing happened.

"Probably three days to a week," Erin responds.

"Last time Andre and Fred fought, niggas' families came up here, shit got too real!" Tanjaneka giggles.

"They brought their family up here?" my mouth drops.

"Yup, niggas' mama's was out there thumping and everything!" Erin adds, making us laugh.

"Damn, I know that was crazy!" I shake my head.

"Yeah, they got expelled after that though," Tanjaneka confirms.

"Right, the school didn't let they ass come back!" I joke.

After lunch, Tanjaneka and I walked Erin to her class, then we walked back to ours. It's so funny because today is the first day I've noticed Tanjaneka. I hadn't realized she was in my class this whole time. I've been changing schools like diapers lately, and I can't keep up with people anymore.

"Yo, Robert, here go my playlist." Terell hands Robert a white piece of paper and five dollars in class.
"Damn, nigga', I told you to be low key. I don't want Ms. Brown's nosy ass to start hating." Robert snatches the paper and money quickly.
"Ms. Brown know better. Anyway, I'ma need the CD by tomorrow."
"Tomorrow?" Robert sound stressed out.
"Yeah, nigga', I most definitely need it for the weekend," Terell confirms.
"Alright, man, I'ma see what I can do," Robert tries to blow him off.
"Stop playing, Robert, I'm serious," Terell frowns.
"I heard you! I got you!" Robert confirms.

Once the conversation is over, Terell walks back to his seat after taking a quick glance at me. He is so freaking fine! He's tall with a caramel skin tone, hazel eyes that match his light brown hair. He looks like he has a girlfriend. He doesn't come off like the player type either. He is well behaved, and he participates in class, unlike Cortez. I have a bad boy crush and a good boy crush, and they're both in my class. How lucky am I this year in 7th grade? I wonder if they have a crush on me. I guess I'm just going to have to wait and see because I refuse to ask either of them myself.

The end of the day is here sooner than expected. I'm excited but at the same time nervous about dance practice. Lanae was supposed to be here today. I wonder why she missed school again. I was looking forward to learning the dance with her. Now I'm just going to be by myself, but it's cool though.

On the way to the dance room, I run into Cortez. Before he speaks, I begin smiling anticipating something funny to come out of his mouth.

"Dang, girl, I haven't even said anything, and you are already blushing," Cortez smiles.

"Boy, because I know you're about to say something crazy!" I giggle.

"Where you about to go?" Cortez looks at me suspiciously.

"Dance class." I start walking off slowly.

"Can I come to watch you dance?" Cortez looks at me sideways.

"No, boy! Bye!" I continue to walk off.

"Whatever! Wit yo' fine self!" Cortez yells down the hall.

Oh my god! Where does he get his game from? He must have an older brother or something," I think to myself as I walk in the dance room.

"Alright, class, listen up! Class starts immediately after school. If you're more than five minutes late, you will run ten laps around this dance room. In life, you will have to learn how to be punctual, so we're going to start now!" Ms. King announces to the entire dance class.

First everyone changed into their workout clothes, then we stretch out before starting the routine. Then I hear the beginning of the song Temperature by Sean Paul come on the radio. When the song comes on, I can tell this is going to be my favorite dance. Everybody's face just lit up with joy since this song is pretty popular right now.

Two girls already know the beginning of the routine. I don't know if it's because they're like the dance captains or if it's because they're just the teacher's pets. One girl is on her left, and the other girl is on her right, so if you can't see Ms. King, you're bound to be able to see one of the other girls. The beginning of the routine is similar to the music video. I've seen this video several times because we have cable at D's house.

"Okay, class, let's start from the top!" Ms. King replays the song and everybody repositions.

I'm learning this routine pretty fast. It's not too hard, but the moves are kind of fast-paced. So far, this dance is sweet! We haven't even finished the routine, and I can't wait to perform it already.

"How was dance class?" Mom asks with excitement.
"It was fun! We doing a routine to that Temperature song by Sean Paul."
"Temperature?"
"Yeah, the one that be like, "In the wintertime cold, I wanna' be keeping you warm. I got the right temperature to shelter you from the storm." I sing it out in my best Jamaican voice.
"Oh, yeah! That's a good dancing song!" Mom smiles.
"They copied some of the dance moves from the video too," I continue.
"Oh really?" Mom giggles.
"Yeah, but the routine still sweet though."
"I have good news!" Mom smiles.
"What?" I ask quickly.
"We're moving into our own place sometime next week."
Final—fucking—ly!"
"Where at?" mom got my undivided attention.
"Just right around the corner from D in a four-family flat," Mom explains.
"A four-family flat? I didn't know those exist."
"Yeah, they're smaller than the two-family flat, but at least we will have our own space."

"Can we ride past the one we will be staying in?" I'm eager to see it.

"Yeah, we can." Mom seems cool about it.

Since we don't live that far from Joy Middle School, it takes us no time to get to the block we're going to be living on. This block looks worse than the D's block, but like Mama said, at least we will have our own spot. I'm so happy we will be leaving D's house soon. I mean, I guess it's better than living out of the car, but at least the car doesn't stink. Sometimes I have to double-check my clothes and myself to make sure I don't smell like D's house when I go to school. It's really disgusting, but he's a nice guy, and that was nice of him to let us stay for as long as we did, but I'm ready to go!

I don't know where my mama met these people, but I have a strong feeling that this is going to be a drunken night for her. She's already blinking slowly like she's fighting her sleep. As I become more embarrassed while watching Mom, I hold onto Koko tightly as she sleeps in my arms. I would lay her down, but I'm sitting on the only clean-looking part of the couch. I've never seen these people a day in my life, so I'm sure they don't give a fuck about how drunk she is or how many kids she has with her. I'm scared her drunk ass might drive Koko and me off the road and kill all of us tonight.

As the night goes on, I make sure to grab her phone in case I have to make an emergency call. I hate it when she drinks like this! Damn, I miss my daddy, Key, and my grandparents. I still can't believe she's keeping us away from them and that I haven't seen or heard from them in months. Thinking about it always tends to bring tears to my eyes, so I try not to think about it. But times like this I would at least have Key here with me. Koko is just a baby, she doesn't know what's going on. I've never felt so lonely in a room full of people before.

Mom finally wakes up from her nap, and it's about 3am. She still looks like she's drunk and she's still acting drunk. She didn't sleep long enough to be sober. Here we go again, having to get in a vehicle with her tired ass. No one is going to say anything because she's grown. I pray we're not far from D's house. I have never wanted to get to his house as much as I want to right now. Before we pull off, I make sure Koko is strapped in her car seat nice and tightly, then I make sure I put my seat belt on. When I look over at Mom in the driver's seat, I notice she doesn't have her seat belt on.

"You not gone put on yo' seatbelt?" I ask shyly, expecting to get yelled at.
"Shut the fuck up! I know what the FUCK I'm doing!" Mom snaps.
"God, please get us home safely," I say a silent prayer as Mom pulls off.
Trying to keep her alert, I continue to make conversation "D been calling you."
"And did I ask you? Just mind yo' motherfucking business Miko!" Mom slurs her words.

About ten minutes within the ride, I see the McDonald's that's right across the street from D's house, so I know we are close. Instead of this drunk bitch going home, she wants to get something to eat. Here we go again in the drive-thru and she's passed out, only this time, it's Koko and me in the car, and we're on the ghetto ass east side of Detroit. Anything can fucking happen to us right now if somebody notices that she's passed out in the driver's seat. I try several times to wake her up. I try tapping and shaking her, but she's not budging. She's definitely still breathing though, so that's good. Then out of nowhere, Mom's cellphone starts ringing. When I look at the caller id, it reads Irene, so I answer.
"Hey, Irene," my eyes begin to water as I get out of the car to talk.
"Miko? What you doing up this late?" Irene asks.
"I'm with my mama. We at this McDonalds on Mac and she's

drunk and passed out in the car." Tears begin to fall.

"Passed out?" Irene sound scared.

"Yeah, and it's weird people, crack heads, and everything over here walking around."

"Are y'all over there by the church?" Irene tries to calm herself down.

"Yeah," I can't help but to cry.

"Oh, my goodness! It is dangerous over there! Y'all are too young to be out there alone! And she's been drinking! They are going to call the cops on her ass, and I hope they do! This is not right, I would come to get y'all, but Amanda has the car, and she's at work."

"The last time this happened, the restaurant called the cops, and they had to escort her to the hospital," I add.

"You mean to tell me that this is not the first time she's been passed out drunk at the drive-thru?"

"Right," I confirm.

"Joyce needs to really quit it! Y'all are still young! She can't be doing stuff like this! Now I'm over here worried!" Irene confesses.

"Miko," Mom's voice sounds like a ghost from behind me.

"Huh?" I turn around.

"Who are you talking to?" Mom frowns with bloodshot red eyes.

"It's Irene, she called." I hand her the phone nervously.

Mom snatches the phone away from me as if she's so angry. I'm the one that should be angry! We've been out here for too long waiting on her to wake up. Mom talks to Irene for about five minutes. I can tell Mom doesn't want to hear what Irene has to say. As soon as she gets off the phone, she checks me.

"Everything is alright, Irene. Thanks for your concern," mom then hangs the phone up quickly in Irene's face.

"And what the fuck was that?" Now she sounds sober.

"She called... I answered..." I shrug my shoulders.

Before I could finish my sentence, she slaps the rest of whatever I was going to say out of my mouth.

"What did I tell you about running your motherfuckin' mouth?" Mom screams at me.

That slap to the face hurt so bad that I couldn't say anything. Out of anger and fear I decide to run to D's house on foot.

"What's going on? Where ya' mama at? I been calling her!" D answers the door nervously.

"She's at the McDonald drunk as hell!" I yell as my face is soaked in tears.

"The one at the corner across the street?" D asks frantically.

"Yeah, she passed out in the drive-thru again with me and Koko in the car!" I spill all the beans out of anger. Now, I feel fearless and fed up.

"Aww, shit, she still passed out?" D puts on his shoes quickly.

"No, she finally woke up after a hour or two." I pace back and forth.

"After a hour or two? Why you just didn't call me?"

"Because I didn't want to get in trouble!"

"Now why would you get in trouble?" D sits down.

"Because I'm always getting in trouble over stupid stuff!" I vent as Mom walks through the door with Koko.

"You left these babies in the car at the ghetto ass McDonald's at this time of night?" D looks at my mom like she's the dumbest person walking on earth.

"Miko, go upstairs!" Mom says sternly.

All she about to do is make up a lie to make herself sound better than what she is. I swear to god, I'm not letting her whoop me tonight. If she thinks I'm about to lay across any of these fucking beds, she got me fucked up!

"I can't stand her ass!" I say loud enough for only me to hear. As I continue to pace the room, tears steadily fall down my cheeks as I hear Mom walking in the upstairs hallway.

"How many times do I have to tell you to stop telling people our business?" Mom looks me dead in my eyes.
"I want to live with my dad!" I ignored her question.
"You can live with him when you turn eighteen." Mom keeps her tone of voice stern but only loud enough for me to hear inside the room.
"Yea, whatever all you do is lie!" I lash out
"Watch your fucking mouth when you're talking to me!" mom says sternly

I know she's mad that I told D where we were tonight. I'm surprised she didn't try to whop me for running my mouth, but everything I said is the truth, and that's something you just can't hide forever.

CHAPTER **FIFTY-EIGHT**

THIS FOUR-FAMILY FLAT is so raggedy inside. We live on the second story left-hand corner unit. When you first walk through the door, the living room is the first room. To the right is Mom's room and to the left is the kitchen. The bathroom is next door to the kitchen, and my room is next door to the bathroom. Even though we live in a raggedy area, Mom makes sure we keep our small apartment squeaky clean and comfy, which makes the place feel more homey and comfortable.

"Ma, can I go over Tanjaneka's house today?" I ask, expecting for her to say no.
"Who is Tanjaneka?" Mom frowns in a weird way at the unfamiliar name.
"My friend from school. I don't think she live that far from here," I add, trying to be convincing.
"Did her mom say you could come over?"
"Yea, she asked her mom first."
"Okay, you can go. I'll take you in a few after I get Koko dressed." Mom looks away.

I'm in shock! I can't believe she's letting me go somewhere further than the porch. Before leaving her room, I call Tanjaneka to get her address and to tell her I'll be on my way soon. Wow, she's never let

Key go over to her friend's house from school before. That's why I was sure that she wasn't going to let me go. She barely used to let us go across the street over to Patricia and Porsha's house. This is about to be so much fun, and I'm so happy! Before we leave, I make sure to grab my small piece of white paper with my dad's number on it and place it in the strap lining of my bra. Usually, I would put it in my sock, but it's the summertime, and it's too hot to be wearing socks.

"Pick it up!" Mom yells at Koko because she dropped some food on the floor.

"YOU HEARD WHAT I SAID!" Mom hits Koko's hand as hard as she can then she pinches her arm until it's red.

Koko begins to scream to the top of her lungs from the pain.

Damn, she's only two years old. She's still learning how to understand everything, I think to myself as I watch.

"Shut up! Don't nobody want to hear that crying shit!" Mom looks angry.

"If you don't shut the!" Mom grabs her house shoe and begins whopping Koko like she stole something.

Like that's going to make her shut up! I frown. "This is the type of shit that makes me want to just bring Koko with me. She's just a mean ass bitch."

This is exactly why Key didn't mind me rolling with her because Mom acts like she gets a thrill out of hitting on us. She is beating on a baby for not listening to her the first time she said something. No remorse, no kisses or hugs after the beating. Just straight cold blooded. I want to go pick Koko up so bad, but the last time I tried to console her after she got a whooping I got in trouble for being nice to the baby. This time I didn't have to go pick Koko up. Koko runs to me when she notices I'm standing nearby, unable to resist her sobbing cries. I pick Koko up as soon as she get close enough and let her cry herself to sleep in my arms as Mom picks up the little bit of food from the floor that Koko spilt.

Stupid bitch, that's why I hate her ass now. I continue to rock Koko to sleep in my arms.

"See, I told you your mama was going to let you come over!" Tanjaneka has a huge smile on her face.

"Girl, my mama is very strict and mean. I'm so surprised she said I could," I giggle as I suck on my popsicle.

"She doesn't seem mean at all to me." Tanjaneka looks at me like I'm crazy.

"Yeah, you're not the first to say that, but she's only mean to her own kids. She nice to everybody else's kids."

Tanjaneka's neighborhood is much nicer than the neighborhood I live in. This neighborhood reminds me of my old neighborhood off 7 Mile on the west side. All of the houses look occupied, and it's clean for the most part. As the summer day continues, we play outside games with the other kids. Tanjaneka has some boys as friends that live around the corner, and they are so cute and fun!

"I like it over here, and it's a whole bunch of kids around here too!" I smile.

"Yeah, I basically grew up with all of them." Tanjaneka ties her shoe.

"Reminds me when I used to live on the west side in my old neighborhood," I reminisce.

"I forgot you from the west side. You seem like a west side girl too," Tanjaneka giggles.

"What is that supposed to mean?" I size her up in a joking way.

"It is what it is. Erin is going to be so jealous when I tell her you came over here." Tanjaneka gives me the side-eye.

I giggle, changing the subject. "Those boys were cute too!"

"Who, Tim and them?"

"Yeah."

"Girl, they are some hoes!" Tanjaneka rolls her eyes.

"They cool as hell, though! They had me cracking up!"

"Yeah, they are silly as hell. I'm surprised they left so early. They usually stay out all night," Tanjaneka explains.

"Aye, do you have a cellphone?" I switch the subject like I'm on a mission.

"My grandma does, you want to use it?"

"What? Your grandma has a cellphone?" I laugh.

"Yeah, girl, she think she young. I'ma go get it!" Tanjaneka gets up from the porch stairs to walk in the house.

"I'm surprised my mama hasn't called yet," I whisper to myself.

Tanjaneka comes back with the phone in no time. I reach in my bra to grab my small white paper and dial my dad's number as quick as possible.

"Hey, Da!" I get excited after he answers on the second ring.

"Mik Mik! Hey, boo!" Dad sounds happy to hear from me. "Where you at?"

"I'm over my friend's house right now on the east side," I explain.

"Where at on the east side? I'm over here too!" Dad asks.

"I'm not sure. I have to pay attention to where it is next time. But Mom is on her way to get me," I add in case he was thinking about pulling up.

"See, what I tell you about paying attention to your surroundings?" Dad catches me slipping. "So, where y'all living at now?

"We live on the east side off of Mac and Conners."

"Damn! That's the hood hood!" Dad laughs. "Did y'all get a house over there?"

"We live in a four-family flat over there."

"Who the fuck she know over there?" Dad sounds surprised.

"Some guy named D. He's older than her, dark-skinned, kind of chubby guy."

"How long y'all been over there?" Dad continues with questions because we haven't talked in so long.

"A few months after we left off of Coyle. When we left Coyle, we didn't have a place to stay. We slept in the car at the park for weeks," I spill the tea.

"What?" Dad sounds flabbergasted.

"Then she got in touch with Irene, who was living at the Holiday Inn hotel, so we ended up going to live at the hotel for a few months too."

"At a hotel? Oh my god, what the fuck is Joyce thinking? Why did she leave the house on Coyle after her parents just got it for her?"

"I guess because she doesn't want you to know where we live."

"That's got to be the dumbest shit I've heard all year!" Dad exclaims.

"I know, right? Left a fully furnished home to be homeless," I still can't wrap it around my head.

"What took you so long to call, Mik?" Dad asks softly.

"Well, this is the first time I'm able to be alone and away from her. I hadn't been in school or nothing," I explain.

"Right, so y'all living over there by that McDonalds, huh?" Dad sounds sure.

"Yup."

"Okay, how is Koko doing?" Dad asks.

"She's doing good. She got a whooping today for spilling some food on the floor. Mama gave her a whooping with a shoe and was pinching on her. She's just a baby."

"Ain't that about a bitch!" Dad sounds like he's in deep thought. "Yeah, I'ma get y'all back someway somehow, boop."

"This mama calling on the other line." I instantly get nervous.

"Okay, boop, stay in touch! Love you!"

"Love you too!" I click over to the other line.

"Hello?" I try to sound normal.

"I'm on my way to come get you." Mom sounds sober.

"Alright, we outside."

It took Mom about fifteen minutes to arrive. It's the weekend and I know she like drinking on the weekends sometimes. Thank God she's not drunk today!

The last week of school seems pretty empty. I wonder if Robert is coming back one of these days so he can make me one last CD.

There are only like eight people in the class today, so Ms. Brown is just letting everybody do their own thing.

Cortez walks back in the classroom. "Ain't nobody in this bitch."

"Where you go?" I lean over in my desk.

"I was just roaming around." Cortez sits in Robert's seat.

"I'm not coming tomorrow," I giggle.

"Right, me either. So, we gone keep in touch over the summer?" Cortez side-eyes me.

"Yeah, we can, what's your number?" I open up my binder to write it down.

"313-755-**** Save it under boo thang!" Cortez smirks, and I can't help but to laugh.

"Alright, boo thang!" I continue to giggle at his sense of humor.

"You not even gone call me!" Cortez smacks his lips in disbelief.

"Yes, I will," I smile.

"Okay, we will see." Cortez gets up and walks right back out of the classroom.

"Cortez, where are you?" Ms. Brown stops in the middle of her sentence as Cortez runs out of the classroom.

I must admit, the east side brought some cool people. I met a lot of cute boys over here and some cool friends too. I know we just moved into our own place, but I have a feeling we're not going to be over here for too long. I don't have a clue where we will be going next, but I'm pretty sure the voyage is not over.

It's the middle of the summer, and it's hot in Detroit city. Just as I guessed a few months back at the beginning of the summer that we would not be on the east side for long, and we weren't. After my dad popped up on us at the store near our house, I guess Mom felt like she needed to relocate. This moving from place to place shit is so stressful and overwhelming. Especially since I'm moving all of the bags because Mom is always complaining about her back pain. What she fails to realize is I don't have the best back either. My scoliosis is getting worse as I get older. My waistline is kind of imbalanced, and it's becoming more noticeable.

Now we're living in Southfield at an apartment complex called Pebble Creek with another unfamiliar man. Mom swears he's a friend of the family on my granddad's side, but I've never seen or heard of this man. His name is John and he's a very tall dark-skinned, grey-headed old man. He doesn't talk to me much. He has a weird personality, and most of the time, he acts as if he doesn't want to be bothered, so I don't say much to him. Despite the fact that we live with a weird old man, it's so much fun living over here. I thought the east side of Detroit was fun but living over here is ten times better. I mean, I do miss having my own room, but it seems to be a lot safer over here.

There are so many kids that are my age and older that live in the complex. Even the kids that live in the houses behind the apartment complex, comes over here to hangout. My closet friends are Jessica and Yana. They have been living over here before me. I don't think they're that close to each other. They tolerate each other because I'm their mutual friend. They're both in high school already, so they tease me for being the young one a lot. I'll be going to the 8th grade after the summer while they will be going to the 10th grade. I tell them all the time I'm used to hanging around people older than them. I told them I have an older sister that is five years older than me. They always ask where she is, and I just say she lives with her boyfriend. I don't make it a habit to tell people about my family business. I guess being trained to not speak on family business has grown on me. Plus, I wouldn't want anybody throwing anything in my face. Kids can be cruel. Sometime people will try to take advantage and use things they know about you against you. I would hate to have to beat somebody the fuck up for teasing me about something personal. Until a person has shown me their true loyalty, I feed them with a long spoon.

It's a nice summer day outside, but I don't see anybody outside, surprisingly. It's freaking freezing in this apartment. John's old ass loves to keep it deep freezer cold. We already live in this one-bedroom small apartment, so it gets really cold in here fast.

"You cold, huh?" I joke with Mom as she sits on the couch with a thick throw covering her legs.
"It's cold as hell in here," Mom giggles.
"Can I go outside to warm up?" I ask.
"Yeah, take Koko with you," Mom adds.
"Alright." I pop up to grab Koko's shoes.

When Koko and I get outside, I see Dominique and a couple of her friends playing. Dominique is Jessica's little sister. If you had to guess, you wouldn't think Jessica and Diamond were even related. Jessica is dark-skinned with short hair. Diamond is high yellow with long hair, and their facial features are completely opposite.

"Hey, Miko!" Dominique runs towards Koko and me.
"What's up, Dominique?" I hold Koko on my hip.
"Who is this? She is so pretty!" Dominique grabs Koko's hand.
"This is my little sister, Koko."

"I didn't know you had a little sister! Why you don't ever bring her over our house?" Dominique asks.

"Because she's a baby, she be with my mama most of the time."

"Can I hold her?" Dominique holds her hands out.

"If she will go to you." I lean over trying to give Koko to Dominique as Koko leans back the opposite way.

I giggle ."She don't want to come to you."

"Aww, man!" Dominique pouts. "Why you don't want to come to me, pretty baby? Huh?" Dominique tries to talk like a baby.

"Where Jessica at?" I ask.

"She in the apartment. You want me to go get her?" Dominique asks with her hyper eight-year-old energy.

"Yeah, tell her to come out." I put Koko on the ground so she can walk.

Dominique runs off, heading towards the front door of their apartment. Before Koko and I could get to the Gazebo across the street, Dominique comes back outside rushing to her friends.

"She said here she comes!" Dominique yells from across the street.

"Come on, Koko boo!" I let Koko chase me to the top of the Gazebo.

Once we get to the top of the Gazebo, we sit down on the ground to play Patty Cake. About five minutes later, Jessica comes walking over.

"Aww, is this your baby sister?" Jessica smiles.

"Yeah."

"Hi, Koko! Can I hold her?" Jessica looks excited.

"Yeah, if she let you. Dominique was trying to hold her earlier, and she wouldn't go to her."

Jessica laughs. "That's because Dominique ugly."

"No, she is not!" I laugh as Koko lets Jessica hold her with no problem.

"See, she likes me. Hi, pretty baby, you want to be my fake daughter? Huh, cutie?" Jessica talks to Koko in a soft baby pitch.

"Why you got that sweater on?" Jessica notices out of nowhere.

"Girl, because it be cold as fuck in my apartment. I'm just now starting to unthaw," I tell half of the truth.

"Y'all want to come over to my place? It's hot as fuck out here!" Jessica wipes her forehead.

"Okay," I shrug my shoulders.

The main reason I like wearing my sweater is so I can hide my scoliosis. Being that my spine is curved, it makes the right side of my hip poke out a little bit. I was born with this condition, and I believe it's hereditary since Mom was born with it too. I don't know if it's that noticeable to other people, but if you pay close enough attention, you can most definitely see it. What bothers me is people are always paying me a lot of attention, so wearing my sweater makes me feel secure, covered, and comfortable. When I used to hang out with Kesha and Kansas, they noticed once, and I had to explain the condition I have to them. I wasn't embarrassed or anything because they are my best friends.

"Have you heard that new Chris Brown song called "Say Good-Bye?" Jessica grabs the remote.

"Yeah, I like that song!" Koko and I flop on the couch.

"Yes, girl! I love that song, and I love Chris Brown's yellow self!" Jessica turns on the video.

"Oh yeah, I know you like them yellow boys!" I give her an evil smile.

Jessica can't hide her blushing. "Be quiet!"

"You and De'vall still talking?" I ask.

"Yeah, we are with his annoying ass," Jessica rolls her eyes.

"He popped that cherry yet?" I laugh at myself.

"I didn't tell you?" Jessica looks surprised.

"Nah."

"Girl, yes, we did it already! More than once too!" Jessica laughs.

"Really? How was it?" I get comfortable being nosy.

"Girl, it's good! But he didn't pop my cherry. Another boy did." Jessica gets up from the couch to mimic the Chris Brown video routine.

I burst out in laughter. "You know the routine?"

"I been practicing." Jessica mimics every move Chris Brown and the girl is doing in the music video.

CHAPTER **FIFTY-NINE**

"MA, LOOK AT my hips. You see how this one stick out further than this one?" I point so she can see the difference.

"Yeah, it's because of the scoliosis. You'll probably just need to wear a brace. I have it too, and when I went to go get checked for it, that's what the doctor told me. We can go get you checked out sometime next week."

"Okay, cool," I smile.

Mom does a lot of crazy things at times, but I can say when it comes to getting business done, she's always on top of it. When it comes to school, health or anything doctor related, she is superman. Just like the time I caught a wart on the bottom of my foot from playing in the volleyball court, Mom made sure we got the wart remover for it immediately.

Everybody is at the park tonight, even a few unfamiliar faces. I'm hanging with Yana and a couple of her friends tonight. Jessica was out here with us, but her mom made her go home.

"Jessica mama made that ass come in the house early tonight!" Yana teases.

"Right, her mama wasn't playing any games!" Jennifer eggs Yana on.

"Jessica mama said get that fast ass in the bed right now!" Yana makes everybody laugh.

"Y'all stupid," I laugh, shaking my head at their jokes.

Yana is cool with Jennifer and all of her other sister's. Jennifer is Farod's — Yana's older brother — girlfriend. Farod and Jennifer appear to be so in love, but I hardly ever see her. I see more of him since we all live in the apartment complex. I think Jennifer and her family live in the houses behind the apartments. I secretly have a little crush on Farod, but since I know he has a girlfriend, I would never try to talk to him in that way. Even though I have a lot of space and opportunity to try to shoot my shot since I'm friends with his sister, I also believe in karma, and I wouldn't want another chick to try to get with my boyfriend knowing that we're together.

Yana is light-skinned, short, with big curly hair. She has three older brothers, and she's the youngest. All of her brothers are cute to me, and I believe they all have girlfriends. Jennifer is light-skinned, sort of taller with super long naturally curly hair. Jennifer and all of her sisters have extremely long curly hair as if they're biracial or something.

"What y'all ugly little girls over here talking about?" Dion walks over out of nowhere.

"We talking about how Jessica's mama made her ass go in that house!" Yana laughs.

"That was her mama in that car that pulled up?" Dion giggles.

"Hell yeah!" Yana continues laughing.

"Ahh, Jessica was about to get her little ass whooped!" Dion jokes, making all of us burst out in laughter.

Dion is Yana's second oldest brother. He looks identical to Yana; they literally could have been twins. They sort of have the same kind of personality too. Dion is always joking on somebody.

"She was not about to get a whooping," I laugh taking up for Jessica.

"Miko, shut yo' skinny butt up!" Dion jokes.

"Boy you shut up! You skinny, too, nigga'!" I laugh.

"So? I still look better than you!" Dion laughs, walking towards their apartment.

"Shid! You wish!" I speak louder to make sure he heard me.

"That nigga' always trying to bake somebody!" Yana laughs.

"Right, just like you! Y'all act alike, and y'all look alike! I can't with y'all!" I laugh.

"I don't look like his bean head ass!" Yana giggles.

"Y'all do look just alike, Yana!" Gabriel, Jennifer's sister, breaks her quietness.

"That's just like saying you and Jennifer look just alike," Yana tries to make a point.

"But we don't!" Jennifer laughs at Yana's ridiculous comparison.

"I mean, y'all favor each other. Y'all have the same kind of hair, but that's about it!" I examine Jennifer and Gabriel's sisterly features.

"I look just like my dad. Gabriel looks more like my mama. But you and Dion damn near have the same face!" Jennifer agrees with me.

"I don't see what y'all see at all. I think me and Farod look more alike than me and Dion," Yana stands behind her opinion.

"Nah, Farod and Brandon look alike. You and Dion look alike," Jennifer corrects Yana.

"Brandon is the oldest brother?" I ask.

"Yeah, he lives with my dad, that's why you never see him," Yana confirms.

"Oh, okay, who is that chubby light-skinned guy over there with Farod and them?" I ask aloud for anybody to answer.

"You talking about Zach fat ass?" Yana ask.

"Yeah, you know him?" I continue to look.

"Yeah, he lives over in the houses. He goes to Southfield Lathrup with us," Yana explains.

"Why? You like him?" Jennifer gives me the side-eye.

"I mean, I don't really know him, but he is cute!" I giggle.

"Ugh, Miko a chubby chaser!" Yana points at me while all of us laugh.

"Girl, shut up before he hear yo' big mouth ass!" I push her.

"I don't think Farod is that cool with him, but Ralph is friends with him, though," Jennifer spills a little tea.

"Ralph friendly ass, friends with everybody." Yana smacks her teeth.

"I'ma have to get the scoop from Ralph then," I smile hoping to get some good 411 on this Zach guy.

Ralph is like one of my best guy friends around here. I don't even remember how we met, but I just know he's a Scorpio like me and we've been tight ever since we found that out. Ralph is a brown-skinned guy, tall with pretty teeth. It's something cute about him, but I just can't put my finger on it. He's never tried to get with me, flirt, or have sex with me. When we hangout, it's just a simple, genuine friend thing. He's in high school as well. He makes me feel like a little sister most of the time, and I love it because I've always wanted a big brother.

Today I'm taking X-Rays of my spine at the doctor's office. I'm not too nervous because my mom has scoliosis as well. She's always tells me I will just have to wear a back brace. She's never worn a brace before, and she's fine, so I should be too. The doctor is taking longer than expected. They told me I couldn't eat anything a couple of hours before the X-Rays, and I'm starting to get a little hungry.

"You nervous?" Mom asks with a comforting smile on her face.

"No, I'm hungry though," I giggle.

"Yeah, I'm kind of hungry too." Mom put Koko down to walk on her own.

"I wonder what's taking so long." I adjust myself on the table.

"They probably have a lot of patients in today," Mom assumes.

About twenty minutes later of waiting and dragging along conversation, Dr. Fischer finally comes into our room.

"Sorry for the wait. We had some unexpected solutions in your results." Dr. Fischer opens his folder.

"Oh really?" Mom sounds surprised.

"Yes, I'm sorry to have to tell you guys this, but Kimiko is going to have to undergo an operation." Dr. Fischer's words sounds like they're coming out in slow motion as he looks me dead in my eyes.

"An operation?" Mom's eyes pops out of her head.

Dr. Fischer pulls out X-Ray sheets with writing on it and places it on a small white square-shaped light board.

My heart feels like it dropped from my chest to my toes. I want to burst out in tears, but I can't. I can't let anybody see me cry.

"This is her spine. It's at a 69-degree curvage." Dr, Fischer points at the board.

"This is the only option? She can't wear a brace?" Mom sounds nervous.

"The curve in her spine is too severe. Anything under a 45-degree curve could be fixed with a brace," Dr. Fischer explains.

"Oh wow, and she's way past that," Mom finishes his sentence.

"Exactly, and trust me, if there were any other options, we would try to execute them before taking the surgery route. Since there isn't, I must go over the risk and possibilities that could happen while under operation." Dr. Fischer pulls out another set of papers.

"You have several nerves in your spinal cord. While under an operation, if one of these nerves become irritated or damaged. It could cause you to be paralyzed from the waist down. Excessive bleeding can cause several issues. Blood clots are a major risk.

A shortage of bone formation and any kind of infections can

open doors to other risks.

If there are any kind of infections, a repeat surgery will be necessary."

"You alright, Miko?" Mom asks.

I just nod my head, afraid that if I speak, I will start crying like a baby.

"The fact that you're not experiencing any pain is great news. If you were in pain, I would suggest for you guys to set up the operation date ASAP." Dr. Fischer gathers his belongings.

After the long talk with the doctor, we are finally able to leave. We didn't set any dates for surgery just yet, being that we're not stable and don't know where we will be in the next couple of months. The ride home is very quiet. Mom doesn't try to comfort me; she doesn't try to share any kind words of encouragement either. Not that I'm expecting it anyways. I don't remember the last time she showed any kind of affection towards me anyway.

"I wasn't expecting that," Mom tries to spark up a conversation.

"Mmmhmm," I nod my head looking out of the passenger window.

I guess Mom is getting the hint that I don't want to be bothered, so for the rest of the ride home, silence fills the car. As soon as we pull up to the apartment complex, I feel my stomach drop, sort of like an aching feeling. Once we get inside the apartment, I rush to the bathroom. When my foot hit the inside of the bathroom, a waterfall of tears begin to pour. I try not to make any weeping noises through my mouth, but it's so hard. I'm going to have to get surgery, and none of my family members is going to be there to comfort me. My mom doesn't even know how to express her love. Why do things have to be this way? Why can't we just get along like regular families? My parents don't have to be together. It was hell when they were married anyway. But damn, I just don't understand why things can't be civil. Yana's parents aren't married, but she's able to go visit her dad whenever she wants. The difference is Yana's mama cares about how her kids feel to a certain extent. My mama doesn't give a fuck about how any of this is affecting us. All I want to be able to do is be around my loved ones, including my mom, but she's making that impossible. And that alone is just making me hate her guts even more as each day passes.

"What you gone be for Halloween?" Janae asks in the seat behind me.

"I don't know. I might not even dress up this year," I explain, less excited than her.

"Why not? You tripping!" Janae is surprised by my lukewarm energy about Halloween.

"What about you? What you dressing up as?"

"I think I want to be something scary like Freddy Krueger or somebody." Janae looks so serious.

I burst out in laughter. "Freddy Krueger? You the one tripping."

"How? My brother and them dressing up in something scary too," Janae giggles.

"Everybody gonna' think y'all a group of little boys running around." I laugh at my own joke.

"I don't care." Janae shrugs her shoulders, unable to hide her tomboy ways.

Janae is one of my close friends at the Academy of Lathrup Village. I still can't believe I'm back at this school for 8th grade after all of these years. Surprisingly, there are a lot of people from elementary school that never left. One person I was especially happy to see when I first started was my old friend Will. He looks just the same. He's still chubby and wears glasses. He literally looks like he just got taller. I wish Will and I could be close friends, but I can tell by the way he looks at me that he likes me more than a friend. He tries to put on this outgoing personality, but when it comes to flirting with girls, he's really shy. I don't want to have to let him down, so I kind of keep it short with him.

CHAPTER **SIXTY**

IT'S A FRIDAY night and it's Halloween, and I don't have anything planned. I'm not dressing up, and we're not going to hang out over anybody's house. This shit is wack, and I'm ready for this night to end. John's old ass is in his room, and my mom is doing her nails. Right before I get comfortable, the doorbell rings.

"I'll get it!" I hop up from the couch and head down the stairs to the door.

"Yo, what you doing?" Yana seems hype.

"Shit, being bored as fuck," I express after closing the front door to walk on the porch.

"Dog, come with us over to the houses. Jessica and them out there too," Yana suggests.

"Really? I wonder why she didn't come to get me," I add.

"Because that bitch fake as hell. I seen her with some other people. It look like she was with family or something," Yana explains.

"Y'all about to go over there for trick or treating?" I ask.

"Hell yeah, you know all of those people that live over there got money! They about to have all the good candy!" Yana laughs.

"We don't even have on costumes. They gone be looking at our grown asses like…" I make a funny facial expression.

"Shidd, I'ma tell them I'm O-Dog from *Menace II Society*!" Yana laughs.

"Bitch, you don't even have braids!" I laugh at her.

"Those rich White people not gone know who O-Dog is!" Yana continues to laugh.

"You stupid!" I burst out in laughter. "Okay, hold on, I'ma be right back." I rush back in the apartment to see about going trick or treating.

"Ma, that's Yana outside. Everybody is over by the houses trick or treating. Can I go?" I ask quickly.

"Yeah, take Koko too so she can get some candy. You want to go trick or treating, mama?" Mom talks to Koko nicely.

Damn, now I gotta lug Koko around too."

Mom quickly gets Koko's shoes and coat on and off we go.

"Well, if you are O-Dog then I'm Stacey sister and this Caine baby!" I close the front door as Yana and I share laughs about the old black classic movie.

It's been about thirty minutes of walking around, and I'm already exhausted. There are kids everywhere, and almost every house has the porch light on.

"Thank god it's not freezing out here!" I put Koko down to give myself a rest.

"Right, it's a little nippy, but it's not bad." Yana rubs her hands together.

"I'm happy Koko is being a big girl and not a cry baby." I hold Koko's hand as we walk.

"Koko always being a big girl! Ain't that right girl?" Yana bends down to give Koko a high five.

"Nah, Koko got some lungs on her. When she cry you would think somebody was hurting her or something," I explain.

"Look at Farod and them, looking like some big fucking kids!" Yana points.

"Ahhh, that is them! Look at Ralph, De'vall, and is that my boo thing?" I squint my eyes for a clearer vision.

"Yeah, that's Zach fat ass!" Yana giggles.

"Ooo, I gotta' tell Ralph to put a word in for me," I giggle with excitement.

"I don't see what you see in his slick hair high yellow ass anyway," Yana jokes.

"The same thing you see in De'vall slick hair high yellow ass!" I return the joke.

"I don't see anything in that hoe! That's Jessica's boo! He fucks her and everybody else in Pebble Creek!" Yana laughs.

"They fucking?" I act surprised to get more information.

"Girl, yeah, and everybody know it. He thought he was going to fuck me too. I was looking at him like he was crazy." Yana shakes her head.

"Do Farod know?"

"Nope, if I told Farod he would whoop his ass! I'm not trying to do boy like that," Yana sounds certain.

"Let's go over there," I suggest.

"For what?" Yana looks confused.

"I don't know, to say what's up." We both know I just want Zach to see me.

"Alright." Yana leads the way.

As we walk toward the group of boys, I begin to get a little nervous, but I calm myself down quickly.

He doesn't know you like him yet so just be cool," I repeat in my head as we approach them.

"Lil Miko, what's up? Ooo, who is this pretty little baby?" Ralph walks over and gives Koko and me a hug.

"This is my little sister!" I smile.

"She is so cute, what's her name?"

"Her name is Koko."

"Her full name is Kee-oa-ko," Yana corrects me.

"Hey, baby Keoako, hey!" Farod plays with her hand.

"Dang, I want my daughter to look like her!" De'vall brags.

"Right, she pretty as hell!" Zach agrees.

"That's 'cause they Asian or something, you heard them names!" Farod laughs.

"Right, and Miko full name is Kee-mee-ko," Yana continues to put all the business out.

"Damn, Yana, tell them my social security number too!" I frown in a playful way.

"For real? That's your full name?" Ralph looks amazed.

"Yeah, and?" I roll my eyes.

"Dang, I thought we were better than that. How I'm supposed to be your big brother and I didn't even know your real name?" Ralph makes a fake sad face.

"I just don't tell people my whole name because people never pronounce it right anyway. Miko is easier to remember. I'm surprised Yana annoying ass remembered how to pronounce it," I put Koko down.

"Why y'all out here trick or treating with no costume on?" I laugh, gearing the conversation in another direction.

"Right, looking like some grown-ass kids!" Yana jokes.

"Fuck a costume! A nigga' needs some candy!" Zach gives De'vall a five and everybody laughs.

"It's getting dark, let's go drop Koko off and we will be back." I look at Yana.

"Alright, we will see y'all later." Yana, Koko and I walk-off.

It didn't take long for us to get stacked up on candy going trick or treating by the houses. I'm excited to meet back up with the boys after we drop Koko off. They are so much fun, especially when everybody is all together just kicking it.

After we drop Koko off at home, we see everybody at the park. So instead of going back over to the houses, we walk down to the park. Once we got to the park, we learned that everybody we seen earlier is here. Yana is right about Jessica having her cousins with her. Jessica is acting a little different, but I really don't care because my boo is here.

"Look at Jessica dick sucking ass. All in De'vall face," Yana leans over to me closely.

After I checked out Jessica and De'vall, Ralph comes over to me. "Little sis, come here."

"Where we going?" I let him guide me.

"Let's take a quick walk." We walk toward the Gazebo.

"What's the deal, Ralph?"

"So, I heard you got a little crush on Zach," Ralph smiles.

"Oh my god! Does he know?" My eyes pop open.

"I think he does," Ralph giggles.

"Nigga' you know if he know! That's your friend!" I give him the 'yea right' stare.

"What I do know is that he is a dog, so whatever little thing you have for him, you need to lose it." Ralph looks serious.

"Really? He a player, huh?" I try to get more details.

"Player is an understatement. That's all the nigga' do is fuck 'em and leave 'em." Ralph continues with the juice.

"And I'm not even like that." I shake my head.

"I know you not. That's why I'm giving you the scoop on him. He probably think I'm over here putting a good word in for him. Man, you too young for that, and he's not looking for a girlfriend. He just looking for something he can smash and pass." Ralph looks down the street from the Gazebo.

"Well shid, I appreciate the 411 for real, big brother!" I play punch Ralph in the side of his stomach and his jaw.

"Oh, you know I got you! You know you my little dog for real!" Ralph plays fight back.

———∞———

April is here before we know it and today is Key's birthday, and mama hasn't spoken a word about her. I think she's turning eighteen today. I wonder what she's doing and how she's been. I miss her so much. I hope with everything in me that she's doing good. Last time I talked to my grandparents, they said she was doing fine and that her and my daddy was living over there at the house on Coyle. I miss that house too, it was a nice size, and it felt like a newly built home. A lot of houses in Detroit are so old and ran down, but the house on Coyle was well kept. My mom is a fool for leaving with nowhere to go with two children.

Now we live with another unfamiliar man. This time I believe she's dating this man. His name is Donte and he looks about the same age as my mom. We live in a small duplex off of Warren and Evergreen. I'm surprised my mom wants to be so close in the city with the chances of running into people like my dad or Key. The last time we ran into my dad when we were living on the eastside, she started acting like nobody could be trusted, and soon after we ended up moving again.

The new school I'm attending is called Ruddiman. It's not really a good school, but one of the things I do like about it is everybody gets their own schedule. It reminds me of how people explain high school to be. I don't have a homeroom class, I have my own schedule, and every class has different people in it. Again, I'm the new girl who doesn't know anybody which is so aggravating. Surprisingly, it's not like it's been at other schools. Everybody isn't looking at me like they have never seen a new person before. I don't feel like the center of attention, which I really like. It's pretty chill, a couple of fights here and there and that's it.

I don't have many friends here, which I'm fine with because there is nobody at this school I really want to be friends with anyway. There is this one cool chick I've been vibing with named Chrystal. Chrystal is a dark-skinned complexion, short and she always wears her hair in braided styles. I've never seen her real hair, so I don't know how long it is. She's pretty cool and knows a few boys, so when I hang around her, I always meet a new boy, which is fun.

"Chrystal, how old are you?" I ask out of curiosity because of her maturity.

"I'm 16. My mama started me in school late," Chrystal answers quickly.

Yeah, fucking right."

No wonder why I get along with her so much, it's because she's older.

"Dang, Chrystal, who is your new friend?" Armon creeps up out of nowhere.

Chrystal laughs. "Boy, don't be popping up out of nowhere asking stupid questions. And she right here, ask her yourself."

"I think you might be in my last hour." Armon looks at me in a flirty way.

"Yeah, I think I am." I'm just going along with him because he's cute.

"My name is Armon, what's yours?" Armon smiles.

"I'm Miko," I return the smile.

"Oh, well, you should take my number down so we can keep in touch," Armon suggests with a cute smirk on his face.

"This nigga' Armon think he got game!" Chrystal instigates in the middle of our conversation.

"Yeah, write it down on something," I suggest.

"Okay, come here." Armon grabs my hand softly, spreads it open and begins writing his number on the palm of my hand.

"I got all the game!" Armon pops Chrystal's head with the pen and runs off.

"Boy!" Chrystal started to chase him but changed her mind.

"I'm about to walk home," I add.

"Me too! Where you live?" Chrystal follows me in the same direction.

"On Evergreen."
Chrystal laughs. "Straight up?"
"Yeah, fool!" I giggle wondering why she's so hype.
"I do too!" Chrystal laughs.
"What if we live like right next door to each other?" I laugh.
"Right, that would be too funny!" Chrystal and I continue to walk.

Come to find out, Chrystal and I live right down the street from each other. She lives a little closer to Warren than I do. When I walk into the house, I overhear my mama lying to Donte about our situation. She's talking about how everybody wants nothing to do with her after her divorce, and how her ex-husband doesn't want to help her out with us. She literally makes me sick to my stomach. Then she calls me in the room to second everything she's saying and I'm very nonchalant about everything. All of my responses are just "Mmmhmm" and "Yup," and I can tell that's pissing her off. From Donte's body language, he can tell that something is off. I know she's going to have a mouthful to say to me when he leaves for work and I don't give a fuck.

Donte's occupation consists of doing something in the police department, but I don't think he's a police officer because I have never seen him in a uniform. Donte is very nice to Koko and me. He gives me lunch money every day, and he tries to make sure I'm comfortable in the house. Mom told me that he's friends with her good friend Charece's husband, who also works in the police department. Mom also told me that Charece said that Donte used to beat on women and that one time he threw a lady out of the second-story window. While she's telling me this story, I'm thinking in my head, *And you want to be with this man? Are you insane?* I don't know if she thinks it's cute or if she's concerned. She doesn't seem concerned. She just shared the story like it was a normal story.

Ever since my mom told me about Donte being a woman beater, I've been looking at him differently. He hasn't shown any signs of being a woman beater while I'm around, but I don't know how he acts when I'm in school. Today, my mom is pretty late picking me up from school. This not about to be a repeat of me sitting here waiting for her until the nighttime. I'm not waiting at this school all day. I could have walked home by now.

Just before I started to get worried that something happened to my mom, she pulls up.

"What took you so long?" I'm aggravated as I get in the car.
"Donte and I just got married!" Mom smiles.
Did this bitch just say what I think she said? I roll my eyes with my head facing away from her. "Oh."
"No congratulations or nothing, huh?" Mom cuts her eyes at me.
"Congratulations," I add nonchalantly so she can know I don't mean it.
"Thanks," she responds quickly.
"When I was with my dad, Big Mama was really sick. If she passes away, will you let us go to the funeral?" I ask randomly.
"No…" Mom adds slowly then corrects herself. "Well, I guess, but y'all will have somebody there watching y'all. And as soon as it's over y'all will have to come back with me." Mom sounds sure of her decision.
Oh, this bitch is crazy! I have to figure out a way to get away.

CHAPTER **SIXTY-ONE**

"YOU SMOKE?" CHRYSTAL asks as she's rolling a blunt of weed.

"I do now," I giggle.

Chrystal laughs. "You silly!"

"Yo' mama know you smoke?" I study how she's rolling up the blunt.

"Yeah, but she don't like it," Chrystal smiles.

"What she be saying?"

"She be cussing me out but…" Chrystal shrugs her shoulders and licks the blunt in a circular motion.

I haven't smoked since we all lived on Manor when I was too young to know what I was doing. When my parents were married, I remember the times when my dad would be high. He always acted normal for the most part. The only difference in his personality was that he was usually a little bit nicer and laughed a little bit easier. Completely different from when my mom gets drunk.

"This feel chill." I blow smoke from my mouth after inhaling some of it.

"Puff, puff, pass, my dog!" Chrystal laughs.

"I hope this high wears off by the time it's time for me to go home," I add, feeling a little paranoid.

"It should, this is just some Reggies," Chrystal adds, smoking like a pro.

"Some Raygo! A nigga' feel like drinking a Faygo!" I joke with the blunt in my hand making Chrystal laugh.

"You stupid, man!" Chrystal finally catches her breath.

"Why you talk like that?" I pass Chrystal the blunt.

"Like what?" Chrystal looks confused.

"Like you have a different kind of accent," I try to explain.

"It's probably because I'm from Lima, Ohio." Chrystal hits the blunt.

"Lima?" I double-check if that's what she said.

Chrystal laughs. "Yeah, nigga'."

"Shit, nigga', it's probably because I'm from Lima, Ohio," I mimic her in a funny tone of voice.

Chrystal burst out in laughter. "Aye, you play too much, dog!"

"Chrystal!" Chrystal's Mom yells from inside the house.

"Damn, you think she can smell it?" I ask.

"I don't know, here you go. Hold this real quick." Chrystal hands me the blunt to smoke.

Less than a minute later, Chrystal is back on the back porch talking on the cellphone.

"What y'all over there doing?" Chrystal puts the boy on speaker.

"Nothing over here, about to get high," the boy laughs.

"Oh, well, catch up, nigga', me and my homegirl Miko over here blowed right now." Chrystal reaches for the blunt.

"Miko? That name sound familiar," the boy adds.

"She go to Ruddiman too, but she kind of new." Chrystal hit the blunt.

"It's the end of the school year, don't nobody know me," I giggle to myself.

"That's her? Let me talk to her," the boy sounds excited.

Chrystal hands me the phone. "Hello?" I keep him on speaker.

"Damn, you sound sexy as hell!" the boy adds as Chrystal and I laugh.

"Thank you," I blush.

"Oh, we gotta' meet!" the boy continues as I hand the phone back to Chrystal.

"Come through, fool, and bring some weed with you!" Chrystal giggles.

"Alright, because I know y'all not over there smoking on no Purps!" the boy brags.

"Call me when you get close." Chrystal and the boy hang up.

"Who was that?" I ask, hitting the short tail of the blunt.

"Oh, that was Dijohn," Chrystal flicks her hand like he's nobody.

"Y'all talking?" I try to get the scoop.

Chrystal laughs. "Nah, he just cool! Sometimes he be acting like he be crushing, but these little boys can't be trusted."

We ended up getting so high and eating up the entire kitchen. Out of nowhere, Chrystal turned into Chef Boyardee. Chrystal's mom didn't end up tripping like I was expecting. It's probably because we were outside and the smell wasn't stinking up the house. When we were smoking, it felt so forbidden, like Chrystal's mom wasn't the only person we didn't want to catch us. It felt like we had to hurry up so the cops wouldn't catch us. Smoking weed is not like having a drink of alcohol. Alcohol is sold at every liquor store and grocery store. It's legal, and it's out in the open. Marijuana is not legal and is sold by the doughboys in the streets. You have to know somebody that sells weed to buy it.

I've never been drunk before or even taken a drink, but from what I've witnessed with my own eyes is that alcohol makes a person loud and obnoxious. Marijuana is the complete opposite. It calms you down and brings you to a level head, so in my opinion alcohol should be illegal.

After we get finish eating and cracking jokes, I notice the time.

"Aww, damn, its ten-thirty. My mama probably wondering why I'm not home yet." I jump up.

"You still high?" Chrystal asks.

"A little, but after I ate it brought me back down," I smile.

"Oh, you had to be brought back to life, huh?" Chrystal jokes.

I laugh. "Right, but I'm about to get out of here before it get too late."

"Alright, I'ma walk with you because I want to stop by the store." Chrystal puts her shoes on.

After I gather my things and Diamond gets what she needs, we head down the street towards my house.

"You should tell Dijohn and them to come over tomorrow so I can smoke with y'all," I suggest.

"That's probably what they will end up doing anyway," Chrystal sounds sure.

"Okay, cool, I'ma ask my mama can I just spend the night so I won't have to be tweaking if they come later on tomorrow."

"Right, or have to leave extra early," Chrystal agrees.

"You think your mom will let me spend the night?"

"Yeah, she won't care."

Chrystal and I split up at the corner, and in no time I'm home. When I walk into the house, I see Mom, Donte, and Koko all in the living room looking like a family. I make sure I speak to everybody and take my butt right upstairs to fall asleep.

"Hey, Miko, you alright?" Donte seems concerned.

"Yeah, I'm alright," I answer quickly.

"You want to ride with me to the store real quick?" Donte asks trying be friendly, and I take up his offer.

"Yeah, okay." I put my sandals on and follow him to the car.

Once we get into the car and drive off, I can tell Donte wants to talk about something.

"So, what's really going on? Are you really good? When you're at home you just seem so unhappy," Donte expresses.

Oh wow, how thoughtful of him. He notices something my mom seems to overlook everyday.

I think twice before speaking, "Well, to be honest…" I'm hesitant about telling the full truth or just part of the truth.

"Come on, you can tell me." Donte notices me holding back.

"I really just miss my family. I miss my dad, my sister, and grandparents. I know all of the stuff my mom has told you about them, but it's a lie, all of it," I unfold.

"All of it? So, your dad?" Donte sounds like he wants more information.

"My dad is looking for us right now. My mom and dad have been going through a custody battle for years. She is keeping us away from him. She's keeping us away from my sister and my grandparents too. Her own parents!"

"But why?" Donte frowns.

"Because she's good at holding grudges. She's mad, for whatever reason, over something that happened years ago, so since she doesn't want to be bothered with these people, she's keeping us away from them too. My dad, sister, and grandparents are the closest people to us." My voice starts to crack.

"Wow, so he's not around because she's not letting him be around?" Donte asks.

"Correct, but he wants to be," I confirm.

"Okay, I'm going to try and talk to her," Donte looks determined.

"Yeah, I doubt if that works. My mom is a liar, she will make you think that she's listening, but she really has another idea in her head," I explain.

515

"I mean that is still y'all father. That's wrong of her to be keeping y'all away from him. She's been making it seem like he doesn't want to be involved the whole time." Donte shakes his head as he drives.

"Now why would you say that?" Mom grabs my hair and tries to throw me against the wall, but I resist, using my strength to make her let go.

"It's the truth!" I yell.

"Bitch, you must be really trying to get fucked up! Keep my motherfuckin' name out of your motherfuckin' mouth!" Mom looks me dead in my eyes as we stare each other down face to face.

She's clearly livid because I told Donte the truth about our family and how much of a liar she is. Donte must have tried to talk some sense in her like he said he would. I knew whatever he said to her was going to go in one ear and out of the other. She couldn't handle the truth if it politely kissed her on her hand. As much as I want to beat this bitch the fuck up, I still have too much respect for her to hit her first, but if she puts her hands on me like that again or throws a punch, I'm not thinking twice about defending myself. Mom or no mom, flat out. That little tussling shit she just did wasn't shit. I don't mind spazzing out on her if need be.

I'm surprised my mom let me go over Chrystal's house today being that I know she's probably still mad at me. Ever since I smoked with Chrystal for the first time, we've become smoking buddies. Sometimes we smoke by ourselves and just kick it. Other times we might link up with some boys to smoke. Either way, a blunt is being rolled and passed when I go down the street. Of course, my mom doesn't have a clue. I wouldn't dare open up to her about anything I do because we don't have that kind of relationship. My mom is not the kind of mom you can be honest with. If it's not something she wants to hear, she doesn't have an understanding bone in her body. I know I'm too young to be smoking, but when I smoke, I feel stress free. When I'm high, I don't get drowned in my own thoughts and emotions about missing family I'm used to seeing or talking to every day. It's a stress reliever and the people I smoke with I trust. I would never hit just anybody's blunt. I'm smart with the moves I make. As of now, I don't see Mary Jane (marijuana) leaving my to-do list anytime soon.

"Why you been acting all off today?" Chrystal inhales the weed.
"Man... me and my mama got into a little scuffle earlier." I look off.
"For real? You and yo' mama? Why?" Chrystal's eyes get big as she passes the blunt to Dijohn.
"Because she's a fucking liar." I summarize the story, not feeling like going into details.
Dijohn giggles. "You too pretty for all of that."
"I remember my older sister fought my mama when I was younger," Chrystal giggles.
"Really, who won?" I ask.
Chrystal laughs. "My mama gave it to her ass! She was stupid for stepping to her. That's exactly what she get!"
"Aye, I bet y'all can't do this?" Dijohn hits the blunt hard and blows out the smoke with O's coming out of his mouth.
"I know how to do O's, boy, stop playing!" Chrystal smacks her lips.
"Let me try!" Only smoke comes out of my mouth, no O's.
"Let me show you how to do it!" Chrystal reaches for the blunt.
"Hold on, shortie, you moving too fast." I hit the blunt again as Chrystal and Dijohn laughs.
"You not even doing it," Chrystal adds.
"I wasn't trying to that time. You was about to mess up the rotation." I hand her the blunt after hitting it again.

Once Chrystal hit the blunt, she was able to make small O's, but she didn't do it as good as Dijohn did. As the summer night gets older, we continue to smoke and bullshit before Dijohn eventually went home.

Today is the eighth-grade dance of the year, and I'm sitting in this hot ass house. I know I don't have that many friends at Ruddiman, but I really wanted to go to the dance. Chrystal said she is going, and I know Armon is going too.

This stupid ass bitch gets on my last nerve! Then she won't even tell me why I can't go. It's not like it's a formal event, so I have something to wear. The tickets are free for eighth graders, so I don't have to pay. She doesn't have to use her gas because I can walk. She just wants to be an annoying mean bitch.

"We're going to be moving out in a couple of weeks," Mom speaks out of nowhere.

Oh, my fucking! "Where?" I look at her with a straight face.

"It's looking like it will be into our own house," Mom explains.

"A house?" I'm a little more interested.

"Yeah, you remember Bruce and Paulette's old house?"

"Yeah," I nod my head.

"Well, they're going to let me rent it out, and I can finally get that stuff out of the storage." Mom looks at her cellphone.

"Oh, okay, that's cool. Hopefully, this is the last time we're going to have to move," I add as Mom ignores my last comment.

The news just put me in a better mood. But what I'm really wondering is why we're moving, and she just got married. I would ask her, but I know she's going to lie about it. I figured since she had gotten remarried, we would be here for a long time. Or maybe Donte is coming with us, and she forgot to mention it. I'm honestly okay with him coming with us or staying here. I'm just happy about having my own room again and reuniting with all of my old favorite toys that are in the storage.

Once Donte came back home from work, I noticed some tension between him and my mom. They aren't as friendly and welcoming to each other like usual.
Oh, yeah, something's up. He's not coming with us to our new house. I can feel it."

When Donte gets comfortable in the living room where my mom and I are chilling, Mom gathers her stuff and goes upstairs.
Damn, she don't even want to watch TV with his ass.

"I don't know if your mom told you, but I told her she has to leave." Donte takes a sip of his beer.
"Really? Why?" I play stupid.
"Because it's true what you said. She's a boldface liar and I can't have that in my life right now," Donte explains.
"Yeah, I told you." I look at him with assurance.
"She hasn't told me where she's going, but I told her there is no rush and that you and Koko can stay for as long as she needed." Donte sounds genuine.
"What did she say about that?" I yearn for more information.
"She said I was a damn fool if I thought she was going to leave you guys here with me." Donte chuckles.
"Wow." I just shake my head.
"I can honestly say I moved way too fast with her. She really has some serious issues, but I just wanted you to know that if you ever need some help finding your dad or any family members, I'm here for you," Donte sounds sincere.
"Thank you so much," I'm appreciative of his honesty.
"Miko!" Mom calls me from upstairs.

CHAPTER SIXTY-TWO

OUR NEW HOUSE isn't as big and nice as the house on Coyle that my grandparents bought, but it's better than being in somebody else's space. It's so funny that we live here now because I remember coming over here when I was younger for Halloween. Bruce and Paulette have three boys. One is Key's age, one is my age, and the youngest one is a few years younger than me. It feels amazing to be back in our own house. My mom still has the storage, but most of the stuff is in the house now. I miss all of my old toys, especially my American Girl Dolls and my Pokemon cards. All of these toys just remind me of home and family. They remind me of everybody I miss so dearly. I wouldn't have ever thought things would be like this. As much as my parents used to argue and fuss, sometimes I wish they would just be back together for stability's sake. Everything has been so crazy after the divorce.

"Miko, I'm going to hang out tonight. I won't be gone for too long," Mom proclaims.
"Alright."
"Y'all will be fine with staying here alone, right?" Mom asks with little interest.
"Yeah, I guess."
"I'm going to leave my cellphone here with y'all," Mom continues.

"Okay," I nod my head.
"And Pierre called you when I was on the phone too," Mom adds.
"Can I call him back?" I ask.
"Yeah." Mom hands me the cellphone from off of the sink.

I haven't seen or talked to Pierre for so long. When he answered the phone, I almost didn't recognize his deep voice.

"Can I speak to Pierre?" I ask.
"This is me," Pierre laughs.
"Boy, where you get all that bass in your voice from?" I laugh.
"Nah, you the one sounding like your mom, I thought this was Joyce calling me back!" Pierre laughs.
"Really? Ugh, I don't want to sound like her!" I add as Pierre cracks up.

Pierre and I talked for hours on the phone, catching up, laughing, and reminiscing. I miss him too. When he asked if I could come to the skating rink with him and all of our mutual friends from Cherry Hill, I had to take a rain check. When he asked why, I was honest with him because he knows about how strict my mom is, so it isn't surprising to him. Pierre knows a lot about my personal business because I trust him. I don't think he would go around telling my business, even though he has a lot of other friends outside of our mutual friends. By the time we got off the phone, I see my mom getting ready to put on her shoes.

"Okay, Miko, I'm headed out. Koko is sleeping so you shouldn't have to worry about her. Don't answer the door for anybody. You know the front door is weird, and it locks from the outside. I will be back in a few hours." Mom grabs her purse from the kitchen table and head out of the side door.

When the door closes, I instantly have an urge to call my dad.

Every time I get a chance to be alone, this happens. I run to my room to look for the small piece of white paper with Dad and Key's number on it. I call Dad's number first, and I got no answer. I try a couple of more times, and I still, no answer. Then I call Key's number, and she picks up on the second ring.

"Hello?" Key sounds the same.
"Hey, Key, it's Miko!" I smile.
"Hey, Miko! Where you at?" Key asks with no hesitation.
"I'm at home. We live in Bruce and Paulette's old house." I get a little nervous.
"Oh, how long y'all been over there?" Key asks.
"For maybe a month now." I pace around the living room.
"Where my mama at?" Key sounds like she's in the car.
"She just left to go out," I explain.
"You want me to come get you?" Key giggles, but I can tell she's serious.
"Ummm, I don't know." I get even more nervous.
"I'm already in the car. I remember where Bruce and them used to stay too," Key tries to convince me.
I pace around the living room nervously, wanting to say no but dying to say yes. "Okay, okay, come on."

I can't believe what just came out of my mouth! Key is really about to come and pick us up. What if everything goes wrong and I have to come back here. All of these negative thoughts are racing through my mind. Then out of nowhere, Key is outside faster than meals on wheels. It feels like it only took her five minutes.

"Miko, come on! I'm out here!" Key sounds excited over the phone.
"Did you talk to my Dad?" I ask over the phone.
"Yeah, I'ma take y'all over Shoody's house because mama don't know where she lives," Key explains.
I'm pacing back and forth, contemplating on if I should really go

or not. "Okay, I don't know about this, Key."

"Come on, I'm right across the street." Key doesn't budge.

"Fuck!" I utter.

"What?" Key asks.

"I can't just walk out of the front door," I add.

"Why not?" Key sounds confused.

"Because the door locks from the outside. I think mama locked it and took the key." I jerk the doorknob back and forth.

"What about a side door?" Key suggests.

"We have an alarm, and I don't know the code."

"Alright, y'all can just jump out of the window." Key thinks of another idea.

"Okay, cool, but these windows have bars in the front of them." I put my shoes on.

"Alright, I'ma come over and help y'all get through." Key gets out of the car and runs to the house.

All of a sudden, it feels like I'm on the show Cops, running from the police. After Key and I get off the phone, I leave Mom's cellphone on the kitchen table. I didn't have enough time to put any clothes on or pack any clothes for Koko or me, so after I put my shoes on, I go to grab Koko to put her through the window bars first. It was pretty easy getting Koko through the window. It was more of a struggle for me to get through, but after some squeezing and pulling, I'm through and free.

"Jihod! Come look at the TV, y'all on the news!" Shoody calls us from the other room.

"What happened?" Dad is just as shocked as me.

"Joyce put an Amber Alert out on the girls," Shoody giggles.

"This bitch is crazier than I thought." Dad looks like he can't believe what's happening.

"She had pictures of the girls up there and everything." Shoody shakes her head.

"And you were just sitting here watching it the whole time? Why you didn't call us in here sooner?" Dad looks at cousin Shoody like she's stupid.

Shoody is my dad's first cousin. She's really cool and loving towards me, so I like being over here. As Shoody and my Dad bicker back and forth, I noticed the news has our descriptions on there and everything. My mom spoke for a short time for an interview. In her interview, she didn't seem nervous, scared, or even bothered at all. Usually, if someone puts an Amber Alert out on their kids, they're hysterical and emotional. She knows we're okay and, most importantly, safe.

"Why is she trying to keep you away from the kids anyway?" Shoody asks.

"Because she's crazy as hell. She tries to keep them away from everybody," Dad frowns.

"Yeah, she's not even letting us talk to my grandparents," I add my two cents.

"Her parents?" Shoody seems even more confused.

"Yeah, anybody she calls herself being mad at, she dismisses them," Dad continues.

"Dang, well, what did y'all do to the lady?" Shoody giggles.

"Nothing, maybe told her a thing or two about herself, but that's it. She act like she can't do no wrong. She can't take the truth, that's the problem!" Dad goes on.

"Wow, now everybody about to know who we are." I put my face in my hands, dreading the attention.

"Mik, you got Scoliosis?" Shoody asks.

"Yeah, how you know?" I'm confused.

"She put that in your description," Shoody points toward the screen.

"Oh my God! That is so embarrassing!" I speak loudly.

"She acting like you walking around with a damn cage over your head or something!" Dad frowns.

His comment makes me giggle. "Right!"

"You can't even tell you got it!" Shoody adds.

I will never forget this day. My dad is getting so many calls from friends and family. People he hasn't heard from or seen in years are going out of their way to contact him to make sure we're okay. All day I've been super paranoid. Everywhere we go, I feel like people are going to notice us from the news. No one has said anything yet, but it's so embarrassing to have been on the news for an Amber Alert. Some family members are calling my dad to say my mom had stopped by their houses with the police looking for Koko and me. I just can't wait until the drama is over.

"My mama put an Amber Alert out on us today," I catch my grandparents up on the drama over the phone.

"An Amber Alert?" both of them speak at the same time.

"Yeah, but she know we with my daddy," I explain.

"That girl is really losing it!" Granddaddy adds.

"Why would she do that?" Granny asks.

"We left last night when she went to hang out. Key came to pick us up and dropped us off to my dad. Y'all should've seen her on TV looking stupid," I giggle trying to find some humor out of this nonsense.

"She was on TV looking stupid?" Granddaddy asks like he didn't hear me.

"Yeah, talking about 'If you're a mother, you can relate to my pain.' Not a teardrop in sight, though," I laugh.

"Oh my goodness, this needs to stop!" Granny sounds fed up.

"My daddy already talked to child protective services. I think we're scheduled to meet in court sometime this week," I explain.

"Good, I don't know why they just won't send y'all down here to us since they can't be adults and do things the right way." Granddaddy sounds like he's frowning.

After a long conversation with my grandparents, I learn that Granny have been diagnosed with Breast cancer. With all of this drama going on, that information didn't make anything any better. I'm sure my granny has been going through a lot of stress with not talking to my mom, whom she's used to talking to every day. With not speaking to us and being unaware of our whereabouts. I'm sure all of the drama has caused her some stress. She doesn't sound sick over the phone, which makes me feel better. She said that she will be starting chemo soon and that she will be fine.

Today feels like the scariest day of my life. Today we will have to face the judge and speak in court. I'm praying we will not have to leave with my mom. If that happens, I know for sure I won't be seeing anybody for a long time. I love my mom, even though she irks my soul, but I also love my other family members as well. If I could have it my way, I would want to live and be able to see both of my parents, but I can't trust my mom because she is so mean and vindictive. I can't trust that she will put everything behind us and be normal for five seconds, so on that matter, I will choose my family if I have to.

All of my immediate family on my dad's side are here today in court to show support. My mom looks so pissed. Ever since my parents' divorce, I've started praying at night before I go to sleep. I've been facing all kinds of stress and depression. My prayers give me hope and make me feel mentally and emotionally stronger about the future. After my mom went on about my dad being a drug dealer and a bad example for us, my dad got a chance to talk. He spoke about how she's an alcoholic and unfit. He also brought up several times she fell asleep at the wheel with us in the car. When he brought up certain events, the judge wanted me to talk about it and to say if it was true or not being that I'm a witness. When I was told to speak and tell the truth about events I was present for, I did. With me telling the truth, the judge granted my dad temporary custody until our next court date. My mom walked out of the courtroom without speaking or saying bye to anybody.

"I'm surprised she just walked out without speaking to the kids." Aunt Lora lights her cigarette and rolls down the window.

"If it was up to me, we wouldn't even be going through this court bullshit, letting the hoe ass White man tell us how to handle our kids. Telling us when we can see them and when we can't!" Dad expresses.

"Right, I can't believe she's even taken it this far, but at the same time, I'm not surprised," Aunt Lora continues.

"Did you hear us last week on the radio?" I ask from the back seat.

"Nah, y'all was on the radio?" Aunt Lora giggles.

"Mik was!" Dad looks proud.

"Yeah, I was talking to Coco and Foolish and them. Telling them that Koko and I were safe and that my mom was making all of that stuff up."

Aunt Lora laughs. "Wow, that's crazy, I'm sorry y'all have to go through all of this for nothing."

"For absolutely the fuck nothing," Dad agrees.

After court, Dad, Aunt Lora, Koko, and I went out to eat, and later we ended up at Aunt Lora's apartment. Dad left us with bags of clothes, and Koko and I stayed with Aunt Lora and her daughter, Tae. With my dad not having a stabled home, Koko and I went back and forth from Aunt Lora's apartment to Big Mama's house for weeks. After several court dates of Mom not showing up, Dad was granted automatic custody of Koko and me. I wouldn't have ever thought it was going to end that way, but it did. I have no clue when the next time I'm going to see my mom and it's fucked up.

CHAPTER **SIXTY-THREE**

"WOW, KEY REALLY got it junky in there," I giggle.

"Yeah, she letting that nigga' Cory just run the house to the ground. They don't ever clean up. He got it looking just like Betty's house." Dad seems pissed at the thought.

"How long he been staying here?" I ask standing in front of the car.

"Ever since I left. They make me not even want to be in there it's so nasty," Dad goes on.

"Didn't you say you bumped into Tina the other day?" I change the topic.

"Yeah, she said she was going to stop by, her and the girls." Dad's attitude changes slightly.

"Oh, okay, I haven't seen them in so long!" I bite into my popsicle.

Tina, Raven, and Micha got to the house later on in the summer night. Raven, Micha, Key, and I are having so much fun catching up with each other and reminiscing about the old times. When they asked about my mom, they were very surprised to hear that we hadn't heard from her. They went on and on about how much fun it used to be coming over our house and how fun our parents were. All of us sat outside enjoying the nice summer night while my dad and Tina stayed in the kitchen talking.

"Miko, you should see if your dad will let you come to camp with me!" Micha suggests.

"Ooo, I always wanted to go camping! He should be cool with it!" I get excited knowing my dad is lenient.

"Yeah, I can tell my mama to sign you up," Micha explains.

"Okay, cool, when do it start?" I ask.

"It start next week. You can sign up for a week or just for the weekend. I usually go for the week. Last time, I got kicked out because I fought this ugly-ass bitch named Tammy," Micha explains.

"For real? Why y'all fight?" I ask giggling at Micha because she's always fighting somebody.

"The bitch talk too much," Micha adds in her slight southern accent.

I burst out in laughter. "You stupid, but yeah, I'ma see if I can go too!"

After everybody chilled and spent time, Tina, Raven, and Micha get ready to leave to go home.

"Don't forget to ask your dad about camp!" Micha turns around before getting in the car.

"Oh yeah, Dad, can I go to the summer camp with Micha?" I asked immediately.

"Yeah, you can go. What's the name of it?" Dad asks.

"It's called Wildwood Ranch Camp. It's a Christian camp." Tina smiles.

"Oh, okay, that sound pretty cool. So how do she sign up?" Dad asks.

"You just have to fill out these forms. I have some extra ones at the house. I can fill them out for her. Micha go back next week," Tina explains.

"Alright, good looking out, I appreciate it!" Dad walks Tina to the car and closes her door.

Wildwood Ranch is a boys and girls Christian camp. We do different activities every day. We go to the chapel right after dinner. Just before bed, the cabin full of girls creates a circle on the floor to read and pray. The cabin leader reads us nice Christian stories. The chapel is pretty fun too. We sing all kinds of gospel songs and go over different kinds of lessons. This camp makes you feel like you're out camping in real life. The cabins are out in the wooded area, and before we eat breakfast, lunch, and dinner, we have to drink one cold cup of well water. I've never drunk well water until I came to this camp. The well water stinks, and it has a weird taste to it. They say it's supposed to be healthy for you, but I'm not positively sure.

"You drunk your cup of well water already?" I watch Micha guzzle down her cup of lemonade.

"Shit no, that well water nasty as hell." Micha pops a couple of ice cubes in her mouth after finishing her drink.

I burst out laughing at her disobedient ways. "I feel you."

"I saw you talking to that ugly little boy earlier," Micha gossips.

Giggling, knowing exactly who she's talking about I ask. "Who?"

"I don't know, some little boy. The dark-skin boy with the braids." Micha eats her food.

"Oh, you talking about Rico! Girl, he was just asking me something." I wave my hands towards her.

"He look like he wanted to ask you for a kiss," Micha continues.

"Girl, no, he didn't!"

"From where I was standing he did," Micha sounds sure.

"Yeah right, Micha, you probably need glasses or something anyways, blind ass!" I laugh at my own joke.

"Nah, I can see, and I know what I saw," Micha stands her ground.

Micha has been coming here for years now. Raven used to come too, but I think she's too old for this camp now. For the whole week, Micha has been telling everybody I'm her cousin, similar to when we went to Bagley together. I don't know if she had friends here before I joined the camp. If she did, she's been acting very fake towards them since I'm here. Micha doesn't want to hang around anybody but me, and she doesn't want me to hang around anybody else. It's kind of cute, funny, and annoying at the same time how she's territorial over me. She's funny and cool to hang around, so it's fine, but it would be nice to meet new people too. There aren't that many cute boys at the camp, but I think I might have a crush on Rico. He's dark-skinned with braces and braids. He has an older brother who's really cute as well named Brian. They are like the camp's cutest boys, in my opinion.

"If that bitch, Tammy, look at me wrong I'm going in her shit again." Micha looks around for Tammy.

"Didn't you already beat the girl up?" I watch Micha.

"Yeah, but she think she slick. You got my back if her friends try to jump me?" Micha asks.

"Hell yeah! I'm not about to let nobody jump you girl!" I respond with certainty.

"Alright, cool, because these bitches around here will try to catch you while you slipping." Micha paces back and forth.

This girl can't wait! I laugh.

Being back over Big Mama's house is kind of a bummer. I'm ready to move into our own house so I can have my own space. It's so small and cluttered in here. It's sad seeing Big Mama sleeping with a breathing machine. Now that she's sick, she's not able to color her hair blonde like I'm used to seeing it. Her silky black hair makes her Indian features stand out. Since I don't have my own space here, I've been sleeping with Big Mama. I thought since I'm older now Big Mama wouldn't want me to sleep with her, but surprisingly she still doesn't mind. She's been coughing a lot, smoking her cigarettes, and drinking her Pepsi. I overheard Aunt Lora say she's not supposed to be drinking pop or smoking cigarettes, but she's doing it anyway. I've been running little errands for her, doing as much as I can for her around the house. She doesn't complain much she just chills in her room like she's known for doing.

"Hey, Daddy!" I smile.
"What's up, Mik? What you doing?" Dad flops on the couch.
"Nothing, being bored. Can I go back to camp this weekend?"
"Yeah, you can go back. By the time you get back, the house should be ready," Dad adds.
"Yes! Because I'm tired of staying here!"
"You always talking about you tired of something. I'm tired of you!" Dad flicks my nose playfully, and we both share laughs.
"Where you about to go? I'm hungry." I follow him to the porch.
"Come on, let's go grab a pizza!" Dad leads the way to the car.

When we get into the car, Dad cuts the Fugees on, and Lauren Hill's voice guides us on our way.

"Ready or not, here I come, you can't hide. Gonna find you and take it slowly."

"She can sing and rap, I like her!" I bob my head to the song.
"Yeah, Lauren Hill, the truth!" Dad confirms.

This weekend camp was so much fun. Micha wasn't there, so I was able to actually meet other people and make other friends. Rico and I were able to get to know each other a little better this time around, and we exchanged numbers so we can keep in touch. I accepted Jesus Christ as my Lord and Savior and learned how to pray in detail. No one forced me to make this huge decision; it just felt right. Praying on my own and having the church experience as a kid with Big Mama may have encouraged my thoughts and feelings about Christianity. My parents aren't huge churchgoers or super religious, but I know they believe in Jesus Christ, so accepting Jesus Christ as my Lord and Savior seemed like it was meant to be. It was an amazing weekend, and to top it off, we're moving into our house today.

Our house is off of Puritan and Linwood on a street called Normandy. It's a decent house in a rough neighborhood. There are nice houses on our block, which makes it a little better, but like I always say, 'it doesn't matter where we live. I feel the safest with my dad.' The house has three bedrooms, one bathroom, a basement, and a huge den area. The house does need a few repairs, but I have my own room, and Koko has her own room. It's perfect for our little family.

"You want to come with me over Tina and them house?" Dad asks after we finish unpacking.
"Yeah, I don't care," I shrug my shoulders.

When we get to Tina's house, Raven, Micha, and Breana are here. I haven't seen Breana in so long. She lives with her grandmother, so she's never around when I come over. She seems happy to see me.

"Hey, boo!" Breana reaches her arms out for a hug.
"Where you been?" I smile at her.
"Girl, working and stuff." Breana sits on the couch.
"And with her boyfriend!" Micha adds in a smart way.
"With one of them!" Raven rolls her eyes and walk towards the back.
"Y'all can shut up!" Breana frowns.
"And if we don't?" Micha test Breana.

"Come on, Miko, let's go to my room!" Breana leads the way.

I don't know why it seems like Raven and Micha don't get along with Breana that well. Breana seems like a nice big sister, or at least that's how she acts towards me. I know Raven and Micha get into it often, but the energy they give Breana is different. After catching up with Breana, I go to see what Raven and Micha are up to.

"What y'all doing?" I sit down against the wall.
"Trying to figure out why we been seeing your dad over here so often," Micha gets right to the point.
"For real?" I'm shocked by the unexpected gossip.
"Yeah, and we don't even have to see him to know it's him because we can hear that BMW when he pulls up," Raven adds.
I giggle, "Right, that car is loud. Wow, that's annoying. I didn't know he was coming over here like that," I frown.

All of a sudden, from the news, I'm not so happy to be here anymore. I pray Dad and Tina don't call themselves liking each other. That's going to make everything so weird and awkward. Things are just starting to get normal for me, so I'm praying to God that we're all just overthinking the situation.

"So, Miko, Tina and them are going to be moving in," Dad casually adds out of nowhere.
"What? Why?" I instantly catch an attitude.

Everything he's saying is going in one ear and out of the other. I can't believe they would have the audacity to be together then on top of that, act like we're a happy fucking family!

"Why do y'all even think that's a good idea? You know she's like a sister to my mama! They are like our cousins! I can't believe y'all think it's cool to be dating! That's disrespectful as hell!" I snap.

"But she not your mom's sister! And she hasn't seen or spoken to your mom in years! And like I said, we're not going to be staying here for long! We went half on the house on Normandy and the house around the corner on La Salle. We're going to move into the house around the corner. It's nicer and bigger. It just needs a lot of work done to it. Uncle James and a few other guys and I are working on it," Dad explains, trying to make everything sound like it's under control.

"And like I said, it's disrespectful and crossing the line!" I roll my eyes.

So, Raven, Micha, and I were actually underthinking the whole situation. These motherfucka's are really about to move us all in the same house like we're the fucking Brady Bunch. Now I have to move to Koko's room, and Raven and Micha are taking my room. This is some all around bullshit! I'm so mad at my Dad for doing this. I could have stayed over Big Mama's house for this shit! Just when things in my life seemed like they were getting better, shit is going to another level of fucked up! I don't know how much I can take of either of my parents!

CHAPTER **SIXTY-FOUR**

WE'VE BEEN AT the hospital all day today. Big Mama has been on a ventilator for hours. My daddy told me her organs are shutting down and that she might not have long to live. Those words sounds like knives slashing my heart, but I'm blessed to be here, right now with my family. All of my Big Mama's kids and their kids are here. Extended aunts and cousins are present too. I can't imagine being with my mother right now. Her mean ass probably wouldn't have let me come to the hospital.

Once the family decided that Big Mama should be laid to rest. Everyone gathers around her frail body in the hospital bed. Prayers filled the room softly, as we say our last goodbyes before giving the doctors permission to take her off the ventilator. It's hard to believe I won't be seeing Big Mama anymore. It doesn't seem real to me at all. The intense emotions pouring from everyone is forcing the hard truth. Big Mama has gained her heavenly wings and she's going to meet her Father.

School is back in effect, and 9th grade is already aggravating me. I'm attending Highland Park High by mistake, and I feel very salty. My dad enrolled me in the wrong school. I was supposed to be going to the school upstairs. Highland Park High has three stories. I don't know why the other school is using this third floor, but I do know it's supposed to be a charter school. That's the school I was aiming to sign up for.

We can't wear our own stylish book bags at this school. Everybody is ordered to wear these see-through book bags, and we have to walk through metal detectors every day. This is why people are always late to class. We can't just walk through the door. There is always a line at the front door.

After I finally got through the security, I'm able to drop all of my stuff off in my locker and start my first period. I heard a whole bunch of rumors about freshman Friday and blah blah. All I know is I will be fighting and getting suspended if somebody thinks they about to bully me because I'm a freshman.

"Dang, your hair is super long! Is that all of your hair?" this light-skinned girl next to me blurts out of nowhere.
"Thank you, and yeah, it's all mine."
"What you mixed with?" she asks.
"Umm, nothing really." I shrug my shoulders, not feeling like giving details about my family.
"Girl, you gotta' be mixed with something! Look at all of this hair on your head!" she smiles.
"Probably a little White and Indian," I add.
"Yeah, because you can tell. Anyway, I'm Claire."
"I'm Miko."
"I think I might try out for the cheer team," Claire shares politely.
"When is the tryouts?"
"Tomorrow, are you going to try out too?" Claire asks.
"Probably not, I'm more of a dancer. I'll probably stop by, though."
"You should try out!" Claire tries to talk me into trying out.
"Nah, I'm straight. What class do you have after this?"
"I have Math. What about you?"

"I have Science. I hate Science." I roll my eyes.

"I hate being a freshman. My older sister and her friends be teasing me." Claire laughs.

Claire seems cool for now. In all honesty, I wish I could try out for the cheer team, but I don't like to show off my body shape. My scoliosis is getting worse as I get older and my hip still sticks out a little, and I'm insecure about it. On top of my scoliosis condition, I have a perspiring issue as well. It doesn't matter how hot or cold I am, I'm always sweating under my arms. That's why I always wear sweaters to cover up my scoliosis and my sweat. Thankfully I don't be musty, but it's still embarrassing. I've noticed over time, people really be studying me, paying me all types of attention. Girls and boys look at me and observe my body type and overall just be all in, so I'm going to pass on the whole cheerleader thing.

"What's up, pretty!" a dark-skinned smooth guy sits next to me in Science class.

"Hey," I giggle at his sense of charm.

"This my first time seeing you, what's yo' name?" he smiles.

"Miko." I didn't ask him what his name is because I peep him trying to run game.

"Oh, Miko, you might have to be my girlfriend!" he continues with a smile.

I laugh. "Boy, bye."

"What, you got a boyfriend already or something?" he looks confused.

"Those lines just don't work on me, playa'." I look him dead in his eyes.

"Oh, so you different, huh?" he looks intrigued.

"Yeah, a lot different." I give him a confident smile.

"I like different, you should call me sometime. You seem like a cool girl." He starts to act a little normal now.

"What's your number?" I pull out my razor flip phone my

grandparents sent me money for.

"313-423-**** and it's T-Money." He licks his lips.

I burst out laughing. "Boy, what's your real name?"

He giggles. "Alright, it's Ray, but everybody call me T-Money."

"Text me now so I can have your number," Ray adds as he walks out of the class to go to next period.

Ray isn't that cute to me, but there's something cute about him. He seems like he will be fun to kick it with. I've met a lot of guys at this school already. The girls don't seem that friendly here, but it's cool because the boys seem way more hype anyway. As I was heading outside to see if my dad is here to pick me up. I coincidentally bump into my childhood best friend, Nessa.

"Oh my God! Miko!" Nessa laughs.

"Nessa! It's been too long!" I feel overjoyed.

"Girl, I'm so happy you are okay! I saw you on the news in the summertime!" Nessa looks serious.

"Oh my God, that is so embarrassing!"

Nessa burst out in laughter. "Why? What happened?"

"Girl, nothing! I was with my dad the whole time!" I express quickly.

"So, you were safe the entire time?" Nessa laughs.

"Yes, girl, safe…safe!" I give her a half-serious look.

Nessa laughs. "You are stupid! Take my number down so we can keep in touch! We have to catch up, girl! I miss you!!"

"I know right! I miss you too!" I pull my flip phone out. "Alright, and do you go to the Charter school upstairs?"

"Yeah." Nessa puts her number in my phone.

"Girl, that was the school I was supposed to go to. My daddy enrolled me in the wrong fucking school," I shake my head.

Nessa laughs. "Damn, that would have been perfect if you were up there with me."

"I know, right? But I'ma call you later! I see my daddy car." I wave goodbye.

Off to the "hell hole," I go. Raven, Micha, and I reference the house we live in as the "hell hole." It's been so depressing living with Tina, Raven, and Micha. Before we all moved in together, everything was cool. Now that we all live under the same roof, I don't even look at Tina if I don't have to. My relationship with Raven and Micha has even changed. We don't kick it the same anymore. Micha and I talk more than Raven and me because Raven tries to stay away from this house as much as possible. She's always with her boyfriend or with her friends. I try to leave every weekend to go over Key's house when my dad isn't being an asshole. Sometimes he tries to tell me I can't go over there because he feels like Key lets me do whatever I want. I mean, she does, but I'm not doing anything that's out of the high school normal. When I'm over Key's house, I smoke a lot with her and her boyfriend, but my dad knows I smoke, so that's not a secret. Key didn't turn me on to smoking. I started smoking when I was living with my mom. He also doesn't like that Key's boyfriend Cory always has different guys over there. He doesn't like how Cory's favorite little cousin, Boo Bear, is always over as well. He always has smart comments to say about it like "You want to go over there so you and Boo Bear can be together?" But I don't look at Boo Bear in that way. Yes, Boo Bear has tried to holla' at me, but he just plays it cool since the feelings aren't mutual. I guess overall, my Dad just doesn't think Key is the best influence right now.

"Yo' let me get that Lil Wayne CD up out you. I got that new 40 Water album! Here you go." Zeak hands Cory the CD through the passenger window.

"Fasho!" Cory trades the CD.

"Good looking, C!" Zeak walks away.

Zeak is a dope dealer who lives across the street from Key. I think Cory works with him from time to time. One thing I do know is Key doesn't like Zeak at all. She's always telling Cory that he's not a real friend to him. I don't think Cory listens to Key, but from the stories she's told me, it doesn't seem like he is a true friend.

After they trade CDs, we pull off. It's always Key, Cory, Boo Bear, and me in the car seventy percent of the time. Boo Bear is just now finishing rolling the blunt. Key and Cory are in the front seat, and Boo Bear and me are in the back seat.

"Man, I shouldn't of traded that Wayne CD out for 40 Water!" Cory smacks his teeth at the CD player taking too long to play the CD.

"You smoking, Miko?" Boo Bear passes me the blunt.

"You already know!" I take the blunt and hit it a couple of times before passing it.

Once the CD player decides to work, a lady's voice starts rapping through the speaker's acappella.

"Sixty-eight inches above sea level. Ninety-three million miles above these devils. Play me in the winter. Play me in the summer. Play my in the order, any order."

Everybody is silent waiting to hear what's coming next from this weird sounding lady. The lady repeats herself.

"Play me in the winter. Play me in the summer. Play my in the order, any order."

Out of nowhere, this sweet beat with so much bass starts banging through the speakers. Everybody starts bobbing their heads at the same time in the same motion. Then slowly but surely, E-40 starts murdering the beat with his unique artistry.

"I'm tryna' get my beak wet. I'ma let you shoot the dice, and I'ma sign that. Still, hungry just ate—my game the same size as a dinner plate. The bay ain't been the same since I took a break. Where you been 40? Buying real estate?"

Cory cracks up laughing. "This nigga' said "I'm tryna get my beak wet!" making everybody laugh.

After we make a few runs smoking and driving, we stop at Coney Island to get food and head home.

"Girl, I hate living there with Tina and them," I express at the dining table.

"Why? What they be doing?" Key asks nonchalantly.

"Nothing, it's just awkward as fuck because they suppose to be our cousins. With my daddy and Tina being together, it's just not comfortable," I explain.

"You probably over exaggerating." Key bites into her Coney dog.

"So, you don't think it's wrong that they're a couple? I look Key dead in her face.

"I do think it's wrong. That's why my mama never took her around my daddy. She knew Tina was a hoe, but my mama not even around to have a clue about what's going on," Key states her opinion.

"My daddy always say that too. 'We didn't even know each other.' Like that's supposed to justify the shit." I roll my eyes.

"My point exactly. That's exactly why they didn't know each other." Key giggles

"That's not the point, though. The point is, it's still disrespectful. Raven and Micha be saying the same thing. They hate it there too," I continue to complain. "You just don't give a fuck because you don't have to live there. You come over and you leave. Shit, I wouldn't give two fucks either if I didn't have to live there," I continue.

"This is true," Key admits.

I shake my head. "Anyway, guess who I bumped into at school yesterday?"

"Who?" Key doesn't try to guess.

"Nessa from Cherry Hill! You remember her?"

"Oh yeah, I do!" Key adds.

"She go to the school upstairs on the top floor. I wanted to enroll in that school, but Daddy enrolled me into the wrong school," I explain, "I'm about to call her and catch up!"

When I dial Nessa's number, one of her sisters answers the house phone. Once Nessa got on the phone, she sounds really excited to hear from me. We talked for hours, catching up on everything. It feel just like old times as if we didn't go years without talking. After our conversation came to an end, I see Ray's name pop up on my caller ID as "T-Money." I started not to answer, but then I wasn't doing anything else, so I just pick up.

"Hello?"

"I didn't think you were going to answer the phone." Ray sounds like he's smiling.

"Why not?"

"I don't know, maybe to try and play hard to get." Ray giggles.

"I don't play hard to get. I am hard to get."

Ray laughs, "Oh, for real?"

I smile secretly over the phone. "For real... for real."

"Oh, I like you, you funny as hell," Ray chuckles. "You coming to school Monday?"

"Nah, my Big Mama passed away this week. Her funeral is tomorrow."

"Aww man, I'm sorry baby." Ray sounds sincere.

"It's okay, but I know tomorrow about to be so sad. I hate funerals, it's about to be hard," I shake my head.

Surprisingly, Ray and I stay up on the phone all night, talking about all kinds of stuff. He seems like a pretty cool boy for the most part, but I don't like him as a boyfriend yet. I still have to figure him out before I get too close to him. But I don't mind being his friend in-between time.

CHAPTER **SIXTY-FIVE**

OBSERVING MY BODY in the mirror, I don't feel that confident. Most girls at my high school are proportioned differently than me. The girls have shapely bodies and big booties, and I don't have that at all. Everything on my body is small, skinny and long. My legs are skinny and long. That's probably one of the reasons people ask me if I'm mixed because I'm shaped differently than most black girls. Boys from Detroit seem like they praise the big titties and big booties. Even though I'm shaped like a White girl, I still get a lot of attention from boys at school and outside of school. The boys never complain about how skinny I am. They always tell me how pretty I am and what not, but I still have my own insecurities.

I'm on my way to meet up with this guy named Ricky that I met over the summer. I met Ricky at the summer job I started working at right after camp. Tina helped Micha, and I get summer jobs. Micha and I ended up getting placed at different locations, though. I got placed at a senior citizen's home right down the street from Key's house on 7 Mile and Greenfield. Ricky worked there with me too. My dad lets me drive the car even though I don't have my license yet. I'm usually very careful when I'm driving because one of the brake lights is out, and I believe my dad's tags are bad too. I appreciate him letting me get the car; it low key makes me feel like the man. On top of that, he doesn't give me a curfew either. I know not to come back at a crazy hour, but the fact that he trusts me makes me feel really good.

"Da, we have to go to the doctors for my back." I grab the keys from next to him.
"Why? Your back be hurting?"
"Yeah," I lie to exaggerate my point so he can take me seriously.
"Okay, call the doctor this week then, and we can go up there." Dad fixes himself something to eat.
"Yeah, so we can get a surgery date set."
"Right, where you about to go?" Dad asks.
"Over Kesha and them house," I lie.
"Oh, okay," Dad bobs his head in approval.
"I'll be back later." I grab my small purse.
"Aright, see you."

My Dad is cool, and I can talk to him about boys, but he's not that cool. I don't feel comfortable telling him I'm going to meet up with a boy. It's almost like I'm going over Kesha's house because Ricky lives in the same area as she does. When I start up the BMW, it is as loud as a motorcycle engine. I roll the windows down and connect the aux cord to my iPod and select Gucci Mane - I'm Up.

You can't tell me anything while I'm behind the wheel with my hair blowing through the wind, Gucci Mane's cold beats banging through the speakers as loud as the volume can go.
It took me no time to get to Ricky's house. When I pull up, it looks like his cousin is still over.

"Hey, baby!" Ricky walks up to the car door looking goofy and excited at the same time.
"Hey, Ricky."
"Damn, nigga', let her get out of the car!" his cousin yells from the porch.
"Boy, shut yo' fat ass up before I slap the shit out of your little

brother again!" Ricky yells back.

"You not gone do that shit to me though!" his cousin looks unbothered.

"Right, but yo' little brother gone reap all the repercussions!" Ricky giggles, making me laugh.

"Miko, this my bully fat ass cousin. This my soon-to-be wife/baby mama and everything else." Ricky grabs me from behind and starts giving me quick kisses on my cheek and neck.

"Stop, Ricky!" I laugh, playfully pushing him off of me.

"Y'all trying to smoke?" his cousin pulls a rolled-up blunt out of his pocket.

"Where the fuck you pull that out of? Yo' ass?" Ricky looks serious, and I can't help but to laugh.

"Bro, I'm about to go spark up, you can stay here and keep making jokes, dummy." His cousin walks towards the backyard.

I finally catch my breath. "Y'all are stupid!"

"I'm serious! I been with this nigga' literally all day, and I didn't see him roll a blunt none today. Yo' stingy ass kept acting like you didn't have no more weed." Ricky sits down on the chair.

"Yeah, nigga', cause you kept fiending. If you had calmed down, you would've seen me roll another blunt!" His cousin sparks the blunt.

"You smoking with us, baby?" Ricky asks politely.

"Yeah." I cross my legs on the car I'm sitting on.

"Have you ever smoked before?" his cousin asked as he passed the blunt to Ricky.

"Nigga', you don't have to check up on my girl! I'm right here!" Ricky snaps in his playful way.

"I'm not talking to you!" the cousin snaps back.

"But I'm talking to you!" Ricky begins coughing.

"Learn how to smoke, little nuts!" his cousin teases.

I laugh while grabbing the blunt from Ricky. "Yeah, I've smoked too many times."

"Damn, yo' girl can smoke better than you," his cousin jokes.

"Nigga', I choked in the middle of my sentence, Panda Express." Ricky clears his throat.

That's one of the reasons I'm attracted to Ricky, because he's so funny and he has sort of a wild side to him. He and his cousin cracked on each other all night and kept me crying laughing. When it was starting to get late, we all went into the house to chill. Ricky guides me to his room, and at this point, I'm as high as a kite.

"Can I have a kiss?" Ricky slowly moves closer to my face.

Instead of talking, I just nod my head in a yes motion, and he leans in to kiss me. Next thing I know, we are tongue kissing on the bed. After kissing for a few minutes, Ricky puts his hands on my vagina. My pants are still on, and he claims he can feel how wet I am through my pants. Without permission or rejections, he takes my pants off slowly and then my panties and starts giving me some head. All I can think of is, *I'm getting some head right now. I'm getting some head right now.* I can't believe it! After giving me some head for a few minutes, he comes back up and ask if I want to have sex.

"Where is your mom?" I ask out of nervousness.
"She's at work. She work the night shift. I told you she's a police officer. She'll be gone all night." Ricky explains.
"Nah, Ricky, I gotta' get home." I get up to put my pants on.
"Okay, that's cool. You wanna' stop by Coney real quick?" Ricky asks.
"Yeah, we can go." I grab my purse and keys, and we head to my car.

After Ricky buys us food, we pull back in front of his house to eat in the car. Then I leave to go home. On the way home, I still can't believe what just happened, so I decide to hit up my best friends, Kesha and Kansas, to spill the tea.

"Hello? Are both of y'all there?" I make sure the three-way is working correctly.

"Yeah," Kesha adds.

"Yeah, I can hear you," Kansas confirms.

"So, guess what?" I paused quickly.

"What?" Kesha sounds excited.

"What nigga'?" Kansas sounds anxious to hear the news.

"I just got some head!" I laugh, and Kesha and Kansas join me.

"Okay, Mickey J! Kesha hypes me up.

"Heel-toe on 'em, then!" Kansas jokes.

Kesha burst out in laughter singing the Too Short song. "Right! D.T.E… Hustle…!"

"So, how was it?" Kansas ask for more detail.

"It was fun, and I'm over here high too. I'm about to go home and fall straight to sleep!" I laugh.

"Oh my God! Miko is such a low key weed head!" Kesha jokes.

"Right, low key as hell!" Kansas giggles.

Today is the day I'm set to undergo back surgery. The doctors told me I couldn't eat for up to eight to ten hours before my surgery. My grandparents are in town for help and support. I'm hungry and scared. I know all of the negative things that can go wrong with this surgery. That's heightening my anxiety and making me extremely uncomfortable. Everybody is surrounding me as my IV is easing through my veins. All of my close family members are here except for my mom. Sometimes I wonder why she never tries to reach out to us. I mean, at least Koko because she's only a baby. I haven't seen or heard from her since the day she walked out of the courtroom almost two years ago. She knows I have to get surgery, and that wasn't important enough for her to check in or keep in touch. The thought of my mom brings tears to my eyes as everybody in the room starts to get really blurry.

"Mickey, you up?" Granny stands on the side of my hospital bed.

"Mickey, can you hear us?" Granddaddy is behind her leaning towards me.

"She probably can't hear us yet," Granny answers Granddaddy's question.

"Well, how do you know, Mary?" Granddaddy frowns, catching a slight attitude per usual.

"Well, I don't but—" I cut Granny off.

"Hey," I speak slowly.

Everybody looks excited to see that I'm up and doing okay.

"How do you feel, Mik Mik?" Dad asks with a big smile on his face.

"Was I sleep for a long time?" I ask slowly as my own voice sounds unfamiliar.

"Yeah, you kept waking up on and off yesterday when you first got out of surgery." Key smiles.

"You were cussing up a storm too," Granddaddy adds making everybody laugh.

"For real?" I don't recall.

"Yeah, you were high off that morphine." Dad giggles.

"I don't even remember that. I don't remember going into surgery either." I try to move a little bit, but it's painful.

"I don't think you want to remember going into surgery, boop," Dad jokes.

"Was I in there for a long time?"

"Yeah, for about eleven to twelve hours." Granny moves my hair out of my face.

All of a sudden, there's a knock on the door.

"Come in!" Dad yells quickly.

Expecting it to be a nurse coming to check on me. Turns out it's my childhood best friend Pierre.

"Hey, Pierre!" Key welcomes him with open arms.

Pierre giggles. "Hey, Key!"

"Hello, here I'll take these and put them with the rest of her flowers." Granny grabs the small bouquet of flowers from Pierre's hands.

"What's up, Kimiko!" Pierre has a big goofy smile on his face.

"Just call me Miko. You sound like a childhood friend," I drag out in exaggeration.

Pierre laughs. "Well, I am a childhood friend."

"Don't mind her, she probably still a little blowed from the meds." Key sucks her two fingers like she's smoking a blunt.

Pierre and Key burst out in laughter. "Oh, you just came out of surgery?" Pierre asks.

"I feel like it!" I lean back, starting to feel more pain from my incision.

"She got out yesterday," Dad answers for me.

I don't remember Pierre saying he was going to come and visit, so it is a good surprise to see him. Pierre seems to blend right on in with the family. My Granddaddy seems to be acting unusually friendly towards Pierre for whatever reason. My daddy remembers him from elementary school, so he's like family.

"Hey, Koko! How old are you?" Pierre plays with Koko.

"I'm 4." Koko tries to act shy at first.

"Koko, you don't remember him?" I ask.

Koko shakes her head.

"The last time I saw her, she was talking about being a Gemini!" Pierre makes everybody laugh.

"A Gemini?" Granny giggles.

"What you know about a Gemini?" Granddaddy asks Koko in a playful way.

After a few laughs and reminiscing, Pierre heads home.

"Mickey, who was that?" Granddaddy asks as if he's been waiting to ask all day.

"He's been my friend since like 4th grade," I respond less excited than Granddaddy.

"You think he got a crush on you?" Granddaddy tries to stir up some gossip.

"No!"

"Is he gay?" Dad asks.

"I low key think he might be," Key adds her two cents.

"No, he's not gay! He used to like me when we were kids, but he doesn't anymore," I explain cutting all of their silly thoughts short.

"I don't think he's gay!" Granny takes my side.

"Yeah, because you don't know him." Key giggles.

"Right!" Dad laughs.

I shake my head. "Y'all childish! Y'all don't know him either."

"Sike, nah, I don't know, he might not be. It don't really matter he cool either way," Key shrugs her shoulders.

"He probably still like you, but you just don't know it yet!" Granddaddy continues with his crazy assumptions.

"I don't think so because I can tell when a boy likes me or not. We're just friends," I correct everybody.

"Miko, I spoke with Deanna, and she said she don't mind if you recover over there at her house since y'all got that bunk bed in the room." Dad switches the subject.

"Okay, good!" I smile, happy to know I'll be living somewhere I actually want to be.

"Yeah, and we're going to get you a comfortable bed to go into the room you'll be sleeping in," Granddaddy assures.

"Okay, thanks! I have to use the bathroom." I try to get up, and everybody jumps out of their seats, motioning for me not to get up.

"The nurse said you have to stay in bed for the whole day today," Granny explains.

"So, what am I suppose to do about the bathroom?"

"You have a catheter in you, so you can just pee right now," Dad explains.

"Right here right now?" I look around at everybody.

"Yeah!" Dad chuckles.

"What if some spill out?" I'm nervous because I've never used a catheter before.

"It shouldn't, and if it does, that mean they probably have it in wrong," Key adds.

"Go ahead, Mik Mik, you should be fine!" Dad confirms.

Like everyone said, the catheter caught every drop of my pee. It feels weird peeing in the bed. I feel like a senior citizen, but it's happening and that's my life right now.

CHAPTER SIXTY-SIX

I STAYED IN the hospital for a couple of weeks. Midweek, I had to start getting out of bed to learn how to walk again. The nurse helped me walk down the hall with a walker every day. I brought that same walker home with me to Aunt Deanna's house.

I'm so happy I'm able to stay with Aunt Deanna and them for my rehabilitation. I don't know what I would have done if I had to stay in the hell hole they call home. I have pain medication that I have to take every five hours, and I'm on a restricted diet. My scar is on the left side of my body instead of on my back. I hope it heals quickly because these stitches look so nasty in my skin. I feel like I'm so delicate and fragile. Just the thought of going back to school and possibly getting into a fistfight or even a play fight with the boys is terrifying. *What if I'm in a fight and one of my metal rods in my spine slip. Or I get hurt really bad and have to come back to the hospital,* I whisper to myself as I lay in the bed my grandparents bought me. I'm praying to God I don't have to face a situation where I have to fight or even horse around. I don't even have to be in a hardcore fistfight for a mistake to happen. My mom messed her hip up from a fall in the gym when she was a kid. That labeled her disabled for the rest of her life. This recovery got me all kinds of paranoid. I fall in a deep sleep, as I get lost in my own thoughts.

"Dang, fool, what were you doing in there?" April giggles as she focuses on the laptop.

"I was knocked out. I think those meds are getting to me. What you doing out here?" I place my walker to the side to sit down in the chair.

"I'm on that YouTube website looking at the 'Aids Man'. This nigga' sick in the head!" April looks uncomfortable, as her eyes stay glued to the computer screen.

I giggle. "What he on there doing? Turn the laptop this way." I motion for her to show me.

"This nigga's on here wearing a mask, naming all the women he intentionally gave Aids to." April turns the laptop so both of us can see.

"What? Now, why is he doing that?"

"He mad because he got Aids. The person who gave it to him didn't tell him they had it, so he said he not telling no woman he got it until it's too late," April explains.

"So, he said he not forewarning nobody?" I ask in a smart, goofy way.

April laughs. "I swear to God this fool said that. I'm about to start it from the beginning. I hope the police find his crazy ass."

"Dang, he got these hoes first and last names and everything!" April and I laugh at my joke.

"I can't believe we still haven't seen or heard from my mama!" I spark up a conversation with my dad in the room.

"Yeah, me either, how can a mother just say fuck her kids like that?" Dad just shakes his head.

"She didn't even come to see me in the hospital. She didn't send a postcard, a letter, or nothing." I giggle, avoiding my true feelings about my mom's abandonment.

"Right, that shit not right. I know she has her animosity against me, but that shouldn't have nothing to do with y'all." Dad explains remorsefully.

"Granny and Granddaddy said they heard she was out there with Brenda in Atlanta," I continue.

"They probably drinking like fishes down there together too." Dad giggles.

"And Brenda divorced too." I add only imagining the drunken picture of my mom and auntie.

"Brenda and her husband got a divorce after fifty years?" Dad's eyes grow big.

His facial expression forces me to laugh. "Yeah, Brenda and Charles are divorced now. I heard he left her for a young woman."

"What? Damn that's crazy!" Dad still looks like he's in shock.

"I know, right? That's what I said."

"And your Granny down there sick with breast cancer. She hasn't called and checked up on her or nothing, just pathetic." Dad looks like he's in deep thought.

"Right, and if she is down there with Brenda, she know that my Granny is sick. You know Granny and Granddaddy still keep in touch with Brenda and them," I assure.

"Yeah, I can't believe Joyce ass either. She was treating y'all that way, mean and cruel. It's Key fault y'all was going through that." Dad frowns.

"How?" he catches me by surprise with the comment about Key.

"Because for one, she's the oldest. She could've stood up to your mom or spoke out or said something." Dad backs up his opinion.

"My mama used to be beating the crap out of Key. She was scared to stand up to her. All she used to do was bully us. Key got it worse than me."

I wouldn't have thought I would be missing my mom the way I do, being that I dreaded living with her. I wonder how she would take the news with dad and Tina being together. I wonder, would she be mad or just wouldn't care at all? I do miss her, though. Sometimes I wish I had a way to tell her. I wonder if she feels the same way. If she does miss us, her actions haven't expressed that thus far. I knew my mom was cold hearted, but I never knew to this extreme. I knew my mom could hold a grudge, but I didn't think she would hold a grudge against us, her own daughters, for so long.

Tenth grade is feeling a lot like ninth grade, as I'm still attending Highland Park High. My dad, Koko, and I went up to Detroit Community High last week, and I'm so happy to be starting there soon. I'm not a huge fan of switching schools, but I'm not learning anything at HP, and I'm ready for a change. I ran into one of my best friends from sixth grade named Rachel at Detroit Community High. She seemed happy to see me. Seeing her made me really excited to start at DCH. My dad is going to be taking a coaching job for the Junior Varsity basketball at DCH, being that my dad used to be like a hood basketball celebrity growing up. It seemed like the coaches and a few of the other staff members knew him already, so I'm sure he's going to get that coaching job easily. I'm also excited to be back wearing uniforms again. We don't wear uniforms at HP, and I don't like it at all. I feel weird about having to repeat the same outfit sometimes. People probably don't notice, but I just don't like it. Wearing uniforms is just easier to me. The end of the semester is almost here, and I can hardly wait.

"Miko baby, come here!" Ray walks fast from behind me.

"You annoying!" I roll my eyes in a playful way.

"I called you yesterday. Why you didn't pick up?"

"I figured you should be calling your girlfriend!" I fold my arms in a challenging manner.

"I told you I don't like that girl. Her and her friends are crazy as hell!" Ray tries to laugh it off.

"Boy, bye! You lying!" I put my hand in his face and try to walk away.

"I thought we had moved past that. That shit old!" Ray looks confused.

"I just answered your question." I shrugged my shoulders.

"So, can we talk tonight?" Ray grabs my hand.

"We will see." I look him in his eyes before walking away.

Today, my dad is parked across the street at the gas station. The speed bumps in the school's driveway are really high, and it causes everybody to drive around super slow, so from now on until I leave, I'll just be meeting him over here.

"I thought you were going to be late today." I throw my bookbag in the back seat.

"Yeah, my schedule got changed today," Dad smacks on his candy.

"So, on your workdays, I'll just walk down the street to Aunt Jo Jo's house?" I confirm.

"Alright, and take this with you." Dad hands me a pocketknife.

"We have metal detectors at the school." I put the knife in my bag.

"Just place it under that garbage can over there and go back to get it when school is out." Dad points at the black garbage can near the gas station door.

"Alright, so am I going over Aunt Jo Jo's tomorrow?" I ask.

"Yeah, but I don't know why you don't just want to walk home. It's just a straight shot up Puritan." Dad looks annoyed.

"Puritan is too raggedy! Nah, I will just wait for you over Aunt Jo Jo's house." I look at him like he's crazy.

"You gone have the knife for protection," Dad tries to make sense out of it.

"I don't want to! That's a long shot up Puritan anyway." Dad can hear the aggravation in my tone.

"See, that's that spoil shit I be talking about!" Dad continues to drive.

Just because you grew up over here in the fucking slums doesn't make me feel comfortable walking through it. I didn't grow up over here! I keep my comment to myself as we ride past the ghetto rundown neighborhoods.

"What about the trucking company my granddaddy was helping you out with?" I change the topic since he wants to be annoying.

"That didn't end up working out. I'ma do the coaching instead. That will be fun too. You know I used to be a basketball star back in the day!" Dad goes on.

Yeah, what the fuck ever. I know it's his fault the trucking company didn't work out. He's so used to being in the streets that he doesn't know how to be legit and turn the street shit off.

I can smell Tina's cooking as soon as I walk through the door.

"You want some chicken and potatoes?" Dad looks excited.

"No." I straight face him and continue for the stairs.

"Today is your dish day too!" Dad yells up the stairs so I can hear him.

Fuck you.

I guess he made it his business to tell me to wash the dishes because last time Tina told me to wash the dishes, I didn't. Lord knows I'm hungry, but I don't want to eat Tina's food. It's obvious that I try to avoid her as much as I can. I hate living here, and I can't wait until we move around the corner to our own house. I'm low key miserable here! I hate coming home! I hate being in this house! I was just in an okay mood, then as soon as I opened the door to this hell hole, the shit went south.

After settling in, I put my pajamas and my back brace on, then pull out my homework and help Koko with hers too. Later, when everybody navigated to their bedrooms, I made my way downstairs to start the dishes. The water in the kitchen sink doesn't work, so we use two buckets. We put water in both buckets from the bathroom sink. One bucket has soap water in it, and the other has clean water in it. As I'm washing the dishes, I feel my phone vibrate in my pocket. Once I'm able to get my hands dry, I see a missed call from Ray.

"What's that you got on?" Raven comes out of nowhere from the other room.

"It's a back brace; it's supposed to help my back stay aligned after my surgery," I explain.

"I probably need something like that. My back be hurting from dancing." Raven places her plate on the stove.

After our small talk, I decide to call Ray back.

"Hello?" Ray answers on the first ring.

"Playa'... playa'..." I sing like I'm about to start rapping the Biggie Smalls song.

Ray giggles. "You got all the jokes, huh?"

"I got a few!" I smile.

"What you doing? What took you so long to call me back?"

"I'm washing the dishes right now. And I called you right back, boy!" I giggle.

"Can I ask you a question?" Ray sounds serious.

"What, Ray?"

"When you gone stop playing with me?"

"When you gone stop playing with me?" I continue to play.

"That's where you wrong. I'm not playing with you. I'm trying to make you mine," Ray runs game.

"And who else, Ray?" I sound serious.

"Nobody else."

"I don't believe you." I'm not convinced.

"I swear to God, I mean, other chicks be trying to get with me, but my attention on you," Ray tries to flatter me.

"I don't know, Ray, I mean, I like you, but I can't trust you. Ever since your girlfriend called me damn near crying. I just don't know. You have to gain my trust," I stand my ground.

"That was some bullshit, but alright, I will try," Ray gives in.

"Aw, You will?" I ask in a cute way.
"Yeah, you smiling?" Ray sounds like he's smiling.
"Yeah, I like when you make me do that," I giggle.
"Okay, let me take notes!" Ray jokes.

Tonight so many of my other guy friends are calling trying to chop it up, but they're all getting the voicemail since I'm on the phone with my boo thing. Ray and I talk all night and eventually talk our selves to sleep on the phone.

CHAPTER **SIXTY-SEVEN**

DETROIT COMMUNITY HIGH seems like a good school overall. We wear black or khaki pants with our DCH red, white, or grey shirts. My schedule is pretty cool; the only class I don't really care for is French. I just feel like I'm not going to do well in this class.

"I'm thinking about switching that French class to Spanish." I walk with Rachel in the hallway.

"Why you transferring? That's the only class we have together." Rachel looks like she is stargazing at the upperclassman.

"French is hard. I think I'll do better in Spanish. Girl, what you looking at?" I look at her like she's stupid.

"Right, I feel you. I will be right back." Rachel heads over towards the seniors and adds herself in the conversation.

Wow! What a dick-sucker! I continue to walk like I was never with her.

So, I guess I'm going to have to find some new friends around here because all Rachel does is sniff the seniors' asses. I know she has a crush on that Nygee guy, but it doesn't seem like he likes her as half as much as she likes him. I might be a lot of things, but one thing I don't have in my blood is to be a dick-sucker. It's so hard for me to try to be somebody's friend who's clearly not interested in a friendship with me. If the work being put into a friendship is not mutual, I fall back immediately. I don't care who you are, how popular you are, or how cute you may be. And if that means I walk alone, then so be it.

My next class is computer class. This class is one of my favorite classes, and I love my teacher, Ms. Lee. The classroom has like seven rows with four to five computers on each side of the room. Each row has a level above, like a wide staircase. It kind of reminds me of a college classroom. These new Mac computers are pretty sweet that we work on. We didn't have these computers at HP. These computers have cameras on them and different filter settings. We're learning how to use the different programs on these types of computers. Ms. Lee is always so patient with everybody and kind, but she also doesn't put up with anybody's mess. I think I'm one of Ms. Lee's favorites. Sometimes I stay after computer class and chill with Ms. Lee to kick it. I feel like I can trust her. She kind of reminds me of an Aunt or something. I've told Ms. Lee about some of my personal business, and the look on her face is always amusing. She looks at me like she can't believe the stuff I tell her about my life. Sometimes I just feel like I want to talk to somebody outside of people in my family.

"You saw Ms. Lee out there?" I ask Tony.

"Nah, she wasn't out there when I was in the hallway." Tony sits down next to me. "How you get to that?" Tony looks at my computer.

"It's called Photo Booth. It's on everybody's computer." I show him where the icon is on his computer.

"Oooh, come here! Come get in mines!" Tony giggles as we take pictures together until Ms. Lee starts class.

"So, how you liking your new school?" Kansas asks as she lights her Black n' Mild.

"It's cool! I like it way better than HP," I giggle.

"Is it a lot of cute boys that go there?" Kansas tries to hand me the Black.

"Ugh, I don't want to smoke that!" I toot my nose up.

"Come on, dog! I be smoking with you!" Kansas looks at me like I owe her.

"Yeah, smoking w-e-e-d nigga'! They say Black n' Mild worse than cigarettes!"

"Man, I never heard of that!" Kansas looks unconvinced.

"I swear it's true!"

"Hit the Black, dog!" Kansas puts the Black n' Mild closer to me.

"Dang, peer pressure Patty!" I roll my eyes and snatch the Black from her hand.

"That's how you be with me about weed, like you Smokey from *Friday*. 'I'm about to get you high today man!'" Kansas mimics the movie *Friday*.

I cough from trying not to laugh. "Shut up, I do not be like that!" I hand her the Black.

"I swear you do. I'm about to head down the street in a minute to my lil' boo thang house." Kansas does a little dance.

"Ugh, y'all nasty!" Kansas and I laugh. "I got a new lil' boo on the low too," I smirk.

"For real? Who?" I got Kansas' full attention.

"His name is Rome. He lives a few houses down," I smile.

"How you meet him? How old is he?"

"I met him through Porsha's boyfriend, and he's like a junior or a senior in high school, so he's like seventeen or eighteen," I blush just thinking about him.

"Is he cute? Because you know how you do!" Kansas burst out in laughter.

"Yes, he is fine as hell! He's tall, brown-skinned with braces! And I know you not talking because you done had you some ugly's too!" I laugh.

"Who?" Kansas challenges me.

"Everett!" I straight-face her.

"First of all, he doesn't even count!" Kansas tries to explain.

"Get the fuck out of here! Yes, he do, dog! Stop playing! That was your boo, too!" I burst out in laughter.

We hear people coming through the side door, so we quiet down.

"Y'all in here chit-chatting it up, huh?" Cory passes us to go in the den as Boo Bear follows.

"Hey, Kansas." Boo Bear has an awkward smirk on his face.

"Hey, Boo Bear," Kansas speaks back quickly.

"Dang, Blue Balls, she the only one you see?" I joke.

"Miko dog, I see you all the time!" he throws his hand up.

"Looks like that's my cue!" Kansas gets up to get ready to leave.

I giggle. "You childish, I still can't believe Boo Bear gave you some head last night," I whisper so only she can hear as I grab her bag.

"I know, me either," Kansas giggles in a sneaky way.

I give Kansas a quick hug before she leaves.

"I'll be back tomorrow," Kansas assures.

"Okay, cool, see ya' later!" I close the side door and walk back to the dining room table.

"Where Kansas go? To her lil' boyfriend's house?" Key asks sarcastically, already knowing the answer to her own question.

"Yeah," I giggle.

"Her mama know she got a boyfriend down the street from here?" Key teases.

"Probably not," I answer shortly, feeling Key's annoying vibe.

"Her mama gone pop up on her one of these days. She better watch out because I'm just gone play stupid, like "oh, I thought you knew." Key giggles in a serious way.

"Speaking of boos and boyfriends, can I invite Rome over tonight?"

"To spend the night?" Key frowns.

"Nah, just to chill and smoke for a few hours," I correct her.

"I don't care. Speaking of smoking, y'all trying to roll up?" Key yells to the back den to Cory and Boo Bear.

"I'm two steps ahead of you, Key!" Boo Bear adds with a blunt in his hands.

"Boo Bear back here rolling up as we speak!" Cory puts some weed on a scale.

After mine, Key, Cory, and Boo Bear's smoking session, we all sit back in the den, watching The Boondocks. After cracking up all day and having the munchies, Key makes nachos, and then I decide to message Rome. Rome is a guy I have a crush on from down the street that Key noticed a while back. When she told me he was fine, I knew she wasn't lying because she has good taste. Come to find out, we have mutual friends and finally met up, exchanged numbers, and been in touch. Every time I'm about to message him, I always get extremely nervous. I hate how nervous he makes me feel. Usually, when Rome and I hang out, we're either at his place or at my place chilling and smoking. Sometimes I feel like I can't be myself around him because my nerves always take over. I wish I could just calm down and be the normal silly, cool ass me. I've been trying to ignore the fact that I feel like I'm more interested in him than he is in me. I just like him so much, and I really want the feeling to be mutual, but my womanly intuition is always reminding me otherwise.

As soon as I hear the knock on the front door, my heart instantly drops to the floor.

"Okay, Miko, be cool." I inhale slowly and exhale quickly.

When I open the door, Rome is looking so good in his smooth brown skin and his straight back braids. He stands so tall over me, and I love it.

"You tryna' blow one?" Rome pulls a blunt out of his pocket.

"I'm already high," I giggle nervously.

Rome flops on the couch. "Good, since you already high, you

can't get any higher."

"Says who?" I challenge him.

"It's factual!" Rome sparks the blunt like he's Scarface or somebody.

As we're in rotation, we exchange kisses and shotguns, mouth to mouth. He's doing all of these smoking tricks, making me feel like such an amateur.

No wonder why he can't take me seriously. I catch a slight attitude with myself.

"Come here, look at this," he pulls out his cellphone.

"Who is this?" I'm so blowed from the weed and caught off guard from his dick picture he just pulled out.

"It's me, girl!" he giggles.

"Duh! Of course, it's him! Why would he be showing you pictures of other niggas' dicks?" I'm low key embarrassed at my response.

"Right, I'm too blowed!" I try to laugh off my idiotic question.

His dick pictures are nice. His entire penis is all the same color, thick, and long. He's straight packing! That's exactly why he's a player now. He's fine as hell with a big dick, that's what all the girls want. I don't know what to say to his dick pictures as he scrolls. I don't know how to compliment a dick, and I'm for sure not about to say put it in my mouth! Even though I'm sure he would love that. I don't even know why he's showing me these pictures. We weren't even talking about anything freaky just now.

You do know why he's showing you pictures of his dick! He want to fuck you! That's all he wants from you! S.E.X! That's it!" My intuition won't let me be naive for one second.

Out of nowhere, Rome and I are making out heavily on the couch. I don't know who kissed who first, but I know he's a good kisser and his kisses feel so good. Everything about the way he moves is just perfect in my eyes, especially right now. His kisses are so soft, and I'm getting super horny. At this point, I'm ready to risk it all. Even though I know he's not good for me, I just feel ready for whatever is going to come. Just as I was about to take him upstairs to my bed and give him my virginity, I hear the deepest baritone voice I could ever imagine.

"DO NOT DO THIS. YOU WILL REGRET IT"

This voice was so loud it startled me in the middle of my make-out session with Rome. The voice spoke so clearly and stern but not in a scary way, more in a cautious way. It was so loud to me, I almost asked Rome if he also heard it. Thankfully, I saved that question, which saved me from looking like I was tripping. Right in that second, I decided that I should just pass up this thrill. When Rome noticed I snapped out of whatever I was just in, he got the point without me having to write it down.

"Dog! Guess what?" I walk in Key's room dying to spill the tea.
"What?" Key giggles at my excitement.
"I was about to do it to Rome last night!"
"What happened?" Key looks confused.
"When we were kissing and touching, I was just getting so horny and right before I was about to tell him to come upstairs, I heard this loud, deep, powerful voice," I explain as vivid as possible.
"Man, you were probably just high!" Key laughs.
"Nah! It wasn't that, because I don't hear voices when I'm high, dog! I've never heard a voice while I was high, and I been smoking for a while now! If I heard voices while I was high, I wouldn't smoke!" I laugh at her sick assumption.
"Like I was saying, the voice spoke to me right before I was about to take him upstairs, and it said "DO NOT DO THIS. YOU WILL REGRET IT," I continue. "I mean, it was so loud and clear I thought Rome heard the shit too!" we both burst out in laughter.
"I think it was God himself speaking to me, man!" I look at Key dead into her eyes.

"I don't know, maybe it was!" Key sounds a bit more convinced.

"I think I'm about to try and slowly distance myself from him," I sadly admit.

"Why? I thought you said you like him?" Key plays with her gum.

"I do, but he doesn't like me the way I want him to," I try to explain.

Key looks at me like I'm stupid. "Now that sounds crazy. You can't control how somebody feels so soon," Key adds.

"I know, and I can't change his mind, so I'm just going to leave him alone. He doesn't look at me the same way I look at him, and it be making me feel so stupid," I vent to Key on her bed.

"Well, y'all only been talking for a few weeks, right?" Key asks.

"Yeah," I side-eye her.

"You never know how he might feel if you give it a little more time," Key suggests.

"But I know how I'm going to feel. More in my feelings, fuck that. So I'm straight on him. He not about to play me."

"Well shit, don't talk to him no more. It's plenty of fish in the sea!" Key finally jumps on my side of the boat.

"So, when are we leaving?" I catch an attitude with Dad.

"I told you to give me a few more months, damn! You know the house on LaSalle need a lot of work done to it." Dad tries not to get angry at my frustration.

"You been saying that for like two years now," I continue to challenge him with a straight face.

"Uncle James has been going over there a lot. It's just two of us working on the house. It's going to take time." Dad talks fast as if he's done with the conversation.

"Well, can I move in with Key for the time being? I hate being here!" I come up with a quick solution.

"Hell nah, with Key? For what? So you can be over there smoking all day and being under Boo Bear!" Dad doesn't think twice.

"With Boo Bear? Boo Bear is a nonfactor..." I add very slowly so he can understand.

"Nonfactor, my ass!" Dad stands his ground.

By his last comment, I know moving in with Key is not going to be easy, but my determination still gives me hope. Maybe I should still try to move my stuff over there and see what happens. Key has already told me plenty of times that she doesn't mind me moving in. I have my old room that I can sleep in upstairs. Even though the house is ran down from when we used to live there with my mom, it still beats living up in here with Tina and them. The energy here is just so depressing. You can tell the only people that are trying to act like this situation is okay are Tina and Dad. Koko doesn't really know what's going on because she's so young. She doesn't know my mom, and she wasn't born back when my parents were married. When I open up about my current living situation to people, they always say "that's fucked up," and they "wouldn't want to live here either," so I know I'm not tripping. I've been trying to be patient with my dad, but I think he's feeding me a whole bunch of bullshit. I don't think he has any intentions on moving off of Normandy any time soon. I'm honestly done with this entire situation. If he wants to be with my "Aunt," I don't want any parts.

CHAPTER SIXTY-EIGHT

THIS WEEKEND I overpacked to come over Key's house. I'm hoping that my dad gives in with letting me stay with Key. I'm planning on calling him to tell him I'm staying for the week or I might wait until he reaches out to me.

"Girl, and when I suggested for me to stay here with you, his face got to frowning up, talking about 'Hell nah, and all you gone do over there is be under Boo Bear.' Calling us little Key and Cory. I've told him plenty of times that I DON'T LIKE BOO BEAR. He talking about, all I'm going to be doing is smoking all day, like I'm about to move over here and be a dropout or some shit!" I fill Key in, per usual.

"And he really don't care if you smoke. He know you smoke, so I don't understand. It's not like he forbids it or something. And that Boo Bear shit is just some slick, smart shit to say. He's just saying that because he doesn't like Cory. He's never really liked him, so bye!" Key seems angry.

"Well, I'm going to go to school from here tomorrow. I'm not calling him to ask him to pick me up tonight," I shrug my shoulders. "Then the other day I asked him about the trucking company and why he never started it. He talking about 'it never worked out,'" I continue.

"The shit didn't work out because he didn't want to pay for his registration to keep the truck. My granddaddy bought him a Class 4 delivery truck. All he had to do was get his trucking license and pay his yearly registration. His irresponsible ass didn't want to do either one. He always trying to make it seem like he don't want you over here and like I'm such a bad influence, but what kind of influence is he?" Key is clearly heated.

While Key goes on with her rant, my Lil' Wayne ringtone cuts her short, notifying me someone is calling. When I look at my phone, I see it's my dad calling. I pick up the phone, ready to get into an altercation.

"Hello?"
"What's up, Mik, what you doing?" Dad sounds calm.
"Nothing, just chilling over Key's."
"Is she dropping you off soon?" Dad asks.
"Nah." I cut my explanation short.
"Why not?" Dad sounds concerned.
"Because I want to live over here until we get our own house," I express calmly.
"Did you not hear what I said the other day! No! You are not staying over there in that junky ass house with Key and her bum ass boyfriend! As a matter of fact, I'm about to come get you myself!" Dad hangs up the phone on my face.
"What he say?" Key is anxious.
"He said he's on his way over here." I put the cellphone down on the table.
"And he better not come over here thinking he about to dog no motherfucking body! You know how he get! Now he coming to get you? I'ma tell that nigga' he need to come get you all the time! Instead of being petty like he don't ever have no gas, making me drop you off every time like somebody stupid!" Key looks like she's ready for the bullshit my dad is about to bring with him.

It literally took my dad less than fifteen minutes to get to the house. He's never pulled up over here so fast. As soon as he comes into the house, Key and my dad immediately get into an argument. Key is taking up for me, and he's not having it at all. Dad is basically saying fuck how Key and I both feel. There's so much hostility and anger in the room. I feel bad that I even started this mess. Dad and Key already have a bad relationship, and this little incident is probably just going to add to the fire. Finally, a fight breaks out, and I'm stuck in the middle trying to break it up. Dad is manhandling Key against the wall as she punches as fast as she can.

"Stop! Stop! Get off of her!" I scream to the top of my lungs, pulling Dad away.

"I don't know who the fuck either of y'all think y'all are, but y'all got the shit twisted!" Dad points at me. "You! Get your shit and get in the fucking car!" then points at Key. "You worry about you and your own fucked up love life!" Dad yells.

"Like yours is better!" Key snaps back in tears.

"It's better than yours!" Dad doesn't hold back.

"Yeah fucking right! You had to go date one of my mama's best friends to get a girl! You picking through leftovers! Get the fuck out of here!" Key waves her hand in the air at him.

I get my stuff packed as fast as motherly possible so we can hurry and leave before shit gets worst around here.

"So, things didn't go as planned at all, huh?" Ms. Lee giggles at my story in computer class.

"Not at all, I think I know what I have to do. It's not plan A or ideal, but..." I look off in deep thought.

"And what's that, young lady?" Ms. Lee looks at me with suspicion.

"I think I'm going to have to leave on my own," I continue to look off.

"You mean like run away?" Ms. Lee looks worried.

"Yeah, after this junior year is over during the summer. But run away to my grandparents' house in North Carolina," I explain myself in more detail.

Ms. Lee exhales. "Oh, okay, with somebody you know, because I was about to say."

I giggle. "Yeah, not to just run the streets and get killed, but similar to what I did to my mom when I left her to go with my dad."

"Right, when you guys ran away to your dad, okay." Ms. Lee bobs her head in understanding.

My eyes get watery. "Yeah, didn't think I would be going through this with him. I really wish we would just move into our own house, but I can tell he really likes Tina. And I'm literally miserable when I'm in that house. I don't like going home, and I hate the feeling of not wanting or liking to be at home. Like home is supposed to be home, comforting, relaxing, and peaceful," I vent.

"The place you call home is supposed to be peaceful and comfortable," Ms. Lee agrees.

"I know, and it's the complete opposite for me. It almost reminds me of when my parents were married and my dad would be gone a lot, and we would be at home with my mom. I used to dread being at home with her. The only place of peace in that house was my bedroom. In my bedroom with all of my toys and American Girl Dolls was my safe place. I controlled what I wanted to in my own little world." I giggle at the thought of my childhood memories.

"Oh, so your parents were married once before?" Ms. Lee asks.

"Yeah, for ten years. We all lived in the same house, and we seemed to be financially stable. All of the moving around and living with people wasn't even a thought then. I'm used to having my own space. I know sometimes in life things change, but damn, didn't ever think in a million years it would be like this," I let my face fall in my hands.

"I don't know why I thought you were always with your father," Ms. Lee adds.

"Because my mom decided she didn't want anything to do with us anymore. She walked out of our lives after the divorce. I haven't seen or heard from her since." my tears finally fall.

Ms. Lee walks over to give me a hug. "I just never heard of a mother walking out on her own children after raising them. Something just isn't right with your mom."

"She doesn't know how to love. She shouldn't of ever had children," I continue crying.

Today is Rose and Candle. It's a celebratory event that honors the juniors and seniors. The juniors are given roses for the seniors, and the seniors are given candles for the juniors. The program isn't that long, and at the end of our ceremony, we do our exchange of roses and candles. Before our exchange, a selected few, including me, got a chance to sing "The World's Greatest" by R. Kelly. Once the program is over, everyone is mingling.

"Miko, what you doing after this?" Victoria asks.

"I don't know, what about you?"

"We thinking about going to the River Walk. You should come! You can ride with me!" Victoria offers.

"Okay, let me go tell my dad so he won't be looking for me." I go to look for Dad and Koko.

Victoria is this chick I met earlier in my junior year in journalism class. She's a cute, brown-skinned girl who always wears blonde hair. She's pretty mature, and we just went from not talking at all to hanging out a lot. She drives too, which is cool because I feel like I'm the only one that's driving out of my few friends in high school.

I thought the girls we would be hanging out with at the River Walk would be from our school, but these girls don't look familiar at all. Even though I don't know these girls, they seem pretty cool and friendly. Everybody is just chopping it up and taking pictures.

"I can't believe we about to be seniors!" Victoria smiles looking over the water as the wind blows.

"Right, it went so fast!" Kianna adds.

"I'ma miss you, Vee!" I give her a side hug.

"Where the hell you going?" Victoria looks at me like I'm crazy.

"Girl, I'm moving to North Carolina with my grandparents."

"How you just gone leave our senior year?" Victoria looks confused.

"I'ma try to come back and go to prom with you and Aaron." I ignore her question, trying not to get too personal in front of her friends.

"I'm holding you to it too!" Victoria gives me a serious but goofy look.

Koko is watching me intuitively as I pack the heaviest suitcase I've ever packed to go to "visit" my grandparents.

"Koko, why you don't want to come?" I ask softly.

"Because it's boring down there. I don't have any friends down there." Koko shrugs her shoulders.

"Well, always remember, you can always come with me, okay?" I look Koko in her eyes trying not to get emotional.

"Okay." Koko nobs her head.

I instantly hug Koko as tightly as I can, knowing I wouldn't be seeing her in a long time. I try my hardest not to cry, and thankfully it worked this time. I don't want my dad to feel how heavy my luggage is, so I use all of my strength to carry my own suitcase down the stairs and to the trunk of the car.

This summer is going by so slow. I don't know what I would do if I didn't have my Sims game to keep me occupied. It is "boring" down here like my sisters always say, but it's also calming and relaxing. I don't have to worry about somebody robbing me when I go to the gas station. I don't hear random gunshots at night. The crime level is nowhere near as high as it is in Detroit. It's a guarantee that I eat breakfast, lunch, and dinner every single day. That alone brings me inner joy.

My granny is one of the best cooks I know. Unfortunately, she's not in the kitchen as much as I'm used to her being because her cancer has gotten worse. It's literally eating her from the inside out. I can tell she doesn't want me to worry about her, but I secretly do. Her nails and toenails look like they're disappearing. Sometimes she tells me they ache. Both of her breasts are removed. We drive her about an hour out every other week for chemo treatment and I pray it's helping, but it doesn't seem like it is.

"Granny, you want me to help you out in the kitchen for dinner tonight?" I ask.

"No, Mickey, I'm fine. How does barbecue pulled pork, greens, and macaroni and cheese sound?" Granny smiles.

"Oooo, that sounds really good!" I do a silly dance to express happiness for the food.

"It would be nice if you came out of the room sometimes," Granny suggests.

"Yeah, she stays in that room!" Granddaddy adds his two cents from the living room.

Damn! Ear hustling ass!

"What do you do on your laptop?" Granny asks nicely.

"I be playing The Sims game." I twiddle with my fingers.

"You haven't won yet?" Granny asks.

I laugh. "It's not a win or lose kind of game. It's a game where you can create and control your own world. You create your own neighborhoods and families. When you create the people, they have features on the game that give you the ability to literally create and distort their faces to make them look like you or whoever you want. You can pick their clothes and what kind of personality they have. It gets deep."

"That sounds boring," Granddaddy chuckles.

Who asked you?

"No it doesn't, Jim." Granny takes up for me.

"It does to me!" Granddaddy continues to joke.

"Well, that's why you don't have to play it," I add in a friendly sarcastic tone.

Granddaddy smirks. "Yup! You got that right!"

"Anyways, you get to pick their careers, and if you know cheat codes, you can make them have a lot of money and make them live longer as well.

"That sounds like a lot," Granny adds.

"Yeah, you can build the Sims houses, or you can buy the houses that are already built. If I really like the family I'm playing with, I'll custom build their house from scratch. I guess it's a kind of game you have to have patience to play," I giggle.

Since my granny said I should come out of the room more, I decide to sit with them after dinner instead of going straight to my room. My grandparents usually chill in the living room until it gets late, then they go to their room.

"You ever watch Martin?" Granddaddy grabs the remote.

"Not usually, but I have seen it before." I sit down on the couch next to Granny.

"You're not missing anything." Granny grabs a catalogue.

I can't help but laugh at Granny's honesty. "You don't like Martin?"

"No, he tries too hard for me." Granny makes a grim facial expression.

"She's never liked Martin," Granddaddy adds.

"I thought Martin was funny, last time I remember." Now I'm a little excited to watch Martin since it's been so long.

"He is, I don't know what's wrong with her!" Granddaddy stretches his legs out on his sofa chair as Martin comes on.

As the Saturday night goes on, Granddaddy and I die laughing at Martin as Granny makes little night snacks for us to munch on. This Saturday night is the complete opposite of what I would be doing if I were in the city of Detroit. I would probably be turnt up smoking or drinking with Kansas and them, or I would be pulling up on some boys that I know. But I'm having fun with my grandparents as well, if I do say so myself.

CHAPTER **SIXTY-NINE**

"OH! YOU BRING yo' ass back home! I don't know who the fuck you think you are!" Dad yells from over the phone.

"No, I'm not! I told you I hate living in that house with you and Tina!" I yell back as tears fall.

"I don't give a fuck what you want or what you like!" Dad sounds sure.

"I know you don't! That's exactly why I had to remove myself from the premises! You and my mama don't care about nobody but y'all selves!" I continue to scream.

"If her daddy said she has to go home, she has to go home," I overhear Granddaddy speaking from the living room.

"I'm not going back to Detroit! I don't care what he's saying over this phone!" I correct my granddaddy loud and clear from the front room.

"Well, I guess I'ma have to call the police, then!" Granddaddy challenges me.

"Well, I guess you will because I'm not leaving!" I hang up the phone on my dad and rush to my room.

After the heated conversation between my dad and I, plus my granddaddy's smart remarks, all I can do is cry. I hate the parents I was born with! I wish they would get their fucking lives together! If not for themselves, at least for us, their "children." They are selfish motherfuckas, and I'm sick of it. Having to deal with two selfish parents only leaves me to have to fend for myself. I have to make the best decisions for MY life and myself because they're only worried about themselves. They don't give two fucks about how anything affects us. They continuously put us in fucked up situations because of their own self-centered ways, so it's time for me to be self-centered as well by default. I know my dad feels like I shouldn't live here with my grandparents because of the way they raised my mom. They spoiled her rotten, and it got her nowhere, but they don't treat us the way they treated her. I feel like they learned from their mistakes with raising her, and essentially that's what matters. They don't spoil us rotten. They give us stuff we want sometimes, but most importantly, they provide us with things we need, and they pick up my parents' slack. My grandparents make sure that we know that in life you have to earn things and you have to work for a living.

The end of the summer is approaching, and it's time for me to be enrolling in school. I don't know what got into my dad, but he has had a change of heart. My guess is Tina talked him into believing me living down here is a good idea. Whatever the case is, he's totally fine with me living with my grandparents now. A couple of weeks ago, I flew back to Detroit to get some papers from the courts stating that my grandparents are my legal guardians. I need this paper to be enrolled in West Brunswick High in Shallotte, North Carolina. All of the kids at my church go to West Brunswick, so I know a few people that go there already. It's so weird and lame, going to a new school in my senior year of high school. But I have to do what I have to do. The kids from my church are sort of lame to me, but they're nice, so I'm nice in return. Honestly, I'm just looking forward to college. I'm praying this year goes by as fast as possible.

As I'm sitting in Social Studies class, I notice most of the kids in the classroom are White. I must admit, it's a culture shock attending this predominately White school. Coming from the city of Detroit, where your only chance of seeing another race is maybe behind a counter, at the hospital, or a store. I'm used to only seeing Black people everywhere I go, back at home.

"This class is super boring, right?" A White girl sitting next to me smiles.
"Yeah, it is," I giggle.
"I'm Laura, what's your name?" she flips her blonde hair behind her ear.
"I'm Miko,"
"Are you new here too?" Laura asks.
"Yeah, are you?"
"Yeah, I moved from Indianapolis. That's my hometown," Laura explains.
"Oh, okay, I'm from Detroit, Michigan." I look at Khadijah ear hustling from the other side of Laura.
"Yeah, this class is extremely boring," Khadijah "C" her way into the conversation.
"I was just telling her the same thing! I'm Laura." Laura smiles at Khadijah.
Khadijah is one of the girls that go to the same church as me. She's cool, but sometimes she can be a suck-up.

The kids down here are so different. When I talk to kids from the church, they always proclaim how much they want to attend Historical Black Colleges. The reason is that they were all raised around White people. All of them long to be around Black people, and my life is the complete opposite. Growing up in a black city I wouldn't mind going to a college with different races. My dream college is Full Sail University. It's a college specifically geared toward entertainment, media, arts, and technology. I haven't heard about too many Universities offering degrees in these kinds of artistic fields in the year 2010. I absolutely love music, and I want to go to school to be a music producer. I dream of learning how to use those programs producers use to create sounds and beats for songs.

"Yo, Khadijah, did you hear about that party from last weekend?" a Black guy with short locs asks.

"Whose? Fred's big brother's?" Khadijah ask in her country accent.

"Yeaaah," he smiles.

"Yeah, I heard a lot of people showed up." Khadijah nods her head.

"Man, I was so high the whole time!" he giggles.

Now he got my full attention! I get a little excited.

"George, what were you smoking on? Some weed?" Khadijah laughs.

"Yeaaah, I was sooo high! I was sitting in the middle of the dance floor the whole night," George explains.

"Oh, you were fucked up, huh?" Khadijah confirms.

"Right," I laugh at George. "So you were sitting in the middle of the dance floor while everybody else was dancing?" I ask to make sure I'm hearing him clearly.

"Yeah, it was crazy! I was soo high!" George laughs at himself.

"What kind of weed were you smoking?" I take note in my head for precaution.

"It was some "Wet Wet". They dip it in embalming fluid," George explains excitedly.

What the fuck? Oh noooo!!

"Never heard of it." Laura looks lost.

"I'm just as lost as you, Laura." I giggle.

I'm really in another neck of the woods. I'm really in the fucking sticks! Right when I was about to get excited about getting some 411 on the weed man, this nigga' talking about being blowed as fuck off some bullshit. I haven't hit a blunt in a long time, and from the looks of it, I might have to get comfortable in the sober lifestyle. George's story just made me nervous about smoking with anybody out here. I'm not trying to get laced. I'm not used to shit like this, so I'm just going to play it safe out here and stay weed free.

As the year goes on, meeting a few people outside of the church people is relieving. This chick name Keirra is really cool from California. I met her in music class, and she has a huge love for music too, so we clicked instantly. She seems like the only person around here that's near my lane.

"Girl, these people out here are country as hell," I giggle.

Keirra burst out laughing. "You noticed too, huh? They are always asking me where I'm from because of my accent. They tell me I talk White."

"You talk proper, but you don't sound like a White person to me," I add

"I know, right? That's how people from California talk. It's sort of like a proper accent," Keirra explains.

"Are you cool with a lot of people out here?" I ask.

"No, not really. I know a couple of cool White girls out here, but that's about it. My mom said we might be moving back to Cali sometime next year. If that's true, I can't wait!" Keirra crosses her fingers.

"I know you can't! I can't wait to graduate and get up out of here myself!"

"What college are you going to go to?" Keirra asks.

"Hopefully, I can get into Full Sail University. It's in Winter Park, FL. My grandparents said we're going to take a trip there after graduation and check the school out. I'm excited about that! You got one more year, right?"

"Yeah, and I'm hoping I don't have to spend it here. It's boring as hell down here." Keirra and I share laughs before class starts.

One good thing about this school is the yellow school bus will come to pick you up and drop you off from your house if it's in the scheduled route. Since my grandparents are too scared to let me drive back and forth to school, I take the yellow bus. When the bus pulls into Sea Trail (the resort I live in) a random little White boy turns around and blurts out.

"So how does it feel to be the only Black person that lives in Sea Trail?"

I look at him weird because I don't know if he's trying to be smart or if it's a compliment. "I don't know, it's alright." I get up from my seat and head off the bus.

I should've asked him 'how does it feel to be a white boy who looks Asian?'" I talk to myself as I walk into the house a little aggravated at my slow comeback.

Summer dropped like a bomb that I had been waiting to explode for the longest time. My senior year was an okay year. I passed all of my classes and was able to walk across the stage to receive my diploma. Dad and Koko flew down for my graduation, and Keirra joined our entourage to celebrate. I was able to go to two proms this year. I went to my school prom, which I didn't take seriously at all because all of the underclassmen were invited. I didn't even dress up for it, because it didn't feel like a real prom. Thankfully, I got a chance to go back home where I had a date and a real prom dress. Family and friends came to see me off in Detroit, and I got a chance to enjoy prom with my good friend Victoria and her date.

I have a summer job at the Food Lion right around the corner from where I live, and I hate it. I don't like working the cash register, and I don't like anybody that works here. It's tourist season, and every day these lines are to the door. I don't care how fast you go, everybody is shopping to go to the beach to party or going golfing.

"Hey, Key." I take a bite of my sub sandwich on my lunch break.

"What you doing?" Key asks over the phone.

"On lunch break at Subway," I talk with a mouth full of food.

"Oh yeah, I forgot you working at the grocery store. I remember when I used to work at the grocery store. How you liking it?" Key asks.

"I hate it."

Key burst out laughing. "Why? You work the cash register, right?"

"Yeah, I hate when people come in with checks and WIC cards and food stamps. I just don't like it. I can't wait to leave for college, but I don't know where I'm going. I got low ACT scores, and Full Sail doesn't take government assistance. I have to be rich or have hella scholarship/grant money" I explain, feeling down at the thought of not being able to go to college.

"Dang, I remember you said you called Jenna for help. What did she say?" Key asks.

"She sent me some of her ACT sample study books and was telling me I'm going to get into somewhere. She was just trying to encourage me, but I'm lost. I don't know what to do. Summertime will be over before I know it." I daydream outside of the window.

"Yeah, and you know Jenna went to boarding school and got prepped throughout high school for college. That's why she was able to get into one of the best colleges," Key explains.

"Yeah, I was so mad when we took our trip to Florida and got more detail about the payment process and everything else. At this point, I just want to go anywhere," I continue.

"Like Jenna said, you will be fine. Something is going to come through for you," Key assures.

Finally, the night has come, and there are only two people in my line. Thankfully, both of them are paying debit or credit. Those kinds of transactions are the easiest. After counting my drawer and making my deposit, I'm good to go. It's time for me to clock out.

"Miko, before you leave, remember tomorrow is going to be just as crazy as it was today so I won't have time to come over and help, so you have to remember those different transaction methods when you're on the register," Shawanda explains.

"Yeah, I just get so nervous when these lines get so long, and my mind goes blank."

"Alright, well, sharpen up tomorrow." Shawanda give me a fake serious look.

I hate this stupid ass job!

After weeks and weeks of researching media colleges and coming short of what I was actually looking for. And busting my balls at the annoying ass Food Lion for minimum wage, Granddaddy brings some light to my exhausting summer.

"Miko, pack up. We're driving down to Columbia, South Carolina, tomorrow!" Granddaddy sounds confident.

"What's in Columbia?" I'm lost in the sauce.

"Benedict College. It's an HBCU. Clive called me yesterday and gave me the hookup with this guy that works there. I called him today, and he said he can get you in ASAP!" Grandddaddy smiles.

"He said the sooner you can get down here, the sooner he can get you enrolled," Granny adds in a silly voice making Granddaddy laugh.

"Oh! So, I'm going to college? I'm going to college!" I do a dance then race to my room to begin packing.

"Mickey, you have to call Food Lion and let them know you're leaving!" Granny yells from the front of the house.

"I'll call them on the way there!" I wave my hand in the air not worried about the job, but excited about my college days ahead.

The Beginning

MAJORING IN MASS Communications, at Benedict College in Columbia, South Carolina, for my first year of college was my introduction to the real world. I lived on campus alone and met all kinds of black people from around the world. During my freshman year of college, I had an epiphany that I wanted a "boyfriend." Not a husband, not a life partner, just a boyfriend. Every single night I said my normal prayer and added my wish for a boyfriend. Serving the God that I serve, he gave me just what I prayed for. At such a young age, I was oblivious to how detailed and perfect Jesus himself was. At age 18 my boyfriend prayers were answered. I lost my virginity and I fell in love. In the middle of my love life starting to unveil, I lost my Granny to breast cancer. With my mom neglecting us, Granny was the closest thing to a mom, my sisters and I had.

Sophomore year of college, I changed my major to Audio Production and moved back home where my family and boyfriend remained. I transferred to The Art Institute of Novi and worked part-time at Motor City Soul Food during the summer. After the summer I got a job at Twelve Oaks mall, working for Victoria Secret Pink for the rest of the year.

Three years went by as fast as I could count. I endured heartache, pain, and, most importantly, wisdom. Being immature, young, and in love caused my boyfriend and I to break up eventually. In addition to that, hearing my father tell me out of his own mouth, he is addicted to drugs caused an abundance of agony and confusion. Out of all the distress that was affecting me, I could only feel sorry for my baby sister Koko. Being raised without a mother and a drug addict for a father, I felt a plethora of sorrow. I guess those "lies" that Key and I thought my mom was telling us about my dad doing drugs came out to be true. Assuming that my dad was calling out for help when he decided to share the bad news, I recommended he go to rehab. Soon afterward, I learned he didn't have any intentions of breaking his habit.

As the stew continued to stir in Detroit, I grew to lose my interest in Audio Production and decided it was time for a change. I switched majors from Audio to Video Production and transferred to The Art Institute of Charleston. It worked out perfectly because Granddaddy lived 2 1/2 hours from the college. So I did the commute from my Grandparent's house in Sunset Beach, North Carolina, to college in Charleston, South Carolina, for one year. For my last year in college, I ended up rooming with a nice Caucasian woman from class to save on expenses. I also picked up a job in the hospitality industry, working at the front desk at The Hampton Inn, while going to school.

As I was finishing up in college, I watched my Granddaddy slowly but surely become sickly. On top of that, things at home with my immediate family were becoming more and more dysfunctional, feeling helpless and all around, just mad. I continued to pray for things I knew I couldn't change. I continued to pray for my family, friends, and my future. I continued to pray for happiness, healthiness, and peace. I believe keeping my relationship with the spirit of the living God and Jesus Christ close, got me through a mental storm.

While living with my Granddaddy, I was able to become more in tune with my spiritual self, and I was blessed with the opportunities to travel and see the world. One of my first girl's trips was when I turned 21 in Miami. After Miami, there was New York and London. As my spiritual walk became stronger, I learned obedience by fasting on foods I craved like sugar and meat for two years. During my journey of fasting and enlightenment, overall, I was enjoying my singleness. After so many years of being single and fasting, I decided I wanted to practice abstinence in my dating life. Practicing abstinence is to restrain from sex until one is married or in covenant.

My dating life had already been slow before I decided to practice abstinence after breaking up with my first love. I hadn't connected with anybody or had sex with anybody after him anyway, so I figured it was a sign to just wait on my husband. I knew that during this abstinence journey, it would be very difficult and challenging. But I believe if God is in the center of anything a person does, it will be blessed and pure. Of course, people judged me and question me about my sexual journey because it's not "popular" or glamorized in music or social media. One thing is for sure when you're confident about the way you live your life/ lifestyle; no one can make you feel bad or uncomfortable about what you're doing or who you are.

After receiving my Bachelors degree in Digital Filmmaking and Video Production, I decided I was done with the "dirty south." I saved up money while helping my Granddaddy around the house until I had enough saved to move to Las Vegas. I felt kind of bad wanting to leave my Granddaddy, but the industry I was pursuing wasn't offering any opportunies in the southern area, where I remained. Before leaving, I made sure my Granddaddy felt comfortable with me, leaving him alone. He assured me that he didn't help put me through college, for me not to use my degree. Granddaddy didn't usually say stuff he didn't mean, especially when it came to education and handling business.

Nine months after obtaining my degree, I packed my bags in my small SUV and did a cross country trip to Las Vegas, Nevada. Prior to my departure, I kept having visions of me crying in my car. The vision never displayed my reasoning for crying. I assumed that maybe moving to Vegas would bring me happy tears, maybe I would get a good job in my career field that made me cry or get emotional. Or maybe I would cry because I was going to be further away from all of my family. I moved to Vegas with no place to stay and without a job lined up. All I had was the couple of thousands I saved up. I made a one-week hotel reservation and grinded to find an apartment within that week. Gods willing, I found an apartment that didn't need proof of income on the last night of my reservation.

Once I settled into my apartment, I continued my grind to find a job either in hospitality or in my career field. I was going to take whichever opportunity came first. After applying for jobs online for weeks and not getting any interviews. I decided to dress up every day like I had an interview with the companies I applied for and personally gave the hiring managers a face-to-face visit. Soon after, I got my first offer at The Golden Nugget Casino, working at the front desk. After orientation, I got the worst phone call ever as I was getting in my car to leave. One of my Granddaddy's good friends called me to tell me my Granddaddy had passed away in the comfort of his home. And there goes my vision coming true, me balling crying in my car in Vegas.

I lost one of my biggest support systems, both of my Grandparents. Coming from a broken immediate family, it was a hard pill to swallow. While burying my granddaddy in Detroit, Michigan, I got a call from Channel 3 News offering a position in my career field as a News Editor. As there were things to be sad about, there were also things to be happy about.

In life, you have to take the good with the bad. You can't dwell on the negative causes and expect positive effects. If you're not happy about something negative in your life, take steps to change it. Don't ponder on tribulations your childhood, environment or life brings you. Learn from those mistakes and mishaps. Understand that your current situation is not your final destination. Work on becoming a better you and change up your routine. Change is scary, but it's much needed. The saying "comfort can kill" is a real thing. It can kill slowly or expeditiously. Overall, no matter what, never stop. Never stop at reaching your higher self. You can slip, fall, and stumble but never stop or give up on yourself.

Never judge a book by its cover. You never know what a person is going through. You never know what that person has to face when they close the front door to their home. Just because a person is physically pretty on the outside, doesn't mean they're pretty on the inside or everything about their life is perfect.

Last but not least, love God, one another, and, most importantly, love yourself.

Pretty can be Ugly,
Kimiko Lewis

Facebook: Pretty can be Ugly

Instagram: @PCBUreads

YouTube: k3 Pictures

Twitter: @PCBUreads

www.ingramcontent.com/pod-product-compliance
Lightning Source LLC
Chambersburg PA
CBHW051047230426
43666CB00012B/2591